An Englishman in Riyadh

An Englishman in Riyadh

David Urch

The University of Buckingham Press

First published in Great Britain in 2009 by

The University of Buckingham Press
Yeomanry House
Hunter Street
Buckingham MK18 1EG

© The University of Buckingham Press

The moral right of the author has been asserted.

All rights reserved. No part of this publication may be reproduced, stored or introduced into a retrieval system or transmitted in any form or by any means without the prior permission of the publisher nor may be circulated in any form of binding or cover other than the one in which it is published and without a similar condition including this condition being imposed on the subsequent purchaser.

A CIP catalogue record for this book is available at the British Library

ISBN 9780956071651

Dedication

For Dick and Onar Benge;
our very good friends in Riyadh and Vienna,
and all the Benge family.

AN ENGLISH MAN IN RIYADH

Contents

The Buckingham Bangladesh Scholarship	i
Introduction	v
Prologue	xv
1. Making the Desert Kingdom	1
2. Black Gold	25
3. Riyadh 1383/4 (1964)	49
4. The Way of the Prophet	81
5. Open Government	103
6. Through the Gateway	123
7. Disguised Matriarchy	131
8. Learning and Understanding	147
9. Enjoying Ill Health	187
10. Safely through this Foreign Land	205
11. Soldiers of the King	237
12. A Band of Brothers?	251
13. Tales and Adventures	283

BUCKINGHAM BANGLADESH SCHOLARSHIP

An Englishman in Riyadh is a title that reflects my first impressions of David Urch. Then he was my teacher at Bury Lawn School, but over the years we have become good friends. David is a remarkable man who has always given me the encouragement, the intellectual and moral support so crucial both in education and in life. The most important thing a teacher can do for his pupils is to get them interested; in other words, he must be a good storyteller. David was more than a good storyteller – he was a master storyteller – and most of his stories were about his years in Saudi Arabia. David's accounts of his adventures were fascinating and sometimes hilariously funny. But in my case, there was something else. As a Muslim, I was especially interested in what David had to say about the birthplace of Islam, marvelling at the way he could balance all the mystery, spirituality and splendour with simple stories of human goodness and decency. I always wanted to hear more, to learn some of the secrets of history of the desert kingdom, from the footsteps of the Prophet

Abraham (Makam-e-Ibrahim) in Makkah to the peace and tranquillity of Madinah.

I was so impressed that I came to see David as my mentor and inspiration. Even when I was at Bury Lawn School, I promised him that, one day, his stories would be published – in part to thank him for everything he has done for me, but also to allow others to read his stories and in the process to learn what he thought about Saudi Arabia and about Islam. I am delighted to be able to keep my youthful promise so that, through the pages of *An Englishman in Riyadh*, readers can travel through time with David and catch a glimpse of the old Arabia, and then continue their journey by exploring the impact of the oil rush and all the complications it has brought in its wake. The impact has been huge and, in barely a generation, Saudi Arabia has passed from being a land of tents to one of skyscrapers. David is far too subtle an observer to think that the changes have been either all for the good or all for the bad; he shows that some have been positive but others have perhaps been too fast. Above all, his work is a celebration of the Saudi people who, David believes, display a vigour and sagacity that should stand them in good stead – whatever happens to the oil. In *An Englishman in Riyadh* we certainly meet some remarkable people. .

But it is well worth remembering that some of Saudi Arabia's wealth and success rests on the contribution made by workers from other lands. Many are Muslims and many of these come from Bangladesh. Here it is important to mention David's first book, *Crescent and Delta,* also published by the University of Buckingham Press. *Crescent and Delta* tells the story of the people of Bangladesh, many of whom are now spread all over the world. Told objectively by an outsider, in some ways it is a very sad story – terrible injustice, colonialism, poverty, corruption, war, natural disasters and much suffering that should have been avoided – but it shows that, in spite of everything, the Bangladeshi people have achieved a great deal and have the potential to achieve much more. Everyone knows – or think they know – about Saudi Arabia, but Bangladesh is often overshadowed by its bigger neighbours or sidelined by the media. As *An Englishman in Riyadh* will change what we think about Saudi Arabia, *Crescent and Delta* will either change, or more likely create, views about Bangladesh.

An Englishman in Riyadh and *Crescent and Delta* are wonderful books in their own right, but it is important to see them in a wider context. Both form essential parts of "The Buckingham Bangladesh Scholarship Scheme". This project is unique in the way it links literature with learning.

I should explain that, after Bury Lawn, I studied at the University of Buckingham, Britain's only independent university. Buckingham too has been an important part of my life. Now, with the support of the University, and the help of my former tutor, Professor John Clarke, David and I are creating a scholarship that will enable a British-born Bangladeshi or a Bangladeshi from abroad to come to study at Buckingham. Some universities seem to discourage original ideas but Buckingham is not like that; our alumni come up with new thinking – and I like to think that the Bangladesh Scholarship Scheme is a good example of that.

Proceeds from both books will go towards a scholarship fund managed by the University Foundation. Uniquely, those who receive this award can choose to study any academic discipline at Buckingham. Above all, Buckingham Bangladesh Scholars are not beholden to any interest group or individual. In the great atmosphere of Buckingham, they can be true to themselves as they grow in knowledge and wisdom – strengthening their characters and integrity as they learn to become bridges between all that is best in the traditions of Britain and Bangladesh. This is an inspiring vision and one all who purchase *An Englishman in Riyadh* and *Crescent and Delta* can help to realise.

Dean M Junayed Miah

The Buckingham Bangladesh Scholarship was formally launched at the House of Commons at a reception hosted by the Speaker, the Right Honourable John Bercow, MP.

INTRODUCTION

An Englishman in Riyadh, David Urch's account of his years in Saudi Arabia, belongs to a long-standing and important tradition – works by English authors describing their encounters with Islamic societies. They range from the *Letters of Lady Mary Wortley Montagu* to T E Lawrence's *Seven Pillars of Wisdom* and the works of Freya Stark. Consciously or unconsciously, the best examples – of which *An Englishman in Riyadh* is undoubtedly one – reflect aspects of Islamic and Arabian culture; above all they reveal a sheer delight in story telling. Thus David Urch's book really belongs to two traditions rather than just one – the other is that of the *Arabian Nights*. David's stories are wonderfully told: the sense of timing, the pace, the humour, sometimes the pathos, the impending disaster, the unexpected twist and – usually – the happy ending. All of the essential ingredients are there. Something of Arabia has surely rubbed off on David.

Good books may be read at several different levels – perhaps another way of saying that *this* book should be read several times. It could be read with pleasure and profit simply as a collection of marvellous stories – and there would be nothing wrong in that. But there are also deeper levels, more challenging to the reader, to be explored if anything like the full significance of *An Englishman in Riyadh* is to be appreciated. Most, though not all, of the stories involve David himself; in other words, they are not just accounts of events, but also describe his own feelings, interpretations and reflections. In short, this is a work of autobiography.

By definition, autobiographies can never be really objective, because the author and the person he is writing about are one and the same. Autobiographies are thus essentially subjective. They are statements of how authors see themselves, or at any rate of how they wish the world to see them. It is up to the reader, or perhaps the editor, to supply the element of objectivity – to assess the author's portrayal of himself, preferably sympathetically, but ready to question motives and interpretations and willing to speculate about things only hinted at in the author's own text.

John Clarke

Probably the most significant thing about a text is its title. If that title is well chosen, it sums up what the book is all about and assists understanding of its significance. Frankly, when the title of *An Englishman in Riyadh* was first put to me, I thought it seemed a little dull but, on further reflection, I realised that it was a very good title indeed. Most good titles involve two distinct categories, though these concepts can either be complementary (for example Gibbon's *Decline and Fall*) or they can be contrasting (for example Austen's *Sense and Sensibility* or Stendhal's *Scarlet and Black*). Perhaps the most intriguing are the ones where you are never quite sure whether the categories are complementary or contrasting – and, in the last resort, *An Englishman in Riyadh* is like that.

At first sight, however, *An Englishman in Riyadh* seems a straightforward case of a "contrasting title." David tells us that, when looking through an Atlas as a child, he was strangely attracted to the town of Riyadh, not least because it seemed to have no obvious links with the outside world – no roads or railways. His fascination, and his determination to go there, increased when he learned that Riyadh was accessible only by camel. Early anticipation of major developments in later life can be seen as extra-sensory glimpses into the future, as evidence for the idea of fate or destiny or, more prosaically, of particular traits of character. David, it seems, is drawn to places unlike his native land. Of course, we know that opposites can attract – but, when all is said and done, England and everything that goes with it do not seem to have much in common with Arabia, certainly not the Arabia of the early 1960s.

David actually underscores the contrast in his title. He does not call his book *A Teacher in Riyadh* or *Mother and Son in Riyadh* – as he might have done, although with those titles they would have been different books – but *An Englishman in Riyadh*. David may be a rather unusual Englishman, but no-one who reads this book could have the slightest doubt as to the author's nationality. He may learn Arabic, he may wear Arab dress, he may appreciate and understand things most Englishmen do not – but he is still English to the core. This book is most emphatically *not* about someone "going native." In fact, it actually tells us as much about what it is to be English as about what it is to be Saudi. We recall W S Gilbert:

> In spite of all temptations,
> To belong to other nations,
> He remains an Englishman,
> He remains an Englishman.

David's essential Englishness has a number of implications. It means that his stance is ultimately quite detached. We learn how he comes to admire and respect the people of Saudi Arabia, but he never seeks to present himself as one of them – he realises that would be impossible and in any case it is not what he wants. For example, he fully understands the absolutely central role of Islam and writes sympathetically and perceptively about it, yet insists that his years in one of the most profoundly Islamic countries in the world have only served to strengthen his own Christian faith. As a genre, autobiography is essentially subjective, but that does not preclude objectivity within it. Objectivity can only be achieved through detachment; the detached observer, the foreigner, can often be more perceptive than any "native" about his host society, precisely because he is not part of it. This is as true of England itself as of any other country. If you really want a balanced assessment of the strengths and weaknesses of Victorian Britain, read Léon Faucher's *L'Études sur l'Angleterre*. David Urch does for Saudi Arabia what Faucher did for nineteenth century Britain.

Of course, David's assessment is sympathetic rather than hostile. He knows only too well that many in the West view aspects of the Kingdom of Saudi Arabia with considerable distaste. They believe that it is an oppressive theocracy where human rights and freedoms are grossly violated, where the position of women is appalling, where the system of government is flagrantly undemocratic and where there is idleness, hidden decadence, massive corruption and waste. He demonstrates, very convincingly, that most of these charges are either untrue or grossly exaggerated. It seems that what is admittedly a theocracy is not really that oppressive and that the position of women is quite carefully protected. He shows that some practices that might seem corrupt to outsiders really involve a proper sense of obligation to friends and extended family. Above all, he shows a monarchy astonishingly open – in the literal sense – to the complaints and problems of ordinary people. *An Englishman in Riyadh* offers a wonderful corrective to the view that Wilsonian democracy represents the only acceptable form of government – regardless of previous history and culture. Although David concedes that the Saudis may have their shortcomings in some areas, it seems that their besetting national weakness is hypochondria – which as weaknesses go is surely relatively innocuous.

But David appreciates that it is hard to generalise about national character, especially in times of rapid change. If there is one word that sums David up it must be that he is a traditionalist, a traditionalist to an extent rarely encountered even in Buckingham and never – surely - in Milton Keynes. To paraphrase Gibbon's comments about the Fellows of Magdalen in the eighteenth century, I fear his constitutional toasts may not have always "been expressive of a lively loyalty to the House of Hanover", David does not tell us a great deal about his motives for leaving England for Saudi Arabia in the early 1960s. True, he wanted a job and he certainly wanted to teach, but I cannot imagine that he ever had much time for pop-music, permissiveness or any of the other signs of the "swinging decade." For a true traditionalist, England must have been rather an unappealing place at that time; somewhere *really* traditional, even if the precise forms of that tradition were as yet unknown, would have been correspondingly attractive.

I have one major unanswered question about *An Englishman in Riyadh*: how strange and incomprehensible did David actually find the desert kingdom? Of course, externally it was very strange indeed, but was it so strange inside? David shows an instinctive understanding of Saudi culture and mores – kindness and hospitality to strangers, bravery, deep faith, a curious blend of hierarchy and equality, honour, loyalty, a sense of membership of groups, deference to mothers and to the elderly – serious qualities indeed though often displayed with a charmingly light touch. I suspect that David did not really find these things strange at all – not least because they represented values he already subscribed to. Although they took a specifically Saudi form, they were really the core values of traditional societies, Muslim and Christian alike. So there may be no contradiction in the title after all.

In the best sense of the word, there is something "Medieval" in David's account of the courtyards, the hidden gardens, the towers and above all the people of Riyadh. It is as if the psychological traits of Medieval Europe, described in the abstract by Jacob Burckhardt, are coming to life before our very eyes. David is an Oxford man and Matthew Arnold tells us that Victorian Oxford was "still whispering the last enchantments of the Middle Ages." I wonder if, after glimpsing hints of that enchantment at Oxford, David pursued it further, to Riyadh itself.

In fact, "The Medieval Dimension" is crucial to the underlying themes of this book – the relationship between the West and the Arab world, between Christianity and Islam. At first sight, the relationship between

Christianity and Islam was at its most confrontational in the Middle Ages, but things were more complex than that. There was a great deal of interaction and many of the most important features of European Medieval civilization actually had their origins in the Islamic world – ideas of chivalry, mathematics, architecture, the universities and much more besides. Strangely the time when Christianity and Islam were most obviously in conflict was perhaps also the time when the underlying cultural differences between them were narrower than either before or since. My, very Western, response when entering the courtyard of the great Mosque at Karrouan in Tunisia was, "this reminds me of an Oxford quad." Of course I had got it the wrong way round; I should have said to myself, "an Oxford quad reminds me of this." I think it may be precisely because he is rather a "Medieval man" that David actually found himself so at home in Saudi Arabia. If others could discover their own "Medieval roots" – which I am sure are not far below the surface in most of us – that would represent an enormous step towards a better understanding of Islam and of the Arab world.

But while the Saudi Arabia David encountered on his first visits could properly be described as "Medieval" – and I use the word, as I am sure David would, in a flattering rather than a pejorative sense – it is much harder to apply the same description to the Riyadh of his later years. Things would be fairly straightforward if it was just a matter of a traditionalist providing an objective, though sympathetic account of a traditional society. But what David is actually describing is a society in the throes of an extraordinarily rapid transformation, as almost unimaginable riches poured in, together with foreign workers and experts and – inevitably - new values and customs. In effect, we are told what oil has done to Saudi Arabia.

I have described David as a traditionalist, perhaps a bit "Medieval" in some ways. It is tempting to say that he is a Romantic – a term applied to many admirers of the Arab world. But I don't think it really fits in David's case; Romanticism is too self-indulgent, too self-absorbed to describe David or the qualities I associate with him. But I would never call him an obscurantist. That would be both insulting and untrue. In any case Medieval Europe was not all obscurantist – witness its willingness to take ideas and technology from the Muslim and Arab world. And I think that David's approach to the transformation of Saudi Arabia is of a piece with this. He does not at all object to many aspects of the modern world; he likes things to work, he well understands the benefits that modern medicine, transport and education can bring. Although individual projects may have gone disastrously wrong, his basic stance is that the rulers of the Kingdom have genuinely tried to give their people better lives and he thinks that on the whole they have succeeded.

David is a religious and cultural traditionalist rather than a technological one. He clearly does have concerns about the effects of oil wealth and its associated preoccupation with money on values he admires and to a large extent shares. The traditional societies David admires exhibit a strong sense of the collective. Yet the pursuit by individuals of money, or indeed of anything else – regardless of traditional constraints or obligations to others must be corrosive of the old community sense. But there is more. Wealthy individuals are liable to attract the wrong kind of "foreign friends," manipulative and insincere flatterers who draw them away from the paths of virtue by inflating their vanity, encouraging them to vice and separating them from all that is noble in their own culture – so much so that they ultimately incur the loathing of the more reflective members of their own society.

Thus the balance sheet of "modernisation" is rather uncertain, but David is ready enough to admit that it has had its down side. While he stresses that excesses of greed or depravity are actually quite rare, he still finds them disturbing. But if there has been a moral deterioration, where has it come from? Is it the inevitable consequence of oil revenues – which it seems unlikely that any Saudi would wish to forego – or is it due to the culture that has made itself so dependent upon oil? In other words has corruption and decadence come from the West? Those who think it has may be described as Islamic fundamentalists – often young and apparently well educated, with experience of life in the West, yet thoroughly disillusioned with secularism and all its works. David's sympathies are more with the House of Sa'ud, balancing uneasily between championship of Wahabism and the continuing need for oil revenues. David realises their task is difficult and thinks they have actually done rather a good job, but he does understand the feelings of the fundamentalists and radicals.

In the Middle Ages, the Islamic and Arab world provided Europe with a wealth of intellectual and cultural treasures, the essential basis of "The Renaissance of the Twelfth Century." It is hard to see this contribution in anything other than positive terms. In the last century, especially during the past fifty years, the "contribution" has been the other way, from the West to the Arab world. Is this contribution essentially positive or negative? It is almost impossible to say whether the technological benefits have outweighed the alleged cultural, social, political and even spiritual damage. The traditionalist in David is clearly dismayed by some of the things that have happened, but what can we learn from his book about why they have occurred and what is the right response to them?.

While David understands the position of the fundamentalists and radicals, I don't think he shares their analysis in its entirety. Yes, some of the tensions, strains, even the worrying if limited signs of decadence, may be attributed to the malign influence of Western governments, companies and individuals, but David never suggests that this is the whole story. There is another strand of analysis in *An Englishman in Riyadh* that also requires investigation. David stresses that, while its cultural and other roots go back thousands of years, Saudi Arabia is actually a very new nation. The story of the birth of nations may be heroic but it is usually quite painful as well. Even on its own, the creation of a new political – and to some extent spiritual - entity brings challenges, leading some to question old ways and others to defend them with new determination and even ferocity. But it was not just a matter of making a nation; the process was accompanied by an amazing economic transformation, turning what had been an impoverished society into one of the richest in the world. Whether or not the West had been involved in this economic transformation, it would be naïve to suppose that it could have been achieved entirely without pain.

Following the example of the great Arabic historian, Ibn Khaldoun, it is always useful to look for patterns. Of course two situations are never exactly alike, but there can still be significant similarities. I would say that it is more or less inevitable that all societies experiencing dramatic economic change will also experience some turbulence. The consolation is that the worst turbulence comes relatively early on in the process, at any rate in the first fifty years or so. If the society concerned can "get over" the period of danger and potential revolution, there is a good prospect of achieving stability and security. The case of Britain in the eighteenth and nineteenth centuries is instructive. The economic transformation of Britain really began in the 1780s with the advent of something later described as an Industrial Revolution. If there was ever a time when British society was in danger of political and social revolution – even of counter revolution – it was between the 1790s and the 1840s. By the 1850s, the real danger had past.

There are significant indications in David's book that Saudi Arabia may be quite well placed to follow the same pattern. It seems that there are three essential ingredients: rulers who do not panic; a readiness to root out excesses of corruption and decadence; and respect for religious values. This is what saved Britain and it could well save Saudi Arabia too. A certain amount of religious "tightening" may be necessary – remember that Victorian Britain was far more "respectable" than the same country had been in the eighteenth century.

Of course there are dangers. In particular there is a danger that disgust at what can be presented as the corrosive influence of the Western presence – which is actually essential for the economic development of the country – could spill over to produce almost unimaginable chaos. There is an answer here and it is implicit in David's book, though of course he is far too modest to mention it or perhaps even think it. It is important to demonstrate that Western influence is not destructive or corrosive of the best traditions of Saudi society – of course not the same, but still understanding and supportive. David Urch himself embodies precisely these qualities.

There is, however, one final message to be drawn from *An Englishman in Riyadh*. We have talked of the Islam's technological and cultural contribution to Medieval Europe and identified the important Western technological contribution to the Arab world, particularly to Saudi Arabia, in recent years. The vital question now must surely be whether the West can make an equally important cultural contribution to Arabia? If it could, that would really "even the score" and provide a proper basis for mutual respect.

It is well known that Islamic societies are not usually very receptive of cultural influences whose origins lie elsewhere. At first sight, therefore, it seems hard to identify any "gift" likely to be acceptable. But the "gift" might be acceptable if it was in some senses Islamic itself. While David is clearly devoted to his former pupils – as every good teacher should be – it is clear that he was sometimes frustrated in his professional work by the attitudes of his students, and even more by those of the authorities. In many cases it was not a matter of ill-will, laziness, or lack of ability, but rather of different understanding of what education should be all about. David politely singles out hypochondria as the Saudis' chief failing, but he is clearly not very keen on the tendency to think that rote learning is all that can be required of a pupil. David is such a good teacher that he was able to inspire some of his students, so that they came to appreciate that there is more – there is explanation, interpretation and exploration of implications.

There may be some who think that such things are "un-Islamic." Although not a Muslim, I think I know enough about history to be able to say that this is nonsense. The greatest Islamic gift to the West in the Middle Ages was one of philosophy, as revealed in the works of great thinkers like Avicenna. Their essential message was that education was all about logic and reason and much of the later achievements of the West rest on this foundation. For whatever reason, it seems that this tradition has faded a little in the Arab world and that is a shame. To the other qualities I believe Saudi Arabia needs for a successful and stable future, I would add one more: clear thinking. It is really a matter of returning a gift with grateful thanks to the original donor.

But let us return to basics. Before you can get pupils excited by logic, reason and clear thinking, you have to get them interested. You have to tell them stories and then get them to think about what lies behind and beyond those stories. As David shows in *An Englishman in Riyadh* he is very good at doing that. I may or may not have interpreted his ideas aright, but I truly believe that they provide an explanation and possible way forward when dealing with some of the most profound issues facing both England and Saudi Arabia.

John Clarke

PROLOGUE

"Is Riyadh really the capital of Saudi Arabia, Daddy?"

I was, I suppose, between five and six years old, and precociously fascinated by maps. The capitals of all the countries in my Atlas were printed in Capital Letters, which made them easy to recognise: from all of them, with one notable exception, roads and railways radiated, and many were on rivers. Only in Saudi Arabia – in those far-off days – was there a great blank in the middle of the Arabian Peninsula, broken by just one name.

My father told me that, yes, Riyadh was the capital of Saudi Arabia. Looking back, I am surprised he knew: Arabia was an unknown land in those days, but I expect that he had just looked over my shoulder, seen the capital letters, and, with the assurance of his years and experience, had understood with certainty that they signified a capital city. This, however, did nothing to explain its isolation.

"How do people get to Riyadh?"

"They still go on caravans of camels."

As far as I remember it was to myself, silently, that I made the promise; but it may equally well have been aloud: anyway, I never forgot it. "Well, one day, even if I have to sit for weeks on the back of a camel, I am going to get there." In the event it did not take me weeks – it took me about forty minutes on a Boeing 720-B, then the pride of Saudi Arabian Airlines, comfortable, elegantly decorated, with soft music playing. We flew from Dhahran to Riyadh at midnight and the then new terminal building was still being constructed. On the other hand – using a different time scale – it had taken me almost thirty years to reach my goal.

***

In the summer of 1964, when Mr Macmillan's "Winds of Change" were blowing not only through Africa but through everywhere else as well, I was negotiating rather ineffectually to go and teach Palestinian Refugees in Jordan. My previous experience of teaching Arabs had been with cadets from the Royal Iraqi Navy, preparing for entrance to the Royal School of Navigation at Southampton. The date proposed for the start of my teaching in Jordan was twice postponed (for financial reasons, I understood) when I happened to read in *The Times* that Saudi Arabia was now recruiting teachers of English. The fact that I was not a specialist English teacher in no way deterred me. I immediately wrote to the address mentioned and received, by return, a letter giving particulars about the available posts, and an appointment for an interview the next Friday.

At that time, in my naivety, I was not surprised at this. As I now sit writing and looking back, it strikes me as one of the most unusual events in my long association with the country. Certainly, in all the years that followed, I never received a letter by return from any government body – often I never received a reply at all. I like to think that this first encounter with the Saudi Authorities had a unique flavour, something that marked the day with a white stone.

But I was surprised by the appointment on a Friday as I expected the Saudi Embassy to keep Saudi rather than English working hours; and, as the date given for the appointment was, in fact, that of the Thursday, I telephoned to confirm the day. It was correct, so on the Friday I duly presented myself in York Street, off Baker Street, for an interview. Two Saudis were present, rather disappointingly dressed in well-cut suits, and a shirt sleeved Briton, who had been teaching in Damman in the Eastern Province, and was assisting in both the English and the French sense. The leader of the group, the man who made the decision, was the Director of Education for the Eastern Province, Sheikh Abdul Aziz Al Turki, for many years the Cultural Attaché of the London Embassy. As he will not appear again, I would like here to say that, throughout the many meetings I was to have with Sheikh Abdul Aziz over the years, I always received unreserved help and kindness from him. This, as I hope to explain later, was normal. The senior Saudis, whether civil servants or businessmen, were almost always courteous, kind and ready to go out of their way to be helpful, or at least they were when I first went to Riyadh. There were of course many in junior positions who were equally helpful, but "man, dressed in a little brief authority" can behave just as annoyingly in Riyadh as anywhere else, and troubles and delays, as they were bound to come, emanated from the lower echelons.

The interview was rather odd. We talked for a while about living conditions, and the sort of schools that were looking for English teachers. I said I wanted to go to Riyadh – which provoked general amazement. "Everyone else wants to go to Jeddah or the Eastern Province" they told me, "Nobody wants to go to Riyadh." I gave them (carefully selected) names of referees who might be contacted – although in the event none were approached. I was asked for my Degree Certificate and said – as it happens inaccurately – that Oxford did not issue such certificates, but that they could look me up in the Oxford Year Book. They asked for some sort of official letter; but when I tried to get one I was told that Oxford did issue these certificates, especially for people working abroad. It was strange that they were so insistent on the evidence of a degree. The Briton on the "interview" board not only had no degree himself, but had falsely claimed a degree which didn't actually exist. He described himself as "BA Edinburgh", but some years later when we had an "MA Edinburgh" teaching in Riyadh, most of us learned that Scottish Universities did not award BA degrees. I said nothing (he was doing good work in the Eastern Province as far as his students were concerned) but there was gossip that finally reached the authorities and he was summarily dismissed. He continued – somehow – to teach abroad and I am sure deserved the OBE he was to receive later from a grateful sovereign for his educational services in the cause of promoting the English Language.

At this point the interview seemed to peter out. As I had no more questions I stood up, saying something like, "Well perhaps you will write to me when you have made a decision," but Sheikh Abdul Aziz, looking mildly surprised, said "Don't you want the post?" He then produced a contract: I sat down again, signed it, and we all shook hands.

"Can you come to Saudi Arabia on Tuesday week?" was the next question. There seemed no reason why I shouldn't and I was told to send my passport to the Consulate for a Visa, and then to turn up at Victoria Air Terminal – if possible with a Degree Certificate, "as you will need it in Riyadh." On my way out I spoke to a very pleasant older man whom I had talked to earlier in the hall that served as a waiting room: "I've signed a contract already and I'm going to Riyadh on Tuesday week," I told him. "Then I'll ask for Riyadh too," he said, "Perhaps I'll see you on the plane." Ralph Ellis, who had worked in Egypt for many years in the Thirties and Forties and had a fair smattering of Arabic, was a tower of strength to me and was to support my uncertain footsteps during those early days in the Desert Kingdom.

***

About a couple of dozen of us turned up at the Air Terminal and met our cicerone, the ubiquitous Briton from the interviews. All tickets, visas and reservations were in order, a circumstance which at the time stuck me as normally efficient, but would later have appeared almost miraculous. At Heathrow we boarded a Comet of Middle East Airlines to Beirut, a flight marked briefly by a six hour delay in Paris, where we were lunched and wined at the Airline's expense. Possibly through some oversight, the waiters continued to serve carafes of wine all afternoon: as none of us paid anything we assumed the Airline did. I spent most of the time talking to Ralph Ellis, who I had been delighted to see at the Terminal. We discovered that we were the only men going to Riyadh, which set us apart. People tended to speak to us as though we were candidates selected for some task of extreme danger, the relief of some Arabian Mafeking. This attitude was encouraged by our cicerone who addressed the others with gusto. "I wouldn't be them," he exclaimed, "flying up to Riyadh. Terrible old planes, literally tied together. More than your life's worth." Even in my ignorance I thought that he was mad.

It is an odd thing that there are some Billy Bunter-like people who must tell stories even if they know that they will be found out almost immediately. This story-teller must have known that even in those days Saudi Arabian Airlines had modern, well-maintained jet planes, which we would be using in a matter of hours. At the time his remarks had their effect on the rest of the group. They set Ralph and me apart as if we were already doomed men. As with the terminally ill, there was a difficulty in finding topics of conversation.

We saw very little of Beirut which we reached very late at night. Ralph and I, with one or two others coming and going, sat for a good while in a pavement café sipping beer. At dawn I took a taxi up above the city and down again to the Pigeon Rocks, a Tourist Viewpoint. It was very fresh and beautiful, but the trip allowed little time for bathing, shaving, and resting before breakfast. I was not the only one to feel sorry that Middle East Airlines, on its Beirut-Dhahran flights, did not serve any sort of pick me up, in deference to laws prohibiting alcohol in Saudi Arabia.

***

Flying over Saudi Arabia in daytime was an uncanny experience. How is it possible, one felt, for there to be so much desert? Contrary to popular ideas, very little of this is actually sand desert: most of it is barren, rocky, with little of no settled habitation, but probably providing at least semi nomadic grazing. In his incomparable book, *Arabian Sands*, Thesiger gives a misleading picture of Saudi Arabia, because he was writing about the one really big sandy area. The early books of St John Philby give a better idea of the territory.

From above, however, the whole countryside looks to be sand covered, and for nearly an hour and a half we flew over nothing else. Suddenly, signs of life appeared – tracks in the sand, visible from a plane – then the inescapable detritus of civilization – a wrecked vehicle carelessly abandoned by a driver who was presumably not the owner – oil drums – unidentifiable shapes of metal – compounds enclosing nothing – more shrubs and bushes – and then a place inhabited by the human race. As the plane descended, moving dots could be seen on the roads – think of it! Down there were cars driving on Saudi Arabian roads, and probably being driven by Saudi Arabians! No longer was Saudi Arabia a rather vague blank in the atlas; it was real and soon we would actually be treading its soil.

The later new, functional, terminal buildings at Dhahran are more efficient, designed to meet the ever increasing number of travellers passing through, but the old buildings at which I landed in 1964 constituted what far more experienced travellers than I declared the most beautiful airport terminal in the world. Elegantly arabesque halls, slender towering pillars opened onto fan-vaulted ceilings: it was usually cool and, in 1964, uncluttered. Tired and jaded I was far too hot (to keep down excess baggage I was wearing the winter suit I was assured I should need in Riyadh in December and January). The average mid-September temperature was 90°F, with very high humidity, and it was midday. On that day Dhahran Airport seemed an oasis indeed. Our cicerone dealt with the passports very quickly and then began issuing orders. Ralph and I were to catch a plane to Riyadh at twelve noon the following day: the others would be put up at the Dosary Hotel until they could be sent to their various assignments.

As nobody seemed to have made any arrangements about us, and as neither of us was a novice traveller, Ralph and I found our luggage, took a taxi to the International Airport Hotel (a very modest place in those days) and booked two rooms. We then returned to the group in the Arrivals building to find consternation prevailing. We had disappeared and nobody knew where we were and the cicerone was said to be furious. He certainly seemed so when he reappeared, and he made various unnecessarily caustic remarks about people who didn't do as they were told. (Of course, he had told us nothing except that we would not be staying at the Dosary Hotel, and would fly to Riyadh the next day). He then informed us that we would be flying to Riyadh at twelve midnight and not at noon the next day, and so we would not need the rooms we had booked. Then he disappeared again, presumably chasing missing luggage, and so Ralph and I took another taxi back to the hotel, where we explained the situation to the manager: he was very understanding and cancelled our reservations free-of-charge. Then after retrieving our baggage, we returned to the Airport: here consternation and alarm prevailed again, possibly in a greater degree than before. We had disappeared again!

This time the cicerone lost his temper. I remained meekly silent and left it to my older and more senior friend to speak for us. At last peace was restored and eventually we all set off together in a bus for the Dosary Hotel in Damman. This place did not inspire me with confidence, although it certainly seemed clean. We sat like owls in a rather long and narrow "lounge" upstairs. There were not enough chairs and sofas and what there were reminded me of the sort of furniture that, in England, is only offered by the cheapest suppliers to their least discriminating customers. A meal, we were told, was being prepared; but as an additional piece of information, came the news that Ralph and I, who would not be residents, would not be eligible for this feast. The cicerone, now recovered in temper, advised us to go to The Automatic Restaurant – "Clean, air-conditioned, jolly good food" – and gave us directions. It was quite near but it was now half past three in the afternoon, and I was still wearing my dark, three piece suit of Reid and Taylor cloth, which used to be advertised on the top left hand corner of the *Daily Telegraph* front page, as "the world's most expensive suiting." That day it felt like it.

I remember nothing of the walk to the restaurant, except that I concentrated on putting one foot in front of the other. The restaurant turned out to be where we had been told it would be, and it was air-conditioned. I did not see any actual dirt, but by now I was collapsing with fatigue and the afternoon-after-the-night-before. Inside The Automatic Restaurant there were a fair number of very smeary Formica-topped tables, together with chairs in keeping. Two or three tables had been put together and asleep on top was a large, stout individual, unshaven, in pyjama bottoms and sleeveless vest, neither anything like Persil White. Nobody else was in sight. With some difficulty Ralph roused the figure and ordered food. There wasn't any, he was told; but we could have water-melon if we liked. I sat, miserable and silent amid the flow of Arabic, and finally accepted a plate of pink fruit. It was the first time I had eaten it and I have disliked it ever since.

***

In spite of the minimal attractions of The Automatic Restaurant, I did feel better when we returned to the Dosary Hotel, which the rest of the group, who had been served their meal, had already christened The Doss House. A settled gloom had descended and the only thing that cheered them was the thought that they were not going to Riyadh. It wasn't long, however, before two Saudis from the local Education Office came along to meet the group. They were especially attentive to the two of us who were Transients, and offered to take us for a drive to see something of Damman and Al-Khobar, the "town" of Dhahran Airport. There was no time for more than a very general look, and I was struck by the fact that most of the buildings in those Eastern Province towns were low, two or three storeys at most. We looked at two or three schools from the outside, and went to view the sea. It was a confusing and disorganised ride, of which I retain only scattered impressions, but it was a kind thing to have done, and the two men added to their kindness by saying, on the way back to the hotel, that they would return at ten o'clock to drive us to the airport. Night had fallen, in the rapid way it does in the tropics and sub-tropics, and the surroundings looked a good deal better after dark. The general litter and the lack of organized tidiness (or cleaning) is so softened by lamplight that it ceases to be offensive to all but the most fastidious.

The evening passed in desultory conversation. Some of the group seemed to have gone out "to see Damman by night," but returned rather soon having been unable to find it. We were advised not to have a meal and so contended ourselves with cups of coffee interspersed with glasses of coca-cola, at that time not on the Boycott List. Generally speaking it was a relief when, very shortly after ten, our two friends of the earlier evening returned, and we collected our bags, again bade farewell to our cicerone, and those of the group who were still around, and set off for the Airport.

Even in those days domestic flights were a simple process: our luggage was collected and our friends handed us our boarding passes almost before we knew what was happening. The cicerone's dire predictions about the plane had secretly rather alarmed me, and I was relieved to enter a large modern aircraft (a Boeing 720B was a big plane in those days); immediately all lingering doubts and fears vanished. As music played on and smiling hostesses brought around sweets, I felt that I was at last, after nearly thirty years, setting off on the last lap of my journey to Riyadh – my object for so long. I may add that this mood of euphoria lasted through many vicissitudes, through all the long years of my time in that city, and has never really left me.

Arriving at Riyadh Airport was a bit of an anti-climax. As I mentioned earlier, the Terminal Building was under construction. There were pillars and a roof, but most of the floor was still sand and there were few rooms partitioned off. There were various tables, at which uniformed men sat, and through a doorway could be seen what looked like an inflamed mob of rioters, but which was actually a group of taxi drivers, trying to break in to secure their fares. I was a little unhappy to see how the guards forcibly kept out this horde, using their rifle butts to clear a way through, but Ralph reminded me that we were in the Middle East now. There was a rudimentary Passport Control to go through, but merely to check that our visas were in order, and that we had passed through either a border or airport passport control on arrival in Saudi Arabia. In those days no International Flights came directly to Riyadh: all went to Jeddah or Dhahran. There was only one International Flight a week out of Riyadh – on Thursday mornings – and that went first to Dhahran. My adventures on one such flight I shall recount later.

The bags took a long time to come and were dumped haphazardly on the ground. There was a sort of automatic "customs" clearance, although we were supposed to show ownership of the luggage. We were then assured, in Arabic, that we were free to go and, as we emerged with the yelling crowd outside, I was no longer even mildly critical of the rifle butts, but thankful that the drivers were prevented from carrying out their apparent intention of tearing me apart to get possession of my baggage. Without any Arabic the situation could have been very tricky, but Ralph sorted out an obliging taxi-driver, haggled over the fare, and gave the man orders to take us to the Semiramis Hotel.

The lights of the Airport soon died away behind. There was, even at that date, a dual carriageway from the airport to the city but, except for the Ministry of Petroleum and a few villas, there was really nothing else until the main block of ministries was reached. There was – possibly for that night only – no street lighting for a couple of miles, and I wondered how far out of town the Airport was. The sudden burst of light and the procession of large and imposing buildings on the right – all ministries – whose names the driver rattled off, and the Yamama Hotel, on the left and looking through the trees appropriately first-class, was quite a revelation, and then, after another shorter empty road, we reached a roundabout filled with trees and the Semiramis Hotel.

I mean no criticism of the hotel if I say that I would not have chosen it myself. It was on the advice of the Saudis from the Eastern Educational Office that we went there. We had asked their advice on the best hotel to stay at, and they had been quite definite: the two best hotels were the Yamama and the Sahari Palace, but they were very expensive if we had to stay a long time. They thought that it might be quite a while before we found suitable accommodation – in contradiction to what we had been told in London – and therefore recommended that we take one of the air-conditioned rooms at the Semiramis and eat at the Yamama.

We secured a three-bedded room for our exclusive use. It was the sort of hotel where people could, and usually did, take a bed in a room. The room and the beds looked clean, however, and so did the Bathroom and the European lavatory, which were, unfortunately, not for our exclusive use. It was half past two in the morning and I was worn out: I thought that I could hardly keep my eyes open, when Ralph showed his true superiority, as a friend and travelling companion. As I started the minimum of unpacking to get out my night-clothes and sponge bag, he produced from the spacious pocket of a mackintosh he had carried over his arm all day, a whole bottle of White Horse Whisky! And he went out to order glasses, water, ice, nuts, cheese and olives. I was stupefied with amazement.

"How did you get through the Customs?" I gasped.

"In my pocket," he replied, "these people never search your pockets unless they suspect you of smuggling something. There was nothing in my bags to worry them." The order soon arrived and we got into our beds with a table loaded with refreshments between us. I have never known a bottle of Scotch to vanish so quickly. It must have been nearly three when we began, and by half past three, relaxed, refreshed, and ready for whatever the morning would produce, we turned off the light and, on my part at least, was very soon fast asleep.

***

The next morning we woke, unreasonably fit and alert, at about half past eight. Coffee, bread, cheese and jam were produced in the room for the breakfast (the empty bottle having been tactfully concealed, and no reference was ever made to it; it was later removed by a cleaner). At about nine-thirty or a little afterwards, we set out to walk to the Ministry of Education. We had rather misjudged the distance, which we had covered swiftly in the car the previous night. It was quite a long walk in a sunny September morning, clad formally in London suits and stiff collars, although I for one was more lightly attired than on the unforgettable day before. We commented cheerfully on the efforts of the local Council to plant flowering shrubs up the centre of the dual carriageway; and at last we reached the Ministry of Education, the title of which, over the gates, Ralph could read. During this walk we saw only a handful of people and not more that half a dozen vehicles passed us: before I left Riyadh the traffic on Airport Street was almost nose to tail from dawn to long after sunset.

Inside the Ministry, we had some initial difficulties. We announced ourselves as the new English teachers (at least I remained silent but smiled amicably) but of the few people wandering about nobody knew – or apparently cared – where we were supposed to go. In the end some bright soul had the idea of taking us the Translation Department, possibly imagining that we were going to work there. We found a Saudi Office Manager and an Egyptian translator, Mr Amin Hussein, who was to become a good friend, as hospitable in Alexandria as he was helpful in Riyadh. The two chuckled over our laughable mistake: we shouldn't, it seemed, have come to the Ministry at all, but to the Zone Office of Education, miles off in another direction. However, we were told, it didn't matter; we must stay and have tea and then the Manager would drive us there. In the meantime they would phone the Director of Education for the Riyadh Zone, and tell him that we were on our way.

It was my first experience of drinking Saudi tea – and I cannot compute how much more I was to drink, so I will diverge for a moment. Personally I like to drink tea or coffee without milk and with little, or in the case of coffee, no sugar. As a result in England I hardly ever drink tea which is generally made too strong for me (They do the same in Iraq; many Saudis refer to tea in England or Iraq as 'black tea'). Saudi tea is much weaker, sometimes almost straw coloured, sugared before it is served. It comes in little glass cups with handles, about two and a half of which would fill an average English tea cup. The water is boiled in a vessel that serves both as kettle and teapot, or at least it did so in my day. As the water boils the tea and even the sugar are put into this vessel and boiled together for a few moments. At least in Riyadh, these kettles, or teapots, were normally enamelled and often quite nicely decorated; for some reason they seemed to come from Yugoslavia. When the tea is presented to you it is the height of bad manners to refuse it – even if you don't like it. At least the glass must be taken, although you don't have to drink all of it. It is polite to accept two glasses and then refuse more, although with close friends you can, and sometimes do, take a dozen. The glass should be accepted, and drunk from, using the right hand only, and, after the second glass, or whenever you decide to refuse the next, the accepted procedure is to cover the glass with the right hand while smilingly shaking the head; or if a man is walking round pouring out the tea to the guests, to hold it out to him in the right hand – waggling it slightly from side to side. The same gestures are used with Arabic coffee cups, about which I shall have more to say later.

At the moment, however, Ralph and I were having tea with the Director of the Translation Department. After a short time we went out with him to his car in the three – quarters empty parking space, and we set off down town, past the Semiramis and down what was, in a sense, the main street of Riyadh. Called Bat'ha, it was a wide dual carriageway and followed the somewhat winding course of the Wadi Hanifa – dry almost all the time and open, a sort of rubbish pit, very occasionally cleaned out. There were buildings on both sides of Bat'ha, a few four or five storeys but most lower, and they looked pretty ramshackle and in need of paint and cleaning. That first impression was not particularly favourable. At one point, about half way down, on the left there was a big open space with a lot of cars (which I later found out to be taxis) and some animals. I was delighted, on that first morning, to see a Cadillac stop and a sheep get out of the back seat.

Our reception at the Riyadh Education Office helped, I suppose, to colour the glasses through which I have since regarded Riyadh. We were taken to the Directors Office, and introduced to him. The Sheikh was not very tall, plump, extremely short-sighted and with a really benevolent expression. He spoke no English and so had prepared himself for our arrival by having a Palestinian translator ready. He rose to greet us, shaking hands with each of us and afterwards placing his right hand over his heart after doing so to show that he was giving us a sincere and heartfelt welcome. Then as we all sat down he made a very short speech – translated sentence by sentence – in which he thanked us for coming to Riyadh, the first British teachers to do so, and hoped we would be happy working in our schools. When Ralph replied in Arabic, thanking the Director in his turn, there was general pleasure that he had some knowledge of the language, and I felt slightly ashamed, on being questioned, to have to admit that the only Arabic I knew were the numerals one to ten which I had copied down from Ralph's dictation during our potations' of the night before. In fact one of the last things Sheikh Abdul Aziz Al Turki had said to me in London was, "Now remember, we're not sending you to Riyadh to learn Arabic. You must use English and make your students use English to you." For sheer self-preservation, however, I had to ignore, in part at least, that last injunction.

In a short time tea was inevitably produced and then the Director said, through his translator "Now I expect you would like some money." To our amazement, for Middle Eastern countries have a reputation for being dilatory over payments, he told the translator, who seemed also to be the cashier, to bring the papers necessary for the payment of our housing allowances, equal to three months salary. We, in turn, produced the contracts we had signed in London, our passports and a number of passport photographs, (we had been warned in London that we should lay in a good supply of these) and in less than an hour we had not only signed all the necessary papers, but the money – it seemed a vast pile of cash – had been counted out on the Director's desk and handed over to us.

Meanwhile the Director had not been idle. He asked us where we were staying and advised us to share a flat, as there might be some difficulty, and delay in finding accommodation that we would like. However there and then he telephoned the Headmasters of our respective schools saying that we would arrive on the Saturday morning (readers may remember that we had left London on the Tuesday, had spent Wednesday getting to Riyadh, and it was now Thursday, the last day of the Muslim working week). He asked that English speaking teachers should be available to help us, and also urged each headmaster to request his staff to spend their weekend looking out flats that would be suitable for us to inspect. When all this was done and we had stuffed our pockets full of money, the

Director wished us a pleasant weekend and told us to come to his office at nine o'clock on the Saturday morning, when he would have a car and a driver ready to take us to our schools. As we left the office and for days afterwards, we wondered how two Saudis with little or no English and going to teach Arabic in England would have fared if left to the mercies of our English Local Government Authority!

***

Having what to us seemed an enormous amount of cash in our pockets, our first thought was to go to a Bank. As the National Commercial Bank (whose name was in English as well as Arabic) was just across the road from the Education Office, we went in there. It was of course, Thursday lunch-time, the equivalent of Saturday lunchtime in London, when we tried to open accounts and deposit our money. The teller told us to come back after the weekend. When we expostulated that we couldn't carry all this cash around with us he looked at us quite uncomprehendingly. It was our first intimation that personal property (I write in sorrow "at that time") was absolutely safe in Riyadh. Even so we felt nervous all weekend. One of us always stayed in the room with the money and when we went out to meals we clutched at our pockets and walked around suspiciously, in a way that must have attracted the attention of anybody who saw us.

The Yamama Hotel was, in those days, a very comfortable seeming hotel. The large lounge, occupying most of the ground floor, was filled with groups of big chairs and sofas, grouped geometrically round low tables. The food was not Cordon Bleu, but with the awful memory of the Automatic Restaurant in Damman, a large, reasonably appointed Dining Room, with white, laundered table cloths and napkins, and heavy cutlery – where well-trained, silent-footed Sudanese waiters served food that was always edible and often appetizing – seemed the epitome of Lucullan delights. The Yamama, being opposite the Ministries, was also a place where everybody doing business seemed to go for coffee in the mornings and, as with so many other places, it was a favourite saying that if you sat long enough in the Yamama lounge you would see everybody who was anybody eventually pass through it. Only visitors so exalted that they were invited to stay at the Royal Guest Palace would fail to appear at the Sahari Palace or the Yamama Hotel. In both hotels, the government kept suites for VIP guests permanently reserved.

The weekend passed pleasantly enough. The Yamama was discovered to have a bookstall with a small selection of English books from which we bought with the prodigality of our temporarily boundless wealth. On the Saturday morning, we repaired to the Education Office where we were shown to a car with a driver who then took us to each of the two schools. Ralph, as befitted his senior status, was at the Royal School, then known as The Mahad Anjal, later renamed The Mahad Al-Asema, the Capital Institute. This school, founded by King Sa'ud for his sons and other members of the Royal Family, comprised kindergarten and elementary, intermediate and secondary departments, each housed in a separate wing of the main building. An associated School for Girls was completely separate. I was at the Yamama Secondary School, then the only purely secondary school in Riyadh, and at the time said to be the largest in the Kingdom. The name Yamama, which appeared not only in a school and a hotel, but also in a road, a printers, a grocery, a laundry and doubtless many other places, was one of the names of a very favoured region of farms some fifty miles south east of Riyadh.

At both schools we met the Headmasters and a selection of staff, most of whom spoke English very well. Virtually all were Palestinians, although some of these had Jordanian passports. They had a number of properties for us to view, and we arranged to meet that afternoon at our hotel and go and look at them. Some were frankly awful, the buildings so dark, so noisy and depressing that, although individual flats might not be bad, the heart sank at the thought of actually living there. I can't remember now what I was expecting. I suppose it was something like pictures of the Kasbar in Algiers I had seen in old copies of the *Boys' Own Paper*, but with Dolphin Square type flats inside. Anyway the ones we saw were nothing like that.

There was, however, one flat that stood out from the others. On what we thought of as the main "European" shopping street, Wazir Street, where the shops had plate glass windows and notices in English, was a large modern block of flats on a street corner opposite a mosque. It belonged to one of the King's sons who it seemed had just mortgaged it to a bank. His secretary's flat was vacant and was for rent. It had excellent carpets and curtains throughout, and air-conditioners were installed everywhere: there was also a certain amount of comfortable furniture and a fully equipped kitchen. It was big, with two entrances, five large rooms and some smaller, with two European bathrooms. There was however, a snag: the Syrian teacher from the Mahad Anjal who had found this treasure wanted one of the rooms and a bathroom for himself and a friend. The room was self-contained, quite shut away, and they would not, he said, trouble us in any way or come into "our" part of the flat. On the first day this snag made the scheme seem impossible, but after looking at other flats of increasing impossibility, we were wavering on the second day and on Monday we took the flat. I have no doubt now that the year's rent we paid in advance also covered the rent of our new "flatmates" and probably included commission and a finder's fee; but of that even Ralph was, I think, unaware. The comparatively few things we had to procure were found quickly, and within a week of our arrival we were installed. Our Syrian co-tenant, whose name I have forgotten, was little trouble, although the following year, when I had moved to a house in the Old Quarter, Ralph told me that he thought the man had stolen several hundred pounds from a locked suitcase, but he may have been mistaken. His friend was a Palestinian Science Master: after the forced abdication of King Sa'ud this teacher was in trouble because of his connections with some of the King's sons who were *persona non grata* with the authorities. He was forbidden to teach but for the remainder of his contract he worked as a laboratory assistant. He was a tall, bespectacled, good-looking man, very quiet with an easy sense of humour and pleasant, unassuming ways. In any dealings I had with him, he was kind, helpful and thoughtful. His name was Mohammed Oudah, and he was to become better know to the world as Abou Dawoud, one of the leaders of the Palestinian Resistance and supposedly the mastermind behind the Munich Olympic Games massacre.

***

So at last I was installed in Riyadh, a city so different now to what it was in 1964 that one reason for writing this book is to record, or try to record, something of what it was like then. Although it is getting on for half a century ago, I made rough drafts for parts of this book in 1980, while I was still living in Riyadh, and I had luckily written long and detailed accounts of my adventures to my mother, who, as mothers do, kept them. That is how, at this distance of time, I can say exactly what happened and how and why in those early days. Even in 1980, I felt there had already been profound changes apart from the obvious physical ones. As the face of the city had altered, so had the character of the people changed, under the twin stresses of too much money and too many foreign workers with their foreign ways and customs. I do not regret all change, always preferring the old for its own sake, nor am I a fanatical Arabist, distrusting all non-Arab influences; but I was fortunate enough to live in Riyadh during a time of great social upheaval unequalled perhaps in any other major city. In 1980, it seemed to me a matter for regret, but nevertheless for noting carefully, that the quality of life in Riyadh during my sojourn had deteriorated – however much it might have appeared to have improved materially.

In 1964 Saudi Arabia was already an important country in that it was a major oil producer, and had a lot of money to spend; but beyond a limited number of people with a particular interest it was still no more than a name. I believe that many of my friends and relations had to recourse to an Atlas to find out precisely where Saudi Arabia was in relation to its neighbours. At the end of the year or early in 1965, my mother tried to send me a cable. The telephone operator was extremely dubious and advised her to go to the General Post Office in Worthing. Even then there was a long delay: the man in charge of Overseas Cables had never heard of Riyadh and didn't believe in it. There was, he said, a town with a somewhat similar name in Jordan, perhaps I was there? It says something of my mother's persistence that the cable eventually arrived. Only a dozen years later, at every international crisis, the world waited and wondered about Riyadh's reaction and the procession of VIPs visiting the King seemed unending.

In part, the dramatic change was due to the increased importance of oil in an energy-hungry world, but in my opinion, it was also due in no small part to King Faisal. The King was a statesman whose impact on the world's stage was so great that I believe – even without his country's enormous revenues – he would have made Saudi Arabia the leader of the Arab and Islamic worlds. In the magisterial *The House of Sa'ud* by David Holden (completed after his murder by Richard Johnson), the authors criticise King Faisal and allege that he was paranoid about Israel. But I know what the feeling in the country was during that time, and more and more we felt safe while King Faisal was at the helm of the ship. I remember when rumours were going around that something frightful had happened, I telephoned the Radio Station to get private information and was told that it would soon be announced officially that the King had been murdered. I turned to my mother, who was beside me, and told her and she burst into tears. I can think of no better tribute.

As the whole world wanted oil, and at that time the Middle East was the most prolific source, so Riyadh's influence increased and the combination of factors – great wealth, great power and being courted by the nations of the world – had a shattering effect on a people who, as I shall try to explain in later chapters, until a dozen of so years before my arrival, had been the most tightly enclosed of all inhabitants of capital cities, with the possible exception of Lhasa in Tibet. I can offer one story to illustrate the point. A little before I left Riyadh a youngish middle-aged man came to my house. I did not recognise him until he introduced himself as one of my senior pupils during my first year at Al-Yamama School; I had not seen him since. He had heard that I was leaving and wanted to say good-bye. He spoke faultless English which with more politeness than accuracy, he ascribed to the grounding I had given him at school. We talked of the changes I had seen in the city and in the people: "You know," he said, "when you came here if two men wanted to do business they agreed terms and shook hands. There was no need of documents: the handshake was enough, it made the thing rock-solid. Today, if I was doing business with my own brother, and we had a legally binding contract approved by my lawyers, I would not feel easy or confident until I knew that my brother's money was in my bank account." I think this sums up the change rather well.

We used to laugh, back in 1964, that the Islamic date of 1384, that is the number of years from the Hejira, the flight of the Prophet Mohammed from Mecca to Medina, was more appropriate to our life than the corresponding Gregorian date. This exaggeration, pardonable I think, had an element of truth. Some things had changed little in the six or so centuries that separated the two dates, and although many innovations were already pouring in, people who had been in Riyadh in the early 1950s entered a city that would have caused little surprise to a medieval Arab time-traveller.

This book is not a formal history or geography of Saudi Arabia, although in the next chapter I have to touch on both to explain the background to a country that, after all, was technically younger than I was! It is a book about the people of Riyadh, and what it was like as an Englishman to live there for many years in a time of great change. It is nearly a quarter of a century since I left, and there have obviously been enormous changes since then. But I am sure that if I were to go back to Riyadh at any time and look up old friends, I would be welcomed in the true Saudi tradition, as if I had left them only a week or two before.

Arabs have a different concept of time to most Westerners. It is a fact always to be remembered that Arabs are not Europeans – we are different people. Spaniards are more like Swedes and Germans more like Greeks than any of them to Arabs. People used to talk to me in Riyadh about the "arrogance" of the Saudis, because they were not interested in the views or opinions of the people who complained about them. Yet it seemed to me then, as it still does, that it was equally arrogant to assume that they should be interested,

After I had been a couple of years in Riyadh, I considered myself an expert on Saudi affairs; and after ten I laid down the law to all and sundry in what must have been a most trying way. I was often invited to meet visiting businessmen or personalities, so that, over luncheon or dinner, I could give them the distilled essence of my experience and prognosticate about the future. By the time I left I was no longer sure of anything.

During those long years I was faced with the usual number of problems and frustrations faced by all who work in the Middle East. But I had also been the fortunate recipient of an incredible amount of kindness, generosity and help. I think I learned patience in Riyadh and, even in the most difficult times – as the would-be philosopher said to Dr Johnson – "cheerfulness would keep breaking in." I write this book with no illusions about the people of Riyadh, but with a deep affection for them which I have never lost.

CHAPTER 1
Making the Desert Kingdom

I do not propose to write a History, or even a Geography, of Saudi Arabia; but I think I should write a couple of chapters that combine something of both, in order to explain how the country in which I found myself in 1964 had come into being. It was not an old country; as I have said, it is younger than I am.

For centuries, for millennia even, life in the arid centre of the Arabian Peninsula changed little. There were two sorts of inhabitants: the Bedouin, who moved perpetually with their herds of camels and flocks of sheep and goats, seeking food for their animals; and the settled inhabitants of the oases. Between the two groups there was always an uneasy balance, between a sense of mutual dependence and a corresponding tradition of mutual distrust. The Bedouins' role was to provide meat, milk, and camel hides, together – crucially – with protection for the oasis dwellers when they travelled. These oasis dwellers built towns with walls around them, which the Bedouin could not penetrate, but they controlled the water, as well as other supplies the Bedouin needed.

These Bedouin raided each other often, usually in search of camels: they were very active, very impulsive, very light fingered and, between energetic bouts of violent action, very lethargic. That is, I believe, partly why Arabs have found it difficult to establish anything of permanence. It may, perhaps, have something to do with the effects of the climate, about which I shall have something to say later; but here I can point out a certain pattern. In the century after the death of the Prophet Mohammed an Islamic Jihad (Holy War) spread the power of the new Islamic Empire, the Caliphate, all over the Middle East, across North Africa, and into Europe; but it soon broke up, and, although nearly all the lands remained Muslim, they were no longer united. Much later, in the eighteenth century, the Al Sa'ud family rose, collapsed, rose again, collapsed and rose for the third time in the twentieth. Now more than a century has passed and the

House of Sa'ud is still going strong. The Bedouins have always considered themselves the aristocracy of the Arab World, and, indeed, their innate superiority seemed to be acknowledged by others, as practically every Saudi family I met could – or claimed they could – trace their ancestry back to Bedouin roots. My mother once complimented a young – and very well connected – Saudi wife on the excellence of her English. "Well," the girl said, "I was educated in a Catholic Convent by English teachers; but of course, I am really a Bedu."

I don't know how things were in pre-Islamic times, but during the last fourteen centuries the Bedouins have become very religious Muslims. I call them "religious" rather than "pious," because, in Catholic terms, the implications are different. Yet I acknowledge that the Bedouin could well claim to be "pious" in the Roman sense, as that Latin word implies doing one's duty to the will of God and to one's family.

Until the last seventy-five years, the Arabian Peninsula was never a settled place. There were a number of tribes who had become oasis dwellers, of whom the Al Sa'ud family was only one, and not the most important. David Holden states that the family was originally part of the nomadic Duma tribe from Oman (which still has a reputation for breeding excellent camels) and one Sheikh, Mani Al-Muraidi, was invited by the inhabitants of the Wadi Hanifa to settle among them, possibly with an idea that their own camel stock would be improved. The camel strain was known as Dara'iya. More than four centuries ago, Sheikh Mani founded a little settlement, called Dara'iya and this became the capital of the principality that grew there. One of Mani's descendants was named Sa'ud, and – for a reason I cannot tell because I do not know – gave his name to the family.

Mani's great-great-great-grandson, Sheikh Mohammed ibn Sa'ud, who flourished in the middle of the eighteenth century, is the first figure in the family who could be described as "historical." It was he who laid the foundations for the future greatness of his family by his role in a movement of religious reform. More than a thousand years earlier, when the Prophet Mohammed travelled through those lands "which once were Christian," he had found sloth, corruption and indifference, and immediately began to preach a call for a return to the old simple and direct relationship with God. In the middle of the eighteenth century, a new travelling preacher found the same faults among his Muslim contemporaries. Sheikh Mohammed Abdul Wahab was a Najdi who, if I may make a Christian comparison, became the John Calvin of Arabia. He found so-called Muslims praying to Saints, declaring statues, stones, even trees to be "sacred," decorating mosques elaborately and ignoring the Laws of the Holy Koran. To make matters worse, the tribes of the Najd were lawless and in a state of almost constant warfare. In such a situation even a sublime preacher would have found it hard to spread his message – that is, unless he had powerful secular backing. Sheikh Mohammed Abdul Wahab found the help he needed in the Emir, Sheikh Mohammed Al Sa'ud of Dara'iya. There is a story that the Emir's wife, convinced by the Sheikh's preaching, persuaded her husband to give the necessary practical support. I am reminded of the story that it was the Christian wife of King Ethelbert of Kent who persuaded her husband to welcome Saint Augustine to England – which is why, 1411 years later, Canterbury is still the headquarters of the worldwide Anglican Communion. If I may continue the English comparison, at much the same time that Sheikh Mohammed Abdul Wahab was crossing the Najd, preaching against corruption and indifference, John Wesley was preaching against the sloth and indifference he found in the Church of England.

To cement the alliance, in 1744, the Emir's son, Abdul Aziz ibn Mohammed Al Sa'ud was married to a daughter of Sheikh Mohammed Abdul Wahab. The sheikh's family soon became known as Ahl Al-Sheikh, The Family of The Sheikh, and they were still so called when I lived in Riyadh. They have continually intermarried with the Al Sa'uds (King Faisal's mother was from that family) and have acted as the spiritual advisors to the Al-Sa'uds. Hence they have had a considerable influence on government, in particular on education – which was, until recent years, almost exclusively religious.

What came to be known as Wahabism spread over the whole of the Najd and the verbal swords of the preachers were backed by the very material swords of their secular supporter. It was ultra-puritanical and very strict, and by no means welcomed by the more relaxed Hejazis of the Western Province, or those living in Al-Hasa Province in the East. There are different "schools" in Islam and, among the Sunnis throughout the world, the Wahabis are regarded as the strictest – except in Saudi Arabia, where the word "Wahabi" is never used. To a Saudi cleric, the term Wahabism would suggest that another Muslim sect had been founded, whereas what had really happened had been a return to the purity of the original faith. In other words, the followers of Wahab were the "real" Muslims and everyone else was out-of-step. The only permissible term was "Muwahidin" or – to use a Christian term – "Unitarians" (Wahid means One) for they stressed the oneness of God. "La Illah Ha Illah Lah" (There is no God but God) is the bedrock of their faith. Since God is omnipotent, omniscient and omnipresent, all life, including all political and religious matters, is indivisible. And so, almost unconsciously, a completely theocratic state was born, one that has proved extremely difficult to steer through the cataclysmic changes of the twentieth century and beyond.

Just as the Prophet Mohammed's preachings were enough to launch that first Jihad – which spread Islam over so many lands – so, on a much smaller scale, the preaching of Mohammed Abdul Wahab, with the powerful support of Mohammed Al Sa'ud, spread over much of Arabia. In theory, the whole of the Peninsula was part of the Ottoman Empire, but in reality the Turks only controlled the Hejaz – where, as Khalifa or Caliph, the Sultan was the Protector of the Holy Cities of Mecca and Medina – and they also had some influence further south in Asir and Yemen. They did control the North, including Palestine, Syria, Iraq and Kuwait, but their influence down the Arabian side of the Gulf as far as Oman was nominal rather than real. The Turks certainly never had much influence in the Najd, where they contented themselves with playing one tribe off against another. The Bedouins, inflamed with puritanical zeal, extended their onslaught right across the Peninsula from the Gulf to the Red Sea. Above all they took the two Holy cities, where their iconoclastic activities reminded me all too well of those of some of Cromwell's soldiers – who destroyed much that was priceless in English Churches. Some Bedouin bands even probed towards Damascus and Baghdad, but it was the loss of Mecca and Medina – which he was supposed to be protecting – that stirred the Sultan to somewhat ponderous activity. The Ottoman Empire was already in decline, although it would be more than half a century before it was officially described as "the sick man of Europe." The Sultan did not actually do anything himself, but he asked – or rather ordered – his new Viceroy in Egypt, the energetic Mohammed Ali, to expel the desert invaders.

It took Mohammed Ali seven years to complete the task, but by 1818 (the Sultan's call had been in 1811) the Viceroy's son, Ibrahim Pasha, had not only "freed" the Holy Cities and retaken the Hejaz, but had also moved 500 miles further into the heart of Arabia, to punish the Al Sa'uds once and for all. He surrounded the little town of Dara'iya for weeks and, with cannon all round the town – their emplacements are still shown to visitors – simply battered most of Dara'iya to pieces. The British would have liked him to go on as far as the Gulf to deal with those they designated Wahabi Pirates. At that time the British – in India – were doing a lot of trading in the Gulf, and they had drawn up agreements with many of the coastal sheikhs – culminating in a series of treaties that lasted until 1970. It all worked quite well – the coastal tribes had protection and the British got on with their trade: if any local ruler was so foolish as to step out of line, a British warship came along and bombarded him.

To the disappointment of the British, Ibrahim Pasha had had enough of Arabia and turned for home, taking time only to send the Saudi prince to Constantinople – where he was beheaded – collecting all available food from the area and destroying the date-gardens of Dara'iya. The oddest incident in this story is that the British, wanting to show their appreciation of Ibrahim Pasha by presenting him with a sword, despatched George Forster Sadleir, a young army captain. Sadlier arrived at Dara'iya and Riyadh, a village further down the Wadi, but the Egyptians had already left. The first European to reach Riyadh, Sadleir found the people helpless and starving. Being "British", the Captain pressed on, unavailingly, and completed the crossing of the Peninsula – more than a thousand miles – in eighty four days: this was the first recorded crossing of Arabia by a European. I have never discovered whether the gallant captain pursued Ibrahim Pasha into Egypt, or sent the sword, or whether, indeed it ever reached its intended recipient.

It took the Al Sa'ud family more than twenty years to recover from this setback, and perhaps inevitably other tribes made the most of their opportunity. In particular, there were two "noble" Arab families – the Sudairis from Al-Qassim, north of Riyadh, and the Al-Rashids from Ha'il, some three hundred and fifty miles north. The Al-Rashids were powerful and were paid by the Turkish authorities to keep other Arabian tribes in order.

When the Al-Sa'uds came back to the Najd they did not return to Dara'iya. The place had proved "unlucky" and nobody wanted to live there. A new "capital" was established a few miles down the Wadi in the village called Riyadh, where many houses were built and a wall, with gates, erected around them. The first re-settlement came under Turki, Mohammed Al-Sa'ud's "grandson", or more probably great-grandson, but it was Turki's son, Faisal, who carried the new emirate much farther.

Faisal ibn Turki Al-Sa'ud was a desert warrior of the storybook kind, and is now regarded as the founder of the modern family's authority – which also meant that of the Wahabis – over most of Central and Eastern

Arabia. As might be expected, however, Faisal's success roused opposition. In the East his progress alarmed the British, who liked to look at the Gulf as – in the main – their preserve. In the centre the Turks were also concerned, remembering what had happened in the previous century. They began intriguing seriously with the Al-Rashids, with a view to subduing these Najdis. Even the French became involved as part of their campaign against British interests in the Middle East. In 1862 the Emperor Napoleon III sent a spy to Riyadh to report on the situation: William Gifford Palgrave was a very complex character, described as a Jesuit priest in French pay who was also an English Jew who travelled disguised as an Arab Doctor – a disguise never penetrated. Palgrave was the second European to visit Riyadh. He wrote an account – which I have never seen – of his adventures, and it sounds as if it could have come out of the more exciting pages of the old *Boys' Own Paper*.

There was a third European visitor in 1865, and again an English man. Colonel Lewis Pelly came – rather boldly – to warn Faisal not to interfere with British interests in the Gulf. The welcome was not encouraging. Faisal himself was polite but he was old, frail and blind (he died a few months after Colonel Pelly's visit). He was surrounded by friends, antagonistic Wahabi "advisors," who resented the presence of a man who was not only a Christian but also the representative of an Infidel Power. As far as Britain was concerned it was stalemate, but the fortunes of the Al Sa'ud family were about to experience a second eclipse. Sibling rivalry seems to be a fact of life among Arabs. Although, theoretically, the leader of the Family/Tribe is chosen by the elder members of The Family – in the Najd with the help of the Ulemas (Religious Leaders) – there is always the possibility that one or more of those who are not "chosen" may decide to dispute the matter. In the Al-Sa'ud Family the elder sons of the Emir Faisal – Sa'ud and Abdullah – fought a running and costly battle for power for almost twenty years. Abdullah ruled in Riyadh in 1865, when he built the Musmak – the historic citadel in the middle of the old city – but in 1871 he was forced to ask the Turks for help against his brother. I don't know what inducements he gave, but the Turks were pleased to help him, sending troops down the coast from Kuwait to occupy the Eastern Province of Al-Hasa as far as the Sheikhdom of Qatar. At the same time, in Ha'il, Mohammed ibn Rashid – who had murdered most of his closest relations – had emerged as a very vigorous, and undisputed leader of the Ash Shammar tribe. Armed with Turkish money and encouragement he began to harass the Saudis. Attacked from the North, cut off from the

Sea to the East and torn by internecine fighting between the brothers, the power in Riyadh crumbled. By 1881 the Al-Rashids were in charge, although for another ten years they allowed Faisal's third son, the pious but unstatesmanlike Abdul Rahman, to act as governor – for that was all he was. Between them, Sa'ud and Abdullah, had ruined The Family: I like to remember that, a century after her father had been briefly in power in Riyadh, friends took me to the Palace of his centenarian daughter, Princess Sara bint Abdullah ibn Faisal, to take my midday meal.

By 1891, Mohammed ibn Rashid had enough of the Al Sa'uds and forced them out of Riyadh. The future king of Arabia, Abdul Aziz ibn Abdul Raman ibn Faisal Al Sa'ud, was in his eleventh year – he had been born on 24 November 1880 – and with his sister Nura was carried, as desert children used to be, in woven bags slung on one of the camels. They travelled due East and found refuge for some months in Qatar; and then for rather longer with a Bedouin tribe, the Al Murrah, on the fringe of the Rub Al Khali, the Empty Quarter, which the Bedouin call Al-Rimal, The Sands. After some time with the Al Murrah, they moved northwards through the Eastern Province, obviously unobtrusively, since they looked and behaved like Bedouins, and ended up in Kuwait, at that time, nominally at least, a part of the Ottoman Empire. The ruling family, then as now Al Sabah, agreed to give them shelter: the Ottoman Government must have been informed of their presence, for the Al' Sa'uds were offered a small pension if they stayed put and didn't make nuisances of themselves.

In 1897 two events occurred, at the time apparently by no means earth shattering, but which were to have a very important effect on the history of Arabia. I doubt whether the Foreign Office in London, preoccupied with arrangements for the Diamond Jubilee, even noticed what was happening. The first event was the death in Ha'il of Mohammed ibn Rashid, the dynamic leader of the Ash-Shammar tribe, and a new eruption of family rivalry, which had caused so many deaths a generation before. The second took place in Kuwait, where the ruler was murdered by his brother, Sheikh Mubarak Al-Sabah, a man of great energy and ambition – and far more likely to sanction Saudi adventuring than his predecessor had been.

So young Abdul Aziz spent his teenage years in Kuwait, where, according to his family he used to go out of town and sit on a low hill, looking towards Riyadh. He grew into a striking and compelling figure, well over six feet tall and broad in proportion. He towered above his fellows and, although still very young, was recognised as a leader – never the case with his father. When he was nineteen or twenty, Abdul Aziz began to lead Bedouin-style raids – with the permission, perhaps encouragement, of Sheikh Mubarak Al-Sabah. I suspect the objective was to gain experience as much as anything else. Although not always successful, Abdul Aziz started to be seen as a man worth following; in his mind he was already working out a plan to return to the Najd and to drive the Rashids out of Riyadh.

Yet on any rational calculation the chances of success must have seemed slim. Abdul Aziz could only muster a small force, surely not strong enough to capture a walled town, much less to hold it against more powerful enemies. Sheikh Mubarak urged caution but the young man was determined. I believe – on no evidence other than my gut instincts – that Adbul Aziz, a deeply religious man, believed that it was God's Will that the Al-Sa'uds should return to Riyadh, and hence that he would be given the power to achieve the seemingly impossible.

Abdul Aziz set off with forty men and a few slaves, and as they journeyed some Bedouin joined them. Three of Abdul Aziz's companions must be named because they were to play major roles in what was to follow. All three were closely related to their leader; Abdullah ibn Jilawi, and Abdul Aziz ibn Musaid were his cousins on his father's side and Mohammed Al-Sudairi was a first cousin on his mother's side. The little group first went to the Al-Murrah – among whom Abdul Aziz had spent time as a boy – and then moved towards Riyadh. They spent Ramadan at the oasis of Haradh, later to become a station on the Riyadh-Dhahram Railway and the end of a huge oilfield. Here some of Abdul Aziz's party left him, to spend the Fasting Month with their families.

Abdul Aziz was now finalising his plans and, before the month was over, the party moved towards Riyadh. By the time they celebrated the end of Ramadan, they were within eighty miles of the city. The next day they approached it. There are many different accounts of the events of the next hours; David Holden identifies five versions in addition to information he received from members of the Royal Family. I shall put down here what I was told and the reader can accept it or not! All accounts agree that ten men were left to look after the camels, with instructions that they were to go back to Kuwait if things went wrong. Thus, with a somewhat depleted party, Abdul Aziz made his way to the walled city.

My account is that, as the attack was planned for the night, the party hid the preceding day behind high ground – in what was to become the suburb of Malaz, to the to the west of Sitteen Street. I had a villa near there and Saudi visitors used to point to the rocks and say "King Abdul Aziz hid behind there before he captured Riyadh." The party moved down to the city after dark, sometime after the last prayer. They discovered that the walls were in poor condition and had crumbled at one point – so it was easy to place the trunk of a palm tree against the wall and then climb up. Once inside they made their way silently through the streets until they reached the Citadel, the Musmak, where, report had it, the Rashidi governor, Ibn Ajlan, slept for reasons of security, while his family lived opposite in a private house. Beside the house was another belonging to dependents of the Al-Sa'ud family and it was this house that was at the centre of Abdul Aziz's plan. The party moved unnoticed through the dark streets – something that would not have happened a few years later. When they reached their destination they knocked gently on the door. A girl asked who was there, and, on the reply, "Abdul Aziz, the son of Abdul Rahman," she was told to open the door and welcome the visitors. They were shown onto the roof and from there it was an easy task to move over to the roof of the next-door house occupied by the Governor's family. Finding a way from the roof into the rest of the house, the raiding party quickly overpowered the sleeping women and their servants and then settled down to drink coffee and recite verses from the Holy Koran until dawn.

At last the call to Dawn Prayer came from the nearby mosque – then quite simple but much enlarged later. At this point all the accounts are the same, and they puzzle me. It seems that Abdul Aziz and his friends said their prayers and made their way downstairs to watch the gate of the Musmak – through which there came sounds of activity. After about half an hour they heard the sound of hooves as Ibn Ajlan's horse was brought from its stable, the wicket gate of the fortress opened and the governor came out with some of his followers. Now what puzzles me is this: after the call for the Dawn Prayer why weren't the streets full of men going to the Mosque, and later coming back? It can only mean that the Rashids were lax in enforcing religious observance. I am sure that, a year or so later, there would have been a roll call in every mosque, and "absentees" who were not actually ill would have been dragged to the mosque. Even in the governor's house the men-servants would have been expected to attend at all prayers.

On this day Ibn Ajlan and his son had prayed – at least I hope they had – inside the Musmak and as soon as they appeared the Saudis launched themselves across the street crying "Al-Sa'ud" and "Allah Akbar" (God is Great). There was a confused scrimmage in which most accounts say that Abdul Aziz shot at Ibn Ajlan, but missed, and Abdullah ibn Jilawi threw a spear – which also missed, but stuck in the door. The spearhead is still there, and when I was taken to see the Musmak I was told to touch it – although whether this was supposed to bring me luck I do not know. Ibn Ajlan tried to get back inside the fortress but was caught by Abdullah ibn Jilawi and soon killed. Exactly how he was killed is not clear although later accounts give the credit to Abdul Aziz. David Holden tells of an old man who used to sit at the gate of the Musmak and give people his witness account. I never saw him but I was taken to the house of one of my students to meet an old man who had been there at the time – not as a member of the raiding party, but as someone who had lived in the street and had witnessed what happened. The number of Abdul Aziz's followers varies from story to story – from six to nine to fifteen to twenty three. My informant told me "about twenty," and that might have included two or three from the household where they had been given admission.

With the death of Ibn Ajlan the guards were demoralized. A few were killed and the rest surrendered. About an hour, however, after the skirmish had begun, the imposing figure of Abdul Aziz appeared on the battlements of the Musmak and threw the severed head of Ibn Ajlan to the crowd in the street below. He was some seven weeks past his twenty-first birthday and he was now master of Riyadh. Perhaps it was fortunate that his father preferred the role of Imam or spiritual leader and showed no inclination to rule the city once more or even to return to it. But there can have been few on that January morning in 1902 who could, in their wildest dreams, have imagined how far, and how successfully, this young man was to go.

Over the next years Abdul Aziz strengthened his position inasmuch as he gained the support of the tribes around Riyadh, but he still looked on the Rashids as the principle enemy. As far as the world outside Arabia was concerned, he was a very small bit player on the stage. But two factors were coming into play that changed all that: the first was oil, although its significance was not realised at the time. Oil prospecting had been going on in Persia – as Iran was then called – since 1901. On 26 May 1908, oil was found 130 miles North of the Gulf and the Anglo Persian

Oil Company began to build the first regional pipeline down to the Gulf, where the Company built a new city together with a refinery at Abadan. At the time there was little interest south of the Gulf, but in 1911 the Emir of Bahrain was persuaded to sign a treaty whereby he agreed not to sign any oil-concessions without first obtaining permission from Delhi – for the Middle East was in the sphere of influence of the Viceroy of India, rather than of London. In 1913 the Emir of Kuwait signed a similar treaty and agreements were made subsequently with other Sheikhs and rulers of the Arabian Coast.

I said that there were two factors, and at the time the second seemed the more important, for it threatened British trade in the Gulf: this was the sudden interest shown by other European powers in the area. The first were the Russians, who had expanded Eastwards until, in Vladivostok, they obtained a port with access to the Pacific. They also wanted access to the Indian Ocean, as they had done for years, and during the latter part of the nineteenth century they had been playing what Kipling called "The Great Game" – trying to force a way through Afghanistan into India. In 1908, the Russian Consul in Bushire, the chief Persian port on the Gulf, visited Kuwait and met the inaccurately named Abdul Aziz ibn Faisal. To this young man, the conqueror of Riyadh, the Russians offered arms, ammunition and money. They also offered to help Kuwait, and promised to build a railway from Kuwait to Tripoli, on the Syrian coast – it is now in Lebanon – which would allow traders to avoid using the Suez Canal. Russia already shared with Britain a sort of unofficial Protectorate over Persia and was a serious rival. Of course, Russia had recently suffered a major defeat. In 1905, her drive to expand eastwards had been thwarted when the Japanese had completely destroyed a highly regarded Russian fleet – despatched from the Baltic – at the Battle of Tsushima. Russia's prestige was badly damaged but she was clearly anxious to restore it by increasing her influence elsewhere. In other words, the danger was that, "rebuffed" in the Far East, Russia would turn her attention to the Middle East and to Europe; "wounded powers" can be especially dangerous.

And Germany and France were also in the picture. As the world drifted towards War, the British had even less reason to look favourably on Abdul Aziz. His enemies, the Rashids, were protégés of Turkey and if they helped him against the Rashids, Turkey might move into the German camp. In any case, Germany – like Russia – was increasingly interested in the Middle East. The Germans wanted to build a railway from Baghdad to

Constantinople – a very attractive proposition – and they emulated the Russians by offering Sheikh Mubarak a railway from Kuwait.

The French had never had a foothold in Arabia, but that did not stop them trying to infiltrate the area – mainly in order to make difficulties for the British. The French were not very successful because, while trying to bribe the Sultan of Muscat to place himself under French rather than British protection, the French Consul became involved in illicit slave trading and was disgraced. Britain's most potent weapon was "The Very Superior Person," Lord Curzon, the then Viceroy of India, who travelled through the Gulf in 1903. When deputizing for Edward VII at the Indian Coronation Durbar, Curzon had ridden in a golden howdah on a gold bedecked elephant – altogether a more regal figure than the real king would have been. Curzon's visit to the Gulf is still remembered more than a century after the event. This extraordinary figure – fantastic but above all imperial in his white plumed hat and gold braided Vice Regal uniform – certainly made an enormous impression on the Arab rulers he condescended to visit. Sheikh Mubarak of Kuwait ordered a Victoria carriage from Bombay so that Lord Curzon could drive from the landing place to the town. The British Embassy in Bahrain preserves the chair in which Curzon sat as British sailors carried him ashore; it was imperative that he remained dry-shod.

Abdul Aziz (known throughout the world as Ibn Sa'ud; but, as this is a book about Riyadh and he was never called Ibn Sa'ud there, I shall call him Abdul Aziz) still wanted an agreement with Britain, similar to the one made with Kuwait. Anxious to avoid annoying Turkey, Whitehall and Delhi resolutely refused to have anything to do with him – even though the men on the spot, the Political Agents appointed to each coastal Sheikhdom, and answerable to Delhi and to the India Office, took a different view, arguing that it would be wise to assist a young man who was clearly becoming stronger and stronger. Nobody was more urgent, and more interested in Riyadh and all its doings than Captain William Henry Irvine Shakespear who, David Holden writes, not only looked but behaved like a "Boys' Own Paper Hero." He was absolutely forbidden to go near Riyadh, but in 1910 he was lucky enough to meet Abdul Aziz in Kuwait – at a dinner given by Sheikh Mubarak – and to entertain him and their host at a dinner the next day: According to the *House of Sa'ud*, the menu was roast lamb and mint sauce, roast potatoes and tinned asparagus. For some reason Abdul Aziz and Captain Shakespear hit it off at once, and, years later, the Saudi King said that Shakespear was the greatest

Englishman he had met. However the prohibition against a Riyadh visit continued until, at the end of his tour of duty in Kuwait, Shakespear was given permission to visit Riyadh – provided he confined himself to a Geographic Survey and didn't talk politics. Of course, once in Riyadh, he talked nothing else.

Things had not been going the way Abdul Aziz wanted, and there were family matters, which, when I was in Riyadh, it was still Bad Form to mention. I never knew the details, only the very broadest outlines. I explained earlier that when Faisal ibn Turki died in 1865, his elder sons Sa'ud and Abdullah fought each other for years and effectively destroyed the Saudi hold on the Najd. Abdul Aziz, the son of Faisal's third son, had cousins who claimed to be his seniors and wanted to take over his power. Failing to get much support, they moved to Ha'il and threw in their lot with the Rashids. In 1906 they attacked but were beaten in a desert skirmish. The three cousins were captured, yet instead of killing them out of hand – the normal desert practice – Abdul Aziz forgave them and offered them a home and a respected place in the Family. They accepted and were given a family nickname, Al-Araif, the name the Bedouin give a camel that has been captured in one raid and then recaptured in another. The Araif appeared content, but in 1910 there was an amazing story of how two brothers-in-law of Abdul Aziz poisoned the coffee which he always drank after the Dawn Prayer. By tragic chance the wives of the two men, Abdul Aziz's sisters, drank the coffee first; so virulent was the poison that they fell dead within seconds. The husbands fled and sought refuge with the Turkish garrison in the Eastern Province. This was the beginning of another prolonged family quarrel. Abdul Aziz had to fight against the descendants of his elder uncles, and it was six years before they were crushed. So many were killed, that when they surrendered, the survivors really meant what they said.

Meanwhile in one respect Abdul Aziz's standing with Britain had improved. In 1914, the Powers divided into two camps, with Britain, France and Russia on one side, and Germany and the Austro-Hungarian Empire on the other. Turkey, supposed by Whitehall to be Britain's ally, sided with the Germans: the Saudis, those enemies of the Turks, suddenly became the flavour of the month. Captain Shakespear was sent back to Riyadh, to arrange for Abdul Aziz to be recognized as Ruler of the Najd, under British protection. It took the Civil Service a long time to act between Delhi and London but an agreement was formally signed on 26 December 1915. Sadly, Shakespear did not live to see the day. He had ridden with Abdul Aziz some 250 miles north of Riyadh to Jarrab, near Zilfi, to fight the Araif and their Rashidi and Turkish supporters, but there he had been killed when the Saudi forces were put to flight. Abdul Aziz blamed the Al-Ajman tribe for changing sides during the battle. They certainly helped the Rashids to collect the booty afterwards. Should they be blamed for treachery? One would like to think so but I have never read any British condemnation of the treachery of Mir Jafar, when he handed the Battle of Plassey to the English in 1757.

There had been another "plus point" for Abdul Aziz in 1913 when – to the consternation of some British officials, who were about to sign an agreement with the Ottoman Empire confirming Turkish suzerainty over Arabia – the Saudis suddenly threw the Turks out of Al–Hasa (the Eastern province). It seems that the Saudis were responding to a request from the inhabitants, led by the Al Quisaibi family of Hofuf, the capital of Al-Hasa.

In the Hejaz meanwhile matters had taken a critical turn. In 1910 the Sultan appointed Hussein ibn Ali as Sherif of Mecca. The title of Sherif indicated that the holder was descended from the Prophet Mohammed. As a member of the Beni Hashem, and descended on the male side from Fatima, the Prophet's daughter, Hussein was regarded as a man of impeccable breeding and religious distinction. For most of his life, the Turks had kept him an "honoured guest" in Constantinople – largely to keep him out of the way – and he was not very pleased to have to move to the comparative backwater of Hejaz. But he was over sixty and ambitious, and he decided to improve the lot of himself and the Hashemite family, beginning by demanding money "in tribute" from Riyadh, while trying to persuade tribes loyal to Riyadh to change sides. The brevity of Abdul Aziz's reply may be imagined, but soon afterwards his younger brother, Sa'ad, was captured by Hussein's men near the undefined border region between Hejaz and Najd. To secure his brother's release, Abdul Aziz agreed to pay a small annual sum to Hussein ibn Ali and to accept Turkish suzerainty over the Najd. Of course, as soon as Sa'ad returned, Abdul Aziz denounced the agreement on the grounds that it had been made under duress. But an agreement had been made and – at this stage – the British were even more eager than the Turks that it should be enforced. London regarded Sa'ud as Mutasarrif or Administrative Officer of the Ottoman Province of Najd, and the Foreign Secretary, Sir Edward Grey, insisted that he be dealt with "as a Turkish official or not at all." This marked the start of a long campaign of enmity between the Saudis and Hashemites, lasting half of a century and only ending when Abdul Aziz's son, Faisal, and Hussein's great grandson, King Hussein of Jordan, signed an Alliance for Mutual Protection.

The emergence of the Hashemites, at a time when war was becoming increasingly inevitable, presented the British with some difficult choices. I must explain that one difficulty was that most of Arabia, especially the Persian Gulf from which oil now earmarked for the Royal Navy was coming, was under the jurisdiction of Delhi, while the Near East in general was the responsibility of London via its offices in Cairo – Egypt had been a British Protectorate since 1880. London favoured the Hashemites, if only because they were on one side of the Red Sea while the British were on the other, and the important coaling station of Aden was at the end of that Sea. They therefore entered into negotiations with Hussein, even holding out the possibility of an independent Arab Empire under the Hashemites. Hussein had already proclaimed himself "King of the Arabs," and, with the prospect of weapons, £100,000 a month (Abdul Aziz Al Sa'ud got £5000), and a glorious future ahead, he was prepared to throw in his lot with the British. Delhi, which would have preferred to back Abdul Aziz, was in a quandary. Many Muslim soldiers in the Indian army disliked the idea of fighting against the Caliph's soldiers; but if the Sherif of Mecca was also fighting the Caliph, the situation would be changed.

This Anglo-Arabian agreement did at least specify that the future Hashemite Empire should not include any area where the present ruler was under British protection – which would have kept Abdul Aziz safe. But the war situation was so desperate that some moral considerations had to be jettisoned. Thus, the British made an agreement with the French about the dismemberment of the Ottoman Empire, which clearly contravened the terms of the agreement with the Arabs because, under the Sykes-Picot Agreement, France was to control Syria and Lebanon, and Britain Jordan and Mesopotamia (later Iraq). Palestine, as a Holy Land, was to be jointly administered. As if this "Perfidy" was not enough, in November 1917 the Balfour Declaration promised a Home in Palestine for the Jewish people. David Holden quotes a private note from Balfour to Lord Curzon in 1918 to the effect that it had never been intended to stick to the Declaration, but the damage had been done. Indeed, much of the trouble and distress experienced in the Middle East over the past ninety years may be traced back to these conflicting promises.

The War ended in victory for those who had fought against the Turks and the Ottoman Empire came to an end. The division of the Empire caused problems: the Hashemite Empire was not to be, although to do them justice, the British, urged on by T.E. Lawrence, did do something for Hussein's sons, making Faisal (after the French had driven him out of Syria) King of the new state of Iraq – against, I must say, the wishes of his subjects – and his younger brother, Abdullah, became King of the new state of Transjordan, a chunk of desert arbitrarily carved out of land north of where Abdul Aziz claimed jurisdiction. Hussein ibn Ali was left as "King of the Hejaz," and self-proclaimed Caliph.

The part played by T.E. Lawrence – Lawrence of Arabia – is seen as much more important in England than it is in Arabia. When David Holden asked an old Bedouin Chief what he had thought of Lawrence the old man had sniffed and said: "He was the man with the gold." But Lawrence clearly did impress some people. I knew of a young Saudi named after him, Lawrens Sha'alan, whose sister married the present King when he was Prince Abdullah ibn Abdul Aziz. Laurens was in prison in Damascus and his younger brother, Mohammed, told me that Syria was a "rotten country." "Every time we make arrangements for Laurens to escape," he said, "and bribe Ministers, the Police, and the Governor of the Prison, there is a revolution and we have to start bribing a whole new set of people."

Relations between Hussein ibn Ali and Abdul Aziz, always bad, now became even worse. Abdul Aziz had acquired a new English champion in Harry St George Bridger Philby, who struck up a friendship with Abdul Aziz and abandoned the British Mission he was supposed to be on. Philby was never popular with the "official" British Community, nor was he liked by many Saudis – although the King's support kept him in place for quite a long time. He did not survive long after Abdul Aziz died, as his strident and unambiguous condemnation of the way oil was corrupting the Saudi people displeased many of those so corrupted. Thus, in 1958 Philby was to be expelled from the country and driven over the Jordanian border under escort. He was very proud of his son, Kim, and it must have been a terrible shock when Kim turned out to be the "Third Man" with Burgess and Maclean, the Soviet Agents in the Foreign Office.[1]

---

[1] It is amazing that these three lasted undetected for so long; but Sir Roger Makins the Big White Chief in the Foreign Office, could not believe any adverse reports about Maclean because he had been a boy at St Ronan's Preparatory School, Hawkhurst, Kent, where Sir Roger's son was Head Boy.

Abdul Aziz had been forced more and more into the background, as a Prince of Najd who was vaguely on the British side. Neither he nor his supporters liked his comparatively lowly status, below a man who had taken British Christian money to fight against Turkish Muslims, and who now claimed to be the Protector of the Holy Cities – which had already lapsed from that purity they had possessed when the Najdi Wahabis had been in control. It was high time for another Holy War.

As early as 1912 there had been signs of another violently evangelical movement among the Bedouin, as "The Brotherhood," or Al-Akhwan took shape. In a little village called Artawiyah, some 300 miles North of Riyadh, the first of many religious settlements, or Hujar, was founded. Here the pure gospel of Unitarianism was preached to surrounding tribes and with impressive results, as the village soon grew to be a town of 10,000 souls. The Bedouin there changed their ways dramatically: they wore turbans and short robes instead of the "robes" worn by most Arabs; they sold their camels and sheep and devoted themselves to farming, to prayer, and the Holy Koran. Before I left Riyadh, people especially young people, were looking back to the Akhwan with approval.

To start with, the Akhwan were a blessing to Abdul Aziz. We are told that poachers make the best gamekeepers, and in the new Saudi state, the Bedouin – who might have been a major source of trouble – found an ideal role as the religious guardians of the country. Abdul Aziz soon became the leader "I am the Akhwan", he told Harold Dickson, the British Envoy. In 1916 he ordered all Bedouin tribes loyal to him to abandon herding and to come to Riyadh in groups for special religious instruction – to be subsidized by the Treasury. By this means Abdul Aziz furnished himself with a fanatical religious force that would fight with ferocious determination. Death certainly didn't worry them, for anyone who died fighting for God was promised entry into Paradise. Because their main aim was to maintain the purity of what I must persist in calling Wahabisim, they were more virulently opposed to backsliding Muslims than to those of other faiths. There is nothing odd about this: many readers will know that our word "Assassin" is derived from the Arabic "Hashashin," a group that flourished from the eleventh to the thirteenth century in Iran, Iraq and Syria. The Hashashin's aim was the murder of the enemies of Islam, but the worst of these were seen as Islamic leaders and rulers who did not meet the Hashashin's very stringent standards. The name Hashhasin is supposed to reflect the idea that killers were made "high" on Hashish before embarking on their murderous missions.

As I write today we have been seeing something similar in Iraq. There, although Iraqi Christians have been attacked by Muslim zealots, by far the most violent and bloody attacks and massacres are perpetrated by Sunnis against Shi'as and vice versa. The Christian Church is also guilty: in the Fourth Crusade in 1204, the Western Crusaders attacked Constantinople, the Headquarters of the Orthodox Churches, and, in April, sacked it, far more ferociously than any Muslim town they had captured in the Holy Land. The events of 1204 still stand as a major obstacle to the reunification of the Eastern and Western Churches. In the West the wars between Catholics and Protestants in the sixteenth and seventeenth centuries were notable for violence and cruelty; and we have seen in recent times the way members of different churches have treated one another in Northern Ireland.

Although they can sometimes be useful, fanatics are also a source of danger – as Abdul Aziz soon found out. David Holden quotes examples of their behaviour, how they whipped men who had missed attendance at the Mosque, banned not only alcohol but also tobacco and music and threatened death to all Christians not under the protections of the Ruler. Any Muslim, Bedouin or not, who did not live in a Hujar, might become a victim. Even a deeply religious man who did not choose to join them might be killed on their orders. Another man, perhaps less religious, might also be killed – because he could not recite portions of the Holy Koran as well as they thought he should. The Prophet Mohammed was said to have kept his moustache cut short, and any man seen to have a longer moustache had the ends chopped off. It was even said that once the leader of the Mutair tribe, who had been the earliest of the Akhwan, took a pair of scissors and cut off a piece of Abdul Aziz's robe, which he decided was too long.

By 1918 the Akhwan, eager to cleanse the Holy Cities of corruption, were straining for war against Sherif Hussein – who naturally appealed to the British. London and Cairo, still pro-Hashemite, urged full support, wanting to have Hussein on their side when the war came to an end. The pro-Saudi faction, based in India and the Gulf, regarded Hussein as yesterday's man, who would only be a trouble in peace negotiations: they insisted that Abdul Aziz was the up and coming man – and hence the ideal ally for Britain. Diplomacy went on for months, with copious notes and there was even an attempt to arrange a meeting on a British warship at Aden, but nothing came of it: the two men were set on confrontation. In May 1919, the rival armies approached one another at Turaba, a little village some fifty miles East of Ta'if, the summer capital to be. Hussein's second son, Abdullah, soon to be King of Transjordan, commanded the Hejazi Army, numbering 5000. These troops were well trained and armed with modern weapons supplied by the British. Abdul Aziz himself led 1100 camel borne troops. The battle never happened. During the night of 25 May 1919 the Akhwan with Abdul Aziz went off on their own, armed with swords, spears and some ancient rifles: they fell on the Hejazis in the dark, like avenging angels, and by daylight nothing was left of the Hejazi Army (Abdullah had escaped in his night shirt). The guns were captured, the men dead or scattered, the sand wet with blood. The victors fell to prayer and did not bury the bodies of their victims. Holden says that in the 1970s the bodies of the unburied could still be found on the battlefield; but I never heard this. It was a subject not suitable for discussion, or even mention.

Hussein appealed again for British help, suggesting that the Akhwan would descend on Mecca and put the people to the sword. The British sent a Squadron of military aeroplanes and warned Abdul Aziz to control his people. His reply was a model of diplomacy, promising restraint if the British would restrain Hussein. He also suggested that the whole quarrel should be subject to arbitration. London opinion was impressed and began to veer towards the Saudi ruler – in part because Hussein was threatening war, and also talking of abdication if help was not forthcoming. Abdul Aziz did not feel that the time was ripe for a final showdown with Hussein. To the North, the Rashids, though now without Turkish support, were still a nuisance. Indeed Turkish withdrawal from the Province of Asir and the Imamate of Yemen created both opportunities and problems.

Abdul Aziz's diplomacy had its effect. His subsidy from Britain rose from £5,000 a month to £25,000 and he was to be entitled Sultan of Najd and its Dependencies. This title was not very important to the Saudis but it mattered to the British, still hidebound by etiquette and with memories of the importance of titles in India. The point in Arabia was that while the petty Emirs of little coastal states were given a single gun salute, a Sultan would be greeted by twenty-one guns. Provided the new Sultan did nothing to upset British interests in the Gulf, he could be allowed a reasonably free hand in the rest of the Peninsula.

Meanwhile the tribes in Al-Asir were fighting one another and some asked for Saudi help. In 1919-20 an expedition was sent, commanded by the fifteen year old Faisal ibn Abdul Aziz – although his father's cousin,

Abdul Aziz ibn Musaid was with him to advise him – and all the inland part of the Province was taken. There was a rebellion in 1924, but that was put down quickly, and, as the Rashidis had been finally defeated in 1921 by the Akhwan, Abdul Aziz's position was much stronger. The end of Rashidi power was quite dramatic: Hai'il had been besieged by the most violent and fanatical of the Akhwan leaders, Faisal Al Duwish. Massacre looked to be inevitable, but Abdul Aziz arrived with non-Akhwan troops and took personal command. He entered into secret negotiations with the Deputy-Governor who let Saudi troops into the town to surround the Rashid's palace. The long vendetta was over and Abdul Aziz showed his stature by his behaviour. There was no bloodshed and minimal looting, and the surviving Rashidis were taken to Riyadh to live as guests of the Sultan. One, a widow whose husband had been lately murdered in the family feuds, was married by Abdul Aziz and became the mother of the present King Abdullah. Forty years later, Abdullah was to become Commander of The National Guard, which had replaced the Akhwan as the military wing of the Bedouin tribes. The Najdi state now extended so far North that it reached the uncertain ground of the undrawn frontiers with the British protected Hashemite Kingdoms of Transjordan and Iraq; and Abdul Aziz still had the Akhwan, burning with ambition for new worlds to conquer.

That war did not break out in the North was largely due to Sir Percy Zachariah Cox, a calm civil servant who managed to obtain a great influence over Abdul Aziz. Cox's previous post had been in Baghdad where, as High Commissioner, he had installed his protégé, Faisal ibn Hussein as King. Cox understood that there must be a demarcation of frontiers. He persuaded Abdul Aziz to meet him at the little port of Uqair, South of Dhahran and opposite Bahrain. The Uqair Conference of November 1922 was of great importance because, for the first time, the Saudi lands acquired one of the essential attributes of a modern country – fixed frontiers. It is surely a great tribute to Sir Percy that the frontier he drew in Red Pencil on a map nearly eighty-six years ago is still in place today.

It was during and after the Uqair Conference that oil became important to Saudi Arabia. A New Zealand engineer, Major Frank Holmes, had come looking for mining concessions. Since the British had a stranglehold on such concessions from Kuwait to Muscat – with the exception of Saudi Arabia – in 1923 Abdul Aziz signed an agreement with Holmes that allowed Holmes to prospect anywhere between Kuwait and

Qatar. From this agreement Abdul Aziz was to receive £2,000 a year, but he actually hoped that Holmes would find water rather than oil!

With the North, the East, and the South settled, Abdul Aziz could turn again to the West. There, Hussein, King of the Hejaz, was behaving more and more erratically. He refused to allow pilgrims from the Najd to make the Hajj, the ritual Pilgrimage to Mecca; other pilgrims faced extortionate charges from Hussein's agents as well as wholesale robbery from uncontrolled tribesmen. The final straw came in 1924 when the new, secular, government in Turkey announced the end of the Caliphate. Muslim leaders from Morocco to Malaya claimed the right to become the new Caliph, but Hussein ibn Ali – who did, after all control the Holy Cities – declared that, as a descendent of the Prophet Mohammed, it was his duty to take up the sacred burden. However, as part of that sacred burden he banned the Akhwan from performing the Hajj.

During 1923 Saudi forces had extended Abdul Aziz's realm further North, to Sir Percy Cox's frontier, while in the North West they reached Al-Khobar, North of Medina – which certainly infuriated Hussein. In June 1924 a council was held in Riyadh under the Iman Abdul Rahman, Abdul Aziz's father. The Akhwan were joined by tribal leaders and the Ulema. The Akhwan said that they would take the Hajj by force, and the Ulema said the ban was a valid cause for war. By September it was ordered, and the committee representing seventy million Indian Muslims had lost patience with Hussein.

In that month, 3000 Akhwan descended on Ta'if, the summer capital of Hejaz – as in my time it was the summer capital of Saudi Arabia. It was strongly defended by Ali, Hussein's youngest son, but his army fled, to be followed by thousands of civilians down the road to Mecca. The Akhwan caught and murdered some 300 stragglers and then turned on the town. Every house was completely looted and most were burned. Hussein drove from Mecca to Jeddah and went aboard his yacht. He died seven years later in Amman, with his son Abdullah. Before sailing he abdicated and left Ali to cope with what was left.

Again Abdul Aziz moved swiftly to rein in the Akhwan, so when they entered Mecca there was no looting, except for the Royal Palace. Graves of so called "Holy Men" were however destroyed, and all portraits and musical instruments confiscated. When Abdul Aziz arrived in Mecca fifteen days later he came as a pilgrim and led the Akhwan through the Ceremonies. He was anxious to show the Muslim world that he was a worthy Guardian of the Shrines: he was successful in this.

Ali was left in Jeddah – which was in a sorry condition – but as Abdul Aziz held the Akhwan back from the orgy of destruction they craved, the inhabitants dared to hope. Under Ali they had starvation and disease; perhaps it would be better under Abdul Aziz – it could hardly be worse. In December 1925, Ali was persuaded to follow his father into exile and Jeddah surrendered to Abdul Aziz. On 8 January 1926 all the leading men of the Hejaz were summoned to the Grand Mosque in Mecca, where, after the Friday Prayers, Abdul Aziz was solemnly proclaimed King of the Hejaz. A year later he was to become King of the Najd as well. The state he had founded had now changed out of all recognition, for, unlike the population of almost all the Peninsula, his new subjects, the Hejazis, with their own culture and their own ancient cities, were far more worldly and knowledgeable than the Bedouin tribes.

The Akhwan were banned from entering Jeddah, and in the Holy Cities had to be content with whipping men who smoked in public or didn't close their shops quickly enough at prayer time. Smoking was obviously a sore point. The Akhwan insisted that smoking was a sin and must be forbidden and all tobacco stocks destroyed; but the merchants of Jeddah went to Abdul Aziz and complained that prohibition would cost them £100,000 (a very large sum in those days). Not only did Abdul Aziz listen sympathetically, but he allowed the merchants to continue selling tobacco and even to replenish their stocks. Nevertheless, it was perhaps a portent of things to come when Abdul Aziz moved swiftly to curb the merchants' profits by imposing a tax on tobacco sales.

During the Hajj in June 1926 the Akhwan managed to cause a rift with Egypt that lasted ten years (until the death of King Fuad of Egypt). Every year the Kaaba – the holiest building in Mecca which contains the Black Stone, Qibla, to which Muslims all over the world turn when they pray – is covered with a tapestry traditionally woven in Egypt and brought to Mecca in a camel-borne litter, escorted by a contingent of Egyptian troops and a brass band. There were always many Egyptian pilgrims accompanying the soldiers, but in 1926 the whole thing – especially the brass band – became too much for the Akhwan, who attacked the Egyptians, killing some and injuring many more (and scandalizing the whole lot). Only the arrival of Prince Faisal ibn Abdul Aziz prevented worse; but the Akhwan were very powerful and could put between 50,000 and 60,000 men into action at will. As a stopgap measure Abdul Aziz banished them from the Hejaz and told them to operate among their own desert peoples. As Abdul Aziz also put down banditry and the extortions practised upon pilgrims, numbers taking the Hajj rose sharply after 1926. The Saudi Treasury finally had some money in it.

The Akhwan turned their attention to the North again, looking with hatred at the Hashemite Kingdoms. In the years after Uqair, before they had gone into the Hejaz, they had made raids that had been bloody and dramatic. Men, women and children were butchered by the score, and thousands of sheep and cattle were driven back into the Najd. They had been able to act almost as they wanted, because the defences of the new states were not yet properly organized. But when the Akhwan returned to the North after the Hejaz operation, they found the situation changed. In both Transjordan and Iraq, British advisors had mobilized the tribesmen, and armed them with weapons which – though primitive by modern standards – were far ahead of anything the Akhwan had: armoured cars, wireless communications, biplanes that flew over Akhwan positions and reported back, as well as sometimes bombing them. The Akhwan became desperate and one leader, Sultan ibn Bijad ibn Humaid, Chief of the Utaibah tribe, sincerely but fanatically religious, wanted to launch a Jihad (Holy War). In January 1927 Abdul Aziz organised a conference of the Akhwan and the Ulema to judge upon their complaints: on the whole the Ulema favoured the Akhwan but insisted that only the Imam could proclaim a Jihad. A sore point was the Police Posts the British were building in Iraq. Abdul Aziz promised to get the British to dismantle them, but they were not mentioned in the Treaty of Jeddah, signed in May 1927, whereby Great Britain formally recognized the new frontiers. When Gilbert Clayton, former head of the Arab Bureau in Cairo, came to Jeddah in 1928, Abdul Aziz, fearing an Akhwan rebellion, did raise the question, but the British continued to strengthen those border defences, gradually gaining the upper hand. In November 1928, when 10,000 Bedouin attended a Congress in Riyadh, Abdul Aziz threatened to abdicate, but there were cries, "We will have no one else," and he got the support he wanted.

In 1929 the tables were turned. In February Sultan ibn Bijad marched North for another raid. Hearing reports, that the British with troops, armoured cars, and aircraft were ready to oppose him, and knowing that an attack would prove a costly failure – yet unwilling to return home with nothing to show – ibn Bijad turned back southwards and raided other Najdi tribes who lived in the North of the Eastern Province. It was a fatal mistake; so long as the Akhwan confined themselves to attacking the Infidel British and their misguided supporters, their claim to be the Pure

Flame of Islam was indisputable. Once however they showed themselves afraid of the infidels and then attacked their fellow Wahabis, they lost much of their support.

Abdul Aziz raised a new army and marched North into Qassim, where he met the Akhwan at Sibilla, near Jawab – where Captain Shakespear had fallen. He tried to persuade the Akhwan to disband, but in vain, so he attacked them suddenly. The "battle" was over in half an hour; once again Abdul Aziz showed clemency and spared those who survived; but they promptly rebelled again. This time they were crushed firmly and the surviving leaders were imprisoned. Three years later they tried to escape and were transferred to the dungeons of the old Turkish fort in Hofuf: they were never seen or heard of again.

On 18 September 1932 – a little over thirty years from the recapture of Riyadh – Abdul Aziz ibn Abdul Rahman Al-Sa'ud was proclaimed under his final title. The cumbersome "King of The Hejaz and King of Najd and Its Dependencies" was abolished and he became King of Saudi Arabia. This was an act of obvious presumption, for it attached the family name of one tribe to the whole country. David Holden points out that it only stated what was the actual situation, the land being a fiefdom of the Sa'ud Family. I think, however, that it is necessary to look a little deeper. When we remember the importance of Tribal loyalty and Ancestry, and that many tribes considered themselves as good if not better than the Al-Sa'uds, there is a breathtaking arrogance in making everybody, whoever they were and however "grand" their ancestry, become a "Saudi". I cannot say that I was aware of any resentment when I lived in Riyadh, but there was a tendency among people I knew to stress the age and "nobility" of their own family, and Arabs do know about their families. I once heard my Yemeni Major Domo teaching his five year old son his name: it went back thirty five generations.

So the kingdom of Saudi Arabia was now a reality. In the next chapter I shall have to describe the impact of the discovery of oil and the money it brought. Then I can get down to the task of describing what it was like to live in Riyadh in these now far off days.

CHAPTER 2
Black Gold

So King Abdul Aziz Al-Saud was now King of Saudi Arabia, a modern country with (mostly) properly defined international boundaries. The early years were not easy and between 1932 and 1934 there was a successful campaign against Yemen, which resulted in a recognized frontier. Abdul Aziz could have got much more territory but the wily Imam of Yemen left all decisions about peace terms and land to his Saudi "brother" – and Arab etiquette demanded that Abdul Aziz had to be generous in such a situation.

The main difficulty was lack of money. Saudi Arabia was a sovereign state in a modern world, and, although the king was an Absolute Monarch, there had to be some sort of Civil Service – even if of a rudimentary kind. If there were no "Ministers" as yet, there were "Advisors" who had to be paid. Of course, it is the duty of an Arab Head of Family to provide for that family, and so an Arab Head of State is expected to provide for his subjects. Every day the King had to feed hundreds, perhaps thousands of men, who could just turn up at mealtimes and expect a meal. The King's finances had improved when he took the Hejaz, but the benefits were limited by the effects of the Wall Street Crash of 1929 and of the subsequent world depression. The Hajj pilgrims were an important source of the revenue yet, by the early thirties, numbers were barely a third of those attending before the Crash. The state's finances were in the not very capable hands of the King's increasingly alcoholic Treasurer, Abdullah Sulemain, a Najdi who was to remain in control until after Abdul Aziz's death. Abdullah Sulemain was always on bad terms with Prince Faisal, and resigned in 1956 after a blazing row. David Holden makes much of Abdullah Sulemain, but never mentions the man who is of much more interest to me – Sheikh Mohammed Shalhoub Al-Kebir, Treasurer to the Royal Family, whose family I came to know very well. Sheikh Mohammed looked after the King's money, which travelled with him in chests under the Sheikh's strictest supervision. (In old age Sheikh Mohammed kept his money in chests around his room and expected his sons to give him anything they received and he then doled this out as he saw fit. I know they gave him a lot but they must have retained some for their personal use). But, in the old days, when any future king – Sa'ud, Faisal, Khaled Fahad or Abdullah – or any other of the forty five sons of Abdul Aziz, wanted money, they had first to go and ask Sheikh Mohammed and give a reason that satisfied him. In my early time in Riyadh, King Faisal used to visit him regularly, sit on his bed (for the Sheikh was then a centenarian) and call him "Ammi" (my Uncle). His sons and grandsons told me that the old man could not read or write, but had an encyclopaedic memory. After a personal Royal Treasurer was no longer necessary, the Sheikh became a sort of Minister of Bedouin Affairs. As money poured in, the King wanted to reward all those who had helped him, both in the capture of Riyadh and in the early years of conflict. If the original helper was dead, the King was ready to reward his descendants. All claimants had to go to Sheikh Mohammed, who questioned and cross-questioned them. He knew all the details of all the engagements and "who was who" in the various tribes: a claimant making less than justifiable claims had no chance of circumventing the old man; and anyone whose claim he approved was regarded as 100% genuine. The first time I was put into Arab dress was when the Sheikh's grandsons took me to meet him: "Grandfather does not like to see men in trousers," they explained, "He says that trousers are women's wear." Every summer he used to take his extended family to Beirut; his entourage included a good number of ex-slaves who had refused to leave. The King always gave him the use of one of the largest of Saudi Arabian Airlines Boeings. I was told that the flights were experiences to be remembered. Since mountaintops are sacred places – because there one is nearer to God – the Sheikh thought it impious to try to do one better and fly over them. Hence, the pilot was instructed to fly below the mountaintops in Syria and Lebanon and to navigate his large plane through valleys – which was far from safe. I did visit Sheikh Mohammed in Beirut, or rather in the mountains behind the city, but got there under my own steam and never flew in the Shalhoub entourage.

I have, however, wandered from the main point, which is that the King was very hard up in the 1930s, and on a number of occasions it looked as though the young kingdom would go bankrupt. It was not that the King was extravagant in the normal sense of the word: he spent a lot of money – all he had and more – but it was "necessary" spending, on his people. I have already mentioned the crowds who turned up at the Palace at mealtimes. But the king also travelled a lot; it was important for him to visit as many tribes and villages as he could, and of course, to make marriage alliances with as many as possible – because a tribe so linked was not likely to join any movement against the King or the Al-Sa'ud family. The number of Abdul Aziz's wives is not known. He had forty-five known sons by twenty-two different mothers, and at least as many daughters, many by mothers who had no sons – because, with many of those political marriages, a wife was divorced (after she had borne a child).

A Muslim is entitled to four wives at a time. This is not due to excessive libido, but to the fact that desert warfare leads to many fatalities. Had the early followers of the Prophet Mohammed been restricted to one wife, there would have been a lot of girls who remained unmarried and – in a puritanical society – childless, which would be bad for the tribe. Each wife had to be treated in exactly the same way: the husband should spend equal time with them, give them the same gifts and to provide them with a similar house. When I was in Riyadh, there were a number of compounds which had four identical houses, one in each corner, with a larger house in the centre where the husband lived and entertained. In the 1960s there were few people who had four wives, and those who did looked on this as an advertisement, "Look how rich I am." One of my pupils, Dakheel, who became Head of Security at Riyadh Airport was very upset when his father took a second wife. "I don't mind the marriage," he told me, "but he hasn't bought a new house for the new wife as he could, perfectly well. He expects my mother to share a house and a kitchen with her. It isn't fair."

Treating each wife exactly the same as regards presents must have been comparatively easy when it was just a question of a new cooking pot; but in my time in Riyadh the wives of rich men could want very expensive presents indeed. If one wife hankered after a luxury apartment overlooking Lake Geneva then the husband was supposed to buy four; and as for decorated cars…! I was once caught in a traffic jam on my way to school beside a Rolls-Royce covered in beige suede. I told the boys about it in my first lesson saying "I've seen everything now," but while most of them tittered dutifully, one princeling said, crossly, "That car belongs to my Aunty."

The King had not only to look after his four wives but also those he had divorced who were mothers of his children. I think there were also wives who had not had children, who had been married for entirely political reasons, and some of these were subsequently remarried to somebody else at Court. The last wife of Sheikh Mohammed Shalhoub – and his widow – whom I met (with my mother) had been, we were told, the King's fifty-third wife.

On all the King's travels round the country he stopped again and again with tribes or villages. The minimum stay was two nights but it was often more than three or four. On the first night the King gave a great feast to the whole populace, and on the last he was the guest at an equally lavish spread. On the next morning, however, before the King's departure, a party of elders would present a bill for the previous evening's extravaganza (and I don't expect that the costs were underestimated) with an intimation that prompt payment would oblige. It still puzzles me as much as it did when I was first told of this practice, because the Arabs must be the most sincerely and genuinely hospitable race on earth. That the King was expected to pay for his own entertainment can only be explained by the fact the he was the King, the Father of his People, and the Provider of all. I am sure that if these same people had been entertaining Abdul Aziz ibn Abdul Rahman *in propria persona*, everything would have been done to give him the best that could be found.

Meanwhile, as money became tighter and tighter, there was nothing hopeful on the oil front. Major Holmes had been unable to find oil on Saudi Arabian soil and he was not popular: he was only paying £2,000 a year for the right to prospect throughout the Eastern Province, and he left without paying for the last two years. He had been luckier on the island of Bahrain, where he had sold his find to SOCal (The Standard Oil Company of California). I think he would have preferred an English controlled company, but the British were not interested. Both Anglo-Persian in Iran and the IPC (Iraq Petroleum Company) were quite content with what they had on the Northern side of the Gulf. When it came to bidding for the rights to explore for oil in Saudi Arabia, the British would not put any money up front, while SOCal, already in Bahrain, offered £30,000 (in gold) at once, with another £20,000 in eighteen months time, with an annual payment of £5,000, (also in gold for the first year and in agreed currencies after that). After the 1929 Crash the export of gold from the United States was very carefully controlled, and SOCal had to buy £35,000 gold sovereigns in London, and ship them to Jeddah. On 25 August 1933 the sovereigns were delivered to the only "bank" in Jeddah, the Netherlands Trading Society. There, on the manager's table, Abdullah

Sulemain counted them one by one, by hand. In November 1933 SOCal created CASOC (Californian Arabian Standard Oil Company) to run its interests in Saudi Arabia. When in 1936 CASOC wanted more capital it invited the Texas Oil Company, Texaco, to join as an equal partner. The new company was called Caltex until 1944 when it adopted its final name, and became Aramco, the Arabian American Oil Company.

Site after site, however, proved oil-less and hopes were fading when, on 4 March 1938, four years after prospecting had begun, oil was found in Damman No.7. Just over a year later, in May 1939, Abdul Aziz ceremonially turned on the taps of the pipeline leading to the new harbour and storage tanks at Ras Tanura. Saudi Arabia's oil age had begun.

The oil age did not bring the anticipated financial rewards very quickly; in fact the Kingdom, which meant the King, still faced frequent shortages of money. Royal Expenditure increased with the perceived growth in income; but the reality did not match expectations. As the King's "generosity" increased, so did the demands of his enormous family. We have to think of these princes, not so young now and no longer having to go to "Uncle" Mohammed Shalhoub for cash. They were classic examples of the Nouveaux Riches, used to managing with very little but now feeling themselves entitled to a lot more. Money was being spent, whether it was there or not, and debts accumulated. One trouble was that the 1939-1945 war occupied all minds and energies. Although oil was of a great importance to the War Effort, there was no steel to spare for oil installations, and Aramco's output fell dramatically to 30,000 barrels a day in the early 1940s. As Holden reminds us, this represented only about four minutes' production forty years later.

The greatest change during the war years was that the Americans deliberately set out to replace the British as Protectors of Saudi Arabia. The British relationship had been long lasting, although it has to be said that the British never displayed much interest or enthusiasm. In the years before 1914 they had refused to back Abdul Aziz against the Ottoman Empire, and instead supported his hated rivals the Hashemites. The British dealings, whether London-Cairo, or London-Delhi-Bushire-Kuwait, were cumbersome and sometimes contradictory. Furthermore, many Palestinians – usually well educated and in advisory positions – came to Saudi Arabia as more and more Jews poured into Palestine. It is hardly surprising that these Palestinians were markedly anti-British. Not only had the British agreed with the French to divide the region into spheres of influence, but they had also promised to allow the creation of a

Jewish national home in Palestine. The behaviour of the incoming Zionists – quite ready to resort to intimidation and terrorism – was blamed upon the British. Thus for many in Saudi Arabia, Britain became a "Most Hated Nation," and there and elsewhere in the Arab world there were hopes of a quick German victory.

The Americans exploited the anti-British mood. When Britain tried to cut back on the subsidy to the King, the Americans offered to provide the old amount "with no strings" – at least not obviously. They also gave the King all sorts of military hardware that the British could not match and might not have done even if they could. In 1943 came something the British could not emulate: on 18 February President Roosevelt issued an Executive Order declaring Saudi Arabia to be vital to the defence of the United States. This meant that Saudi Arabia was now eligible for Lend-Lease Funds. The American takeover had begun and the Americans offered to train the Saudi military, which would include a small Navy and Air Force. One odd result of this was that in 1947, outside the summer capital of Ta'if, a group of British Officers began to train hundreds of young Bedouin. It was the beginning of the National Guard, something to replace the Akhwan. While the National Guard was not exactly in opposition to the Regular Army, it was seen – at least when I was there – as absolutely loyal to the Royal Family. By 1964, the National Guard was commanded by the present King, Abdullah, a traditional conservative who was popular with the Bedouin. The regular Army was recruited from the towns, and its loyalty was not as automatic as that expected from the Bedouin. There was a plot in the 1970s, when the conspirators intended to assassinate King Faisal as he drove from his palace in Ta'if to his office. Apparently the plot was discovered by British Agents in the Gulf States: a hundred Saudi Army officers were said to be involved, and they "disappeared." I have an anecdote about this that illustrates the delightful illogicality of life in Riyadh: a colonel, who lived across the road from me, "disappeared" but later reappeared, and went on as if nothing had happened. I was told he had been pardoned because it was argued (in a "dry" country) that as a heavy drinker he had been habitually so drunk as not to know what was happening or what he was getting involved in. This was his family's defence, and it worked.[1] He was always a cheerful

---

[1] Another example of this double-talk reasoning was when Mansour Shalhoub told me that a friend of his mother's was in trouble. Her son, in Ramadan, had crashed his car into a Police Station wall, when he was driving dead drunk. Mansour was being sent to try to get the young man released. The next time I saw him I asked what had happened.

friendly neighbour and I only once saw him slumped on the ground by his main gate: a ring at the doorbell brought somebody out and he was pulled inside without surprise or comment.

In the years after the war, oil production, and therefore Saudi income, grew considerably, but as the income grew, so did royal expenses. Most of the King's sons were guilty in some degree, but Sa'ud, the eldest, was the most conspicuous. He became King from 1953 to 1964 and almost bankrupted the country. He was very popular with the people because of his "generosity" as he gave presents to everyone in the most lavish "Arabian Nights" style. He was forced to abdicate a few weeks after I arrived in Riyadh, and I was told – too late – that I should have attended the King's Majlis. Every Thursday the King sat in open court for anybody to approach him about anything – and I should have told him how glad I was to be teaching in his Kingdom. He would have bowed, he might even have shaken my hand, and as I went out I would have been handed a purse of gold. When Sa'ud was succeeded by his brother Faisal, the largesse stopped, and in some quarters the new king was called "mean", a serious insult in Arabia. I was even told, with bated breath, that he was mean about food. After a meal in a traditional Arab house, the leftover food was offered to any poor hanging about outside, and what they didn't want went to the dogs. It was whispered that King Faisal had the remains of his modest midday meal put into a refrigerator, to be served up again in the evening. I do not for a moment think that this was literally true, but it is significant that such a story should be told at all. This of course was in the early days and Faisal soon won a very real place in the affections of his people.

In the years after the war the Americans moved in decisively. In 1947 Britain announced that it intended to relinquish the Palestine Mandate, could no longer prop up the Greek Government, and was going to withdraw from India. President Truman, who had succeeded President Roosevelt, pressed hard for the admission of 100,000 Jews to Palestine. The fact that the State Department and the Military were worried about alienating Arab – particularly Saudi – opinion went for nothing to

---

"Oh, we got him out." said Mansour. I asked how it had been possible? "We said," Mansour told me, "that he had been very wrong to have been drinking, especially in Ramadan and of course he should not have been driving; but he was so conscious stricken by what he had done that he drove to the Police Station to give himself up, only he didn't stop the car in time." "And they accepted that?" "Of course, and his mother gave a generous donation to a Police Charity."

Congress or the President. As Truman said, "I have hundreds of thousands of Zionists among my constituents. I do not have hundreds of thousands of Arabs." The trouble was that in a meeting with Abdul Aziz just before the President's death, Roosevelt had promised to do nothing that would hurt the Arabs, and that anything to do with Jewish settlements should be worked out between Jews and Arabs. The President was speaking for himself; but the King – and other Arabs – thought that he was speaking for America. Continued support for Israel has made America very unpopular; and the close connections between the American and Saudi governments have led to some awkward situations for the Saudis.

At first, the Saudis had no conception of what came to be known as "the oil weapon", but they did manage to secure a big increase in their income from royalties following Venezuela's successful negotiation of a 50% of the profits deal – instead of the old meagre few cents per barrel. Saudi income almost doubled overnight, and the reader should remember that, when I write "Saudi", I imply the Royal Family. In the Fiscal Year 1950-1951 the state budget was 490,000,000 Riyals, of which almost two-thirds was for Royal Expenses – State, Palaces, Princes, and Royal Establishments. Most of the rest went on Defence (which included the National Guard), Construction, and servicing the National Debt. "Miscellaneous", which included such minor items as Health and Education, got 26,000,000 Riyals. I am glad to say that – possibly as a result of direction from Faisal ibn Abdul Aziz by 1952-53, Royal Expenses were down to less than a quarter of the whole, and, thanks to Abdullah ibn Faisal, the Health Department had 33,000,000 riyals of its own.

The last years of Abdul Aziz ibn Abdul Rahman, known to the non-Arab world as ibn Sa'ud, were unhappy. He became increasingly incapacitated, finally confined to a wheel chair and virtually blind. It was thought that he did not notice how many of his sons – and grandsons – were behaving, or, if he did notice, he no longer cared. The point was that the fabric of society was changing completely. The religious authorities were outraged by many new developments and accused the King of laxity on moral standards. They particularly objected to football (a football club could be a cover for an undesirable political group) and also considered it immoral for young men to appear in public in shorts. Football was the innovation of Prince Abdullah ibn Faisal, and bazaar gossip – to which of course I listened – had it that the Prince's interest in football arose from a personal interest in the better looking players; but, as I said, this was bazaar gossip.

Far more serious was the consumption of alcohol, about which the Wahabis were especially vehement. Most mistakenly in their opinion, the King had allowed foreigners to import alcohol for their own consumption. It was not until September 1952 that a total ban was imposed because – as some readers may understand – the alcohol had not been confined to foreigners, many of whom had been quite happy to sell it to Saudis. Some members of the Royal Family had become hardened drinkers, although I am sure that Abdul Aziz never touched a drop. I have already indicated that Abdullah Sulemain, the Chancellor, was, at best, a compulsive drinker, whose working day was seldom more than ninety minutes. But the actual banning of all imports resulted from an incident that greatly angered the King: in a drunken episode, his twenty-fourth son, Prince Mishari, murdered the British Vice Counsel in Jeddah. The Prince was imprisoned for life but released in a general amnesty following his father's death in 1953.

There had been a possibility that the American Aramco Compound would be exempted from the ban on alcohol. The King was asked to allow alcohol there and also a Christian Church; and, meaning to grant both, in a teasing mood, said the Americans could only have one – expecting them to choose the Church. When they chose alcohol he lost his temper, declaring that, if that was all their religion meant to them, they should have neither. Aramco therefore produced detailed instructions of how to produce a sort of home-made Vodka, which was given not only to Aramco staff but also to other foreigners, like myself. The drink called "Siddiqi", (my friend) could be quite pleasant. I never went to the trouble of brewing it but many did and sold it to their more indolent friends.

I was always told that King Abdul Aziz had instructed that his sons should succeed him in turn, but can find no clear proof of this. Traditionally, the paramount chief of a tribe – or King of Saudi Arabia – was chosen by the elders of the family and their religious advisers. In other words it was not just a matter of the eldest son taking over regardless of his qualities. When the King's life was drawing to a close in 1953 there was considerable doubt as to what would happen. It was obvious that the King wanted his eldest son, Sa'ud, to succeed him, as he had been proclaimed Crown Prince in 1933, and Sa'ud was popular, because, as I have said, he was "generous". But no-one thought of Sa'ud as a political heavyweight. His next brother, Faisal, who had travelled abroad and made a name for himself as a serious diplomat, was obviously more suitable. He was the Viceroy of the Hejaz and, some people thought, might choose to change that title to King, and split away from the Najd. Then there was the next brother, Mohammed, the favoured companion of his father, very keen on hunting and well in with the Bedouin: some people thought he might raise a Bedouin revolt and try to seize power, and, finally, there was the Eastern Province where it was felt the Jilawi cousins might choose to "go it alone."

Abdul Aziz sent Sa'ud to deputize for him at the Hajj in 1950, and he did so again in 1952; but there had been no family conclave with the Ulema to confirm that the Crown Prince would succeed. The King, dying in Ta'if, seemed to rally, and Sa'ud went down to Jeddah, and so was not present when his father died. He returned at once amid great tension and there must have been a general sigh of relief when Faisal rose to greet him as King and to give him a ring from their father's finger. Sa'ud passed the ring back to Faisal and greeted him as Crown Prince and Heir Apparent. Later, it seemed appropriate that the old King should have died in Faisal's arms, and that Faisal should have taken the body back to Riyadh for a simple burial in an unmarked grave according to Wahabi tradition. At the time, however, it was evident that Sa'ud and Faisal wanted to show their solidarity, and when, in the following days, foreign personages came to pay their official condolences to the new King, Sa'ud always had his Crown Prince beside him to shake their hands: their cousin, Sa'ud ibn Jilawi was also there. Despite the previous uncertainty, it had turned out to be a very smooth transition: only the enigmatic Mohammed ibn Abdul Aziz refused to swear an oath of allegiance.

The first years of Sa'ud's reign were marked by several international incidents that probably deflected attention away from the Royal Family's increasingly massive spending. This was encouraged by the crowd of "foreign" Arabs who surrounded Sa'ud and his sons as "advisors," clearly seeing the King's prodigality as a means of lining their own pockets.[2] One of the most significant events in the Arab World was the overthrow of Farouk, the playboy King of Egypt, by the revolutionary Colonel Gamal Abdul Nasser. It was an important priority of Saudi politics to be

---

[2] This was an accepted principle. About 1980 one of my former pupils was hoping to pull off a major contract. "If I win," he said, "I shall build a splendid villa, and I want everything in it to be from England. You, my teacher, will go to London and choose everything for me, and you will arrange a 5% commission for yourself on everything you buy." I was rather sorry when he didn't win the contract!

on good terms with Egypt – just across the Red Sea and the Gulf of Aqaba and with a large and rapidly growing population. Nasser was stridently pro-Arab and anti-America, Britain and France, and anybody from outside the Arab world who might try to "interfere". Nasser was, of course, leader of the moves against Israel, which ensured general Arab support,[3] and also won plaudits for driving the British out of their bases in Egypt – where they had been for seventy years – and then for nationalizing the Suez Canal. He encouraged Saudi Arabia to attack Britain over the ownership of the Buraimi Oasis (where there might be oil), which was claimed by Saudi Arabia, as well as by Oman and Abu Dhabi – both under British Protection.

Readers may remember that there had been a rift with Egypt between 1926 and 1936 after the actions of the Akhwan, who had attacked Egyptian pilgrims. Anyone reading David Holden's *The House of Sa'ud* is likely to conclude that the Saudis genuinely wanted to be on good terms with Egypt. Personally, I doubt this very much, although I admit that there was fear of Egypt's military muscle. Of course, by the time I reached Riyadh, Cairo Radio was broadcasting tirades of abuse against the Saudi and Jordanian monarchies and, because of the amazing appeal of the aging diva, Omm Kalthoum (The Mother of Song) whose songs were separated by political invective, people all over the Arab word listened, and many of them must have absorbed the politics. Yet while there was superficial unity against Israel (or "occupied Palestine" as we had to call it on Radio or television programmes), I know the truth to be very different. In 1973, during the ill-fated October War, Saudi Arabia sent troops to the front, although I think they were all stationed in Syria. There was a small military hospital on the Gulf of Aqaba, and doctors and nurses were sent there from the Military Hospital in Riyadh: one of the doctors, an Indian Christian, told me that they were given secret orders on arrival. If any wounded Israeli Prisoner of War was brought in he was to be treated exactly the same as a Saudi soldier, or a Jordanian; but if any wounded Egyptian soldiers were brought to the hospital they were to be turned away untreated. On the evening of the day when the Egyptian collapse was announced with the news that the Israelis had occupied the Sinai

---

[3] I have never forgotten a letter I received soon after my arrival in Riyadh from Viscount De L'Isle, the Governor-General of Australia who had been Cabinet Minister in the War Office. "Remember," he wrote, "that Israel is very important to the Arabs. Hatred of Israel is the one thing that keeps the Arab States united. If it wasn't for Israel they would be at one another's throats, as they always have been."

Peninsula, English friends of mine, who lived in the same street as the villa which housed the Saudi Military Officers Club, told me that the officers, drunk on alcohol and excitement, were dancing in the street. That was the truth of the Saudi-Egyptian relations when I was in Riyadh.[4]

While King Sa'ud was prepared to support Egypt financially, for example by allowing her to pay for oil in Egyptian pounds instead of dollars – thus reducing the cost by about two thirds – Nasser refrained from direct attacks on the Saudi Royal Family, although he didn't spare either Hashemite ruler, and his calls for revolution against Imperialism went very uneasily with the Absolute Monarchy of Saudi Arabia. The financial disbursements were crippling the Saudi economy, as the personal expenses of the Princes (and the Princesses) continued to grow as though the oil revenues were continuing to expand – whereas in reality they were static for a time. Saudi Arabia tried to adopt a policy called "Positive Neutrality", which did not call on it to oppose the new Arab powers but did stop co-operation with the Western Powers. As the Americans were training the Army (and Navy and Air Force) and the British were training the National Guard it was rather difficult to be non-cooperative. It is worth noting that the British Military Mission continued to work while Britain and Saudi Arabia were in almost open conflict over the Buraimi Oasis. There was a definite anti-monarchist movement in Riyadh in the 1950s, although the Bedouin and, I suspect, the poor, were not involved. The disaffected, encouraged by some of the educated Palestinians, Egyptians, Syrians and Iraqis who had come to work in Saudi Arabia, were drawn from the ranks of the richer merchants, army officers and rather oddly, some of the Princes – including some of the King's brothers and his mostly dissolute and incompetent sons. The leader of the Royal Malcontents was Prince Talal ibn Abdul Aziz, whose rather different ideas may have derived form his Levantine mother. The Prince spoke openly of the need for a Council to advise the Ministers: two thirds of the Council would be elected. In some interviews, he appeared to intimate that the King agreed with him.[5] In April 1957 Palestinians planning to assassinate

---

[4] The Prohibition of the use of the word "Israel" and the insistence on the clumsy "occupied Palestine," caused me problems in 1972 when I was giving three live commentaries a day on Radio Riyadh's English Programme about the events in the Olympic Games, when the Israel team was kidnapped. I had to get permission from the Saudi Manager of the Radio Station to speak of the "Israeli Team." I'm glad to say he gave the permission without demur.

[5] My favourite story of this Prince is that, in the early 1960s before I arrived in Riyadh, he walked one day into the National Bank, where a clerk, who did not recognize him, told

King Sa'ud were arrested in Dharan and Riyadh. They admitted being under the direction of Colonel Ali Khashaban, the Egyptian Military Attaché in Jeddah. The King complained that this was base ingratitude after he had subsidized Nasser to the tune of £40,000,000. In response the Saudis stopped the cheap oil to Egypt and demanded full payment in US Dollars. But financial stringency may have been another factor; at the same time the Saudis also stopped the £5,000,000 a year they had been paying to King Hussein of Jordan.

Relations with Syria had been deteriorating since 1956 with the Saudis objecting to the growing ties between Damascus and the atheistic communist regime in Moscow. They were horrified when, following a secret agreement in September 1957, Egypt and Syria came together to form the United Arab Republic on 1 February 1958. The Saudi response was swift: at a Press Conference in Damascus on 5 March 1958 the Chief of Intelligence in the Syrian Army announced that he had been offered a bribe of £1,900,000 to arrange for Nasser to be assassinated – by blowing up his aircraft. He had accepted the bribes and produced photocopies of three cheques for £1,000,000 and £700,000 and £200,000. They had been cashed at the Damascus branch of the Arab Bank. The go-between had been one of the King's many fathers-in-law. Syria accused the American State Department as well as the Saudis; but both kept silence. The Egyptians were outraged by the Saudis' willingness to spend such large sums of money to kill Nasser at a time when Riyadh was pleading poverty.

Another shattering event, on 14 July 1958, was the revolution in Iraq in which King Faisal, most of the Royal Family and the Prime Minister were murdered.[6] King Sa'ud was badly shaken, but Crown Prince Faisal remained calm and ordered that no public comment be made. When American Marines landed on the beaches of Lebanon to bolster the

---

him to wait in a queue; upon which he marched into the Manager's Office and demanded all the money he had deposited – in cash. The bank did not have *enough* ready money so he took all that they had and closed the Bank. By 1964 the small depositors, who included a lot of the foreign Arab teachers, had not been able to recover their money.

[6] Some ten years later, at a dinner party in London, I happened to sit next to a lady whose husband had been the British Ambassador in Baghdad in 1958. She told me that he, together with most of the other ambassadors, had been summoned to the Royal Palace by the Revolutionary Guards. There, the young King had been brought in and cut into pieces with swords in front of them. Now, they were told, you can tell your governments that you know the King is dead – it will be no good anyone pretending that he escaped. I often remember this story when, during the time of writing this book, I read of atrocities perpetrated by Iraqis on other Iraqis.

Lebanese Government against possible threats from the UAR (the United Arab Republic) and Britain sent aid to the King of Jordan (who had, after all, been at Harrow), Prince Faisal went to Cairo and had a long talk with Nasser. After that relations were "reasonable" for two years; but the future of Saudi Arabia, especially of its monarchy, appeared uncertain, largely because of the near bankruptcy of what should have been a moderately rich state. After his blazing row with the Crown Prince in 1956, Abdullah Sulemain had been succeeded by a man equally inept: expert advisors were brought in but could make no headway. "How can I reduce expenses?" the King asked an Egyptian economist, "when I have so many palaces?" "Blow them up Your Majesty" was the answer. Of these Palaces, Al-Nasariya in Riyadh, was the most conspicuous, an enormous erection of breathtaking vulgarity and surrounded by a mass of other palaces housing wives, ex-wives, sons and daughters. There was a Mosque and the Royal School was beside the complex, which was surrounded by a red wall, fifteen foot high and seven miles long. One of the first things to happen after Sa'ud abdicated and Faisal became King was that most of the wall came down.

In 1957 that the King was "persuaded" to sign a Decree giving the Crown Prince control of the Government. On the day of the signing Prince Faisal visited the Treasury and found only 347 Riyals there. Steps had to be taken, legal steps, to prevent the King or any of his sons from raiding the state's coffers. In 1958 the King had to sign another Decree insisting that all Government revenues must pass through the Ministry of Finance and National Economy to the different Ministries, or to anywhere else, on the order of the Council of Ministers. The King retained the power of actually signing decrees, but a few days after he had "delegated" the running of the country to his brother, he told a number of people, including the President of Lebanon, that Faisal was only his proxy.

While Prince Faisal set about putting the Kingdom's finances into some sort of order, King Sa'ud, freed from any bothersome work, set about spending as much as he could to buy the hearts – if not the minds – of his subjects. Under advice from the IMF (the International Monetary Fund) Faisal cut all appropriations to the Ministries and, when some Ministers objected, he cut their money off altogether for several weeks – which brought them round. He imposed controls and prohibited the import of many luxury goods. He did, however, introduce one rather expensive novelty: all Civil Servants over sixty years old were retired and given a pension which, in the long run, did save money, and was not unpopular. At the end of the 1950s oil production began to expand once more. The forecast was that this expansion would continue (which, unlike most forecasts, turned out to be true) and so restrictions on imports were partially lifted. Salary scales for the Armed Forces were increased; Faisal's knowledge of what had happened elsewhere in the Middle East meant that he well understood the likely dangers of discontented groups of army officers. The budgets rose and the amount of money set aside to repay debt rose with it. The IMF and The World Bank looked on with approval.

But while this was happening, Sa'ud was digging into his Privy Purse to pay for things which were the government's business, but the King's largesse was rapturously hailed in the Saudi Press and on Radio Mecca. In 1959 and 1960, Sa'ud toured the country with a motorized caravan of hundreds of people and a Majlis Tent the size of the Big Top at a Circus; and he seriously considered collaborating with the "liberal" minded princes led by Prince Talal. Early in 1960 Prince Faisal abolished censorship of the Press – officially, that is. In fact strict observance of everything printed, or said, on the radio remained, although the papers began to write of the possibility of constitutional reform. By the summer the King was thinking along the same lines.

By late 1960 Sa'ud felt able to flex his muscles – although figuratively rather than actually. The King had become weak and flabby through over-indulgence in what were officially described as "Irritating Liquids" (which especially featured Contreau). On 19 December Sa'ud refused to sign the budget presented to him by the Crown Prince. Faisal walked out and did not speak to the King again until 8 August 1961, although he did not resign his position. Sa'ud formed a new Council of Ministers, including several younger brothers, some of his sons who were supposed to be "liberal-minded" and a Saudi technocrat, Abdullah Tariki, who became Minister of Petroleum.

Talal had his proposal for the constitution all ready and on 24 December Radio Mecca reported that it had been submitted to the King. On 27 December, the Director of Broadcasting and Publications declared that no such broadcast had been made, although unfortunately it had been monitored by foreign radio stations. I don't think the princes can have been surprised that the King made no mention of it when he addressed the Council. He said that he would work with all his strength and promised fiscal discipline. The new budget was largely the same as the one produced by Prince Faisal – which Sa'ud had refused to sign – but it did abolish duties on foodstuffs, building materials and industrial tools. On 7

January 1961, addressing the Supreme Planning Board (chaired by Prince Talal) Sa'ud abolished real estate taxes levied by the Municipalities. Radio Mecca eulogized the King's generosity, although many must have wondered how the state would manage without the revenue produced by these taxes. In February Talal again raised the question of the constitution, but was referred to the Ulema, who told him that the Shari'ah (Islamic Law) was the only constitution Saudi Arabia would ever have. Relations within the Royal Family deteriorated, and the Council of Ministers became extremely thin. Through the instigation of Prince Mohammed ibn Abdul Aziz, there was a reconciliation of sorts between the King and the Crown Prince: on 8 August Sa'ud called on Faisal in Ta'if; but Faisal said he could not act unless the Council of Ministers was dismissed and his old powers were restored. This Sa'ud declined and Faisal did not do him the Arab courtesy of seeing him off at the Airport the next day. Moreover things deteriorated: on 14 August Prince Talal gave a Press Conference in Beirut, during which he said – quite untruthfully – that a "National Council" was being considered by the Council of Ministers, and (worst of all) in an aside about his brother, he said "that man has so far been behaving himself!" The King was furious and dismissed all the "liberal" princes.

In Foreign Policy Sa'ud had not done too badly. He had told the United States that he could not renew the American Lease of the Facilities of Dhahran because this exposed Saudi Arabia to hostile propaganda and, following the revolution in Iraq when the new government threatened to absorb Kuwait, after Britain's Protective Treaty expired in July – Sa'ud ordered a brigade of Saudi troops to Kuwait to bolster the defence. In September, however, things became too much for him. Early on 18 September, the Syrian Army took over in Damascus and senior Egyptian officials and army officers were bundled out of bed and sent back to Cairo in their pyjamas. Syria had seceded from the UAR. Nine years later Sa'ud was to admit to Nasser that he had spent £12,000,000 paying people to break up the Union.

Sa'ud collapsed with stomach pains that night and was taken to the Aramco Hospital, where he was diagnosed with severe internal bleeding caused by alcohol. As it was impossible to prevent Sa'ud's family or other people bringing "irritating liquids" to him, he was sent to Boston for treatment. He tried to arrange a Council of five princes of his own choice to run the country in his absence, but had to give way to a general demand for Crown Prince Faisal, who promised to make no changes in government while the King was away. Faisal presented his own budget, which included a significant rise in the expenditure on Defence and Education, but Sa'ud began to interfere. In Boston he had been operated on for cataracts on both eyes and had had a stomach operation. He and his entourage ran up bills of $3,500,000: Aramco paid. While convalescing in New York and Florida, he kept sending instructions to the Ministers he had appointed, and on 7 March 1962 he arrived home, intent on taking control and appointing a new Council of Ministers; but the senior princes, who had hitherto kept out of politics, told him very firmly that only Faisal could form a government. These princes included Mohammed, Khaled, Abdullah and what came to be called "The Sudeiri Seven," sons of Hassa bint Ahmed-Al-Sudeiri, who were Fahad, Sultan, Abdul Rahman, Na'if, Turki, Salman and Ahmed.[7] Faisal did not make a clean sweep of Sa'ud's people – he allowed two princes to remain; but he removed Abdullah Tariki, whose main claim to fame was his part in the creation of OPEC (the Organization of Petroleum Exporting Countries) and replaced him by a charming lawyer from Mecca, Ahmed Zaki Yamani as Minister of Petroleum and Mineral Resources (Petromin). When Faisal had been in power from 1958-1960 Yamani had been the legal advisor to the Council of Ministers. He was clever, hard-working, a born diplomat, and he controlled Saudi oil production for many years to come

Relations with Cairo had become very bad, and abuse from Cairo Radio continued to punctuate Omm Kalthoum's songs. Egyptian workers in the Kingdom were ordered to go home, and, as in 1926, there was trouble over the Tapestry traditionally woven in Egypt to cover the Kaaba. In 1962 it was declared to be of too poor a quality to be used and Egyptian pilgrims to the Hajj were told that Egyptian pounds were no longer acceptable and could not be changed for Riyals. At this point Talal called Nasser on 23 July to congratulate him on the tenth anniversary of the revolution which had overthrown King Farouk, and then gave a Press Conference – wearing Western clothes, which raised Arab eyebrows – in which he spoke of constitutional reforms. He was packed off to Lebanon but moved to Cairo, to be joined by his brothers Fawaz, Badr and Abdul Mohsen, and his cousin, Sa'ud ibn Fahad. These five were called the League of Free Princes as a condition for being allowed to stay in Cairo.

---

[7] These seven – or those in Riyadh, or Ta'if – used to go to their mother's palace every day to lunch. She told them everything that people were saying, which she knew through her "gossip" with other Saudi ladies. There was one sister and after their mother's death the brothers used to go every day to lunch with their sister.

They certainly lost credibility by going there, but such open dissension in the Royal Family was the last thing Faisal – or Sa'ud – wanted.

But more trouble was looming with Egypt, still smarting from the disintegration of the UAR. On 20 September 1962 the death was announced of the Imam Ahmed, who had ruled Yemen since 1948. Cairo Radio declared that King Sa'ud and King Hussein of Jordan were just as dead although still unburied. The Imam's successor was the Crown Prince Mohammed Badr, a friend of Nasser and a man with dangerously liberal views. In 1958 Nasser had persuaded him to travel, with the result that he made trade pacts with Russia and China, and bought $3,000,000 worth of Soviet Arms – paid for with a gift from King Sa'ud. An Egyptian Military Mission arrived in Yemen and young Yemeni officers went to Egypt for training: behind the scenes all was building up for a Yemeni revolution. On 26 September, less than a week after the accession of the Imam Mohammed Badr, the Egyptian-trained officers turned the guns of the Soviet tanks – acquired by the new Imam – on his palace and reduced it to rubble. It was widely reported that the Egyptian Chargé d' Affaires in Yemen had given the signal for the revolt. The new "progressive" Chief of Staff, Brigadier Abdul Sallal agreed, without much reluctance, to become President, and was proclaimed on 27 September. Within four days a contingent of Egyptian troops with Yemeni "leaders" long domiciled in Cairo arrived in Yemen, and more followed on 6 October. Nasser was delighted with the chance to threaten the British in Aden and the Saudis to the North and East.

When the news broke, Prince Faisal was at the United Nations in New York. As usual he remained calm and met the rightful ruler of Yemen, Prince Hassan ibn Yahya, who had been proclaimed Imam when Mohammed Badr's death was announced. Faisal warned Hassan that Saudi Arabia could not give Yemen material aid to expel the Egyptians. However on 1 October, Prince Hassan flew to Jeddah, where King Sa'ud and other princes did promise help, although not direct military aid. They knew that the Republican grip on Yemen was weak, and that outside three or four cities the countryside was still Royalist. I believe that the Saudi authorities did not promise military aid because they could not trust their own armed forces – only the National Guard was absolutely loyal and trustworthy. If so, their fears were soon justified. Supplies were immediately despatched to help the Yemeni royalists but did not always reach their intended destination. A Saudi plane with an aircrew of three flew to Cairo instead of the border town of Najran, and the next day two more pilots joined them in a training aircraft. The whole Saudi Air Force was grounded and two dozen officers were purged. I don't know what happened to them: I expect they "disappeared." When somebody "disappeared," unless you were a very close member of his family you did not make enquiries. Anybody else who asked questions might have been involved in whatever the "missing person" had done. When I asked some friends if they knew what had happened to a pupil of mine who had vanished they told me quite urgently not to ask questions: "It is dangerous."

Prince Faisal was asked to form a new government, and he agreed on condition that he was given a free hand: he sacked the sons of Sa'ud and the commoners that Sa'ud had chosen. Apart from making his brother Khaled Deputy Prime Minister, Faisal's most important appointments were of Prince Fahad as Minister of the Interior and Prince Sultan as Minister of Defence. These appointments were to prove very long lasting; in fact I think that Prince Sultan, although eighty-four years old, is still Minister of Defence.

In America President Kennedy was causing a lot of trouble. He was a strong supporter of Nasser and Egypt received more US aid than any other Arab country. But Kennedy also wanted to remain on good terms with Saudi Arabia – because of the oil. He immediately recognized Sallal's Republican Government in Yemen and brought great pressure on everybody else to do the same. Fortunately the Conservative Government in London refused, and even sent light weapons to the Royalists through South Yemen. This enabled Riyadh and London to set aside their differences over the Buraimi Oasis Question, and before the end of January 1963 diplomatic relations were resumed. Cooperation was arranged between the Saudi Intelligence Service and MI6 – who were preferred to the CIA – although the Saudis later worked with the CIA and with French Intelligence. (One of the charmingly bizarre episodes came in 1965 when MI6 arranged parachute drops to the Yemeni Royalists from Israel with planes overflying Saudi Arabia).

Faisal appreciated that the real threat to the Saudi monarchy came from within the country rather from without and this prompted him to announce a ten-point programme of reform on 6 November 1962. The final point took immediate effect: slavery was abolished throughout the kingdom – although Saudi Representatives at the UN had long denied its existence. Faisal had freed his slaves back in 1956, but he complained that none would leave and insisted on staying on as part of his household.[8]

The American plan was simple. Saudi Arabia must be persuaded to stop helping the Yemeni Royalists, and in return the Egyptians would withdraw their troops, now numbering 40,000 men. The idea was good but there were no means of getting either the Saudis or the Egyptians to comply, even though they said they would. After official recognition by the Americans, followed by recognition by the United Nations, President Sallal boasted that he had rockets that could reach Saudi palaces. The Americans were impressed by the support for the Republic in the main towns of Sana, Hodeida and Marib, while the Saudis understood that the feeling in rural areas was very different.

The war inside Yemen was savage: the Egyptians bombed Royalist villages with poison gas – verbal protests were made but nobody did anything to stop them – and they attacked the Saudi port of Najran with HE Bombs. The Egyptians also dropped several tons of arms in the hills North East of Jeddah, supposedly in an attempt to arm Saudi dissidents. That, at least, was the story, but I think it was merely invented to make mischief – there was no evidence to suggest that such a body of dissidents actually existed.

After a year of fighting it became obvious that neither side could achieve a military victory, although the war was proving more costly to Egypt than to Saudi Arabia. Egypt also faced the threat of the loss of American aid if it did not withdraw from the Yemen as promised. Perhaps it was fortunate that, towards the end of 1963, attention shifted to a quite different issue. Israel planned to divert the headwaters of the Jordan River, thereby depriving Arab farmers of their water. Nasser did

---

[8] I can believe that. When I was in Riyadh the Shalhoub family had fifty ex-slaves who refused to leave. They lived in what looked like a block of studio flats at the back of the property. I never saw any of them doing much work – if any – but they lived comfortably and freely and numbers of them always accompanied the family on holidays. I remember Sheikh Mohammed's widow issuing a tender for fifty stereos, fifty televisions and fifty video-players: when I asked why I was told that she couldn't give a present to one ex-slave without giving to all of them. I also remember a time one year when the old lady wanted to go to Mecca where her sons were with King. She planned to drive down with two or three of her daughters-in-law, but the ex-slaves objected and insisted on going too. In the end several limousines and a 70 seater bus – hired from the Municipality – set off, a small army of servants having been sent ahead to set up a sort of tent city for the whole crowd to break their journey on the way to Mecca and again when returning to Riyadh.

not wish to be involved in another war – which he would probably have lost – and so invited thirteen Arab Heads of state to an Arab Summit to be held in Cairo in January 1964. King Sa'ud attended – his first significant public act since giving power to Faisal in October 1962.

In the meantime, and under pressure from senior members of the family, Sa'ud had spent long periods abroad, usually "for medical treatment". In March 1963, he went to Lausanne and then on to the Negresco in Nice – where he outstayed his welcome. From there he proceeded to Paris for more treatment, allegedly made necessary by his excesses in Nice. From Paris, in mid-May, he went to Vienna and stayed there until mid-September. As Sa'ud was accompanied by a hundred courtiers and many of his family – four of whom bought large properties outside Vienna – rumours spread that, in effect, he had already abdicated and handed the government over to his brother. This was hotly denied by Sa'ud's Chief of Royal Protocol, who insisted that the King was in daily communication with his ministers and was still ruling the country. The rest of the Royal Family began to feel that it would be less embarrassing to have Sa'ud back in Saudi Arabia rather than running loose in Europe.

But back in Riyadh, relations between the King and the Crown Prince became very strained indeed. Tension rose when it became known that Faisal's budget for the following fiscal year would substantially reduce money for the Royal Family. The King began to shower money on the tribes, and, with the help of his sons, attempted to rally support to enable him to force Faisal's resignation. The strategy failed totally and the more impetuous among the senior princes, such as Mohammed, Abdullah, and Sultan, pressed for Sa'ud's immediate abdication, with force to be used if necessary. Faisal would have none of this: he wanted his brother to abdicate, but peacefully and with the consent and approval of the Religious Leaders. There was still a little way to go, but in December 1963 Sa'ud was given a letter, signed by the senior Princes and Religious Leaders, reminding him of the 1962 agreement, which had left him only with the rights to sign decrees and be consulted. At this point Sa'ud set off for Cairo. His trip appeared to be successful and he returned with greater self-esteem. But this was soon deflated. Early in March 1964, Egyptian advisors came to confer with Faisal about ways to improve relations between the two countries; Sa'ud was firmly excluded from the discussions. On 13 March 1964 he wrote to Faisal, furiously demanding that his rank be respected and two of his sons taken into Cabinet: he also threatened to have the Royal Guard turn their artillery on Faisal's palace.

The letter was returned by Prince Mohammed who strode into Nasariyah Palace and flung the letter at Sa'ud's feet. It was reported by "eye witnesses" – or at least people who claimed to have been eye-witnesses – that Mohammed threatened to run his sword through Sa'ud's body. This may be a bit too melodramatic, but it would have been in keeping with Mohammed's ungovernable temper.

This was, in any case, a crisis point. The National Guard was put on full alert. One night, Holden tells us, three of Sa'ud's sons sat on a hill overlooking the National Guard Encampment and jeered at the soldiers: in the morning three empty gin bottles were found. Over the previous six months, between £30 and £40 million had been given in bribes, but still support for the King was ebbing away. Of course, what I may delicately call "subsidies", had been given by the other side – to those tribes from whom the National Guard was raised – to reward their loyalty to Faisal. On 26 March 1964 a deputation of Religious Leaders and Tribal Sheikhs waited on Faisal to assure him of their moral support. That evening the Crown Prince sent a message to the King informing him that in future the Royal Guard would be under the command of the Ministry of Defence. All the Royal Guard Officers swore allegiance to Faisal.

On 29 March a dozen of the leading Ulema issued a Fatwah, or judgement, declaring the King unfit to govern. Some doubts were expressed about the legality of the Fatwah, which had not been issued in the name of all the Ulema. On 30 March, however, further decrees were issued, backed by a letter signed by sixty of the senior princes, including Mohammed, Abdullah, Fahad and his six brothers and the King's uncle, Abdullah ibn Abdul Rahman, quoting "the leading Ulema." Sa'ud was stripped of all executive, legal and administrative powers, and his allowance was halved (183,000,000 Riyals). Faisal became Viceroy.

The situation was still very unsatisfactory. Like some bloated spider in the centre of its web, Sa'ud was still spinning plots in an attempt to overturn the decree. While Faisal and his supporters were coping with revolutionary movements outside the Kingdom and sympathizers within it, Sa'ud was trying to win over the Eastern Province tribes, probably making his own private contacts with Cairo and even – if gossip is to be believed – planning the assassination of Faisal. The Crown Prince himself stayed in Jeddah, leaving only to go to an Arab summit in Alexandria in September and to a meeting of Non-Aligned States in October. At this point I will end this chapter, because it was in September 1964 that I arrived in Riyadh. I don't think this registered on the Saudi Arabian

Richter Scale, but it was very important to me personally, and, of course, the final acts of Sa'ud's reign happened when I was actually on the spot.

CHAPTER 3
Riyadh In 1383/4 (1964)

In the twenty-five odd years since I left Riyadh, thousands of British people have seen it. There have been huge changes in the city I once knew. I must stress too that Riyadh changed out of all recognition during my time there and – as I hope to show – the character of the people changed with the place. However I think I am right in saying that the most profound change of all had happened before my arrival. If a man changes his fourth-hand Ford Escort for a brand new BMW limousine the alteration is great; but it is not as great as when he gave up his push-bike and bought the Ford.

Obviously I cannot talk about the city in the years before my arrival – except by repeating what those who were there told me. I had two main sources of information: one was three elderly Egyptian Inspectors who had come to Riyadh in 1950, when it was decided to create a modern Ministry of Education. I worked with all of them, but the Chief Inspector, Abdul Adthim Sha'aban, was a close colleague for two or three years. My second source was the sons of Sheikh Ibrahim Al-Khamis, Riyadh's most innovative and adventurous businessman. Abdul Rahman, the eldest, was with his father in 1964, but Mohammed, the second son, was my pupil for two years and both remained friends of mine while I was in the city.

In 1950 Riyadh was a walled city, and everyone, yes everyone, lived inside the walls. The gates were closed at sunset and not opened again until after the dawn prayer. Five times a day the call for prayer went up from every mosque: at dawn (when a white thread can be distinguished from a black one); at midday; about three hours later; at sunset (when the sun dips below the horizon); and an hour and a half later. In every Mosque, five times a day, there was a roll-call of all the men in what I will call "the parish." If anyone was missing and not known to be ill, members of the Mutawaeen would visit his home and drag him to the Mosque. The Mutawaeen (the Committee for the Suppression of Vice and the Encouragement of Virtue) were still extremely powerful in 1964, although they were less so later. During the day only men were normally to be seen in the streets. Women were supposed to stay at home, although occasionally one – or rather two as they would not go out alone – might pass from one house to another, heavily veiled. A decent woman must wear at least four layers of veiling, or so said the Wahabi elders: even when I was in Riyadh one man told me that he was quite lax because he allowed the women of his family to go out with only two layers of veiling over their faces. Women never went to the market to shop. After the sunset prayer men could return home (until the last prayer) but it was better to stay in the Mosque and spend the time in religious reading or discussion. Of course, all alcohol, tobacco and music were absolutely forbidden, and when it could have been introduced, the wireless was also forbidden. The Mutawaeen had the authority to enter any house where they believed, or had been told, there was a wireless: nobody told me what happened if the set was in the women's quarters.

As I have said, Alcohol became available to those beyond the power of the Mutawaeen. Some alcohol may have been produced in the odd house, but I should think the smell would have made that too dangerous. Smoking was as bad as drinking (the same verb can be used in Arabic) and Palgrave, an early visitor to Riyadh in 1862-3, tells how the then Prime Minister was beaten to death on the doorstep of his home in the Great Square when he was seen smoking there. My colleagues told me that in 1961 – admittedly in Ramadan – a Jordanian teacher had been beaten to death in Bat'ha, the main street, for smoking in public. As for music, anathema to the Wahabis, Philby tells of sitting with King Abdul Aziz on the roof of his palace before sunset when a herdsboy came whistling through the city gates. The King was aghast; "Doesn't he know how wicked he is?" he exclaimed and sent guards to bring the boy to him, whereupon the boy was severely lectured.

But I must return to my informants about life in Riyadh in the 1950s. When the three Egyptians arrived in Riyadh they were given a house by the government for which they did not pay rent. They received their salaries every month in gold and silver, because paper money was not recognized in Riyadh, but there was nothing to spend it on but food. They had a servant – provided by the government, they did not pay him – and he did their shopping. They were absolutely forbidden to go to the market, as it was feared that the appearance of "foreigners" might cause a riot. Apart from going to and from their office, the Egyptians' attendance at the Mosque – compulsory – was the only time when they appeared "in public." Yet not many years later, people as "foreign" as I were welcomed into the city.

The Khamis family were a source of much information about customs and events not long before my arrival – in other words so near to the present in time that the stories seemed barely credible. Sheikh Ibrahim Al-Khamis was a businessman trusted by King Abdul Aziz to travel out of the Kingdom, and on whose judgement and reports the King relied greatly. He used to travel to Kuwait – where, sixty years earlier, the Al Sa'ud family had been given sanctuary; now under British protection, Kuwait was full of all sorts of Arabs and non-Arabs and non-Muslims. When Sheikh Ibrahim returned to Riyadh from one of his visits to Kuwait it was held that he must have been contaminated merely by being in a place where so many of those viewed with suspicion by the Wahabi authorities were to be found. Thus the Sheikh was isolated for three days before he was even allowed to meet his own family. He needed three days breathing pure Muslim air, drinking pure Muslim water and eating pure Muslim food, before the contamination wore off and he was fit to rejoin his family.[1]

All of this of course was in the days when the city was walled. I have said that nobody lived outside the walls, and nobody did, until Sheikh Ibrahim decided to do so. This revolutionary step involved buying a piece of desert, not just outside the walls but actually across the Wadi (which was to become the Main street, Bat'ha) and on rising ground behind where, later, the First National City Bank was to be built. Having imported and installed the first generator in Riyadh, the Sheikh fitted out his new house with electric light. I was told that it was one of the sights of

---

[1] There was something special about "three days." In 1966 I met one of the young Jilawi princelings, a difficult young man always in trouble with his family. On one visit to me he objected to my dog barking, and, pulling out a revolver, said "stop your dog barking or I shall shoot it." And so I was surprised, after hearing that his cousin, the Governor of The Eastern Province, had put him in prison, to be visited by two elegant young men who told me that "His Highness" was going to escape from prison "next week", and would come to me for sanctuary. As a matter of fact – thinking of the dog and the revolver – I was appalled and went to my friends the Shalhoubs to ask them what I should do. "You have to give him sanctuary," they said, "You can't refuse to give sanctuary to anybody who asks for it, even if he is your worst enemy. But after three days you can tell him to go." "How?" I asked. "You don't have ever to give sanctuary or anything else for more than three days" was the answer. However I was relieved when the young man failed to escape from prison.

those days to go up the walls and see the lights of the Sheikh's house switched on at sundown, every evening, as the call for prayer sounded from every Mosque.

Arabs, at least those I have met, are very gregarious. They seem to dislike, almost to fear, solitude, and, in a way the very narrow streets of the old city, some too narrow for a car to go through, symbolised a structural and moral unity.[2] To break away from such a unit was dangerous and there were denunciations against the man who was setting himself apart in this way. "How would it be, they asked "if something happened after sunset? Once the gates were closed they could not be opened again until dawn." As the house was being built, one of the King's brothers came out to remonstrate. He travelled the few hundred yards by car although, considering the nature of the ground at that time, I think that it would have been easier and quicker to walk. Without getting out of his car, he lectured Sheikh Ibrahim. How could he cut himself off from the city? From the King himself? How would anyone reach him? Supposing the King wanted him? Supposing the King died? In the night? How would he hear the news? Sheikh Ibrahim was very polite, very calm and very firm. He was going to build his house here, outside the city, with fresh healthy air, and would bring his family up there. Sometime later, when the walls were down and land prices rocketing, the elderly prince – who was then himself building a palace still further out, went back to the Khamis house and said to Sheikh Ibrahim, "You were quite right!"

I heard another story from Sheikh Ibrahim's sons that gives an interesting and I think important light on the religious background in the city. Having expanded his business and travelled to Damascus, Beirut, Cairo and even Europe[3], the Sheikh wanted to bring a Lebanese Christian

---

[2] I had a curious experience of this. One evening, visiting the Shalhoubs, I felt oddly unwell, and they insisted on calling their doctor from the hospital to see me. I was put in one of the three guest rooms inside the main gate, and at least twenty people crowded in with me while the doctor examined me. He gave me an injection and said I must stay there overnight. I said that I must go home because of my dog, but when I admitted that it had water, I was told it would be all right until morning. All night people stayed with me, in turns, three or four at a time, talking quietly, playing cards, with a very quiet wireless in the background. In the morning I was taken to a fortunately European bathroom, given a most delicious Arab breakfast, and then driven home; but I could not be left alone, unwell. That was against Arab etiquette.

[3] He was the only Saudi allowed to do business in Moscow, from which he imported cars and agricultural machinery. I bought a Lada for my servants, and a very sturdy and reliable car it was.

to Riyadh to work for him. He went to the King and asked for a visa for the man, but word soon got out – it is extraordinary how quickly rumours used to spread in Riyadh: I wonder if it is the same today? The Sheikh's enemies (and what pioneer does not have his detractors?) made an outcry that he was destroying the Islamic character of the city. In the face of such protest the King could do nothing. He assured Sheikh Ibrahim of his personal support for the move, stressing that he appreciated that it would not represent any threat to the state – but such representations had been made that the King could not ignore them. Without religious sanction he could not grant the visa. Indeed, he would not even be able to offer support should Sheikh Ibrahim be summoned before judges to answer charges of religious deviation.

The man to whom he must appeal was Sheikh Mohammed ibn Ibrahim, the Imam of Riyadh, elderly, infirm and blind (he was still, just, Imam in 1964). As Imam he was the Spiritual Leader of the City, the Final Appeal Judge in all religious matters, reputedly very conservative and rigidly orthodox. It was with some trepidation that Sheikh Ibrahim went to the Imam to explain his position and ask for help. To his surprise he found the old man not only wise but tolerant: he said that he knew changes must come, that Riyadh must be opened to the world, but this would have to be done very gradually to begin with. The Imam encouraged Sheikh Ibrahim to bring this Lebanese Christian to Riyadh, promising his support and even a readiness to suppress any religious charges. He counselled patience and fortitude against the verbal attacks and innuendoes which both knew would be made – and very energetically. So, with unofficial official blessing, a crack was made in the puritanical religious wall.

For the Puritanical Wall had been very real. I do not think that there was any hypocrisy in people who reported their neighbours for listening to the wireless in secret. No doubt secretly, there may sometimes have been a background of old family rivalry, some recent grievance, and I am sure there was a wish to stand well with the religious authorities. But I am still convinced that underneath there was a bedrock belief that the act of listening to a wireless was sinful in itself, and that sin should be vigorously opposed. So far as I could see, there was no feeling in Riyadh that reporting other people was wrong in any way. I was, for example, told that in every class I taught there would be three boys who were "paid" informers. One would report on my teaching to the Ministry of Education through the Headmaster; another would report to the Police as to whether I made any political remarks (which some Arab teachers might do); and the third would report to the Religious Authorities in case I made any unsuitable comment on any religious matter – and with a Christian teacher that boy would be especially vigilant. I don't think the Arab teachers were being untruthful when they told me that they did not know who the informers were. Certainly the Public School code of never "sneaking" to prefects or masters was unknown at the Yamama Secondary School. The question, "Who knocked that chair over" would get an instant response and I was liable, on entering a classroom, to be greeted by a chorus of gratuitous information: "Sir, Sir, Ahmed's poured ink over Mohammed's homework and Abdullah's thrown the board rubber out of the window." How "Sir" should respond was a bit of a problem: I never reproved the informants – it would have been no good – and I did, in a mild way, rebuke the offenders, but I never punished them. Well, I would send "Abdullah" to get the board rubber; but as he would take an considerable time to fetch it, absence from the lesson was hardly a punishment. Of course by 1964 the ban on music had been lifted, and wirelesses blared from every taxi – usually much too loudly. I even found some very respectable Long Playing Records sold on Wazir Street, and Monteverdi's "L'Incoronazione di Poppea" was, I think, my first purchase. I was told, by our cicerone on that memorable flight from London, that the first time music had been "officially" played was in 1963 at the opening of the Dhahran Airport. But like everything else he told us, this was inaccurate[4], as in the Hejaz there had been no ban on music before Abdul Aziz took it over, and in 1958 Prince Faisal had been greeted by a Brass Band in Jeddah.

By 1964, although the rules forbidding alcohol were still absolute, those banning tobacco had also been relaxed, a fair majority of men smoked and almost every shop and stallholder seemed to sell cigarettes. The rules about attendance at prayer had also become less stringent. I do not think they still had roll-calls in the mosques at prayer time (at least not in Riyadh, though I am sure they still did in many of the villages); but the streets were certainly emptied at prayer time. On the first evening of our stay in Riyadh, Ralph Ellis and I were sitting outside the Semiramis Hotel, drinking an innocuous orange juice, when a man shouting angrily came towards us (it was just before sunset). Obviously it couldn't be anything to do with us, so we ignored him; but a waiter came out of the hotel and

---

[4] Later, on visits to Riyadh, he would always refer to my mother, whom he had never met, as "Lady" Urch.

dragged us inside explaining that the hotel would be in great trouble if they were to be accused of allowing "foreign" guests to flout the local laws. I may point out that these laws, in force for more than two centuries, had been made up and imposed by the Mutawaeen and are not an essential part of Islam, although, of course, ideally there would be no men on the streets because they would all be at prayer.

Anyway, by 1964, the whole place had changed, remarkably quickly, from what I was told of Riyadh in the early 1950s. One very important alteration had been the establishment of an Airport north of the city, and the building of a series of very impressive Ministries, which were put up at the same time and lined the middle section of the new and imposing Airport Street that led to the Airport from Bat'ha[5]. I think the Airport was a major influence for change – not least it meant that by the end of the 1950s thousands of foreigners, including non-Muslims, began to flow into Riyadh.

In the autumn of 1964, my mother sent me a copy of *The Times* containing a supplement on Saudi Arabia: on the front page was a picture of a block of modern and rather palatial flats. As I was living in this building, I cut out the picture and returned it, with a red line around the apartment and a double red line round my bedroom window. My flat was on Wazir Street (later King Faisal Street) – in 1964 the nearest one got to a "European" street. Yet that was not an entirely accurate description, because the only really European thing about it was that all the shops had plate glass windows and some of the goods had names on them written in a script I could read. There were three big grocers, full of such comforting things as Heinz Baked Beans, Robertson's Golden Shred Marmalade, Jacob's Cream Crackers and Fray Bentos Corned Beef. There was the Khazinder Bookshop, with English paperbacks – although not many at the time – and English newspapers only two or three days old with some English magazines. There were two outfitters where men

---

[5] Several people told me, with relish, a story about the construction of these Ministry buildings. The electricity system could not then support air conditioning; and so the Government issued one tender for thousands of electric fans for all these buildings, ceiling fans, standard fans and desk fans. There were a number of bids and one, considerably cheaper that the others was chosen; but when the fans were delivered they were not electric fans at all, but the cheapest little hand fans. When the merchant was challenged he pointed out that in his offer he had not used the word "electric" or specified the size or type of fan, only the total number. Taken to Court, the Religious Judges found in his favour, and said the Government Officials should be more careful in future about the details of their tenders.

could buy Van Heusen Shirts and women Pringle's Cashmere and Lamb's wool Twinsets. Even if one didn't want them it was reassuring to see them there. One slightly disconcerting thing was that all shops, except the grocers, sold an awful lot of odd things mixed up with their more regular items. Pringle's twinsets could be mixed up with toothpaste, hair cream, electric light bulbs or a typewriter. I have said that the presence of familiar things was reassuring because, in one sense, I needed reassurance. Although I had wanted to come to Riyadh for so long, and although I had had a feeling of being at home on that first morning's walk from the Semiramis to the Ministry of Education, I soon experienced the sensation of being in a totally alien, even if friendly, environment. People whose travels have been confined to countries which at least use the same letters, even if there are no notices in English, may find it difficult to comprehend the bewilderment of being in a city where, not only can you not speak the language and where almost nobody speaks your tongue, but you cannot read a single sign. This was brought home to me very forcibly when I had been a few days in the flat and wanted some small item – I forget what. My colleagues on the staff at School told me which shop to go to in Wazir Street, and so that afternoon I set out to buy it.

In those days the section of Wazir Street containing European shops was barely two hundred yards long. I walked up and down on both sides of the road, staring, hypnotized, at the signboards over the shops, none of which meant anything to me. Looking in the windows was not much better because – as I have said – except for the grocers and the bookshops, the windows contained a bewildering collection of miscellaneous items. Rather timidly I approached one or two passersby, to be met, at best, with a smile, a shake of the head, and a flood of incomprehensible Arabic, or at worst, with a blank stare and a mutter. I felt totally helpless until sanity returned and I did what I should have done in the beginning. I went to the Khazinder Bookshop where there was a man whom I knew spoke English and asked him to direct me to the shop, which was in fact only a few doors away. It was plainly high time I learned to speak some basic Arabic.

After my initial lesson on the numerals one to ten, on my first night in Riyadh, I had decided to make a list of essential words and phrases that would help me to manage with reasonable comfort in my strange surroundings. On the second morning in the school – classes had not yet begun – I was in the staff room sitting with a very friendly group of English speaking teachers and asked whether they would help me by giving me the Arabic equivalents of the words and phrases on my list. They professed themselves delighted to help, and I produced my first list of ten phrases: rather ambitiously I had decided that I could manage to learn ten words a day, (more than I would expect of my pupils) and so we settled down for the first day's task.

The first phrase was an innocuous greeting. What was the Arabic equivalent of "How do you do?" Immediately I was given a large variety of versions of this simple phrase. With everybody talking at once they argued which version, or versions – and how many versions – I should learn: I sat back astounded. As I was to find out in time, the trouble with Arabic is not just that it is a very rich language, but there are regional variations that can become complicated.[6] Meanwhile the argument over "How do you do?" continued. If, someone pointed out, I only learned one or two greetings, how could I understand if people greeted me using one of the other versions? We went on to some other phrases – I forget what they were – and while new arguments went on I was left grappling with my first phrase. If I could not even say "How do you do?" what was the point of learning others? After a morning spent pleasantly with everybody except me indulging in verbal gymnastics and word plays, the meeting broke up without me being a single word or phrase the wiser.[7] My plans for a gradual but steady mastery of the Arab tongue died a sudden death that morning, and, I am sorry to say, for a disgracefully long time I remained incompetent and tongue-tied, an obedient reminder of Sheikh Abdul Aziz Turki's injunction in London not to learn the language and to use English when talking to the boys.

---

[6] Many years later I was staying in Tangiers, and after a day visiting the Spanish enclave of Ceuta, I returned to find no towels in my hotel bedroom, so I rang Room Service and asked for "Monshaffir" and after quite a long pause my driver-guide, whom I hired from the hotel by the day, and who had just brought me back from Ceuta, entered the room and asked what I wanted. I explained that I had asked for towels. "What word did you use?" he asked. When I told him he said "They thought you were asking for Mon Chauffeur. In Morocco a towel is Foutah." "That's a woman's skirt in Riyadh", I told him. I can't remember what he told me meant a woman's skirt in Morocco, but it meant something quite different in Riyadh.

[7] Of course in time I learned all the greetings. There was one peculiar to Riyadh and when I used it in other countries people used to say, "You're from Riyadh." It was "Schlonak," which literally means, "what is your colour?" This is not really an odd greeting because, after all, in English we say that somebody who is not well is "a bit off-colour," and we used to say - although I haven't heard it recently – that a really fit person was "in the pink."

The city of Riyadh was comparatively small in 1964. The thickly populated suburbs of my later years were just desert. Malaz, consisting entirely of modern villas – there were no mud-houses there – was an isolated suburb reached via University Street. There were no roads between Malaz and Airport Street, although there was a way out past the Zoo to the Dhahran Road. The Nasariyah, or Royal City – which stood behind high protecting walls pierced by two gates – was reached by a special road leading up from the Semiramis Hotel. To the East of the Main street, Bat'ha, there was almost nothing except the Market and Rail Street, so called because it led eventually to the Railway Station, from which one could take a train to Dhahran. I never used this train, a fact I now regret, but Dhahran was an easy drive along an excellent road, and of course, even nearer by air. From Wazir Street there were streets leading North to the very modern Shomaisi Hospital – diagonally across the roundabout from which lay the Shalhoub Mansion. In 1964 only three of these roads were tarmacked and the others were made of hard compacted earth with most of the potholes filled in. The main streets had very good lighting and the side streets – that is to say the tarmacked ones – had lighting that was perfectly adequate. Most of the narrow streets in the old city had no lighting at all, but as many people had a light over their front door, the streets actually appeared quite well lit.

I was able to explore Riyadh in two ways. I went on foot through as much of the old city as I could, and friends took me in their cars for tours around the city and beyond. On my walking expeditions I was an object of much curiosity, being so obviously a non-Arab – and remember how recently such as I could not have entered Riyadh – because almost everyone wore local dress: a long white cotton robe, a "thobe" in summer or a dark woollen one in winter, with a "guttra," a headdress that was white or red and white checked (or, occasionally, black and white check) to protect the head and the back of the neck. The best were made from the finest linen and my mother used to wear them as scarves, particularly in England. Some foreign Arabs wore local dress, while others wore open necked shirts and flannel trousers or very neat and correct business suits. I suppose I just didn't look like an Arab, because as I walked around I noticed people coming out of their houses to look at me. In Riyadh, I was never subjected to any annoyance, although I knew perfectly well that some of the small boys were calling out rude, possibly unmentionable things at me. It was a very good example of the old saying "Ignorance is Bliss," for what I could not understand could not hurt me. If, however, an engaging child said something to me that made an elder immediately yank him out of my way and box his ears, I could only assume that I would have been embarrassed if the child's meaning had been comprehensible to me. While walking around, particularly in the hot weather, I usually wore a shirt and slacks. In school, however, I felt that it was incumbent on me to dress formally, and, in fact, usually taught my classes in pale grey or grey-striped trousers, a black jacket and waistcoat with a white shirt and a stiff white collar. In those days, for many years I had worn gold pinz-nez on a silk cord (the boys called me "The Father of The Cord"). I think at the time I felt I was doing something to uphold the Spirit of the Empire, like dressing for dinner in the middle of the Congo; looking back now, however, I realise I must have appeared as a sort of cross between P.G. Wodehouse and Gilbert and Sullivan. It was not until the end of the year that the Shalhoub boys took me firmly to their tailor to be measured for a thobe, so that I would be fit to be presented to Sheikh Mohammed Shalhoub. As soon as I put the Arab clothes on I felt curiously inconspicuous: it was as if I had been camouflaged, and the thobe was certainly very comfortable.

My exploration outside the city was done comfortably by car. New areas of desert were being opened up very rapidly but in 1964 the development was extremely haphazard. It is true that a Greek firm, Doxiadis, had drawn up a master plan for the future development of the capital, so people knew where the new roads would go. Houses were built in places that seemed impossibly far out, with no foreseeable connection to any water or electricity. I have no doubt that, before I left, many of the owners of these villas, remote in 1964, would have sold their houses and moved further out away from the congested streets.

Many of these exploratory journeys were made with Ralph Ellis, who had become Private Tutor to one of the Princes in the Royal School, a very pleasantly friendly young man who gave "his teacher" (not to mention his teacher's friend) a car and a driver when they wanted to go exploring. The Prince also organised our first Saudi picnic, which I still remember even if I no longer have the copious notes I made at the time. It was certainly very unlike the picnics we used to have on the beach or up on the South Downs when I was a boy!

A limousine with the Prince, a secretary, and a man who worked for the newspapers (and I think broadcast) and appeared to be a sort of licensed jester, arrived at a reasonably early hour and the driver was sent up to the flat to collect us. We drove first up the road past the Nasariyah

Palace complex and into the Dara'iyah road. We went by the Palace of King Faisal, then still the Crown Prince, and on either side of the road we saw palaces in various stages of construction. We learned that all of the palaces belonged to the King's brothers or sons and were told the owner's name of each. I quickly forgot who lived where, except for the Palace of Prince Salman ibn Abdul Aziz, Governor of Riyadh and one of the Sudeiri Seven, who later sold it to his brother Khaled – who became King on the death of King Faisal – and Khaled greatly enlarged it and was living in it when I left. A few years later there was an excellent road leading past Dara'iyah, going via Jubail and Salboukh, to the provinces of Sudair and Al-Qassim, but in 1964 it was impossible to go further than the old capital. The land through which the new road was to go – where the very large campus of Riyadh University was to be built – belonged to the already-mentioned oldest member of the Royal Family, the Princess Sara bint Abdullah, King Abdul Aziz's first cousin but fifteen years older than he. As noted earlier, it was her father who built the Musmak when he became ruler in 1865.

The old road led down to the Wadi and then stopped, but – except after the rains when there were any – the surface of the Wadi was perfectly safe for driving. If I had had a jeep or a Land Rover, I would have thought nothing of driving over it myself; but in a new limousine things were rather different. The driver showed no signs of planning to reduce speed, and we lurched and banged along – not uncomfortably, in the excellently sprung seats – but wondering, or I was at least, whether some vital part of the car might get knocked off. The Wadi was lined with a sort of mini-cliff, and trees grew steeply on either side. The old capital lay on the left, more or less west, while on the East side a new town had already been built, but neither could be seen from the floor of the Wadi. Suddenly the driver swung round at right angles and charged up a steep incline though a gap in the trees just wide enough for the car – and then we saw the old city above us.

That was the most impressive way to view it. Even ruined it immediately reminded me of the tourist postcards of Carcassonne. Once through the walls we found ourselves in a place very like the Old City in Riyadh – except it was in ruins. But even there, near the gate, some houses had been partially restored: the doors had new Yale locks and children poured out to look at us. We left the car in an open space near the gate and went on foot through the winding streets. We saw the palace of the rulers, the Majlis, where they held court and transacted their daily business, the house of Sheikh Mohammed Abdulwahab, the great reformer, and the main mosque in which the teachings of the Wahabi movement were first promulgated. The Prince pointed all these out to us and really seemed to know what he was talking about. He took us up onto one of the less damaged parts of the wall and pointed out where the Egyptian cannons had been placed. It had all happened nearly a century and a half before; but to hear him describe the siege of Dara'iyah it seemed much closer – perhaps when he had been a boy; so are the memories of important events kept fresh in tribal tradition.

After inspecting the old city, we went back to the car, down through the Wadi and then up the other side and through the new town. We didn't stop there but travelled on over rough tracks and then somehow found ourselves in the desert. We were vaguely going East, but to me our route seemed quite random. I knew it wasn't, but only a man who knew the country well could have distinguished between apparently indistinguishable shrubs and rocks. We were making, the Prince told us, for a big tree.

Sure enough, after a while, a big tree appeared on the horizon, a giant tree standing by itself. As we got nearer we could see a red painted canvas–hooded truck standing nearby with a number of figures busy doing nothing in particular. These, the Prince said, were his servants who had been sent on ahead to prepare the picnic for us. Under the tree we found carpets spread – not the familiar mackintosh groundsheet of my childhood, but Persian carpets of such beauty that I would have expected even a Prince to have kept them in his palace reception rooms. Comfortable cushions and arm rests were provided, and the alternate ritual of tea, coffee, tea, coffee began, with only short pauses between until the guests can literally take no more. The tea, lightly sweetened and quite weak, is boiled in a kettle: nearly all those I saw in the early days were pleasantly decorated and came from Yugoslavia. The tea was poured into small glasses: it was obligatory to take one even if you did not want it, because to refuse hospitality is a grave insult to an Arab. It was usual to accept two glasses, although more would be offered; indeed, when visiting a poor man, it would be insensitive to take more than two glasses. The signal that one did not want any more was either to put one's hand over the glass, or hand it back to the servant waggling it slightly from left to right. With Saudi, or Arabic coffee, the ceremony was similar. Saudi coffee is very much an acquired taste which fortunately I acquired early: it is made quite weak and mixed with crushed cardamom seeds, which impart a distinctive flavour, (quite unlike coffee in fact as cardamom is a seed of the ginger family) and is drunk from small handle-less cups and poured from a coffee pot with a long, curving spout and open at the top. A filter, normally made from palm fibre, stops the grounds from getting into the cup, although sometimes the filter does not work very well. As with tea, it is the height of bad manners not to drink at least one cup the first time it is offered. A skilled pourer will hold the pot a couple of feet above the cup and drop in the exact amount with panache. The pourer holds a pile of unused cups, each fitting inside another, in his left hand. The problem for more sensitive Westerners was that there were often not enough cups to go round. Then the pourer would go round the circle and as soon as he ran out of cups would go back to the beginning to pour out second cups. When he had two or three cups from those who had refused more, he would shake the dregs onto the carpet (even the most beautiful carpet was not immune) and then refill the cups for the next guests waiting their turn. This is one reason for not accepting more than two cups – not to keep other people waiting. There was another reason, a relic of the past: coffee was expensive and today's guest may be host tomorrow, and should be mindful of the host's position. In 1964 it was not many years since most people in Riyadh had been poor from a material point of view.

While we were drinking tea and coffee the servants were erecting a square striped tent (about twenty foot square) in which were spread more carpets – a great store seemed to have been brought in the back of a lorry. A sheep had been killed, luckily before our arrival, and was being roasted over a fire of wood and shrubs, of which there seemed plenty.[8] There appeared to be one main cook directing several helpers. The pleasure of lying in the shade of the tree, looking at the scene and breathing really fresh air was enough; but the Court Jester was called to entertain us. As a Jester he was not particularly successful. Arab jokes and stories imperfectly translated not only from one language but from one culture to another, are not very entertaining. When, however, he was able to be

---

[8] I was to go to many picnics later, at some of which the sheep were killed after our arrival. I soon got over my initial dislike of this practice when I realised how quickly the whole thing was over, and – the most important thing – the sheep itself had not been frightened: up to the moment when it was killed – instantaneously – it had been roaming unconcernedly eating bits of grass and shrub. If one is going to eat meat at all I prefer to think of the animal dying like that and not being driven, one in a terrified huddle, to a slaughter house.

serious and explain things about the history of Saudi Arabia, he was erudite and interesting.

At last the time came for us to go to luncheon. The Prince had prayed at noon, together with most though, to my surprise, not all of the servants. The prayers were led by an old man who seemed to have no other duties or occupation apart from drinking a prodigious number of cups of tea and coffee. Luncheon was set out inside the tent, and, in deference to the inability of English visitors to manage their food in accordance with the customs of the country, knives, forks, and spoons were laid out as if for a normal English meal, except, of course, that the tablecloth was laid on the ground and we all had to sit, squat or crouch around it.

The Prince led us to the tent, but luckily, we correctly refused to take precedence and enter the tent first. In the entrance there was a small reception committee: one servant held a large silver bowl in the middle of which was a raised piece, rather like the boss of a shield, pierced to let the water run through and on top of which lay a cake of soap. Another servant held a large water jug, also silver, ornately chased, with a long thin spout: this was poured over the bowl as one washed one's hands. A third servant, who appeared to be the senior and supervising the others, held a pile of towels on which we could dry our hands. We entered, and sat down around the cloth.

The main dish was a great mountain of rice, surrounding the sheep and flanked by chickens. The rice was rich in saffron, dried fruit and nuts and was absolutely delicious. There was a soup made from stock thickened with vegetables to start with, and after the meal there was fresh fruit and caramel cream, a sweet I was to meet more times that I could count. We were shown how to pick up a piece of meat and roll it in rice – all with a swift motion of the fingers of the right hand – to squeeze it in the palm of the hand to extract moisture, and then pop it into the mouth. After Ralph and I had made a mess of our faces, shirts, trousers and the surrounding carpet we were advised to use a plate, European fashion.[9]

As we ate, a servant stood behind each of us, fanning us to keep away the flies of which a good number appeared from nowhere. There was no conversation during the meal, except about the meal itself and, I am sure,

---

[9] It took me a long time to master this art: in the end it came to me as I was away from Riyadh on a trip where I had to eat like my hosts or not at all: in one house, for example, they searched in vain for a spoon. Suddenly I found myself managing, if not with elegance, at least without making more mess than a rather dirty child.

comments on the absurd inability of Ralph and myself to feed ourselves properly. On this occasion the Prince waited until we had both finished and then signed for us to rise. What normally happens at a Saudi meal is that each person moves away as soon as he is finished – the idea is that somebody else can then take his place. There is always far more food than necessary spread out before the guest or guests of honour but, after they have eaten, others will appear, members of the family, hangers-on, servants, and (tell it not in Gath) the ladies who came last. However, as I shall explain in the Chapter on women in Saudi Arabia, I absolutely refuse to believe that they get the leftovers. When food is laid out on a long tablecloth the necessity for retiring to allow somebody else to take your place is hardly apparent, but when it is served up in one big round bowl or platter it makes sense. The traditional dish for serving a number of people is a huge bowl full of rice, on top of which is placed all the meat. Twice a day in the palace of King Abdul Aziz, in Morabba, outside the city walls and close by the Yamama School, there used to be a procession of bearers, four to each bowl, which was balanced on two long beams of wood and two cross beams: the bowls were so heavy that this was the only way they could be carried.[10] The only time I saw one of these giant bowls was when I was taken to the palace of Princess Sara bint Abdullah: then there appeared to be enough food for two or three dozen, and there were, as I remember, thirteen or fourteen of us – so there was an awful lot of food left when we had finished. Fifteen or more men could get round each bowl to eat: the technique was not to sit crossed-legged, which takes up a lot of room, but to adopt a sort of kneeling crouch, with the right shoulder and arm pointing to the centre of the bowl. In this way the diner had free play with his right hand and occupied the minimum of space around the bowl.

But at our picnic there was nothing like that; we followed the Prince out of the tent and went through the same washing ceremony. This time I noticed that our host cupped his hands and washed his mouth and chin. Another difference was that the senior servant not only offered towels but shook cologne over our hands and clothes. Then we retired to the carpets under the tree, to recline, and, again, to drink tea. I should have been very happy to be still and go to sleep, but etiquette again demanded that we should be entertained. A whole group of us, including some of the servants, began to play a most peculiar card game. The details of the

---

[10] Any subject of the King could present himself at the midday or evening meal, and be sure of a welcome. I need hardly say that there was never a shortage of guests.

game had completely escaped me when I came to make my notes, because I had never really understood what I was doing. The object of the game was to make people pay forfeit, which you had to pay if you could not produce a card when asked: the "fine" was a number of strokes with a leather strap (rather like a tawse, now, I imagine, forbidden in Scotland) on the back of the hand. The next person in the game, as I remember, had to choose the penalty, that is the number of strokes from one to three and whether they should be given normally, or gently, or extra hard. If Ralph or I had to pay a forfeit we received "gentle" strokes: once, one mischievous servant tried to order Ralph three extra hard strokes but the Prince immediately interrupted and changed the forfeit. The Prince himself was usually treated gently, but his object, and that of the others, was to strike the Jester as hard and as often as possible. He made a terrible fuss, which was, I suppose, all part of the game; but I, for one, was delighted when the whole thing came to an end.

The next entertainment was shooting. One of the servants had brought an ancient rifle and proposed we should hunt for birds; but as Ralph and I showed such disapproval of this the Prince offered instead a prize for shooting. An old tin can was placed a fair distance away and everybody fired off a number of rounds, with no ill effect to the tin. Ralph and I were then invited to try and the Prince told us that it would be polite to accept. After three shots Ralph said that the sights were so bad that nobody could hit anything: when I tried I hit the tin with my first shot and retired gracefully. Of course I had shut my eyes before I pulled the trigger: I think it was the only time I have ever hit anything I aimed at, if aiming is not too generous a word. When I was in the Army Cadets at school I was so bad a shot that they stopped taking me to the Indoor Range, even for the regular compulsory training, and never let me near the proper firing range at all. I think I was the only cadet to be so distinguished.

After the shooting was over (I was not given the prize offered to the servants), more amusements were arranged. Everybody, except the Prince, Ralph and myself, was ordered to take part in various races. There was a short sprint, which everybody at least finished, and two longer races, although the longest was only a few hundred yards. Few competitors, however, finished either of the longer races, and the majority collapsed, panting and groaning with well-simulated distress – the Jester being the loudest groaner and the most realistic writher in distress. The Prince gave cash prizes to those who won or were placed – one or two hundred riyals for the winners and smaller amounts for the seconds and thirds. A hundred riyals in those days was worth almost exactly eight pounds sterling, worth a great deal more in 1964 than it is today: I think it would have been more than two weeks of the Old Age Pension at that time in England.

After the races we got back in the limousine and the servants were told to pack everything up and go home. We set off for an orchard – where exactly it was I don't know but it must have been North of where Oleya was to be built later. We came to a high sand brick wall, with greenery showing over the top. We asked the Prince if this was his orchard and he said, no, but it didn't matter because he knew the owner. We found a door, which must have been opened by the driver who climbed over the wall – anyway there was nobody inside but ourselves. To me it seemed incredible, here in the middle of the desert, to find an orchard full of oranges, lemons and tangerines, growing on trees with grassy walks between them, and little rivulets of water. I suppose there must have been a well but there was no sound of a pump, in fact no sound at all, and we did not explore much of the orchard. It is hardly surprising that the desert Arab has sought in a garden the imagery needed for paradise, as to the nomadic Jews a land flowing with milk and honey was the goal, while St John the Divine, writing "in the spirit" on the barren island of Patmos, described for the sophisticated citizens of the Roman Empire a New Jerusalem bigger and grander and richer than Rome.

When we had eaten our fill of someone else's fruit, we returned to the car; but the Prince told us to watch the sunset while he prayed. I had at sometime seen pictures from Cairo of sunsets over the Nile, vulgar pictures I had thought them, all lurid orange and purple with black silhouettes. Rather to my surprise, I found that nature used exactly the same colours that night; and the effect was not vulgar in the least. We then set off again, driving rather faster than before although it was now dark, across an apparently trackless desert. There were one or two sickening crashes as the driver failed to miss rocks and once we went into what must have been an extremely large pothole. The car held together, however, and as the owner didn't seem to be concerned there was no point in worrying about it. Eventually we hit the road coming up from the Eastern Province. During our day's outing, we had described an arc round the North of the city, on the far side of the Airport as it was then, and then we were returned to our own flat. The air and the sun had taken their toll. I don't know what Ralph did but I went to bed at about eight o'clock in the evening and slept soundly until the next morning.

The Prince arranged another outing for us a few weeks later, my first visit – and picnic – to Al-Kharj. This – the name means "outside" – is a big agricultural district with an excellent water supply about fifty miles South East of Riyadh. Some members of the Royal Family had farms there and the Ministry of Agriculture ran a number of experimental farms. As used in Saudi Arabia, the word "farm" does not mean what it does in England – it may indeed only be what one would call an orchard or a palm-grove. Until the late 1950s there were no cattle farms as we would recognise them but, among the attractions offered on this picnic was a visit to an experimental dairy farm, where various European breeds were being studied to determine their milk yield under local conditions. The area of Al-Kharj where we ate was more like a large park than anything else, but a park not of wide open spaces, but of small grassy enclosures with high hedges round for privacy, inside which a family could relax and enjoy themselves, without any fear that the ladies could be seen by anybody else. There were trees everywhere to give shade.

We had no tent on that occasion – one was unnecessary – but we ate in a different enclosure from the one in which we had been sitting. Afterwards, instead of other entertainments, we toured the farm, seeing such surprising items as Aylesbury Ducklings, which were disporting themselves in a huge shady pool, and various types of chicken, some homely and some exotic. At last we went to another farm, to look at the cows. I do not pretend to be able to distinguish between these excellent and useful animals, so I cannot say what breeds they were: some were black and white, some brown and white, and some were all brown. They were segregated into species and they all looked very sleek and well cared for; but they were, of course, living under ideal conditions.

There was, inevitably, an odd incident when, after looking at the cows, we went to see the bull. There were notices around saying in Arabic "Danger" and "Beware of the Bull"; but the Prince ordered the Jester, who was once more with us, to go into the walled enclosure and run across to the other side. The man refused at first, then when offered fifty, a hundred, and finally two hundred riyals, and only when the Prince in what looked real – but was I am sure pretended anger – insisted, did the man climb over the wall and scamper across the enclosure. The bull, instead of charging or bellowing furiously, took absolutely no notice. Emboldened, the Jester sat on the opposite wall and carried out a swift piece of haggling with the Prince over the price for going back into the middle of the pen and dancing about in front of the bull. I wanted to dissuade him for it seemed really dangerous to me. A thobe is not a garment suitable for sprinting away from an infuriated bull and leaping over walls. However, the Prince insisted and so the performance began. It didn't last long because the bull finally took exception and ambled over in a leisurely way to examine this capering and gesticulating phenomenon, snorting loudly, upon which the phenomenon ceased capering, picked up its skirts and ran to the wall where willing hands helped him up. I was glad because I had half expected him to be pushed back. I thought it was all staged for our entertainment, but the Prince told us later that this was not the first time that the Jester had "baited the bull."

There was a small incident on the way back as we came out of the little town onto the main road back to Riyadh. This second picnic had taken place not long after the abdication of King Sa'ud and the accession of King Faisal and, although there was no question of any "trouble" there were many more conscientiously performed security checks. We had been warned to have our identity cards with us, and Ralph had his with him, but I had (not for the first or last time) forgotten mine. On the outward journey nobody had troubled us: and we had been waved through the barriers. It was a different matter returning after sunset.

We joined a queue of cars and lorries creeping towards a barrier, and the Prince told us to get out our cards. At this point I confessed that mine was most probably lying on my bedside table but the Prince did not seem particularly alarmed. When at last our time came the driver handed out some papers, including Ralph's card, and presumably said something about me. The policeman appeared mildly truculent and made obvious gestures for me to get out of the car, whereupon the Prince, who had hitherto kept a dignified silence, leant forward and spoke two or three sharp sentences. The policeman leapt up as though prodded by a bayonet, saluted wildly and shouted orders for us to be let through immediately. It was intimation to me that ordinary rules need not apply to members of the Royal Family.[11]

---

[11] I had an example of this later myself. I bought my first car from a Princess's Secretary: it was a Cadillac Eldorado in shocking pink metallic paint (my mother was horrified, but got over it by saying to everybody "Have you seen the car David's bought? It's the most vulgar thing in Riyadh."). I didn't bother to get the number plates changed. One day I was driving down the University Street towards the town centre and saw ahead a Police Barrier and a queue of two or three dozen cars. As usual I didn't have my driving license

Throughout these two expeditions the Prince was kind, polite, and attentive, in fact an excellent host. He was perhaps rather solemn for a seventeen-eighteen year old, and Ralph said that he became more and more preoccupied after the death of his elder brother – of which I shall write more below. I saw him very seldom after this, although Ralph, as his tutor, was often at the palace, and also took him round London in the summer – where he was far more interested in museums and historic monuments than most young Saudis. I have very grateful memories of him, a young man who took the trouble to be very kind to me because I was a friend of his tutor. It is still very difficult for me to reconcile these memories with the fact that, ten years later, this young man, Prince Faisal ibn Mousa'ad ibn Abdul Aziz was to murder his Uncle, King Faisal.

The reason for the murder was canvassed and discussed widely, but most people in Riyadh had a good idea of what had happened, even if they did not share their views with the world outside. Prince Faisal's father, Prince Mousa'ad ibn Abdul Aziz, if not exactly schizoid at least had a dual personality, alternating bouts of hedonism (during which he was very conspicuous in the more notorious pleasure sites in Europe), with bouts of extreme asceticism (during which he did penance for his misdeeds, before returning to Europe again). His elder son Prince Khaled, shared his father's extreme religious views but had none of his pleasure-seeking traits. Like many others in Riyadh, Prince Khaled was very worried by the Ministry of Information's plan to open a television station. As the representation of the human form (or the form of any living creature) is forbidden in Islam – at least, as preached by the Wahabis – it seemed to many very reasonable people that a television programme, a series of pictures of people (including, it was rumoured, unveiled women) was, literally, satanic. It was soon decided that the studio should be destroyed before it could open, and weapons, including bombs, were collected. Whether the authorities had any suspicion of what was planned I do not know but, whether they did or not, I am sure there would have been plenty of guards; everything was guarded in those

---

with me (although I did have a letter from Prince Suleiman, the Governor of Riyadh asking the police to help me. I had got this through Fahad Shalhoub who was the Prince's private secretary), but when an officer walking up and down the line suddenly beckoned to me to come out I thought that I was in for trouble; but all he did was to salute me and wave me through unchecked. Then it came to me, that, as I was driving a car with Royal Number plates, I might be anybody, and must certainly have "connections." It was best for the Police to be on the safe side.

days. Prince Khaled's group were challenged and a number of shots exchanged. The television studio suffered only superficial damage but there were several dead, among them Prince Khaled. The rumours began almost at once. The first story was that he had been killed in the exchange of fire but that was succeeded by a better one: the Prince had been wounded, but not treated and allowed to die because that was better for him than to go to trial. The final version was better still: the Prince had been taken prisoner, and had then been shot because of the complications of bringing him to trial. The execution – the emotive word was used – was of course on the orders of Prince Fahad, the Minister of the Interior; but Fahad would not have given such an order, involving the execution of a member of the Royal Family, without the consent of the King.

From the day of her first son's death his mother, a Rashid, blamed the King personally for what had happened, and urged her second son to do his duty and avenge his brother. We heard – those of us who had reliable access to royal gossip – that she went on at Prince Faisal almost every time she saw him: "When are you going to avenge Khaled?" was her constant cry. He went to University in America, where he became involved in radical politics, and also took to alcohol and drugs in a big way. After a long time "studying" in the States, he returned to Riyadh, and he returned a mess. He was of course greeted by his mother's demands for vengeance. I don't know what the drug position was but he was still drinking very heavily. His Uncle, the King, was very concerned about this troubled young man and gave orders that he would see Prince Faisal at any time the young man sought admission. It did not matter, the King said, if the Prince was completely drunk, he must at all times be allowed to see his uncle.

On what I must call "the fatal morning," Prince Faisal turned up drunk at the office of the Prime Minister – the King acted as his own Premier – as the oil minister from Kuwait was there to see the King. The Prince had known the minister in America, and so when the Kuwaiti went in for his audience Prince Faisal went in with him – in any case the guards would not have stopped him. The King shook hands with the Minister and then turned to shake hands with his nephew, upon which Prince Faisal shot him.

The King was taken to hospital where they tried to resuscitate him, but without success. People seemed to know that "something" had happened, and my servants heard rumours in the Suq (market), and told me. About noon I telephoned a friend at the Radio station who was in a fairly senior position, and he told me, "Yes, the King is dead. It will be announced officially in about half an hour." When I turned and told my mother, who was beside me, she burst into tears, which says something of the feeling even foreigners felt for the King.

***

I have written here about the end of King Faisal's reign before I have told about the beginning, for, of course, King Sa'ud was still ruling when I arrived. In Chapter Two I drew the picture of the end of Sa'ud's reign; but did not describe the actual event, which happened only a few weeks after I had arrived in Riyadh. The whole thing was very odd, because everyone seemed to know all about it in advance. Every Friday afternoon – Friday is the Muslim day of rest – the King would drive around the city, being cheered by the populace. One Thursday in school, the boys asked me whether I had seen this and, when I said I had not, they urged me to see the King on his drive the next afternoon, adding, "It'll be the last time, because there's going to be a revolution next Thursday. You needn't worry, because it'll be quite peaceful." I wrote to my mother to tell her not to worry if she read in the papers about a revolution in Saudi Arabia "because the boys in school have assured me that it'll be a peaceful one." It was an odd letter to write, and to receive. Mother said she had been puzzled: I think she wondered if I had found some illegal alcohol.

On Friday afternoon I went down to the Bat'ha and joined a crowd of people. After some minutes three dark green long wheelbase Cadillacs came along: the middle one had four platforms, two on each side, over the running boards, and four guards stood on them, with rifles slung on their backs, but brandishing scimitars, ready to defend the King against attack. All the people cheered and waved, and I thought how strange it was: if I, a foreigner, knew he was going to be deposed next week, surely everybody there must have known that he was on his way out. If he was so popular, how could the coming revolution be peaceful?

In fact is was: school work went on as usual on the Thursday and the boys told me that Prince Faisal had arrived – I heard he'd taken three days to drive up from Jeddah and there would be an announcement that evening, to the effect that King Sa'ud had abdicated and Prince Faisal had become King. David Holden makes much of the hatred Faisal felt for Sa'ud, which I think was largely a matter of contempt; and I had it later from the Shalhoubs that when they asked King Faisal what he had done that first evening he had said "I went and sat with my brother. He is my brother and I had to be with him."

Everybody was interested in the question "Who will be the next Crown Prince?" Mohammed ibn Abdul Aziz was the "next" brother, and it was widely believed that the throne would descend from brother to brother. Although Holden describes his sometimes violent temper, Mohammed had another weakness, a liking for alcohol, which it was felt – after the example of Sa'ud – would make him unsuitable as a ruler. He made it clear that he would not consider altering his mode of living. He agreed to stand down in favour of his next brother, Prince Khaled, who was conservative, popular with the Bedouin, but not physically strong. Following Khaled there were two brothers, Princes Nasir and Sa'ad, who had misbehaved themselves politically in Cairo with Prince Talal, and were hence obviously unsuitable. Then came Prince Fahad, eldest of the Sudairi Seven, and an extremely able and capable man. For the time being Fahad remained Minister of the Interior, but gossip – to which, fortunately for my readers, I always listened – said that after a few years Prince Khaled would "retire" through ill health and Prince Fahad would become Crown Prince. There was one other item of interest in this matter, which was not gossip but something I had on the most reliable authority. When Prince Mohammed agreed to stand down and not become Crown Prince, he stipulated that he should receive the Crown Prince's salary – as of course did his brother Prince Khaled. And so we all settled down to what I regard as the nearly eleven years of the excellent rule of King Faisal. He was an indefatigable worker, and every morning when he went to his office he took the new pile of papers and put the date in the top right hand corner: when he turned to deal with "past" papers he always looked first at the date when he had first received each one. He insisted that papers addressed to his office should be responded to quickly (Would that all Saudi Ministers could have done the same!) and if nothing had been done after a very few days his secretaries were called in to explain the delay. I know that I am biased; but I still feel what I felt all those years ago, that King Faisal was about the best ruler any country could have had.

Before proceeding to describe particular facets of life in Riyadh as I knew it, there are a number of odd facts, minor in themselves, but which remain fixed firmly in my mind as illustrative of the way I lived in those early days. Everything changed so completely in the years I spent in Riyadh, in particular there was an enormous increase in foreign companies with "foreign" work forces. It was not long before the companies were urged to bring all their staff together in a compound and – even before I left – the bigger compounds had a shop, a sort of general store, within their gates, so that the staff would not have to go outside for anything, and thus not meet any of the "locals." But much of the enjoyment of my years in Riyadh was the fact that I had always met and mixed with those same locals. In my later years, when I could speak at least colloquial Arabic, I would be rather childishly pleased when a taxi driver or a shop keeper asked me if I were a Syrian "because of your colouring; but you've been here a long time because you've got the Riyadhi accent": to reply "No, actually I'm English" gave me an absurd pleasure.

Now, for some of these "minor" items. One concerns the time, because in 1964 there were three different ways of telling the time. Riyadh was GMT +3, and that was the "official" time, in as much as there was one, and was used by most foreigners; but the Americans used Dhahran time, which was GMT +4, and traditional Saudis altered their clocks and watches twice a day, because sun rise and sunset always became six o'clock. If one was asked to any sort of event it was wise to ask, "What time, Greenwich or American or local?" I think by the beginning of my second year everyone had settled down to GMT +3.

Another minor oddity was the question of weights and measures. By the time I had been there a few months, Saudi Arabia officially adopted grams and kilos, but at the beginning one bought fruit and vegetables by the "wazener." At some places I seemed to get more than at others and and so I asked one of the Arab teachers at school: "Oh", he said, "Wazener means weight, and each stall holder has his own weights: they aren't standardized in any way. Sometimes you'll see vegetables and fruit cheaper at one stall than another. But that may be because that stall holder has lighter weights."

Reference to the Americans having different "time" to the rest of Riyadh reminds me of how isolated the Americans were at that time. Most of them, the military mission who were training the Armed Forces, were huddled in the Zahrat Al-Sharq Hotel (the name means "Flowers of the East") on Airport Street between the Yamama Hotel and the Semiramis. All American families were given passes to use the restaurant (the meat was flown in from The States) and to attend the film shows. Many of us from Britian were very kindly offered the same facilities; but I hardly used my pass. Most of the Americans lived lives deliberately isolated and insulated from any contract with the Saudis, except for those they met through their work. There may have been a conscious effort to create a "Little America," like the Aramco Compound in Dharan, which could have been the set for any American Television Soap Opera. Here, I believe, "Arabs" were banned – they certainly had their own compound. Mansour Shalhoub met an American girl at his University in California, who said to him, "I was born in the American Hospital in Dharan and went to the Aramco School there – in fact I've lived there all my life, and you're the first Saudi I've spoken to."

Arrangements in Riyadh were necessarily different, but not so different. Going to the local Suq or market, or taking a taxi, were considered adventures. I met American women who not only washed all their fruit and vegetables in Chlorox but left them soaking for hours. There was an American sergeant at the Base who refused point blank to set foot on Saudi soil outside his car except in the forecourt of the Ministry of Defence, where he worked, at the Hotel, or at the Airport when he was going on leave. So many of these people were welcoming and charming but theirs was an environment in which I could not immerse myself.

In those early days, when English teachers were a new oddity, I was constantly invited out to Saudi houses – something which did not last more than two or three years. Whereas "foreign" Arabs – about whom I shall write later – were not popular, the English were exotics, and were eagerly sought after, although I realized at the time that many of my pupils not only wanted to show "their teacher" off at home, and perhaps practise their English, but also to curry favour. However, at the houses one saw more of the fathers and uncles and elder brothers, who were always most welcoming ("The sun shines on our house when you visit!" was my favourite greeting). I was also sometimes asked – strictly on a business basis – to give private English lessons to a member, or to members, of the boy's family. Early in my time in Riyadh these private lessons took up quite a lot of my time.

I welcomed them, not only as an additional source of income, but because I met more people and I certainly thought then – I know because I made a rather pompous note at the time – that in a small way I was contributing to the educational development that so many people in Riyadh seemed to be talking about. "We know we are a very backward people – you must help us to modernize ourselves" was, with variations, often said to me. It was polite, and truthful, to expatiate in reply on the long History of Arab Civilization and to remind the speaker that he probably knew his ancestors back a thousand years, something uncommon in Europe. And I would try to point out that all that was lacking at the moment was knowledge of the latest developments of Western Technology (a lack soon to be corrected). I am glad to say that even in those early, heady days I had doubts of the wisdom of wholesale modernization. Before I left, I was to see the disintegration of the society I had known in the early days and in which so many of my friends had been brought up. Certainly during my years in Riyadh, the health and the material comfort of the people improved enormously; but it was not such a happy or pleasant place to live in as it had been on my first arrival.

The house I visited most was the Shalhoubs, where I taught Sheikh Khaled's youngest brother, Abdul Rahman. I always went to the Majlis, or reception room for male visitors on the left of the main gate. On the right were three guest bedrooms for male guests who were not family members; and a small Majlis where I used to give Abdul Rahman his lessons. Female visitors or families who were close friends would go to the Great House. Of course I never went there on my own, but later, when my mother was with me, I would go with her to one of the Reception Rooms (there were several, the grandest of which was only used when the King visited – we were just allowed to look at it). The women of the family would be lightly veiled, except for Sheikh Mohammed's last (and, I was told, King Abdul Aziz's fifty-third) wife. She used the privilege of old age and revealed her beautiful and finely boned face. In the mens' quarters the evening's entertainment was always the same, and the same people met there regularly, as I did. There was tea and coffee, and conversation, in most of which I was unable to join but the gist was explained to me. There were arguments, usually over disputes between the speakers' fathers or grandfathers, which periodically animated the scene, in a good-natured way, and might go on for nights. The small events of the day were discussed and if anybody had that day seen a friend or acquaintance after some time of absence, then the man, and all his antecedents, were talked over and stories recalled about various members of his family. Sometimes some of the more adventurous played cards (never for money) and this card playing seemed to increase in frequency until a small group, usually the same players, gathered together every evening. In 1966 television was brought to the Majlis, and, thereafter, conversation took a more and more minor place. Perhaps it was a pity that Prince Khaled ibn Mousa'ad and his friends did not succeed in their attack on the station. Now nearly half a century later, I look back on those innocent early evenings in the Shalhoub Majlis with nostalgia.

While thinking of the Majlis, or the Public Reception Room, I must tell a story of the new Majlis King Faisal had built onto his palace. I don't know who built it but an Italian Company was responsible for the décor and furnishings. When all was ready the King went to inspect it. There were, of course, superb carpets, with elaborate velvet and gilt chairs all round the walls. In the middle of the wall, in which the main doors opened, was a splendid throne: "What's that?" asked the King: "It's your throne, Your Majesty," said the Italian Manager. "Please sit in it and let me see how it looks," said the King, seating himself on one the chairs on a sidewall. After the Italian had sat down on the throne the King looked at him. "Which of us," he asked, "is King?" "You, of course, Your Majesty." "Exactly" said King Faisal, "Whatever chair I sit in becomes my throne. I do not need anything like that. Please take it away." I like this story because it shows the King's humility – in Islam all men are equal in the sight of God – and also his superb self-confidence.

The "best" people never made much of themselves – they had no need to. Sometimes a minor Saudi official would appear to be so occupied with his work, or preoccupied with it, that he hardly had time to look at you, but a "real" prince would rise to greet you when you entered his office, and, when you left, would get up and escort you to the door, where he would shake hands. I do, however, remember a friend being critical of Crown Prince Khaled. The friend had gone to the Cabinet Offices only to find that the King was away at a meeting and was walking away when a limousine drove past him, stopped, and out got the Crown Prince who came back and said "If you're looking for my brother he'll be back soon." I said that I thought it had been very kind thing to do. "No," my friend said, "it would have been kind to have stopped the car, and, when I reached it, to have spoken to me about the King. The Crown Prince shouldn't get out of his car to run messages." I saw his point and see it today but now, as then, I still think it was kind of Prince Khaled.

I suppose that life was not very exciting in those days, but it was all so new and so different to anything that I or any of my English colleagues had known before that it could never be other than interesting. Of course there were always some who couldn't adapt themselves to life, but I loved it. The one thing I did do with the Americans was to play Bridge, and one, Charlotte Speicher, became my bridge-partner for several years. This later developed into quite a large international group which held a bridge drive once a week; but in the early days I used to go once or twice a week to the Speichers for an ordinary evening's bridge. I had an unfortunate experience after one of these evenings – during which Scotch whisky had been generously served. I went down to Airport Street looking for a taxi, and, as most taxis in those days were Chevrolets; I flagged down the first Chevrolet I saw: it was unhappily a Police Car, and the occupants wanted to know why I had stopped them, and, smelling whisky on my breath, carted me off to the Police Station. I saw my self being arrested as Drunk and Disorderly (neither of which, I may say, I was) and sent back to England in disgrace. Luckily there was a very pleasant and sensible young Police Officer who took over my "case", told me, in English, not to worry and, after about twenty minutes, personally drove me home. "I'll have to keep your identity card," he said, "but I'll return it tomorrow. When will you be in?" When he did bring it back he told me that he had made a report that he was a friend of mine, and I had stopped the Police Car so that they could take me to his station. This was my first example of how, in Saudi Arabia, "verisimilitude can be given to the most unconvincing narrative." I never saw him again or even knew his name but I still remember his kindness.

One different aspect of Riyadh life was the way most people went to Barbers' Shops to be shaved – and there were a lot of such shops. I thought that I must try this and was recommended one in Bat'ha where most of the barbers spoke English, so the next day – it must have been a Friday with no school – I didn't shave but went down to this shop, where, as I took my seat, a very fierce looking barber asked we "are you American or English?" "English." I replied, whereupon, brandishing a cutthroat razor wildly in the air he cried "I hate the English!" (I believe he came from Aden), and although I never actually thought that he would cut my throat, it passed my mind that there might be an "accidental" nick on the ear or the cheek: in fact he did the job so well that I became an instant convert, and didn't, in Saudi Arabia at least, shave myself for years. On Wazir Street there was a Barber's Shop run by two Syrians, and every morning one of them would open early and shave me (and trim my hair if necessary) as I walked to school. They charged me something ridiculous like one riyal a day and that's about eight pence in today's money!

I ought to say something about food, which is an important subject to me. I usually made myself one meal in the very well appointed kitchen in the flat and ate out for the other. Sometimes I went to the Yamama Hotel, but in Wazir Street, only fifty yards from the flat, was a small restaurant run by an Alexandrian Greek where the food was very good indeed. Ralph and I often went there; the meals I remember particularly are those during Ramadan, the Fasting Month. While, of course, there was nothing to stop me eating in the flat I felt, even in that first year, that if my Arab friends and colleagues were fasting, I ought to do the same. In fact, all the years I was in Riyadh, I fasted quite as regularly as the strictest Wahabi.

Fasting, which had begun at first light – when a white thread could be distinguished from a black – ended at sunset and the moment was fixed when a religious observer decided that the sun had gone down behind the horizon, and a gun was fired. At the sound of the gun the pious would eat a handful of dates, drink a small cup of coffee, and go to the Mosque to pray, after which they went home for a proper meal. The less pious would have a meal as soon as the gun had sounded; and I hope, went to the Mosque to pray later. In the restaurant we all assembled ten or fifteen minutes before the gun and took our places at a table: it was expected that you would order the meal and then sit and wait. There would be bread rolls and jugs of water put on the tables and it was very tempting to break off a piece of bread or to pour a glass of water, but there would have been consternation if anyone had done so. At the sound of the gun, the doors opened and the meals ordered were brought in and placed on the tables in the sequence in which they had been ordered.

There is one odd feature of that first year which didn't strike me at the time although it does now. We must have used a lot of electricity in the flat, with several air conditioners always running and a lot of lights, quite apart from hot water and what we used in the kitchen; but I cannot remember ever seeing, let alone paying, an electricity bill. Of course, as I wrote in the Prologue, the flat had belonged to a Prince's Secretary and it might easily have been arranged that his electricity was free, or was paid for by some other flat occupant.

The school week was a six day one, but I shall write about the school in the Chapter on Education. Here I will only say a word about the Holidays. Apart from the summer break, there were only two holidays, a week after the end of Ramadan and another week during the Hajj – which was supposed to give one time to perform the pilgrimage. Sometimes extra days were added to allow for getting to Mecca and back again, but with Air Travel becoming normal, this was not always granted. When the holidays came round one could not just "go": it was necessary to get exit and return visas (which could take some time) and, first, to get hold of one's passport which was kept by the Zone Education Office. Before they would relinquish it a deposit was demanded: a sum equivalent to the Housing Allowance (which equalled three month's salary) and a further sum equal to another three-month salary. Now foreigners were expected to pay at least six months rent in advance, and probably the whole year, so there wasn't a lot of the Allowance left, and as, when the first Ramadan holiday came round, we had been in Riyadh barely four months, it was obviously impossible to go away. However, at the time, I was giving weekly English lessons to Sheikh Dammanhouri, the Deputy Minister of Education (who died, suddenly, before the end of my first year), and one day he asked me where I was going; "You must see some other Arab countries while you are here" he said. I explained that the financial requirements made it impossible for me to go anywhere. "Oh," he said, "those deposits aren't meant for people like you – they are meant to stop people coming, collecting their Housing Allowance and some months' pay and then just leaving and not returning. I'll give you a letter so your passport will just be given to you." I supposed the letter must have guaranteed the money, and I had my first (of many) holidays in Beirut.[12]

What I remember most about my second holiday during the Hajj was that, the Deputy Minister being already ill, I might not have got away again had the Shalhoubs not guaranteed me and my return. The Headmaster, Doctor Salloum, who later became a good friend, was not entirely happy: "You have only one week Mr David" he said, "Just because you have friends to guarantee you doesn't mean that you can take extra time off. I shall expect you here at eight o'clock on such-and-such a day." I spent an extremely relaxed week, again in Beirut, and arranged to fly back to Dharan the day before I was due back in the school and then take the evening flight up to Riyadh. However with an inefficiency of which I am too often capable, I didn't check the plane times, and they had altered since my earlier visit. When I arrived at Beirut Airport "my" plane had left an hour earlier and I must take the evening flight. This, as I was to discover in Dhahran, meant that I missed the last flight to Riyadh, and the first plane in the morning would not get me there before eight o'clock. The only thing to do was to find a taxi – and in Dharan most of the drivers could speak English – who would be prepared to drive the odd

---

[12] I'm sorry to say that at the beginning of my second year, in September 1965, a new English teacher and his wife arrived in Jeddah by boat. The man came ashore, reported to the Local Education Office, where he signed the necessary papers, received his Housing Allowance, returned to the ship, and sailed away to the Far East where he had secured another appointment. We never heard of him again.

few hundred miles to Riyadh. I found one easily and we established a cost. I explained my position and told the driver that I didn't have the cash on me; but that we would report to the school and then we would go to the Bank when it opened at nine and I would get his money. We drove through the night and reached Riyadh before seven o'clock. I took the taxi-driver to the flat and gave him – and myself – coffee. Then, a little before eight, we drove to the School. It all seemed very shut up but Dr Salloum was standing outside. I got out of the car and went up to him. "I'm glad to see you Mr David," he said, "We're keeping the school closed for another week. You can have another week's holiday." I was too flabbergasted to be angry, and I believe that my turning up in spite of the difficulties (for the whole story soon went round the teachers in the school) was counted unto me for righteousness. I took the driver back to the flat for more coffee, went to the bank at nine o'clock to get him his money, and then went home to bed and to sleep.

I did not stay in the flat in Wazir Street more than the one year, although Ralph Ellis decided to remain. Mohammed Oudah was leaving and there would be some other unknown Arab teacher there the next year. I had met an Englishman in the Restaurant in Wazir Street: going in one evening I saw a middle aged man wearing a Worcester College (Oxford) tie: I introduced myself at once and learned that Brian Walters had been up before the war, and worked for Shell, but now had a contract with Petromin. He had a villa out past the Showmaisi Hospital, and invited me to dinner there several times. In the summer, a little before we were due to go on leave, he told me that the little villa next door would soon be vacant, as the young Saudi who lived there was going to England for two or three years. The young Saudi was Mohammed Sha'alaan whose brother Laurens was in prison in Damascus. I shall have plenty to write about this villa and my adventures there later in the book; but I think this chapter has already been long enough, and I should now turn my attention to the various aspects of life in Saudi Arabia and Riyadh in particular, during the years I was lucky enough to be there.

CHAPTER 4
The Way of the Prophet

Religion is so important in Saudi Arabia that it deserves its own chapter. I am not going to write in detail about Islam as such, but rather about its place in people's lives and its role in the running of the country.

At Westminster, before they speak, members must first make it clear whether they have an interest in the subject under debate. Similarly, I feel I should state that I am on the side of "Religion." As a "practising" Catholic (Mass four or five times a week), I have my own definite views; but I can only say that these were strengthened and encouraged by my time in Saudi Arabia, where I met so many genuinely God-fearing believers. Over the years, I learnt a good deal about Islam and developed a profound respect for it; this I have never lost. I certainly deplore recent actions by people I can only describe as misguided. Acts of terrorism have nothing to do with the actual teachings of the Prophet Mohammed. In part at least, however, think I can understand the motives of those who perpetrate them. At least I know "where they are coming from" and I would never have been able to do that had I not been so fortunate as to live in Riyadh at such a crucial time.

I have already discussed the prohibition on alcohol and tobacco and described how the streets were cleared at the time of prayer. The call for prayer is always made a little before the actual prayer time, thus allowing the devout to complete any business in which they are engaged. They can thus proceed to prayer without any secular distractions in their minds. The prayer times were at Dawn – when, of course, no shop or office would be open – at noon, mid-afternoon, at sunset and an hour and a half later. Strictly kept in my early days, these arrangements were observed more laxly in my later years. In 1964 people were not to be seen in the streets at prayer times. I had an unfortunate experience – in Ramadan of all times – when I had an appointment (to give an English lesson in Petromin) just after the final prayer. Before the prayer was over, I went out hoping to find a taxi driver who would shortly be emerging from the Mosque. But as I was walking down Wazir Street, a red painted lorry full of what looked like extras from "Lawrence of Arabia" came driving in the opposite direction (why weren't they in the Mosque?). When they saw me, they broke into wild cries and I realised they were the religious police. I took to my heels and ran, hoping to dodge down a side street and get into the market somehow – although I don't think they would have had much difficulty in finding me. Fortunately, an irreligious taxi driver suddenly appeared in front of me, saw what was happening, stopped his car and threw the door open. I tumbled in and we shot off at an alarming pace. The police were left behind and I had just enough breath to gasp out the address to the driver. He was laughing loudly and clearly thought my predicament a tremendous joke.

I contrast all this with the situation some fifteen years later, when Riyadh was at the height of its obsession with money. The shops still stopped trading and people did not walk about the streets, but there were cars about, either driving around or stationary outside the shops. Some of the occupants, often prosperous looking men with their wives, seemed impatient for prayer time to be over. The owner of a fair-sized family run supermarket – who told me he averaged £4,000 a day profit, every day of the year – complained that he lost money when he had to close at prayer time, "and people drive away." I pointed out that the other supermarkets were also closed but he insisted that those who had driven away would be outside a different supermarket when prayer was over. He did not seem to understand me when I suggested that any loss was likely to be cancelled out by shoppers from other supermarkets coming his way. I found it sad then – and still do – that this man was not satisfied with his very considerable profit (and remember Saudis did not pay any taxes) and had come to regard prayer times as "interferences". It had been so different in my first years. Then shopping was a leisurely and social event, usually accompanied by a glass of tea. When I wanted to buy a wooden chest from a stall – which would be considered an "antiques stall" in England – I went every afternoon for a week to drink tea with the owner and argue about the price. The Saudis told me that this was the way to shop and the stallholder actually preferred this and liked me much more than if I had merely paid his outrageous asking price without demur. (In the early days you paid the stated price in Food Shops, but everywhere else, including the food market, barter was the norm).

I think at this point I should say something about the Mutawaeen, or members of the Committee for the Suppression of Vice and the Encouragement of Virtue, who used to walk through the streets presumably looking for both. For many years after my arrival, they played a big part in the daily life of everyone in Riyadh. For generations, the Mutawaeen had enjoyed Absolute Power – and we all know what that is said to produce – and there is no doubt that some of the members had become corrupt, although there were probably not many like that. I suspect that the vast majority were sincere; bigoted zealots certainly, but sincere ones for all that. It may not be too fanciful to compare them to the Lord's Day Observance Society in England, whose members were considered "spoil sports" because they wanted to stop other people doing things the Society considered harmful or sinful. Similarly, I believe that a majority of the Mutawaeen thought it a grave sin to miss any one of the five daily prayers, and hence were prepared to do whatever was necessary to prevent it.

However, people like to hear about the scandals, and so I will record some of those I knew about. The lorries belonging to what I will call the Religious Police could not be stopped or searched by the Customs Officials of the regular police, and therefore were sometimes used to smuggle goods, principally alcohol – potentially a highly profitable activity. There were other rackets too. A man working for Al-Jomaiah, one of the old merchant houses of Saudi Arabia, told me that in the early 1960s the son of the Head of the Mutawaeen used to get his father's signature for orders – and payments – for trucks, spare parts, tyres and quantities of petrol. None of these things were actually delivered to the Mutawaeen; on paper they were sold to Al-Jomaiah Company but at a much-reduced price. At least a share of this discount was then handed to the son – in cash – and he would then use the proceeds to leave the Kingdom for a probably very un-Islamic holiday.

As money started to flow into Riyadh, some of the Mutawaeen began to demand "protection money" from shopkeepers and stallholders in the neighbourhood where the Religious Police gave the call for prayer. A chance acquaintance in Jeddah told me that he was no longer troubled by the authorities, since he had seen his local "religious inspector" in a Cairo Nightclub, flinging money about, with champagne and whisky on the table and the "artistes" sitting with him. He said he had gone over and greeted the man who, between drink and fright, nearly passed out. Later, the Mutawa came to him in Jeddah, begging his silence, and promising that in any future problems he could count on the support of the religious authorities.

In Riyadh, there was a particularly striking Mutawa who used to call for prayer in Bat'ha, a district with wide pavements covered with tables and chairs; there crowds sat drinking tea and coffee for hours. Habitués – and many of the Yamama teachers used to sit there every day – told me that he would intersperse his pious exhortations with the words "white" or "black". The Mutawa was a dealer in smuggled alcohol and his customers sipping less heady drinks understood that when he introduced the word "white" he meant that he had gin in stock, while "black" signified whisky. Amin Hussein, the Egyptian Head of the Translation Department in the Ministry of Education, a good friend of mine in Riyadh and hospitable to me in Alexandria, told me that once, when in Wazir Street, he had found a case of gin and whisky hidden behind a shop door. Of course the presence of forbidden alcohol could have been extremely dangerous to the shopkeeper. Hussein rushed to warn him but the man only shrugged his shoulders with the comment, "The Mutawa left it there and he said he'd be back for it later," he said, "It belongs to him so it's no worry to me."

During my second and third years (after a short time in the villa next to Brian Walters) I lived in the Old Town in a house belonging to a man who had gone to Medina with his son. The owner's brother, a Mutawa, acted as his agent, and during my first year as a tenant – when I lived alone – he was no trouble. Even then I was a little surprised when, after a rare rainstorm, he spent one Friday prayer time on the roof checking for leaks. Things became more difficult during the second year of my tenancy. A friend and his wife came to live with me, and my mother also came to stay – she came for six weeks but liked Riyadh so much that she stayed six months. Now the "agent" was in and out of the house like a yoyo. In the end I went to talk to his sons, who were young middle-aged and quite sensible. They said they were sorry if father was being a nuisance; the reason why he was always coming in and out of the house was that he wanted to get a glimpse of the women. I remarked that he often came at prayer time; didn't he pray himself? "Not often," came the reply; the old man seemed to think that he had done his bit by making other people go. I had a brush with him at the beginning of the second year when I paid him the rent. He demanded more in the shape of a "finder's fee", which in Riyadh – and, I imagine, elsewhere – is payable only when first going into a house (in any case the normal entry fee was two and a half percent of the rent, whereas he asked five). When I refused to pay he threatened to have the water and electricity cut off; whereupon I paid up. For the honour of all concerned, I am glad to report that when the owner heard, he was clearly shocked by his brother's actions and personally repaid me the money. This Mutawa was not an admirable character. I later heard that he had worked for one of the King's brothers, who had put him in prison for mislaying a large sum of money, and he was only released when he remembered where he had put it.

A good friend of mine, a Police Officer from the far North of the country – who often came to have a drink with me in my home – heard that a fellow policeman, also from the same town, was about to return to his old home. He quickly wrote a number of letters and took them round to the other officer's house, intending to ask him to deliver them to various family members. It was mid-afternoon, and it was Ramadan, so he was naturally shocked to find a party going on, with piles of food, bottles of gin and the air thick with cigarette smoke. Among the guests he noticed one or two evidently "religious" figures. Two or three days later and by chance, he met one of these in the street. The Mutawa was calling the faithful to prayer, so he went straight up to him and asked him how he reconciled his conscience after joining – especially in Ramadan – in such a party. The reply was direct: "Look here: you're a policeman and I don't know how you do your job. My job is calling people to prayer, and I do it very well. You do your job and don't interfere with me. If you do I'll make trouble for you."

The threat was open, not veiled or implied. The same thing happened to a young friend of mine who, while still a student, worked as a part-time recording engineer on the local radio. He was so competent that I always hoped to have him for my programmes. He was also a very religious young man, who never drank or smoked and prayed and fasted regularly. One day he went to an old school friend's house and, after a little delay, was shown into an inner room, where a number of men, including a Mutawa, were drinking an orange coloured liquid. He was offered a glassbut, as he lifted it to his lips and smelt it, he asked whether it was alcoholic. Yes, he was told, it was homemade orange wine. He was laughed at for refusing it, and no-one was more insistent that he should try it than the Mutawa, but at last he got a soft drink and remained a while. After a little the Mutawa got up and began a mock call to prayer, going around the room knocking on the doors with his stick and calling "Salah! Salah!" Some of the men rocked with laughter, but the boy, horrified by this act of blasphemy ("I thought was going to be sick" he told me) got up and walked out. The Mutawa followed him and caught him by the front door: "Listen young man" he said, "if you repeat a word about what you've seen and heard today, I'll make bad trouble for you. Don't forget I can make any accusation I like. It'll be your word against mine, and I'll be believed every time. Be careful."

An interesting example of what I can only call "corruption" came in the late 1970s – though I forget the exact year. After the Hajj, a tiresomely pious Pakistani pilgrim decided to visit Medina and pray in every one of the Mosques. He got a list of all the Medina Mosques, presumably from the Ministry of Justice (the equivalent of a Ministry of Religion) and went off to complete his devotions. However, when he reached Medina, he could not find several of the Mosques; the Local Authorities said they knew nothing about them. He went back to Riyadh and took his case to the Minister, who ordered an investigation. It emerged that a number of fictitious mosques had been added to the list and the Ministry charged for the upkeep, the carpets, the cleaning and the stipend of the Muezzin who called people to prayer. Who got the money I never heard; and I am sure Medina was not the only place where this happened.[1]

During his reign, King Faisal did what he could to check the excessive power of the Mutawaeen and to curb their abuses; but he had to be careful not to offend the deeply conservative and religious feelings of the mass of the people. He could only act when there was a definite complaint. Such an occasion occurred in 1968 when an Iraqi Professor at the University – dressed as a Saudi – was shopping with his wife in the market. He was waiting for his change when a Mutawa appeared calling on the stallholder to close his stall, beating on the side with his stick, and ordering the Iraqi to go to the Mosque. The professor replied with the

---

1 The same thing happened in the Ministry of Education. A British Inspector visiting Ha'il came back having failed to inspect the English in two Intermediate Schools. He was ordered to go back – at his own expense – and visit the schools. He came to me and explained that these schools did not exist. There had been a "Third Intermediate" which had been renamed twice. I went to Sheikh Ibrahim Al-Hijji, the Director General of Education, and told him what had happened – he talked to the inspector, and ordered some private investigation, which bore out his account. I don't know what happened to whom, but the point is that the details of two imaginary schools, with the lists of all the staff were sent to Riyadh which sent the funds for the salaries, books, and other expenses, to the Ha'il Zone Education Office, and all the other Inspectors, except the British, had returned detailed reports of these schools to the Ministry of Education.

verse from the Holy Koran that enjoins finishing any piece of business before praying. As there was no answer to this the Mutawa went away, but only, as appeared later, to collect his colleagues, with one or two of his special Religious Police. As the Professor and his wife walked off down the street, he was seized and the black head rope (originally, I was told, used to hobble camels, but now used to keep the head-dress in place) put round his neck. He was then knocked to the ground before being dragged to the Mosque, with his wife hysterically calling for help. The result was that the Professor had to go to hospital, his Iraqi colleagues at the University threatened to resign en masse, the Iraqi ambassador went to the King, and the King used this opportunity to weaken the Mutawaeen. The offenders were sent to prison and a solemn warning issued that any other Mutawa who used physical violence would be treated in the same way.

I have put my account of these discreditable episodes in the early part of this chapter so that the rest can be devoted to the better side of religious life in Saudi Arabia. Among the Mutawaeen there were, I am sure, many sincere and devout men who were not at all fanatical. I went to the house of one, the father of a pupil of mine, and was surprised to see an ashtray on the table in the Majlis and said so. The boy explained that his father was sure that "these days" all young men were going to smoke, whether their fathers forbade them or not. This particular Mutawa had told his son that smoking was less of a sin than deceiving or disobeying a father. Hence my pupil and his friends were free to smoke in the Majlis, although the Mutawa asked that, as a courtesy, they should not smoke in his presence. [2]

The Mutawaeen are a Saudi, or Najdi phenomenon, and Muslims from other countries insist they have no place in Islam at all. The important thing to remember about Islam is that it is not just "a religion," something like the Church of England was a couple of centuries ago – for Sundays only. Rather, it is a way of life and embraces every conscious act and thought of the individual in every possible situation. Islam means submission of the Self to Divine Will and the whole creed is contained within the Holy Koran and the "Commentaries". Of course, the Holy Koran, the Word of God, is written in Koranic Arabic: the authorities will tell one that the Holy Koran can only be fully understood when it is

---

[2] When I was sixteen my father told me that I could smoke when I wanted to: "You are bound to experiment" he said, "and I would rather you did it with my permission than without."

studied in the original Arabic. Some thirty years ago I read an English writer who called the Holy Koran boring and frightening, and complained of the translations. English-speaking visitors to the Imam's office in Riyadh were given a two-volume translation by a Pakistani savant, who had obviously studied the language of the Authorized Version of The Bible. I studied this translation in great detail, because I recorded the complete English version of the Holy Koran after the English Service of Radio Riyadh began in 1968. Subsequently, when slightly more elaborate readings were needed to open and close the day's broadcasts, I "arranged" the whole Koran in "lessons" and three of us English broadcasters (one of whom later went to prison for drink offences) recorded it in batches of fourteen lessons each, a week at a time. When studied that way, the Holy Koran becomes a beautiful and moving religious work; but to leave it at that would not satisfy any Muslim, for whom it means a great deal more.

It is hard for a non-Muslim to understand, and equally hard to try to explain, what the Holy Koran means to the faithful. Once, a notoriously clumsy British teacher knocked a pile of books off a boy's desk. One of the books was the Holy Koran and there was a near riot when the teacher trod on it. I thought at the time that if this had been a senior rather than a junior class, the teacher would have been seriously assaulted. As it was the whole school refused to take lessons from this man, and his particular class did no more work that day. I was called in to make peace, and after assuring the boys and the Headmaster (who was deeply troubled) I helped to concoct a letter of public apology, couched in language sufficiently contrite without passing the bounds of absurdity. Of course I didn't see the Arabic translation given to the boys – that could have said anything.

The point is that the Holy Koran is not only the Word of God, it is so in a way different to the Jewish or Christian Scriptures; each individual copy is a sacred object in itself. The boys I have just mentioned really believed their teacher was making a deliberate attack on their religion when he knocked the Holy Koran off the desk and trod on it. Since the Holy Koran contains God's instruction to the prophet Mohammed, regulating not only belief and worship but also how to behave in all daily events, there is no need for any other book. There are further teachings and commentaries but they are only needed by the learned. These include books on Islamic Jurisprudence, of which there are four schools. Readers will not be surprised to learn that it is the strictest of these schools, the Hanbali, that applies in Saudi Arabia. But for the mass of the people, knowledge of the Holy Koran was all that mattered. It was learned by rote and there was little attempt to provide an understanding of what had been committed to memory. I was assured that this was so by the sons of one of the most eminent – and liberal – of the religious leaders: in the old Koranic Schools, memorizing the text of the Holy Koran was all that mattered. In my days, many lessons were devoted to Religion and there were examinations in the subject every year. It did not matter whether the student was studying history, or science, or plumbing in the Vocational School or was at the Police College – passing all religious examinations was essential.

Since all of God's law is contained in the Holy Koran, a truly Islamic country will have a legal system based entirely on Islamic Law, the Shariah. The Judges are leaned Sheikhs who sit on a bench above the Court. Sometimes there are two or three judges but one is enough.[3] I have the highest opinion of Saudi justice, even if it is not always carried out in ways that would be acceptable in Britain. I myself, in the very early days, had a personal experience that I must explain.

I have already explained how, at the end of my first year, I decided to move into a small villa next door to my fellow collegian, Brian Walters, out in a new suburb behind the Shomaisi Hospital. The sitting tenant had been Mohammed Sha'alaan, who has also appeared before in these pages. He was going on a two-year course in England for the National Guard, though I am not sure where he went. There were still four months left on his lease, so we arranged for me to pay him a third of the annual rent. On the day he was to leave, I would meet him at two o'clock in the afternoon to take possession: later he would take me to the Agent to introduce me and to arrange for me to take over the lease in my own name when the time came for renewal. However, when I turned up at the appointed time, it was Brian who met me with the keys and the news that Mohammed had already left.

The next morning, after my first night in my villa, I decided to go to the Agent on my own. The visit was not entirely successful, because I found that Mohammed had not only omitted to pay the Agent the rent I

---

[3] I once sat on the bench in a Shariah Court! I was on holiday in Pakistan, in Swat, and a young man in Reception at the hotel took me home – as I lived in Riyadh – to meet his father who was the chief Judge of the principality; and I was invited to visit the Court the next day. Once there I was invited to join two judges on the bench, with the Judge's son to translate for me. There were two cases heard, and when the judges had conferred they asked me whether I thought they had reached the same decision as judges in Riyadh would. As their decisions seemed eminently sensible I had no hesitation in saying "Yes."

had given him but had also not paid any of the rent due for the second six months of the year. If I wanted to stay in the villa, the Agent said, I should pay the six months rent: slightly reluctantly, I paid. Some ten days later the water pump failed, and when I went to the Agent he said that the water pump was the responsibility of the tenant, and I must pay for a new one. There were one or two other small sums owing which, to keep everything amicable, I settled. I got a receipt to say that I had paid this money "on behalf of the tenant, Mohammed Sha'alaan". A couple of days later I went back to England for the summer.

I returned in September to find myself the centre of a storm. According to Saudi practice, by paying a bill "on behalf of" Mohammed, I hade made myself his representative in Riyadh, and liable for all his debts, which were, to say the least, very considerable. The Headmaster became very uneasy as day after day Police arrived at the school asking for David Urch's appearance at the Police Station.[4] He was pacified, although I did not know at the time, by the Shalhoub family telling him that they would guarantee me. The bills poured in – some, I am sure, spurious – because Mohammed seemed never to have paid for anything. There was even a claim for manslaughter, because some friend had borrowed Mohammed's car and fatally knocked down a pedestrian, and Mohammed had "guaranteed" him. Mohammed's mother, younger brother and sister (who was married to the then Prince, now King Abdullah) had all been before a judge and had it officially registered that they were not responsible for his debts. I was the only person left.

Then I was notified that I would have to appear before a Judge on a stated day. My English friends were very concerned for me, but not as much so as my "foreign" Arab colleagues at school. They told me that I must scrape up as much money as possible and offer what I could: "they know you can't pay it all, it's your total salary for years," but Saudi friends told me "not to worry." I had to write out a statement of exactly what had happened and have it properly translated into Arabic – something done by my colleagues at school. The afternoon before my Court Appearance, my "private" pupil, Abdul Rahman Shalhoub, came to take me for a drive, "to take your mind off tomorrow." We drove around for a bit and then went to a villa to visit a Shalhoub family friend, a very pleasant elderly man who was an expert on tea. He explained the different local ways of making tea. Cardomom, Mint and Ginger teas were

---

[4] I should say here that on each of my appearances the Police were uniformly pleasant and helpful.

made and they were all delicious. When we left and were driving home, I asked Abdul Rahman who the old man was. "Oh, he's the Judge who is hearing you case tomorrow", he said. "He wanted to see you before the case without you knowing who he was." It seemed very strange to me but I felt hopeful.

The next morning, with an Arab colleague as my translator, I attended the Court and handed in my defence.[5] The room was full, and when the Judge asked who had any claim against this man it seemed to me that more than half the men there started waving papers. The judge then made a brief address and pandemonium broke out. My translator explained that the Judge had told the court that a stranger, who had come to Riyadh to help the children as a teacher, not understanding the custom of the country had, out of kindness, paid a bill for a Saudi friend. He was not liable for any other bill, and nobody would be allowed to leave the Court until he had given a written statement that he had no claim against the Englishman. It couldn't have happened in an English court, but I had no complaint.

Then I was asked to approach the bench and the Judge asked if I was prepared to pay for the electricity I had myself used – the Electricity Bill had been enormous and nobody could have paid anything since the house had been built. Of course I said, "Yes." Did I know what the meter reading had been when I went into the villa? As a matter of fact I did, and looking back I am astonished that I had been so practical – it was out of character. With my translator, the man from the Electricity Company and a policeman, I went to my villa, we read the meter, I paid the very small sum required, and with my receipt – in my own name – I returned to the Court. Almost everybody had gone, and when I handed the receipt to the Judge he gave me a very pleasant smile and told me that there would be no further action against me. As I have said, it was plain that Saudi law was different from English law, but it did seem to be eminently fair and sensible. The idea that "foreigners" would be badly treated was simply not true.

There was one occasion when a Saudi judge was, let us say "prejudiced": in Ta'if a Saudi driver, jumping a red light quite early in the morning was hit, and injured by a British driver taking two or three friends to work. He was found guilty of "drunken driving" on the

---

[5] At the end of my statement, at the Shalhoubs' insistence, I had stated that I would accept the decision of the Court and pay whatever they ordered. "But I can't pay it all," I had said. "They won't ask you to," was the reply, "but if they do we'll pay it for you."

grounds that "all the British in Ta'if are drunk," and no Defence Plea was allowed. Of course, this gross injustice was overturned on appeal to more senior and less prejudiced judges.

A Welsh couple I knew quite well were being evicted from their house: the only possible reason for eviction – apart from refusal to pay the rent – was if the owner of the property genuinely wanted it for his or her own use. There was an appeal, and the case went on for three days. It took so long because the judge continually stopped proceedings to make sure, through the translator, that the couple understood both what had been said and its implications. They told me they were sure that, whatever verdict was reached, it would be the right one: they were evicted in the end, but retained the highest regard for Saudi Justice.

There was another young couple I knew, both teachers, who had a flat in a very small block and were being evicted because their Landlord needed it for himself. But the Judge was not satisfied and adjourned the case for a week. When they returned the Judge told the Landlord, "You lived in a villa and built those flats as an investment. Now, because of greed, you have rented your villa at an enormous price to an American Company. You cannot turn these people out. Use some of the money you've made to rent yourself another villa." This couple were also generous in their praise for the way they had been treated. There is a footnote to my own experience. After two or three years in England Mohammed Sha'alaan returned to Riyadh and we met several times, most amicably, as old friends. Neither of us made any reference to the mess he had left me in, and my mother thought him "a most charming young man."

At the beginning of this chapter I explained that the Saudis were – in my time at least – almost 100% religious believers. The expression "In Shallah" (God Willing) was heard continually, and unfortunately became a sort of joke with English and American expatriates – a joke, I may say, extremely offensive to the Saudis.[6] If, as the true Muslim believes, God is omnipotent and omnipresent, then it is only by His permission that anything can take place. When I asked a taxi driver to take me to the Airport he would reply "Inshallah," which in no way implied that he was unwilling or unready to take me, but that our safe arrival depended on the

---

[6] I was once in the Library of Radio Riyadh, receiving instructions about what I should be doing over the next two or three days. At each instruction I murmured "Inshallah" and at the end a young Saudi appeared. "You sounded just like a Saudi when you said "Inshallah," he said "You really meant it."

permission of the Almighty. Of course, it is also true that if I asked for something to be done "boukra" (tomorrow), I could well be answered "If God wills" from a man who was 99.9% sure that the job would not be finished – but as a fallible human being he did not know. Only God, who could have the thing finished if he wished, knew. I was in Riyadh long enough to know from the tone of the voice and even the way of drawing out the syllables whether "Inshallah" was a genuinely pious aside when the speaker was confident that something would happen, or merely placatory, where the speaker disclaimed any personal responsibility for its likely failure. Whatever the implication, it was never lightly said; and although it used to annoy some foreign Arabs as well as Europeans and Americans, on the lips of a Saudi "Inshallah" meant exactly what he said.[7]

I have heard people argue that the belief in the omnipotence of God means that Muslims are incapable of proper planning – but this is a misconception. Nowhere in the Holy Koran are we told not to make a proper provision for ourselves and our family. Of course, submission to the will of God necessarily requires ready acceptance of what He sends: the farmer plants seeds although it depends on God whether there will be a crop. Insurance against something, which after all must have been the Will of God, was actually forbidden in 1964 (though one could insure one's car through Jordanian companies). The ban was later lifted and the Kingdom's religious leaders, after I am sure much heart-searching, agreed to allow Insurance, while still advising the pious not to use it. Before I left Riyadh I think all businessmen used insurance automatically, but car insurance was still not compulsory.

Islam does not teach the rather depressing dogma of Original Sin; and man's relationship with God is an intensely personal affair. Yet there is also much emphasis on congregational worship, and at public worship backsliders could be castigated with all the fervour of a seventeenth century Cameronian, searching the minor prophets for anathemas to hurl at erring members of his flock. Islam teaches that everything you do is written down by the Recording Angel, and on Judgement Day your deeds will be recalled and judged: on that depends whether Eternity will be spent in Paradise or in The Fire. The Fire was a very real place to the Najdi Muslims. On more than one occasion, in my early days, after I had visited the family of one of my pupils, uncles or father would implore me

---

[7] My maternal grandmother, if writing about something that was to happen in the future, always put DV (Deo Volente); and my father's eldest sister had a house parlour maid, who, if asked to do anything the next day, always replied, "If I'm spared Madam!"

to convert to Islam: "We don't want you to go to the Fire! You've been so kind to..." Abdullah, Mohammed, Ahmed or whoever. It was a real fear for me, inspired it seemed by a genuine kindness. However in all my years in Riyadh, I never met a Muslim who thought that he was personally in danger of hellfire: that was for non-Muslims or Muslims of a different persuasion (I'll have more to say about that later) but, especially among the Wahabis, the sense of Personal Election was tremendously strong. Even those who did not seem to pray appeared convinced that matters could be arranged satisfactorily with the Almighty at the last moment. There seemed little or no fear of death. That is not to say – as I have heard suggested – that there is no mourning for the dead. On the contrary, I have sat for hours beside a father, whose eldest son (a pupil of mine) had been killed in a road accident, when for days the man was almost out of his mind with grief; and I still remember the hysterical scenes at the funeral of King Faisal, when even the radio and the television commentators broke down and wept.

It is always interesting to observe the degree of religious observance where this is obligatory. The compulsory roll call had died out in some Mosques before 1964, but even after that date a senior Ministry of Education official, who lived in the Old Town, was taken to task by his local Mutawa. Abdul Aziz's trouble was that he could not get up in the morning, and so, although he duly performed the other four prayers, the Dawn Prayer was too much for him, and he simply said it at home when he woke up. The Mutawa's advice was straightforward – either come to the Dawn Prayer or we must take official notice. If you just can't get up, go and live somewhere else, like Malaz, where the foreigners live and it doesn't matter. Abdul Aziz went to live in Malaz.

The Mosques were certainly very full on Fridays, but less so on other days. Sometimes I saw only forty of fifty worshippers coming out of a Mosque that could have held a thousand. In some Mosques, where there was a fashionable preacher – perhaps one who also appeared on television! – there would be an extra large congregation, with the sermon broadcast outside to those who couldn't get into the Mosque. But that was only on Fridays; on weekdays even the most fashionable mosques would be three quarters empty. Of course people could – and did – pray where they worked. In 1964 if one was in a bank during prayer time, everybody, staff and customers alike, would pray then and there: each bank and big office had a man best described as a "chaplain". This was also true of the "great" houses and the palaces, where a Mosque was built inside the walls. Yet, before I left Riyadh, much of this had already changed; in a bank for instance some people would ignore the call for prayer and get on with their work: I don't say they did not pray later.

In each Ministry there was a Mutawa who called the employees to prayer at noon – the only prayer time when Ministry employees were at work – but the actual time of prayer was somewhat elastic. It depended on exactly when the Minister was free – I have known it to be an hour later in the Ministry of the Interior than elsewhere – but attendance was expected. But not everybody always prayed – and this was probably chalked up against them as a black mark. I once asked a very religious man in the Ministry of Education why he didn't pray there. He said that he was so conscious of the hypocrisy of some of the other worshippers – who were there just to be seen, preferably by the Minister – that it affected his concentration and he could not put himself in the proper frame of mind to approach the Creator in prayer. He also said that the lavatories were so dirty that he could not bring himself to perform the ablution (which should be made before prayer although as years went on more and more people seemed to omit this).

A very important matter to be considered in any discussion of religion is the attitude of the young and here I watched a pendulum at work. When I arrived in 1964 the boys were emerging from the traditional submission to authority – parental and academic – and were flexing their muscles. They were deciding that prayer was something they would do when they wanted, not when they were told. I am sure that most prayed at home, but many didn't want to pray at school. It was therefore necessary not only to have someone to call them to prayer, and to lead the prayers, but also to have young and active men to go round and chivvy boys out of classrooms where they would linger. Some would even walk out of the school completely; so the gates had to be locked and more young and active men recruited to stop the pupils climbing over the walls. Finally, many schools resorted to a counsel of despair. Lessons began earlier, so that the day's work was over by noon, before the call for prayers. Although prayers were still offered, the authorities had no need to try – usually unsuccessfully – to compel attendance and so no face was lost by anybody.

The attitude of the young to the Mutawaeen in 1964 was definite and unappreciative. There was a feeling, not exactly of fear but more of dislike for the Religious Teachers. Boys who talked to me (not in School!) longed for freedom to make the choice – although I don't believe they would actually have welcomed the freedom if they had it. What they really wanted was a more benign authority to give its blessing to a relaxation of austerities.

But while I lived in Riyadh, there was another, rather dramatic change. As long ago as 1980 a growing number of young men (and women) were becoming all too aware of what we then called "The Islamic Revolution" that was sweeping through other countries. These young people looked, not for a relaxation, but a re-imposition of controls. I was interested to discover that many of these young Puritans had studied abroad, mostly in the United States, and had decided that what they had seen there was not for them – or, at least, was not for them at home. They came back to Saudi Arabia, educated, articulate, and bitterly anti "western" because they had decided that "the West" was morally decadent and corrupt. This did not mean that they became pro-Russian: Communism was atheistic, and was thus even worse.

Before I left, undergraduates at Riyadh University – who included some of my past pupils – had become very cynical about their relations with the government. They told me openly that they knew they were being bribed to be quiet with generous grants and conditions. They were willing enough to remain silent, so long as their grants were paid but, as I noted at the time, religious feelings were moving and hardening.

I do not intend here to write about the differences between the Sunni and Shi'ite Muslims, other than to say that they are as profound as the differences between Catholics and Protestants during the Thirty Years War, or between the Eastern and Western Churches when Constantinople was sacked by the Crusaders in 1204. All my readers will be aware of the religious troubles in Iraq in recent years. By some accident Shi'ite Muslims are in an enormous majority in Iran and in a majority in Iraq, although for many years they were kept in subjection by the Sunnis. On the southern side of the Gulf there were pockets of Shi'ites including some in Saudi Arabia. These villages and small towns were entirely Shi'ite, because Shi'ite and Sunni would not share living space. Shi'ites in countries outside Iran and Iraq (in Lebanon for instance) seemed to be poorer than most Sunnis, and like other repressed people, tended (and I believe still tend) to espouse left wing causes in a sort of sad hope that something better may ensue.

I cannot speak for today but in my time Shi'ites were definitely at a disadvantage. They lived in the Eastern Provinces and those who lived there told me that Shi'ites were always at the end of the queue. This confirmed the impression I had formed when I was in the Ministry of Education. Schools in the Shi'ite areas would write in to say used they had not received essential supplies, perhaps the set-books for that year's exams. But these complaints were rarely acted upon. In short, the Shi'ites were left in little doubt that the authorities regarded them as second class citizens, whose concerns were regarded as a low priority.

The Saudi Shi'ites were completely uninvolved in the extraordinary events in 1979 when, to usher in the Muslim year of 1400 AH, armed men seized the Grand Mosque in Mecca and proclaimed the new Messiah – but they suffered grievously as a result. In Qatif, Safura and in some Shi'ite villages, the National Guards got out of hand and shot down hundreds of people. This was officially denied; but I did not doubt the word of foreign "eye witnesses" who, though forbidden to drive through the area, had heard the shooting and seen the fires. Later they were to see the damage and to discover that many of their friends had disappeared. A man at Riyadh University told me that, of the Shi-ite students, he did not believe there was one who had not lost a relative in the massacre. They had, he told me, become sullen, secretive, refusing to pray with the others, even refusing to wear traditional Saudi dress, and talking together in their own dialect. One of the student leaders told him – "Just wait – our time will come."

In 1980 I thought – incorrectly I am glad to say – that the Shi'ites posed a political threat to the Saudi Kingdom. In the Autumn of 1980 an English friend of long standing and of the highest probity was in Beirut, where, in the house of a friend, he met a Shi'ite from Qatif who revealed that he visited Beirut every two weeks. His purpose was to acquire arms, which he then smuggled into the Eastern Province – so that the Shi'ites would be strong "for the next time." With Saudi Arabia's long desert frontier, at that time it was impossible to keep complete control of what entered the Kingdom, and lorries could enter almost as and when they pleased. In 1979/80 it seemed highly likely that the Shi'ites would cause trouble. Fortunately the danger did not materialise. It is possible that efforts to ameliorate the lot of the Shi'ites in Iraq went some way to appease them. In Saudi Arabia, the 1980 budget was rewritten to include scores more projects in the Eastern Province, to improve the standard of life, and to provide more jobs and money.

I have said that, even in 1980, there was opposition to the Saudi Government, but it was a religious opposition, not political. It seemed ironic to me that a government, one of the few trying to rule according to enlightened religious principles, should be pilloried for being too lax. But "lax" it was considered by the new young zealots, while the Mutawaeen – so drastically curtailed by King Faisal – were already scenting the battle from afar and coming back to preach a return to the fundamental tenets of the Faith and thus implicitly demanding the reversal of twenty years of westernization.

I have mentioned the seizing of the Grand Mosque in Mecca in 1979. Although it should not have done so, it took every body by surprise. The leader, Johaima'an Oteibi, had been on "the most wanted" list for years, and his pamphlets had circulated widely. These were, of course, absolutely forbidden material; but I knew people who had seen them and could admit it, because they had read the pamphlets "officially" – so that they could refute their contents. The pamphlets began, unexceptionably, with the statement that it is the duty of a good Muslim to support a Muslim government and obey its laws. But then they went on to claim that the then Saudi government could no longer be considered truly Islamic and hence had forfeited its right to the allegiance of its citizens. There were two main allegations. First, there had been too much westernization, to the detriment of the quality of Islamic life. Secondly, the pamphlets emphasised the notoriously un-Islamic life-style of some of the senior Princes, including some with important roles in the government of the Kingdom; here it must be said that the writer was on quite strong ground. At that time, many Muslims in other countries were irritated by what seemed blatant Saudi hypocrisy; they found themselves on the receiving end of lectures – which accompanied Saudi money – on such topics as the need for a total ban on alcohol. Nobody minds an austere teetotaller preaching abstinence, but the same advice from a bon viveur, with a large glass of whisky in one hand and a fat cigar in the other, tends to grate, and that, in the late 1970s and the 1980s was the Arab cartoonist's image of a Saudi.

To use a loose term, the zealots who seized the Grand Mosque and proclaimed the Messiah were "Puritans". The Saudi government immediately denounced the Messiah as "false;" but there was a great deal more support for him in Riyadh than I expected.[8] Many of the elderly Mutawaeen and preachers in Riyadh were imprisoned – one of them was

---

[8] The expected Mahdi, or Messiah, was Mohammed ibn Abdullah Al Qahtani, a 27 year old student from Riyadh's Islamic University: the awaited Messiah was to have the same name as the Prophet Mohammed ibn Abdullah, and come from his tribe, the Quraish; and the Qahtani were part of the Quraish tribe.

arrested in the middle of a sermon attended by the secretary of a good friend of mine. His error (or crime) was to say that it was too soon to say whether the claims if this Messiah were true or not; and I was told that there was a considerable feeling in the University of Riyadh that the claims could possibly be true. The claimant appeared to fit a number of earlier predictions. The most important of these, from the students' point of view, was that although all his supporters might be captured and killed, the Claimant himself would escape. Many days before the French Special Forces were brought in to retake the Mosque, an informant from the University told me that the Claimant had been removed secretly to await the next move. To be sure, after the end of the affair, a body was found in the wreckage of an underground room and identified as that of the Messiah. A photograph of a young man, lying in all the careless abandonment of sudden death, was printed in all the papers, and I watched on television as five rather cowed youths, from the family or household of the Claimant, two no more than boys, gave monotonous and stereotyped identifications in answer to leading questions from the interviewer. As a convincing performance I decided it merited nought out of a hundred, and I also thought that more people must have doubts after seeing the programme than before it had gone on air.

Of course the Saudi Government had been in an impossible position. They had either to denounce the Messiah as false, or surrender the government of the Kingdom to him. In the event, on a political level, they handled the situation rather well. It was only the incredible ineptitude of the forces sent to retake the Mosque that made the affair into such high drama. Had the "rebels" – as they were termed – been crushed within two or three days. it would all have been blown over quite quickly. As it was, however, it seemed that the thought that they were fighting to protect the holiest shrine in Islam – and that death in such a cause would open the doors to Paradise – went to the heads of the National Guardsman. I was told that they made their attacks by running straight towards the Mosque in a dense crowd with no thought of cover. Of course, they were mown down by the hundred; and as the pile of the dead and dying grew higher, later comers merely climbed on top of them to be shot in turn. Eventually, in places, the piles of corpses were nearly as high as the walls of the Mosque.

I got my information from a friend, an international lawyer, who had a cousin whose house in Mecca was across the square from the Grand Mosque, and (until the military turned civilians out) telephoned every evening to recount the events of the day. Tariq duly passed the news on to me. That is how I learned that many of the Religious Police on duty at the Mosque had joined the "rebels" – which was the main reason why they were able to seize the Mosque so easily. Another fact, suppressed as far as possible, was that far from being a group of ignorant Bedouin villagers misled by a silver-tongued charlatan, the rebels included some of the best students from the Religious University and their professors.

After the seizure of the Grand Mosque, the reaction of the authorities on a religious level was one of panic. They imprisoned many preachers, including some who had not supported the claimant in any way: the most they had done had been to echo his denunciation of the trends towards westernization so evident in Riyadh – and I imagine, in other cities too. Now mosques were not only guarded but were filled with armed troops. More than one friend told me that there were more troops than worshippers in his local mosque, and a man I knew very well, from a highly respected family and a strict Muslim most punctilious about his duties, told me that he had simply stopped going to the Mosque, "because I can't pray with a loaded rifle pointing at the small of my back."

What might be termed "religious subversion" had been going on for some years before I left: it was aimed at the Government, or certain members of it. Johaima'an Oteibi was captured and executed after the Mecca affair; but in fact he was only one of many. The Pilgrimage, no longer a peaceful and holy time, became fraught with great danger. In 1979 a good friend and his wife went on the Hajj together and were regularly solicited by Iranian pilgrims. The Iranians had brought with them masses of inflammatory pamphlets and papers from the Ayatollah Khomeini, attacking the Saudi regime in particular and Westernizing influences in general. In 1980 the Iran-Iraq war interrupted the main artery bringing pilgrims overland, and many Iranians came through Pakistan. Rumour, ever busy in a city like Riyadh – where finding out the truth depended on whom you knew – had it that many Iranian pilgrims had been seized and imprisoned for possessing compromising documents

It should be is plain from what I have written here – which is based on notes I made twenty-eight years ago – that the Saudi authorities had to walk a religious tightrope. So far they seem to have managed to do this successfully. Nevertheless, one fundamental problem remains, as serious today – if not more so – than when I was in Saudi Arabia. I suspect that a majority in the Hejaz and the Eastern Province want a moderation of the austerities, while a sizable number in the Najd and in the country districts hanker after even greater austerity and compulsion. In Saudi Arabia, there are certainly men we in the West have been taught to call "terrorists" and I believe it when I am told that a majority of the Al-Qaeda are Saudis. After all Osama bin Laden is Saudi. His father's company built the great road between Mecca and Ta'if, and, incidentally, extended and refurbished the Grand Mosque, on which King Sa'ud spent more than one million riyals. During the 1979 siege of the Mosque, the Bin Laden Company was asked to provide the plans of the intricacies underground to help the troops trying to storm the place, and, later, to restore the damage done. I am sure, in my own mind, that Al-Qaeda has a lot of sympathizers in Saudi Arabia, although not many would actually do anything about it.

One trouble is that the strict Wahabis think – like all good believers – that theirs is the only true faith; there are some who even think they are somehow polluted when they mix with non-Muslims or even non-Wahabi Muslims. Yet I have also met a lot of Muslims from other countries who have assured me that the Saudis know nothing about Islam. I have talked to Egyptians, Syrians, Lebanese, Iraqis, Jordanians, Palestinians, Pakistanis, and Malaysians, and discussed religious matters and attitudes with them. They all gave the same opinion: the Saudis did not understand their own faith. These people had, of course, not been talking with theologians, but to the ordinary Saudi man-in-the-street. Taking into account that the main thrust of all education was religious, it was surprising just how ignorant the Saudi public could be. That is until one remembered that during Religious Instruction no explanations were given: the be all and end all was to be able to recite as much of the Holy Koran as possible.

It is difficult for anybody not actually on the scene to judge the degree of religious fundamentalism in the Kingdom at present, but I suspect that there is a lot of private support. I doubt whether there is the same amount of what I must call "spiritual co-operation" of the kind we enjoyed under the guiding hand of King Faisal, who thought that all Believers should work together, especially against atheism and communism. He reminded his people that Christians were The People of the Book, and declared in a broadcast, that, in the eyes of Almighty God, "a good Christian is better than a bad Muslim." He opened negotiations with the Vatican, and we were treated on television to the edifying spectacle of purple-habited Monsignori arriving at Jeddah airport to a full official welcome. This was later followed by the news that the Minister of Justice, the highest religious authority in the Kingdom, had performed his prayers before the High Altar in St Peter's, Rome. I was told by many people, some slightly disapprovingly, that in one of the periodic Italian financial crises, at the direct request of the Vatican – who feared Italian Communists would benefit from economic collapse – Saudi Arabia moved a vast amount of money from American to Italian banks.

There were, of course, some violent reactions from strict religious figures who feared their position was being undermined. This led to some unfortunate consequences. Thus, when the head religious teacher in the Yamama School met an Iraqi Catholic teacher on the stairs, he reviled him as a dog and an apostate; later the same man asked for a separate common room for the religious teachers so that they would not have to sit with unbelievers. The headmaster was forced to put up a notice, "British teachers are requested not to say Good Morning or try to shake hands with the Religious teachers."

How do I sum up this chapter? During all the years I was in Riyadh, I never had the slightest intimation that I was being belittled or set aside in any way because I was a Christian – albeit a "sympathetic" Christian. I was invited into the houses of strict Muslims and always treated with all the hospitality for which Arabs are famous, and my own Faith was strengthened by the general "religious" atmosphere of the city. Of course I was one of the first Englishmen to be very publically in Riyadh, I was there for years and I wore Arab dress (I was told that people spoke of me as "the English Bedu") but in all the time I lived in Riyadh I received the same kindness and help from Religious figures as I did from all the other people in the city where I spent such happy years.

CHAPTER 5
Open Government

When I lived there, the government of Saudi Arabia was paternalistic, feudal, totally authoritarian and extremely rich. Apparently an anachronism by the 1980s, it certainly worked much better than most governments of the so-called Third World – although I do not know whether it could have been so successful without its wealth.

Since this is an account of my personal impressions, I shall only consider three aspects of government in this chapter: the source of power; the executive; and the enforcement of authority. In each case, I shall try to describe them as they struck me at the time. The King is the Head of the Government, and all power comes from him. Succession to the Kingship is not automatic, but the practice is similar to that by which a man becomes Chief of a Tribe, when he is chosen by its elder members. The King of Saudi Arabia is chosen by the elder members of his family and by the religious leaders. It is quite possible for both the Chief or the King to be succeeded by their eldest son – but not necessarily so. The successor must be of the right age and experience and have shown himself to be an able leader. In Saudi Arabia, the first King, Abdul Aziz, was succeeded by his son, Sa'ud, but thereafter the succession has gone from brother to brother: Faisal, Khaled, Fahad and now Abdullah. There is one non-tribal feature in Saudi Arabia, the appointment of a Crown Prince; but on the death of the King, the Crown Prince must be chosen by the family and the Ulema. So far, the Crown Prince has always become King – but need not be. Suitability is what matters, and I have already told how Prince Mohammed was – for a consideration – passed over as Crown Prince and, presumably, King.[1]

However the choice of a Crown Prince does not settle the succession. During King Faisal's reign, the evident ill health of Prince Khaled gave

---

[1] Prince Mohammed was mortally offended at the showing of the film "Death of a Princess," as it was his granddaughter who was stoned to death for adultery.

rise to doubts as to whether he could sustain the burdens of Kingship. There were, certainly, the usual rumours to the effect that some of the illnesses were "diplomatic", while others suggested that Khaled was too likely to use the velvet glove – without first remembering that it should cover an iron fist. Many expected that King Faisal's successor would be Prince Fahad – but Fahad's prospects were dashed when reports circulated in European papers about his enormous gambling debts. Gambling is forbidden in Islam, yet it was alleged that Fahad's losses sometimes amounted to millions of dollars a night. King Faisal was furious and for some time refused to receive his brother. People close to the Court circles told me that Khaled would be brought forward and Fahad gradually eased out of government. This process had only just begun when the King was assassinated. There was still some speculation that Fahad would be chosen to succeed Faisal but, in accordance with the earlier plan, Khaled became King and Fahad Crown Prince. Fahad was always completely loyal to his brother, and was regarded as much more of an international figure than the King or the next brother, Prince Abdullah. However in mid 1979, Fahad gave tacit approval to the Egyptian-Israeli Peace Treaty – which was unpopular in Saudi Arabia [2] – and then he went to Spain for a prolonged "rest". He almost disappeared from the local press but his behaviour and activities, at least as reported in the Spanish papers, were not suitable for a future King of Saudi Arabia. During this time, Prince Abdullah was brought very much into the foreground, with daily reports of what he had said or done. But then came the Incident in the Grand Mosque in Mecca, and the debacle of Prince Abdullah's National Guard, some of whom were rumoured to have joined the "rebels"; suddenly Prince Abdullah was relegated to an occasional mention. It was always officially stated that there was no dissension in the Royal Family – although such statements would have been unnecessary if there had really been no dissension. I was told by people working in the King Faisal Specialist Hospital that when King Khaled spent some time there, gravely ill, and the Princes and the Ministers moved en masse into the Hospital, Prince Fahad and Prince Abdullah were not on speaking

---

[2] My mother and I were staying in Beirut when the peace Treaty was signed, and the whole ceremony was televised on an English language programme of Lebanese Television. We spent the day with the Sayeghs, owners of the Libraire du Liban, who supplied the Saudi Ministry of Education with books. They were very excited and really believed that it was the beginning of peace in the Middle East. As I recollect we drank a fearsome amount of champagne that day.

terms and swept past one another if they happened to meet in the corridors.

Of course, this apparent quarrel was made up; when King Khaled, died Prince Fahad succeeded him and Prince Abdullah became Crown Prince. The Family had chosen and, however much its members might squabble among themselves, they would stand united together against any threat from outside. This unity was and I expect still is necessary, because there was opposition to the Al-Sa'ud family. They are, by chance, or as they would say, by the will of God, the ruling family in the Kingdom; but within the last hundred years there have been other Houses with every bit as much "royalty" as the Sa'uds. The Sherifs of Mecca, the Rashids in Ha'il and the Sudairis from Sudair Province are the most obvious. The power and influence of the "Sudairi Seven"[3] was due largely to the fact that they were "royal" on both sides. Yet there were other, older and more profound forces. The Sa'uds, Sherifs, Rashids and Sudairis were certainly important, but were scarcely equal in some eyes to other families. The Oreibis, one of whom seized the Grand Mosque in Mecca, was such a one. In 1965 I was having a drink in the quite modest house of a Saudi whose name I will not give. My host began to criticise the Government (for whom he worked as a Departmental Director). "We don't have any money today", he said, "but we are a real Najdi family: we've always been here, not like those Sa'uds who only came here a few hundred years ago." "Do you know", he went on, "if the King's son came to this house to ask my father's permission to marry my sister, my father would consider it an insult to our family, and would have him put outside." Looking back I can see that it was partly the whisky talking, and I should allow for exaggeration and hyperbole in the rather excited circumstances; but I quote the anecdote to show how some people felt and spoke – even though if their words had been reported to the authorities they might have received condign punishment.

The Royal family were, and still are, very firmly in control; but I believed then and I believe now that an important part of that control lies in their ability to provide for their people. It is not just that the King, as Head of the Government and the Father of the People, should provide for everybody: individual princes too have responsibilities for tribes who are supposed to be particularly loyal to them. I remember a pupil of mine telling me one day that his family were in difficulties: over a thousand

---

[3] Prince Fahad, Prince Sultan, Prince Abdul Rahman, Prince Turki, Prince Na'if, Prince Salman and Prince Ahmed.

Bedouin had come and camped round his father's palace, to show their continued support, and in return expected – and had to receive – almost unlimited largesse. I asked why his father couldn't just send them away and do without their support? But, the boy said, it was necessary for each prince to show that he had "popular" support.

There is, at the time of writing, an investigation into an alleged scandal over defence sales. Today the "culprit", if I may use such a word, is Prince Bandar ibn Sultan ibn Abdul Aziz. When I was in Riyadh, his uncle, Prince Turki ibn Abdul Aziz – then Deputy Minister of Defence – actually had to resign over a financial scandal concerning jets from Lockheeds. Highly moral foreigners often object to the amount of "Commission" that has to be paid when obtaining government contracts in Saudi Arabia. It seems especially odd that the Commission has to be paid to a Prince who is quite unknown to the bidder. It is not really a question of "bribery" in the normal sense, because the Prince concerned is not promoting the interests of an individual company in return for money. What has happened is that the Prince has been promised a certain amount of money and all the companies bidding – as I noted more than twenty five years ago – have been told to add the commission to their bids. There are also objections to the size of the commission – ten, twenty or even thirty per cent of the overall tender. It could be that some of the commission will be spent on un-Islamic activities, but it is important to appreciate that most of the money will be distributed among the Prince's supporters whose loyalty will be strengthened by renewed evidence of his favour. In other words, Prince X probably never met any of the companies concerned, and was quite uninterested in which was the successful bidder, because his commission was secure whoever won.

In Riyadh, as in many places, money meant, and still means, power and the senior princes and their sons clearly felt the need to be seen to be generous to their supporters. I could not, all those years ago, and I cannot now assess the extent to which they were seeking personal popularity or the general popularity of the Family. I suspect the latter was the more important.

The Saudi system of Government was, I think, unique in the world. The King was the ultimate source of all power and he delegated to his ministers, some of whom were his brothers. But he could still be appealed to by any citizen or by any foreigner working in the country. In no other country in the modern world is free access to the monarch available; in Riyadh, the King's health permitting, he gave a Public Audience every week, and when travelling through the Kingdom, he gave one in every place he visited. In addition, especially in Ramadan, he gave a public breakfast at the Palace to which anybody might come.

The significance of this Audience was obvious to me and to other foreigners, but was taken absolutely for granted by the Saudi People. Soon after Prince Faisal became King, a delegation of foreign journalists arrived to greet and interview him. For some reason I was co-opted by a friend in the Ministry of Information to go along to the Yamama Hotel for lunch and dinner each day to help entertain the journalists – and also to take them shopping and sight seeing. Of the group I found myself most with a very congenial couple: Magdala von Brentano, the niece of the German Foreign Minister,[4] and Constantine, the Middle East Correspondent of the Russian newspaper, *Izvestia*, who was liable to utter very incautious remarks. As I was teaching all morning, I used to meet them first at lunchtime to hear what they had been doing in their official programme. On one particular day they had been taken round a semi-moribund match factory, something I would have kept out of the sight of visitors, but at that time it was one of the few signs of industry we possessed. Only about half the delegation were at lunch, and we were sitting eating when the others arrived. The new comers were greeted with jeers and catcalls: "Where did you all slope off to?", "Only just got out of bed?" But these were silenced when one man announced that they had all been to see the King. The match factory half were instantly bristling, why hadn't they been taken to see the King? "Oh," said Khaled Barezi, my friend from the Ministry of Information, "it was nothing special – just citizens with complaints or petitions going to see the King. It happens every week." "But why were we not invited?" chorused the unlucky half. "Nobody's invited," came the answer, "anybody who wants to see the King can just go and see him." Constantine stood up, his face the colour of borscht, waving his arms like a conductor in one of the more violent passages of the *Rite of Spring* and in what I imagined to be a very Russian manner began bellowing across the Yamama Hotel Restaurant: "Do you mean I've been dragged round that bloody match factory when I could have seen the King? Do you suppose you could just walk into the

---

[4] Once in Wazir Street, after Miss von Brentano had been doing some shopping, I gave her a chaste peck on the cheek as she got into her car. The next day every teacher in the School had heard about my unbridled debauchery. How had they heard about it? Who had seen me, known who I was, and spread the word? Everybody in Riyadh seemed to know everything one did.

Kremlin to see the President of Russia because you wanted to? This is unique! Can't you see that?" The Saudis looked puzzled: "It isn't unique," they said "it's perfectly ordinary, it happens every week." Constantine sat down, "Good God," he said to me, "What a propaganda point those people would have if they knew how to use it. An absolute monarch who is available to his people! What a country to live in!"

This system of availability extended far down the scale, but was especially noticeable as Ministers sat in a Public Audience for an hour every morning. At first sight the system is marvellous because, as well as the Minister, the Deputy Minister, Directors General and Heads of Departments (like the King) have to be available for meetings with the public. The snag comes when too many of the public insist on interviews. Some of the younger graduates in Public Administration tried to adopt a more Western approach so as to get the work done on time. There is also another problem; because of the extreme paternalism, and because the entire religious, social and education system discouraged individual initiative, everything tended to be referred upwards. Unless a request or a paper was absolutely routine – and mine seldom seemed to be that – a junior clerk would refer it to the Head of his Section, who would refer it to the Head of the Department, who would refer it to the Director, who would refer it to the Director General, who might refer it to the Deputy Minister, who might or might not refer it to the Minister. If you were lucky somebody would write "Approved" or "Do It" or something; but if you were unlucky – actually more likely – someone would write "Act in this matter according to the regulations" and then the paper would go back down the chain of command to the original clerk who would say, crossly, "I don't know what to do!" and then write some new query on the paper before sending it once more on its journey up the ladder.

At the same time, these junior clerks were by no means automatic tools in the hands of their superiors. If there was a regulation, they could stick to it as hard as they liked; and skill and cunning had to be exercised to circumvent them. In 1968 I was asked, urgently, to write a pamphlet to be given out in London to all applicants for teaching posts, telling them something about living conditions, the behaviour expected of them, and also something of the problems likely to be met in the schools – both linguistic and disciplinary. When I had written the pamphlet, it had to be translated, and then submitted to the Higher Education Committee for approval. This all took time but it was eventually approved on 10 August. It was supposed to be printed and in London by 1 September, though in fact it was never used at all, and I was free to return to London for my holiday. I went to the appropriate Junior Clerk to obtain a form to take to Saudi Arabian Airlines, where I hoped to exchange it for a government issued air-ticket. I gave the young man, whose name was Abdullah, the letter of release from the head of my Office. He shook his head and smiled: "No tickets," he said.

"Why not?" I asked. "Here's the letter giving me authority to go home now I've finished my work."

"It's within eight days of the end of the Official Leave," he explained, "Your name isn't on a list I was given from the Deputy Minister's Office of employees ordered to work through the summer. If you go, you buy your own tickets."

I went at once to Sheikh Ibrahim Al-Hijji, the Director General of Education, and Acting Deputy Minister.

"Please help me." I asked him, and when I had explained he wrote a letter saying that I had been doing some urgent work for the Ministry and should have my tickets. I took this back to Abdullah who read it. "I'm sorry," he said "I can't give you your tickets. There is a plain regulation and later, when the Ministry Accounts are done, they may say that I have issued a ticket improperly and make me pay for it."

"But" I said, "You have a letter from the Acting Deputy Minister – authorising you to give me the tickets. It isn't your responsibility any longer."

"Oh yes it is," he said, "The order is from the Council of Ministers: no Deputy Minister can override that. No tickets."

I went to the Head of his section who came and argued with him. As we got nowhere we all went together to the Director of Foreign Contracts, who also reasoned, but Abdullah remained obstinate. Then, in a growing crowd we all moved off to the Director of Personnel, who was very sympathetic and talked to Abdullah kindly, firmly and angrily; and as none of these approaches made the slightest difference he stood up and said "We will all go to speak with Sheikh Ibrahim Al-Hijji." In Sheikh Ibrahim's office the whole rigmarole was gone through again. Finally Sheikh Ibrahim offered to write Abdullah a letter in any wording he chose accepting full responsibility for my wretched tickets. Abdullah refused a final time and walked out of the office. We all looked at one another. "What do I do now?" I asked. "Go home," said Sheikh Ibrahim (this had taken all morning and it was past lunchtime). "Go home and come to my office tomorrow morning at nine o'clock."

The next morning I presented myself hopefully. Sheikh Ibrahim was smiling cheerfully. "It is all right," he said, "I've thought of a solution. You and your mother can't have your regular tickets to go home because of the regulations. But I am Acting Deputy Minister and I can send you both to London on an Official Mission. Where do you want to go? I asked for tickets for Beirut, Athens, Istanbul, Rome and London and he ordered his secretary to make out a letter at once to Saudi Arabian Airlines to issue me with the tickets I wanted. Half an hour later I had it. "What do I do about getting back, Sir?" I asked. "I'm going to be late according to the regulations." "Give yourself a month," he told me, and come straight to me when you get back. Have a good holiday." I did have a good holiday and returned, technically late and theoretically subject to all sorts of penalties. I went to Sheikh Ibrahim who took charge of my passport and sent it to Personnel through his own office. I suffered no penalties and no deduction of salary. Some time later I asked an official in Personnel why I had escaped without even an enquiry. "We received instructions," he said, "that you had actually been here all the time but they had forgotten to send up your passport."

There were times when I thought Saudi Arabian bureaucracy was wonderful!

It used to be difficult to find any Saudi official below the highest rank who was prepared to accept that the buck stopped with him, but it could happen, particularly if you could make out that you were a special case.[5] It happened once that money was due to many of us who worked on the English Service of Radio Riyadh for the Ministry of Information. The payment was long delayed and when it did come through I was lying, encased in plaster, after having my foot crushed in a road accident. When I could get about again the crucial time had passed and once more there was no money. Clutching my pay sheets (for two or three thousand English pounds) and hobbling heroically on crutches I made my way with spectacular difficulty to the new director of Personnel in the Ministry of Information, to whom I poured out my tale of woe, gesticulating at my rather obvious disabilities, and told him that it was impossible for me to keep running after the Cashier. He told me to come back to him in seven days and he would have a solution. Sure enough, when I returned, he told

---

[5] People who stood up for their "rights" usually got themselves into all sorts of complications. I learned to go in to any official, whether I knew him or not and say "I am in difficulties. Can you help me?" And always the man became attentive and concerned and did what he could to assist me.

me that all the money to pay a batch of pay sheets – in which mine was included – had been transferred from the Ministry of Finance. He asked me if I could go to the Cashier's office, which would be locked, but I should bang on the door until I was let in. Before I left he telephoned the cashier and said that I was on my way down and was to be admitted: he also gave me his internal telephone number "in case I needed it." I was rather surprised to find that the tactic worked, and, after banging at a large and heavy metal door for a minute or two, I was let in. All down the length of the room there were stacks of money – standing as much as six foot high and two or three foot deep. I had no idea how much it could be but it was certainly millions of pounds sterling. I handed in my humble papers and a smile spread over the Cashier's face. "I can't pay these," he said, "they're out of date. They need the Minister's signature." Without wasting on him the courtesy of "By your leave", I grabbed his telephone and dialled the number of the Director of Personnel, and yelled, "Help! They won't pay me!" There ensued a long argument which ended with the Director of Personnel's voice coming out of the telephone loud and clear: "Pay him and get the minister's signature later. That's an order!" With much head-shakings and tongue clucking over the impatience of the English (the money was only a year overdue), and after a plea that they didn't have any money – I pointed to the mammoth pile and was told that was for something else – I was paid: the notes, mostly in small denominations, were slowly counted and recounted.

With very unchristian pleasure I was delighted to hear, a week later, that this Cashier had been arrested for drunken driving, and for being in possession of quantities of drink and drugs. He also had a very large sum of money in his bank account, which he could only explain by saying that it was more convenient to keep the Ministry's money in his personal Account as he could get at it more easily that way. A little later, when the Government Audits were completed, there was a scandal, immediately hushed up, but which went round the Ministry like wildfire. Ninety million riyals (then almost twelve million sterling) had vanished – in cash – and the Ministry was unable to straighten things out. I couldn't help wondering if the money I had seen had been part of the haul, because I was assured by other people working in the Ministry that a few days after my "vision" the cash office had returned to its normal impecunious state.

I have already written, but I repeat, that this regular practice of "passing the buck" created enormous pressure on the senior officials, who had to approve and authorize almost everything. The fact that there was virtually no delegation of authority was not due to senior officials wanting to keep power in their own hands but because junior officials did not want any responsibility. I don't think this can be called an Arab or an Islamic trait, because I did not find it in other Arab peoples; but I do believe that the Wahabi teachings in Saudi Arabia tended to suppress initiative and independent thought. I found that every minor clerk wanted his printed regulations beside him to consult. I have watched pay sheets being prepared in the Ministry of Information: the clerk would come across a radio programme. He notes the type of programme, the duration, frequency, and the classification of the compiler; and checks these against his list of fees, closes the books and makes out the pay-form. The next programme is identical in type, duration and frequency and is by the same contributor: out comes the booklet and the same information is laboriously checked once more, the booklet is shut and another form is filled in. It is a strong man who can sit through much of this, especially when his own money is involved.

The official working hours were more or less eight o'clock in the morning until two in the afternoon, six days a week, but many senior officials would be at their desks by seven, to try to work before the arrival of the flood of people who had to be allowed to interrupt. Many would go back to their offices at night and work until midnight or after. There was no other way they could get through their work.

The Ministries were full of people whose presence was totally unnecessary, but for whom it was important to provide a salaried job. Every room in every Ministry seemed to be full of desks, some temporarily unoccupied, where clerks sat with vast ledgers in front of them – when they were not out drinking tea, talking to a friend, driving a taxi or otherwise engaged. The purpose of these ledgers was to record the movement of innumerable letters and files; but many merely duplicated and reduplicated other work. Once in the Ministry of Education, I had to take a file to four different tables in one room and at each table it was entered and issued with a new number. The operation took me less than twenty minutes as, by good, luck, all four clerks happened to be there; but had I left it to the messengers, whose job it was to ferry papers round the Ministry, it would have taken four days – one day to each table.

The filing system was not foolproof. I once could not find my passport, but a Saudi friend tried to trace it and took me to an office dealing with people about to be deported – which slightly alarmed me. We introduced ourselves to a very civil servant, who said that he didn't know what he could do to help but he would send for my file. It came and as usual he read it right through while we drank tea: then he held up my passport: "Is this your passport?" he asked. I said that it was. "But you name is not David Jones," he said, and I agreed. "This file is that of a David Jones," he said, "he is the man with the problems. There is nothing about you in here." "Then where is Mr Urch's file?" asked my friend, "I have no idea," was the answer. "And where is Mr Jones's passport?" I asked. A smile spread over his face: "I expect it is in your file," he said, "after all you're both called David."

I was once told, and I believe it, that either the Ford Foundation or the Stamford Research Bureau did a survey of the administration of the Saudi Ministries and came to the conclusion that between 80% and 90% of the employees were superfluous. The authorities explained that it was necessary to provide employment for as many citizens as possible, because working as a government employee in a ministry was one of the few jobs Saudis were prepared to do. It was then suggested (and I must stress that this came to me indirectly) that there should be, as it were, parallel ministries; a small one where the work was actually done, and a much bigger one, where files, and letters, and letters about files could be endlessly circulated, keeping people happy and "employed" without impeding the work. It was an attractive idea for, although there had been a rationalization in some ministries even before I left, there were still an awful lot of people doing no practical work. Many young men who had been trained in Europe or America came back with ideas about reorganizing the government department to which they had been appointed. Usually within a year – although sometimes it might be as much as eighteen months – they were either banging their heads against the wall and trying to get into the Private Sector, or had given up the struggle and were drifting along at the pace set by the clerks in their department.

Although successive Royal Decrees had increased the salaries of the lower ranks of the Civil Service, they still did not compare with the rates offered by the western companies or indeed with the Private Sector in general, and this caused some resentment, even if low-key. What most of the clerks in the Ministries failed to appreciate was that in the Private Sector they would have had to work very much harder and more efficiently. Private companies expect people to come to work and leave on time and to stay at work during office hours. Ministries also expected this but had to shut their eyes to their employees' irregularities. I once asked the Deputy Director of Passports why the passport office was such a mess and why nobody seemed to work. He told me that compared to the inflated salaries of the men who handled passports on behalf of private companies, pay in his office was so low that his staff just didn't want to work and frequently had to be fetched from home in the morning by the Police attached to the Passport Office. But when they were brought to their desks, after a little desultory work, they would say they were going to the lavatory and disappear again for good.

The variation in salary was not only a minor cause of friction between the public and the private sectors, but also between nationalities. The system of fixing a man's salary according to what he would earn in his own country is a very reasonable one in theory – the post being made sufficiently attractive to bring people in. But if three men (with, perhaps, different degrees of competence and enthusiasm) do the same work, and the Sudanese's salary is twice that of the Jordanian, who in turn is paid more than the Saudi, some ill-feeling is inevitable.

I have said that the punctuality was not a notable virtue among the government employees, and attempts to make people punctual led to some absurd subterfuges. In all offices and schools, even in hospitals, people had to sign in and out like factory hands. They were not required to punch a time clock,[6] but had to sign a Register. In some – possibly most – schools the Headmaster would enter the Common Room and draw a line firmly across the page; anyone who signed below the line was considered to be late. In the Ministries the ledgers were collected from each office, a quarter of an hour grace being allowed. Of course, this whole system depended on the man responsible for collecting the ledgers turning up on time himself. He took the ledger to some arcane department where gnomes decided on deduction of salary for lateness or non-attendance. But there were ways round. If a friend was apparently going to be late, you signed his name for him. I think this practice was almost universal, but it could lead to complications – for example when two people signed for the same friend, or the man actually turned up at the last moment and actually signed his own name after a previous version.

One summer's day I was supposed to be on holiday, but was wandering about the Ministry looking for a clerk (the same Abdullah who

---

[6] Time clocks were once introduced in Petromin; but in a very short time they had all gone out of order. The trouble was that the large number of employees who were late tried – in every sense of the word – to put back the clock, to falsify their arrival time.

would not issue me with the forms for my tickets) who was late with my visas. I spent some time with my friends in the Translation Department where they wanted my advice on some nuance of translation. In the corridor I came across the man who made tea in our office (The Research and Curriculum Department) and he told me to go at once to the Director-General's office, saying it was urgent. I went and found Sheikh Ibrahim, the kindest and most equable of men, in a decidedly grim temper. He scarcely answered my greeting and pointed to a seat at the side of the room, where I sat in silence for a short time until I was joined by the Acting Head of the department – who was also curtly told to sit down. The Acting Head asked me in a whisper if I knew what was up: he himself had been down town. Gradually half a dozen more of our elite band arrived and when it seemed that nobody else was coming, Sheikh Ibrahim addressed us. It was the only time I ever saw him angry. He said that he had wanted some information from us and had telephoned the office without reply. Thinking that there was some fault on the line he had gone to our office – which was quite a way away and two floors up – to find the whole department, all four rooms, completely empty. After a while our tea man arrived and professed complete ignorance of where anybody was: he was ordered to find us and send us to Sheikh Ibrahim's office.

The Sheikh turned first to me demanding to know where I had been. When I said I had been in the Translation Department he told me that I didn't work there and would I kindly keep to my proper place. Fortunately I had the letter in my pocket saying that my holiday had started two days earlier, and I was therefore exonerated and dismissed; but I hung about outside until the others came out, perspiring heavily and looking shaken. From them I learnt that Sheikh Ibrahim had collected the signing-in ledger and had demanded to know where all the people who had apparently signed their names that morning actually were. I had signed through sheer habit although I wasn't supposed to be there – but two or three people just hadn't come in. One had been away for a week, although nobody would have known it, and another had taken his family to the summer capital of Ta'if six weeks before, while still preserving an immaculate attendance record on paper. The Director-General had been extremely angry and had extracted a full account of what had been happening. Deductions from salaries and general demotions all round were threatened. I am sure that this was perfectly normal and widely practised: a similar, although innocent, deception actually happened to me in 1969.

I had contracted an extremely unpleasant bout of food poisoning when, hurrying to a lunchtime session on Radio Riyadh, I had bought – and eaten – hot meat sandwiches from an open-air stall. I tottered to the Ministry of Education doctors but it was the last morning before the Holiday and they told me to go to the Central Hospital where Medical Certificates could be issued if necessary. I wasn't exactly thrilled by the scant attention paid me by an overworked doctor in the outpatients department; and a friend suggested that I go to a British doctor with the Air Works Company, and a private Hospital for tests. Without going into details I was ill for several weeks; and at the end of the "holiday" the Head of my office came to see me. "I don't see the point," he said, "of you getting out of bed to come and see the Ministry doctors. You go on with your private doctors, and perhaps they can just give us a note to say how you are." I therefore remained at home, and some work was brought to me – reports that needed writing, reports that needed answering, possible library books that needed to be vetted; and at the end of each of two months I was grateful that all the financial ledgers were brought round to my house for me to sign, upon which my salary was counted out on my bed. At last, when I was thinking I could soon get back to the Ministry, one day, around lunchtime, there was a ring at the door and the houseboy ushered in an English friend from Beirut.

"Well," he said, "what's the matter with you? A bad hangover? Too good a party last night?"

"What are you talking about," I replied, "I'm ill."

"I know," he said, "I went to your office and they told me. They were a bit reticent, said something about you having a bad headache today, and having gone home."

"Well I'm damned," I exclaimed, "What do they mean headache? I've been home nearly two months with acute food poisoning!"

When I did get back to the office I learned what had happened. Since I did not have an official medical certificate I was not officially ill. My name was therefore "signed" every morning: my pay came along perfectly normally, with all the right pages in the ledger signed on the right days: there were reports, tangible evidence that I was working, and if anybody inconveniently asked for me in person I had either gone to the lavatory, to another department, to a school, or, if it was late in the morning, I might have gone home with permission because I was not feeling too well. It seemed that nobody outside my immediate office actually knew I wasn't there at all. I cannot believe that if an almost entirely Saudi staff (we had one Palestinian typist) could cover up so effectively for so long for an Englishman, (and a non-Muslim at that) they did not often do as much or more for their own people.

A close friend of mine, a German, Jean Guerin, worked in the Ministry of Agriculture, and had an excellent translator typist from Jordan. One day the man was missing, so after two or three days Jean asked for a replacement. "You don't need a replacement," he was told, "You have Mustapha," "But," said Jean, "Mustapha is not here." "Yes he is," was the answer. "No, he's not," said Jean, "and I want someone to type my papers. What am I to do?" "Mustapha is here," came the answer again, "Just leave the papers on his desk." This went on for six weeks, and the pile of unanswered letters and un-typed reports mounted steadily on Mustapha's desk, when, one morning, without any comment or unusual greeting, Mustapha walked in, nodded round the room, sat down and began on the topmost paper. Jean went over to speak to him.

"Hello Mustapha," he said. "Where have you been?"

"Me?" said Mustapha, surprised, "I've been down to the Post Office."

And Jean never did find out where he had been during that month and a half.

Finally I come to the ways in which the Saudi Government enforced its will on the country – although enforced is perhaps the wrong word. Certainly the King and his government had greater powers than any modern dictator could dream of, and certainly they were totally untrammelled by any form of democratically elected assembly; but people should not imagine the country was run at the whim of some eccentrically minded Caesar of the sort described by Gibbon. I can only say that I lived for nearly twenty years in what many people called a Police State, with no vestige of any popular assembly; and at the end I decided that I actually preferred living in Riyadh to living anywhere else. Being without a Parliament did not (and does not) necessarily mean being without popular consent.

I have already explained that the King, and everybody to whom he had delegated authority, had to be available to the people at regular times, which meant that "the government" was always aware of the feelings of the people. In fact no step of any importance was ever taken without intensive consultations and sounding the opinions of tribal leaders, religious figures, and anybody who might have an interest in the matter.

The King could therefore very fairly be described as an autocrat who ruled without a parliament but, because his actions were based upon a consensus of the wishes of the people, he enjoyed their approval.

Some decrees were Royal, some Council of Ministers (a Cabinet presided over by the King in his capacity of Prime Minister), some Ministerial and some lower. They could only be rescinded or overruled by an equivalent or higher-ranking order. It was this that had caused the trouble over my air-tickets. There was however, no order that could not be circumvented if there was a good reason. Prince Ahmed ibn Abdul Aziz, one of the kindest and most sensible men it has ever been my privilege to meet, was Deputy Minister of the Interior in my later years. He did most of the work of the Minister, his brother Prince Naif ibn Abdul Aziz, because the Minister was often busy with conferences, state visits and other international activities. Prince Ahmed actually said that it was a part of his job to see that the regulations were applied, but another part was to bend them when necessary for personal or humanitarian reasons. On the few occasions I went to him for help, either for myself or for one of my friends, I found him extremely patient, extremely courteous and if he could possibly help, he would end the matter with a grave smile, and an "O.K. I'll arrange it. Come back at such and such a time." And when I went back there would be the order, or whatever I had asked for, signed and waiting for me. I cannot see the British Home Secretary making him or herself available for any foreign visitor to have a private and personal hearing, and take action within hours. I suppose it was being in Riyadh a long time and knowing a lot of people; but living in Saudi Arabia in those days was made easy.

Many decrees were issued and circulated – so much so that it was difficult for a layman to keep up with this bureaucratic industry. My mother once forgot to take passport photographs when she went to the Saudi Consulate in Eaton Place to get a Visitors' Visa. She was told to come back with two photographs. She brought them in and was asked to return in two or three days. On making her third trip to London, however, she was refused a visa because the Clerk now wanted four photographs.

"You asked me for two" she said.

"There's a new regulation." he replied.

"And when did this regulation take effect?"

"Today."

Upon this my mother banged her umbrella loudly on the desk, and said – equally loudly – "Your desk must by now be stuffed full of my photographs. Take out two of them – I'm not bringing anymore." She was immediately given a soothing cup of tea, the clerk disappeared and in half an hour she had her visa.

On the other hand it is only fair to record that once when I was lying immobilized after coming out of hospital, and my own visa had expired, my mother took the problem to the Embassy in Belgrave Square and nobody could have been kinder or more helpful than the people who attended her.

Sometimes the new regulations came in so thick and fast that there was no keeping up with them. A British doctor working in a local hospital decided to drive back to England and at once ran into problems over his exit visa, and the export licences for the car and various items he had decided to take with him. Receiving so much conflicting information and advice – not least from the office in the Health Department that was supposed to deal with the matter – he decided that the best thing to do was to go to the Deputy Minister concerned and ask him what the position actually was. The man, when questioned, asked his route and then pondered. "Well," he said at last, "I'll certainly give you the latest regulation and tell you what you ought to do; but I'll also tell you the previous regulations, because the chances are that the frontier posts won't know the latest regulations themselves. So you had better be prepared with both." In the end, I understood, the journey went off without any difficulties.

The government's regulations were enforced by a complex series of authorities. There were the regular Police, who kept ordinary law and order, the Traffic Police, the Frontier Guards, the Customs Officers, the Special Security (who wore plain clothes), an Army of informers and observers, and in the Ministries, Inspectors of everything from Attendance Records to School Efficiency to Weights and Measures to Health Care. I don't propose to talk here about the Police because there is a chapter on this important group, whom I admired very much, but I will deal with one small aspect of the regulations as they reached the ordinary people.

As an example I take a Ministerial Decree, which also came from the office of the Governor of Riyadh, ordering all teachers to observe the length of hair of the boys in their classes, and report to the Headmaster any boy whose hair exceeded a decent length. Decrees like this, with an accompanying letter from the Headmaster instructing every teacher to read the decree and sign it, to show that he had read it, were usually brought into the middle of a class to be read, marked, learned and inwardly digested. It was, of course, in Arabic, and although I began by getting the boys to read it and to translate it for me, this usually took so long, and caused such arguments (apart from the fact that some communications weren't supposed to be seen by the boys) that I took to signing each one as it came and asking afterwards what it was about. When I moved into the Ministry of Education, I made it one of my campaigns to try to establish a rule that before regulations were taken round for non-Arabic speakers to sign, an English translation should be attached. This was done for a while in some schools, but in most I imagine it wasn't.

No penalty was attached to breaking a regulation if you could honestly say that you did not understand; ignorance was permitted. But when it was established that an employee understood what he was supposed to do and still broke the regulation, the authorities were normally inexorable. In particular, fines were deducted from salaries for late or non-attendance (hence the signing of other people's names in the Registers). The normal deduction was a day's pay for lateness and two days' pay for absence without a medical certificate. It was, however, possible to escape this fine. Once when I was living in the Old Town – and sleeping on the roof – I used to wake each morning when the sun struck a particular point on the wall and have plenty of time for breakfast and the journey to school – but one day the sky was overcast and I overslept. I had time for nothing but a cup of coffee and I should have been at school before I left the house. When the taxi deposited me at the school I ran in to find the Headmaster in the hall. "You are very late," he said, pointing to the clock. "I'm very sorry," I said, "but the sun isn't shining to day so I didn't know the time." (An argument that would not go down well in England). To my surprise the head Religious Teacher who took prayers and who was in the hall immediately took my side. The clock, he said, pointing at it, was a machine, made by man, which might or might not be right. Only the sun, which was God's measure, was accurate. The Englishman was right – if one couldn't see the sun – and one couldn't that morning, one could not know the time. I am glad to say that I was not fined for being late.

On the whole I thought, when I was in Riyadh, that Saudi Arabia was well governed – and I still think the same. Some of the regulations were a nuisance, but one should not blame the Saudi authorities; there was always a reason behind any new rule. Although many of the expatriates who complained were probably themselves as pure as the driven snow, they had had predecessors, probably from the same country, who had queered the pitch for everybody else by their behaviour. In spite of their isolation and their feeling of elitism, I found the Saudi people very trusting – they probably expected others to have their own high standards of honesty. That things deteriorated so sadly was not the fault of the Saudis. The tragedy was that they not only learnt to expect the worst from the foreigners who came to the Kingdom, but that they also learnt to copy the less admirable traits themselves.

CHAPTER 6
Through the Gateway

In one sense the Saudi household is a microcosm of the state, but in another it is quite different. It is similar because the Head of the family is like the Chieftain of a Tribe and it is dissimilar because, in the household, women have an important role. However, as women have a separate chapter of their own, here I will only write about the Saudi house and the positions of various members of the family.

The respect afforded to age is one of the more attractive features of Saudi life, one now sadly missing in Western Europe and America. In all Arab countries, and in those further East, the elder members of the family are treated with great deference. For example, during my later years in Riyadh, many Bedouin regarded Prince Mohammed ibn Abdul Aziz more highly than his younger brother the King, and, until his death in 1978, Prince Abdullah ibn Abdul Rahman was perhaps the most respected member of the Royal Family. On all important occasions, such as the Feasts, even the King would go to visit the older members of the Family, and would not expect them to come to him. This respect for age was not confined to royalty. I have already noted how King Faisal visited the centenarian Sheikh Mohammed Shalhoub al-Kabir, whom he called "Uncle."

In the family, sons and daughters owed complete obedience to their father – who in turn had to provide them with everything they needed. When I was first in Riyadh, it was not unusual, although less common before I left, for middle-aged men in quite senior positions in government to hand over their monthly salaries to their elderly fathers – who gave them whatever money they asked for, provided of course the father thought the request reasonable. About 1973 I visited an enormous house in Malaz, which, over the years, had had more and more rooms added to it. I discovered that six sons, with their wives and children, all lived under one roof with their father and mother. All money was given to the old man who paid the bills and bought his sons, daughters-in-law and grandchildren everything he thought they required. He absolutely insisted that the entire family should live with him. The practice of having an enormous family house was dying out before I left, although by English standards, most houses Saudis built for their own occupations were still small palaces. However by the late 1970s there was a growing tendency for newly married couples to set up their own home in a flat or a small house – but very often it was the newly emancipated wife, educated abroad, who chose not to live with her mother-in-law.

In return for the obedience they expected from their children, fathers extended total protection. In a few rare cases, there were orphans who seemed to have no family and there were private and government houses to care for these unfortunates. But in general, once you had been born into a Saudi family it would look after you for the rest of your life. Many of the more simple and un-travelled Saudis refused to believe that there were such things as Old Peoples' Homes in Britain. They thought the place for old people was with their families; even if somebody didn't have children, or brothers or sisters, there must surely be nephews or nieces or cousins, for whom it would be a natural part of life to provide for them. I hope that this pleasant attitude has survived in the more Westernized Saudi Arabia of later years.

All the major decisions about the family – where it should live, what it should do – were taken by the father, who might or might not consult his wife. In practice, the mother took all decisions about the upbringing of the children and she ruled her own domain just as surely as the father ruled his. But it was to the father that the children turned for their not inconsiderable wants. During my long stay in Riyadh, Saudi boys stopped pestering their fathers or grandfathers for a bicycle; they wanted a new car, and almost every Saudi boy from at least a middle-class family was given a car as soon as he was old enough, indeed often before he was technically old enough. On his sixteenth birthday, I asked one boy – admittedly a young prince – but still too young to drive officially, whether he had a car; he told me he had seventeen! On a less grand scale I remember a boy in my first year at the Yamama School being given a Volvo because the School gates were too narrow for him to negotiate easily in his Chrysler Imperial.

Generosity was not confined to actual members of the family: all the princes had tribesmen who were their followers and dependents. When visiting a prince who kept traditional state in the evening, I have found myself one of a large group of Bedouin who were there for a free meal. Any man might have to feed forty, fifty or sixty people a day; but they would be "his men" who would, in an emergency, be prepared to fight and to die for him. This had been essential a hundred years earlier, but I could not see the necessity by the time I was living there. Yet it was part of the tradition; and unless these Bedouin hung around one of the princes they had nothing else to do: at least it kept them out of mischief. More ordinary families did not have "followers" but they might still have a crowd of ex-slaves who refused to go away once they had been freed. I have written earlier about the problems old Mrs Shalhoub had with her fifty ex-slaves who demanded constant attention.

Fathers usually took an intense interest in their children, more openly perhaps than most fathers in Europe. It was, of course, a matter of social custom that it was always the father – or, in his place, a senior male servant – who took the children to school and collected them; but fathers did give up a lot of time to their offspring. Just as sons and daughters had a duty of implicit obedience to their father, so they all seemed to have an infinite account with him on which to draw; and, of course, through him to the Head of the Family, who might actually be a Tribal Chief. Even at the time I left, when the *Jeunesse d'orée* might have wanted to escape from the parental eye, I doubt if any of them would have actually refused a father's direct order. One of the most pleasant and enduring traits of the Saudi was his loyalty to his family – and the servants who were regarded as part of it. In my later years, it sometimes happened that a son went into business and made a fortune, while his father remained (comparatively) poor. Then the son's delight was to pour out his wealth on his parents, to give them at least as comfortable a life as he enjoyed himself. One of my old pupils, who became a senior administrator and lived in a beautiful house, told me very seriously of the problem he had with his father – who insisted on staying on in the not-very-big house in the Old Town where he had always lived, and even refused to have modern furniture and fittings. "It looks so bad" the son confided to me, "I'm sure that everybody thinks I am just being mean and not looking after my father properly: they won't believe that he just doesn't want any of the things I have tried to give him."

The system could be described as feudal, but Saxon-feudal rather than Norman-feudal. Under the Saxon system, a man owed allegiance to his overlord and through him to the king; but if the overlord, tribal chief or what you will, renounced his allegiance to the king, all his followers went with him. Under the Norman system, a man owed allegiance to his overlord and a personal allegiance to the king – and was thus supposed to remain loyal to the king, even if his overlord broke his royal allegiance. In Saudi Arabia I felt that the people were loyal to the King because their fathers, uncles or chiefs told them that this was right; but the Kingdom had been established too recently for there to be any real unthinking loyalty to the Royal Family in any part of the Kingdom except in the Najd.

A Saudi household is at once very open and very private. It is an open because the traditional custom of hospitality demands that the reception-room should always be at the disposal of visitors; but it is private because nobody may enter uninvited. Even with very close friends, even if the door were open, I would never dream of going into a house until I had been specifically invited in. There were two ways in which the family's privacy could be ensured: the house could be built round a courtyard with no outside windows[1] at least on the ground floor, with all the rooms opening onto a central courtyard; or a villa could be built in a garden with a high wall round it. Looking into a neighbour's garden was a serious social offence: in one house I lived in I made a new window which I was at once told to fill in because it looked towards the next house and my neighbours thought they might be overlooked. The high walls around the newer houses were pierced by two gates. There was normally a large one – through which a car could be driven – but there was an ordinary door in the middle of the gate to be used by men who came on foot. The second gate, preferably in a different street, was used by the women of the family and their friends. Modern houses had no set pattern but there was generally a room with an outside door into which casual visitors could enter. This room would also have a door communicating with the rest of the house (for the family to use). Larger houses would have one or more reception-rooms near the gate quite separate from the rest of the house (As indicated earlier, in the Shalhoub mansion, there were also guest bedrooms by the gate for odd guests). In this reception room, or majlis, there would be a special stone fireplace, coming well out into the room, and used for brewing tea and coffee. The fireplace was usually backed by a sort of reredos with an alcove of shelves lined with brass and silver coffee

---

[1] In the late 1940s, my uncle Charles, my mother's eldest brother, decided to build a house without outside windows in St Leonards-on-Sea; he had decided that the twentieth century was too vulgar to look at. As he could not get planning permission, he grew shrubs and creepers over all the windows, although my aunt cut a square from the foliage covering her bedroom window so that she could look down over the sea.

pots: they seemed to be for display because I never saw one taken down for use. The "useful" pots were brought in from the house.

The older type of "mud" house was invariably built around a courtyard, even if the yard was very small. When the "front door" of an old house was opened, there was a passage, wide or narrow, ending in a blank wall. To get to the courtyard, you had to go to the end of the passage and then turn a sharp right angle: it was important that no casual passer-by could see the interior of the house if the door happened to be open. Depending on the size of the house, the Majlis might be immediately inside the front door or approached by a staircase up which male guests could go. The Majlis would be furnished with carpets and cushions around the walls – exactly the same arrangement as in a Bedouin tent. During my years in Riyadh, chairs, requiring coffee-tables, replaced cushions in many a Majlis. But the chairs were still placed round the walls – an English style sitting room would be completely out of place. Some people spent enormous sums of money on those furnishings, and in really big houses there would be a number of different reception rooms for different occasions and or the status of the guests.[2]

Personally I felt more comfortable sitting on cushions on the floor. Sadly, when the Saudis abandoned their old dignified simplicity, they tended to go to the other extreme and furnish their houses with furniture designed by Lebanese and Egyptian decorators – who had apparently once had an afternoon tour of Versailles. Towards the end of my time there was a lot of Italian furniture, some if it excellent, but some so ornately vulgar that I could hardly believe it had come from Italy.

Even foreigners like myself rarely got past the official reception-rooms of a house, and for true-born Saudis it was even more unlikely. Occasionally I was invited inside and even met the women of the family, especially when my mother was with me. In all but perhaps half a dozen cases, however, such invitations were always made in households where the couple were young and the wife educated in Europe or America. Such girls would behave in a completely "modern" way in the company of Westerners, but they and their husbands were very reluctant to be equally free with Saudi guests – unless that Saudi came from their own emancipated circle. Outsiders, however, were not admitted lightly to that circle, although there is no doubt (as I hope to show in the next chapter), that Saudi women could be just as emancipated as Western ones.

---

[2] The Shalhoubs had sixteen reception-rooms and the grandest was only used when the King visited.

Sometime in the mid-1970s I remember calling at the house of a Saudi friend: "I'm sorry I can't ask you tonight David," he said, "but my wife and I have a mixed party this evening, and you know that these people don't like an outsider to see them enjoying themselves." They were going to play roulette and the gaming table was set out, as were the drinks. The host was worried that there wouldn't be enough, and, as I could see a whole crate of whisky and five bottles of Gordon's Gin, I asked how many people would be there. "Seven couples," was the reply, but I don't know whether that included the host and his wife. "But surely" I gasped, "seven couples can't drink all that?" "Oh" came the answer," but suppose everybody chooses gin? What happens then?"

Such parties were, however, the exception rather than the rule, and in more than ninety-five per cent of Saudi houses in my time at least, the sexes kept segregated except for family and very close friends – and even that degree of "freedom" would only have been found among the young. There used to be many very orthodox families where the men have told me that they had never seen even their sisters unveiled after the age of twelve. In such houses the women's quarters were completely shut away from the rest of the house, and they were seen only by their fathers, husbands, children and women-friends. It was usual in houses where servants were not kept – and, as wages spiralled, they became increasingly numerous – for the men of the family and their male guests to sit in the Majlis and then there would be a tap on the door, which signified that the wife had left a tray outside the door for her husband to carry in. Even veiled she would not make an appearance in the men's room.

For many years my mother and I were looked after by a splendid Yemeni couple, assisted by the odd houseboy. Admittedly they tended to treat me in private as if I were a slightly retarded child, incapable of coherent thought or action (a typical "conversation". "How would you like the potatoes done today?" "Could we have them fried?" "No. You know the dog doesn't like fried potatoes – I'll mash them.") Although in public, I was treated with the deference due to the Head of the House. Yemenis are nowhere near so strict about veiling as the Saudis, but the wife was very careful about veiling when she was in Riyadh, and she said it was necessary to be so for the sake of her reputation. If her husband and the houseboy happened to be out when I had visitors, she would come into the room and ask what I needed – but only if the visitors were Europeans, or foreign-Arabs known to her and wearing Western dress. If any Saudi was present, or any other Arab she did not know, she would only call through the sitting room door to ask what I wanted and would afterwards leave a tray on a table in the hall – behaving just like any well-brought up women of Riyadh.

It is polite to ask after the father, sons, brothers and family of a friend – in fact this is all part of the ritual greeting that strangers find interminable. But it is not polite to ask after the women of the family unless they are very close friends. I knew some Saudis for many years without having any idea as to whether they were married or not. I imagined they were, because almost all Saudi men were. I also imagined that they either had no children or only daughters: sons would be paraded – daughters were the mother's prerogative. I might sometimes meet a friend in a Supermarket, vaguely escorting veiled figures; but there was no means of knowing whether these were mothers, aunts, wives, sisters or what; and it would have been a rudeness, of which only a foreigner could have been capable, to ask who they were.

The unity of an Arab family was one of the great strengths of the Saudi people. Before I left I could detect a slight weakening of that unity, brought about partly by westernization – but it was still very strong. In Riyadh, for example, it was the exception to find a company in which the partners were not from the same family, because – as a number of businessmen explained to me – differences of opinion within a family were unlikely to cause serious trouble, but this was not the case if the partners were completely unconnected, even by marriage. I knew of men who were obviously unsuited to business life, whose object seemed to be to see how much they could put on their expense account; but the family firm would still back them. There were those who went off, say, to London, to sign a contract, and were expected back within a week; but they were liable to stay away for two months, sending regular S.O.Ss for more money from various pleasure-spots in Europe. Yet still they retained the "confidence" of the partners, with access to the company purse – even if somebody else had to go to London to sign the contract, the original purpose of the journey. The same indulgence would never have been extended to a partner who was not a family member.

There might be arguments within a family, or household, but its members were always ready to stand together against "outsiders." One can take this a step forward and say that, while there might be divisions within a tribe, the tribe would always unite against another tribe. When I came to Riyadh, Saudi Arabia was still too new a country for there to be any certainty that all Saudis would automatically unite against anybody else. It was probably true of the Najd, where I always lived, but I am less confident that the same applied in the Hejaz or in the Eastern Province. I think, however, that by now there must be a much greater sense of National Unity than when I lived in Saudi Arabia.

CHAPTER 7
Disguised Matriarchy

When I was planning this book, I was in two minds as to whether "women" should be included in "The Household" or should have a chapter to themselves. Because they are so important I think I am right to give them the space, and the attention, which is rightfully theirs.

A great deal of nonsense has been written about the position of women in Saudi Arabia. The idea that Saudi women are chattels without rights of their own is as false as the notion that all Arabs have four wives. There has been so much inaccuracy and so much misunderstanding, that what I write in this chapter may surprise my readers; but what I put down is what I knew from the families with whom I was most familiar and from what I was told by Saudi friends, many of them my former pupils.

The most important thing to understand is that a woman in Saudi Arabia is both respected and protected. Of course, critics have stressed that, under Islamic Law, daughters inherit smaller amounts than sons, and, in a Court of Law, a man's evidence is worth more than a woman's. As with most of the Shari'ah Law, these distinctions are based on common sense. Where "evidence" is concerned, as a man goes out and about and sees "the world" it is likely that he will know more about what is going on than a woman who spends her time segregated in the women's quarters. And as far as inheritance is concerned, sons need more than daughters. A man has duties and responsibilities – which cost money – since he must provide for his household, including the women. It is also important to understand that Saudi women have complete control of their own money in a way unknown in England until the Married Women's Property Act, some century and a half ago – and that was only passed against furious opposition. In the Islamic world, since the days of the Prophet Mohammed, a woman's property has been her own and her husband has no legal right to touch it. The possible complications this can cause will be discussed later in this chapter.

One of the popular ideas about Arabs in general – and perhaps Saudis in particular – is that they are obsessed with sex, and that no woman or, alternatively no man, is safe from them. Where this poppycock originated I have no idea, but I think Rudolf Valentino, in his portrayal of *The Sheikh*, gave a very misleading idea of the Desert Arab. I should be sorry to disappoint readers, but I don't believe that Saudis, or other Arabs, were or are any more obsessed with sex than anybody else. I would, however, make one proviso; it should be remembered that a society in which the sexes are segregated has some similarities with that of Victorian and Edwardian England. This was brought home to me when I was reading J.B. Priestley's *Lost Empire* where the narrator goes back to 1913, when his uncle gave him the chance to join a Concert party travelling round the Music Halls of England:

Here I ought to say something about our sexual feelings in those days before the First World War. It will, I hope, save a lot of explanation later. As everybody knows, ever since then, certainly in this country, sex has come more and more into the open, and at the same time there has been more and more sexual titillation, in stage shows, films and advertising. But what many people, especially public moralists, don't realise is that this has cut both ways. The new freedom, even with all the new titillation thrown in, has released an amount of sexual feeling that was, so to speak, unhealthily dammed up in those days. Because less sex came out, there was all the more of it inside, haunting and tantalizing the imagination. It was all the more mysterious and fascinating. You can say that because the girls of 1913 wore so many clothes, covering them from top to toe, we wondered all the oftener and harder what they would be like without those clothes. There was a kind of stifling excitement about the whole thing that I imagine hardly exists now." (This was supposed to be 1964) "I was a fairly normal youth then, neither particularly prudish nor lecherous, but the atmosphere was such – and I think now it was a suffocating and unhealthy atmosphere – that I spent half my mental life prowling uneasily on the edge of sexual discovery and revelation. It made sex much more a delicious thing in itself – Cissie's "naughty but nice" line, which was very common then – and much less a natural urge to be satisfied within a relationship than it is now. On the stage, of course, it was all more free – and easy – and the girls showed as much of themselves as they were allowed to do – and as a rule they had uncommonly good figures – but all this was happening within the strict general rules, which made it all the more raffish and exciting. I don't say that when I accepted Uncle Nick's offer to join him I had sex in mind, but I did very soon find myself infected by a confused sexual excitement, an increasing sense of anticipation, that made hypocritical bosh out of my pretence that I wanted to get to know everybody and be friendly. All I really cared about were the two girls and the women." (Lost Empires, Chapter V)

As I have been told by members of my own family, in the years before the 1914 war girls were very carefully chaperoned. (It was quite different after the war. My mother, who was several years younger than her older sisters, became a Bright Young Thing). In Italy and Spain the tradition lasted much later; but nothing in Western Europe equalled the total seclusion and segregation experienced by the girls and women of the Arabian Peninsula. It was therefore certainly not surprising, or abnormal, if young men – and older ones too – thought and speculated about the women who were under the veils; and indeed about women in other countries who were not veiled at all. It would have been much more peculiar if they had not. I do not speculate on the situation in Riyadh today – where most young men will have access to an almost limitless internet – but what I do know is that in my later years in Riyadh there was a marked revulsion against western license. This did not come from the old and conservative but from the young, who had seen for themselves what life and behaviour was like "abroad" and did not want to bring up their own children in such an atmosphere. In the late 1970s and early 80s the fiercest proponents of the status quo were young Saudis who had spent three or four years at a university in the West (where many of them no doubt sampled the pleasures of the society they then denounced as corrupt) and had returned determined that "that sort of thing" would not be introduced into Saudi Arabia if they could help it.

To me, women in Saudi Arabia were never second class citizens; and the fact that they went veiled, and their husbands insisted on it, does not mean they were oppressed or underprivileged: they were merely protected. The veil may be taken as a symbol of purity, and it was essential wear for the preservation of a good reputation; but it has never really had anything to do with Islam as such. In all Muslim countries, except those where secular law bans "old fashioned" religious observance (readers may remember the argument over head-scarves in Turkey) women go with their heads covered. In some they may wear a veil over the lower part of their faces, which allows them full play with their eyes. Originally, this may have had nothing to do with religion, merely serving as a protection for the throat and nose against dust. In parts of the Gulf women wore a leather mask, which again left the eyes clear. Only in Saudi Arabia was a woman completely anonymous, clothed from head to foot in shapeless black. It is a historical fact that in the time of the Prophet Mohammed and before, decent and respectable women in Mecca went veiled. Others, and there may have been a fair number of these, went unveiled, possibly on the same principle that the "ladies" in the Red Light District of Amsterdam used to stand in their windows displaying their purchasable charms to any interested passer by. The original reason why the women and girls of Mecca veiled themselves completely was to distance themselves from prostitutes and to emphasize their respectability. They would have been subjected to no annoyance from strangers as they walked in the streets.

For walk about they did in Mecca. They were never enclosed like nuns of a very strict order, as were the women of some – if not all – of the Najdi families. Nor were they as strict as some in the towering fortress cities of the Hadramaut – so well described by Freya Stark – where a girl left her father's house to go to her husband's on their marriage, and never went outside again unless she went with the family on Pilgrimage to Mecca (I expect those women of the Hadramaut were very pious!). In Mecca, and in the Hejaz in general, the women walked about, but they walked veiled.

They were, of course, veiled in Riyadh but they could go out, even in the "old" days. They could visit one another, although two or three women would always go together. No woman would have walked out alone, nor, in the "old" days did women go to the market. Shopping, with all its possible dangers of stray encounters, was a man's task. One of the world's great businessmen, Sheikh Saleh Abdul Aziz Al-Rajhi, laid the foundation of his colossal fortune by taking note of this fact. When Riyadh was still a closed city, his father was a money-changer, who would sit with his "change" on the ground in front of him, sometimes totalling no more than ten riyals – although that amount meant something in those early days. His eldest son, realising the untapped spending power of the women, got a hand-barrow, loaded it with household items and clothes, trinkets, anything that would appeal to women who could not go shopping, and wheeled it through the gates (Saleh Al-Rajhi, of course, remaining outside). The result was always the same: the women, who had control of their own money, bought and bought, and there was always a good profit for the man who had thought up this ingenious sales ploy, and took the trouble to carry it out.

Certainly anybody seeing a typical Saudi woman crossing the road could have little idea of what she looked like underneath her black cloaks and veils. A former Minister of Education told an acquaintance of mine that he was not himself very strict – because although the women of his family always wore four layers of veiling he let them wear only two over the face.[1] This is a far cry from the single veil of the thinnest lawn affected by some of the less typical rich young ladies who used to be seen in Wazir Street but later frequented their Jewellers and the French boutiques that proliferated before I left.[2] On them the veil became merely an aid to glamour and became as alluring as a veil would have been to English women a hundred years ago.

This is supposed to be a truthful book and so – although I have much praise for Saudi women in general – I have to say that certain elements were quite as unrestrained and immoderate as anything found in other countries. Of course, I should stress, these young "ladies" came almost entirely from extremely privileged homes. I imagine immense wealth acquired without any effort can have a deleterious effect on the character. Unfortunately – or perhaps fortunately – I have never been tested in this way. Readers must not think I am saying that great wealth always has bad results: over the years I acted as tutor to two princesses, and nobody could have had better behaved or harder working students. One, who had been involved in a car accident and spent months in hospital in England, had missed most of her final University year, including the examinations. She was allowed to take these examinations when others, who had failed earlier, were taking their re-sits. I prepared her and was told that her papers were some of the best the examiners had ever seen.

---

[1] One young Saudi pupil of mine, whose mother was American, said "You should see my mother when she's veiled, sir; she looks like Batman in a storm!"

[2] These boutiques were very popular and many young women opened one: they always did very well for a time, as the owner's friends shopped there. However, a new boutique took away the customers, the owner lost interest, and the boutique failed. Now by Saudi law, while the women had complete control of the profits, she was not liable for the debts; and three of my former pupils had heavy losses to cover from their wives' business ventures.

Admittedly she had the advantage of exceptional intelligence, but I have never known anyone, male or female, who worked with such ferocious single mindedness and concentration.

But even with her, one day, as I left her palace, instead of the exotically custom built Rolls-Royce in which she usually travelled, I saw a small anonymous white Fiat outside: "What's that?" I asked? "That's my car," she explained, "and I use it if I want to go somewhere without anybody knowing where I'm going. I'll send the Rolls with three or four of my maids in it to my mother's palace or to my sister's, and everybody will assume I've gone there." It seemed a very suitable arrangement.

Some of the idle rich – both male and female – were very idle indeed, seldom rising until late afternoon and not going to bed until after dawn; but, especially as far as the women were concerned, this sort of behaviour was confined to a very tiny minority. A fairly mild type of annoyance, luckily of short duration, came about after the introduction of the automatic telephone service. Girls would dial numbers at random in the hope of finding a young man to talk to at the other end. I was myself rung up many times in this way – not by the same girl, the whole point of the "game" was its random nature – and certainly nothing the girls said was in the slightest degree improper. It was mostly just giggles. Some of the calls were, however, less innocent, and – as I know from talking to some of the boys – assignations were made, and it was usually the girls who initiated them.

Another fashionable pastime was what our ancestors used to call "carriage exercise." There were two or three very fashionable pavement cafés, where the young bloods met each evening to walk about and to show off themselves and their latest cars. Young ladies, in their own expensive cars, would tell their drivers to take them past these cafés, and, from behind the gauzy veils and possibly tinted windows, they would survey what I will vulgarly call the "local talent." If they saw a young man who took their fancy, they would point him out to their driver and tell him to find out the boy's car, his name, and where he lived. After that the telephone would be brought into play; but if the telephone produced no result, more drastic action might be resorted to. One evening, as the young man drove out of his father's house to go to his café, his car would be hit by another being very carelessly driven. As he walked angrily towards the driver of the second car, the rear window would be wound down, and a feminine voice would cry, "Oh, please don't be angry. It was entirely my driver's fault. You must allow me to buy you a new car. My name is so-and-so. If you would give me your name and address and telephone number I will arrange for another car to be sent to you immediately." This does sound unlikely; but more than one young man I knew told me that this had happened to him. I think that, even in the decadent West, very few young women would have been so brazen!

Another advantage of the veil is that (as in the instance of the Princess's maids) nobody can tell who is underneath it and as I have already indicated, it was often the car that was the only means of identification. I have sat in a café just outside the city watching the cars streaming in before sunset and my host has named the owner of every car of any individuality. The anonymity of the veil was also used by another group of women, often rich and idle. Weddings are a great occasion in Saudi Arabia, although the elaborate and often costly celebrations are quite different to anything in the West. The guests are segregated, either in different parts of the same house (the men, perhaps, in the garden and the women on the roof) or, in big weddings, in different homes.[3] At a really big wedding, perhaps with a thousand invited guests, it was impossible to keep track of every veiled figure coming through the gates. Some old women, professional gatecrashers, not only attended the weddings but also took the opportunity to go all over the house examining the clothes and the personal possessions of the women of the family. My mother attended one wedding where she was told that the hosts had put everything of value into one room and locked the door to stop prying fingers getting into everything. Of course, nothing was ever stolen on these occasions, but everything was pulled about and messed up – and that was very unpleasant for the family. But, as well as these rather peculiar old women, there were ladies from the highest families, young and not-so-young, who would put on a number of old cloaks and gate-crash a wedding – to which they had been invited and which they would attend later in the evening *in propria persona* – so that they could have a spree incognito, and sometimes just to make as much mess as possible.

I have described all this negative behaviour because it happened, and to conceal it would falsify the story of my experiences; but I must emphasize that it was confined to a limited, over-monied section of Saudi

---

[3] The groom is taken from the "men's" area to the "women's" where he is as it were shown off. He and the bride sit side by side on specially decorated chairs. He would bring jewels, rings, bracelets, and a necklace, which, my mother told me, he would hand to his mother who would put them one by one on the bride.

women, and was in no way representative even of the rich, let alone Saudi women in general.

I think that I should also say something about the Saudi man's attitude to women, as I saw it. It was difficult for an outsider to discover this because it was taboo to discuss the women of a family, unless one was a very close friend. Just as in Victorian England where ladies were not supposed to have legs – at least they were invisible and never referred to – so it might be imagined that some Saudi families came into being spontaneously, without the normal means of reproduction. But I think the following impressions are correct.

The Saudi, particularly the Najdi, tended to put the women of his family on a pedestal. His heroine was his mother and other women were measured against her. Some Saudi marriages failed and ended in divorce – although nowhere nearly so many as popularly supposed – simply because the wife did not meet her husband's exacting maternal standards.

The position of a mother in Saudi Arabia was a very important one. However senior or prominent a man might be, he would drop everything if his mother needed him. I have already noted that Prince Fahad and his six brothers lunched with their mother every day possible (and, after her death, with their sister). Other senior members of the Royal Family, cabinet ministers, big businessmen, would suddenly vanish from the scene, and the answer to enquiries after them came back regularly, "He is in Jeddah – or Ta'if, or London, or Geneva – because his mother is ill and in hospital." I found the same thing when my mother was in hospital after a major heart attack, as I shall recount in the chapter on Health.

With the mother as the central figure, daughters-in-law could sometimes have a very difficult time; I was told that the husband would usually side with his mother rather than his wife. On the whole, however, I understood that mothers and daughters-in-law usually got on very well; after all the mother would certainly have "vetted" the girl carefully, if not actually chosen her. It is true that, before I went away, more and more girls, especially those who had been educated abroad, wanted to live in a separate home. But this was probably due to a difference in education and interests, rather than to any lack of liking or affection.

Virtually all marriages were still "arranged" and, as far as I could see, were certainly as likely to succeed as any freely contracted ones. One of the West's enduring images of the Arab world is of rich and generally unpleasant old men "buying" young wives from greedy fathers. No doubt such things happened, but I am sure only very rarely. By the 1960s, at least, I doubt whether a Saudi father could have forced his daughter into a marriage against her will. In any case, the number of rich elderly men was limited. It is true that some might like to marry and divorce regularly – to show off both their virility and their financial muscle. But there were also some young women, perhaps a good many, who were ready enough to become a very rich wife – with the prospect of becoming, reasonably soon, either a rich widow or a divorcee with a handsome settlement.

There was no stigma attached to a divorce for a woman: indeed I knew of a case where the mother of the girl urged on a most unsuitable marriage with an eye to the subsequent divorce. A very charming English teacher with a drink problem met some young Saudis from a westernized family (two of the brothers were married to English girls). Through the brothers he met the womenfolk and fell in love with their sister. He approached the girl's parents and begged to be allowed to marry her: I was told later that they had many misgivings; but they agreed, providing that he became a Muslim, and that a license was granted for a Saudi girl to marry a foreigner.

No special difficulties appeared: even the scandal when he was found in the Mosque at Dawn Prayer dead drunk, with his dog asleep beside him, was smoothed over. In fact, the couple behaved very much like a rather old-fashioned engaged couple in England, going to parties together, and so, in Saudi eyes, attracting a lot of attention. As the time drew near for their betrothal – which in Saudi Arabia had almost the effect of a marriage ceremony – but before the marriage ceremony proper, the bridegroom's nervousness and general unsuitability became plainer and plainer. He drank more and more, rushing about Riyadh looking for alcohol of any kind, and saying, "You must help me. I've only got so-many days left!" I heard later that the bride herself became very doubtful, at the erratic behaviour of the groom, but her mother urged her to go ahead, and almost as soon as the wedding was over, began to prepare for the divorce. The marriage only lasted a few weeks, after which the girl returned to her parents, leaving the husband in a house where he had already smashed most of the furniture she had provided. When I discussed the whole sorry business with other Saudis – for it ended in him being arrested for a drunken assault on his brother-in-law – they explained that from the family's point of view, a marriage, however unfortunate, followed by divorce, was preferable to a cancellation of the wedding plans. They would be no stigma attached to the girl, who, especially as she was shatteringly beautiful, would have no difficulty in marrying again, this time to a more suitable man; whereas, if she had not been married, after going about with this Englishman and attending many foreigners' parties, she would have been regarded with suspicion, and other mothers would have steered their sons away from her.

While on the subject of marriage, there are three points I ought to clear up. There used to be, and for all I know may still be, an idea that Saudi boys and girls never saw each other before they were married, that divorce was regular and frequent, and that Saudi men had four wives – which, in view of the fact that almost equal numbers of boys and girls were born, seems particularly illogical. To deal with the first point, in traditional Saudi families – which were the vast majority when I lived there – the boys didn't meet their future bride; but they did know all about her, because for years their mothers had been looking at girls of their acquaintance to try to find the right one for their son. In the old days the boy's mother would have described the girl: in my time she would almost certainly have shown him a photograph. It was also very likely that the boy was a friend of the girl's brothers, so he knew the family into which he would marry. If he was happy about the family and his mother reported well of the girl, the chances were that the marriage would be a success. From the girl's point of view, things were rather easier because she could see the boy while herself remaining unseen. In the case of one young couple I knew, the girl had asked her father if she could bring in the tea and coffee as the young man sat with her brothers and her father. As he said to me later, she must have liked what she saw because she told her father later that evening that she was ready to go ahead with the engagement. They had been a very happy and united couple for several years when I left.

The girls do in fact have quite a lot of choice. It so happened that at the betrothal party for this particular couple – men in the garden, women on the roof – my mother met the bridegroom's sister for the first time. My mother told me that the sister, one the most beautiful girls imaginable, was engaged to a relative who was at a university in America. A few months later, when the groom was visiting us, my mother asked him whether his beautiful sister was married yet. "Oh," he said, "She's broken off that engagement. The man wanted to finish his degree in America before getting married which is nearly two years, and my sister says she wants a house of her own before that, so she's going to marry someone else – he's very nice and he's got pots of money." Of course during the 1970s and 80s, more and more families were holidaying in Europe during the summer, and if the parents of boys and girls both happened to have villas outside Geneva, or seafront flats in Cannes, the young people could get to know one another in a more westernized way – although I am sure the girls would be carefully chaperoned. Many business travellers, and others, saw the odd sight of veiled black figures going to the cloakroom soon after Europe-bound flights had taken off from Riyadh, Jeddah, or Dhahram, to reappear a few minutes later minus the veil, clad in some ravishingly expensive little dress from Bond Street or the Rue St. Honoré. Of course it worked the other way as well. A very smart, sophisticated, cosmopolitan woman sitting across the aisle from you would disappear shortly before landing and would reappear in anonymous black.

Sometimes arranged marriages could go to pieces very quickly. There was a much talked of multiple royal wedding when six princes married six princesses in a sort of Hollywood extravaganza (Prince Fahad ibn Abdul Aziz's wife was reported to have had two millions pounds worth of diamonds sewn on to her dress, making it so heavy that she had to be helped to walk from her car to a chair). Several westerners, who did not include myself, were invited. According to rumours circulating Riyadh soon afterwards, five of the marriages ended in divorce the same night when the couples actually met; and the sixth lasted a week. Such a record of failure was, however, exceptional.

In Saudi Arabia, divorce was certainly much easier than in Western countries and could simply take the form of a verbal declaration by the husband that he divorced his wife. Since married couples can have their ups and downs such "divorces" were not rare, but they could, and nearly always were, rescinded by another statement from the husband. If, however, he declared three times that he divorced his wife, that was final. The only way they could then get back together was for each of them to marry and then divorce somebody else: even this complicated and time-consuming contrivance was not unknown. Divorce on the women's side was more difficult. Perhaps this was a sign of inequality, but in practice, if a wife called in her father, or her brother, or a religious figure and asked for a divorce, citing the reason why she wanted it, then it could usually be arranged.

But divorce was not very common. I expect that most of the couples I knew all those years ago are still married today, just as, in the case of the grown men I knew, their mothers and fathers were still securely united. As was once the case in England, in Saudi Arabia divorce was more the occupation of the leisured class. I certainly knew Saudis who had been divorced; but I believe they had parted by mutual consent, recognising their essential incompatibility.

Finally we come to the old chestnut that Saudis have four wives, the maximum number permitted in Islam. In Riyadh only a very tiny minority could afford to have four wives, given that each wife must be treated exactly the same, have her own house, and any present given to one must be given to all. (A new frying pan would be alright, but diamond watches from Kuchinski or a custom built Rolls-Royce would strain most budgets). In the earliest days, when inter-tribal warfare resulted in a high death toll among the men, it was necessary for the survival of the tribe – and for the protection of the women – that a man could have more than one wife, (and there may also have been some idea like the rather grudging admission of St Paul, "It is better to marry than to burn"). Again, in the old days, when travel was difficult and took a long time, a man might spend part of the year in Medina and part in Jeddah, and have a wife and family in each city, rather like the proverbial sailor with a wife in every port. But as having more that one wife was less a sign of virility than of financial muscle, it was becoming less and less common. A very rich man told a friend of mine "I have four wives to show that I can afford it." I have described the typical rich man's compound, with a central house – in which he lived and entertained – and four identical houses in the four corners of the property. They were far fewer such compounds as my time in Riyadh drew to a close.

According to the reports I was given, women who shared the same husband seemed to get on very well together. I only once met two wives of the same man at the same time, and I have to say it was a very strange experience. Sheikh Khaled Shalhoub had taken a second wife, who had become ill almost immediately after the wedding. It was a one of the feasts and my mother and I had gone to visit the family, taking the largest box of chocolates we could find for the invalid. We were both taken to a family room – a sign we were regarded as very close friends indeed. All sorts of preparations were under way; bags were being filled with food and thermoses, together with china and cutlery – just as if we were all going on a picnic. We were told, however, that we were actually going to visit the new wife, who had undergone major surgery the previous day. We were packed into three limousines – there were nearly a dozen of us – and driven to the Hospital, the entrance to which was all of a hundred yards away. Of course, the young Mrs Shalhoub had a palatial suite in the VIP wing, and we were ushered into a sitting room while the invalid was prepared. At last we were taken in to see the poor creature, who lay, deathly pale and unmoving, with tubes coming from her nose and side, but beautifully made-up with perfectly groomed hair. Chairs were placed at the foot of the bed and there my mother and I sat as guests of honour, eating cakes and biscuits and fruit and drinking juices and tea and coffee. The elder wife was obviously very fond of the younger one, but the whole thing struck us as bizarre – if I had had major surgery the day before I wouldn't want complete strangers eating and drinking by my bedside; but we were assured that the new wife was very gratified by the attention we had paid her.

I have said before that in Islam women have control of their own property. The fact that they did not meet strangers to discuss business matters may have been responsible for the notion that they took no part in business. It is true that, in Saudi Arabia, businesswomen must give Power of Attorney to a man to represent them at meetings. Yet many Saudi men used to discuss business decisions with their wives; indeed, I dread to think of what would have happened to any man who used his Power of Attorney against the wishes of the Owner.

There were two areas where women could and did take direct control of businesses. The first was the Boutique, a phenomenon that became fashionable in the late 1970s. Only women were allowed inside, thus removing any objection to the women owner supervising the place. The second was the Beauty Salon, about which there was a running battle for years. They were periodically closed down by decree and then re-opened after promising amendment. There was no objection to a Beauty Salon operated by and for women, but some of the ladies who ran them (Saudi by marriage perhaps but not by birth) used their Salons as fronts for more lucrative activities. Their girls – mostly from Egypt – had skills other than hairdressing. In 1979 a Bank manager I knew well assured me that the Egyptian-born wife of a mutual friend was about to be stoned to death for running a brothel. He had had the news from his wife, who said it was the latest titbit in the Women's College at the University. Fortunately it turned out to be a different woman of the same name. Most expatriates went to some other expatriate who could cut hair, but for some time my mother went to a Syrian woman who employed only her son and her daughter. Once, when the authorities had closed the Salon and placed tapes across the entrance, my mother crawled under the lowest one, about eighteen inches from the ground, so that the boy could cut her hair. Eventually, the Syrian family was expelled.

As I have said, women controlled their own money and before I left a "women only" bank had opened in Riyadh, but even earlier, women were often seen in banks. An English teacher in Badana, on the pipeline in the North, told me that on a number of occasions, he had seen a lordly, cloaked figure, with a pistol prominently displayed, march down the street followed by a mousy little veiled figure. In the bank the man stood aside while the mouse went up to the cashier, took a chequebook and a fountain pen from her handbag, wrote out a cheque, collected her money and followed her husband out. It was quite clear who was lord and master, and equally clear who controlled the purse strings. Some expatriate women used to complain of the practices of men walking in front of women, and of women sitting in the back of cars. That was a throwback to more lawless days when it was a man's duty to protect his wife – and it was certainly changing by the late 1970s. The respective roles of men and women in supermarkets can be very revealing; by the time I left, it was the women who seemed the more enthusiastic. They went around the shelves choosing goodies and putting them into the trolley; the men pushed the trolley and paid for the goods at the checkout.

So, to end this chapter, what is the attitude of the Saudi male to women? I don't suppose it has changed so much from the time I was there. Expatriate women produced breathless accounts of lascivious glances and even pinches – but I took most of these with the proverbial pinch of salt. Everybody who lived in Riyadh knew perfectly well of a few instances when women had unpleasant experiences; but no more – in fact a good deal less – than they might have expect in a city of similar size in Europe. Of course, it should be remembered that, in local eyes, most expatriates dressed as "loose women." My only wonder was that there were not more incidents. Even when she first joined me, my own mother was of an age that should have rendered her immune from unwelcome attentions. At first, however, when I was taking her round the markets, I found myself automatically staring at all the men around, ready to resent as an affront even an unnecessarily prolonged glance – but I did not see any. The men selling perfumes, carpets, dress materials, and antiques were friendly and courteous, and addressed most of their remarks to me. Many walking along would deliberately lower their eyes so as not to seem to be staring. Of course my mother was not alone – in the early years she never left the house unless accompanied by me or by a servant – but as she grew more familiar with the city, against Embassy advice, she regularly took taxis all over the place, sometimes with a women friend, but often by herself. In all those years, she never rode with a taxi driver who was in any way unpleasant. In fact, she insisted they were usually particularly polite and helpful.

In all our years in Riyadh she only reported two incidents, and on both occasions the offender was another woman. Once, she was dug sharply in the ribs by a woman while buying dress materials (the woman also muttered something my mother could fortunately not understand) and once, at a wedding feast, she was pushed over just as she was getting up from the ground. Apart from those two "events" Riyadh had a blameless record. The few "incidents" that occurred were, I think, due to incautious behaviour on the part of the expatriate, like the wife of a teacher who got into a taxi alone late at night and said "Yes" to everything the driver said because she couldn't remember the Arabic for "No." It is hardly surprising that she found herself outside the city and invited to get out of the car. She was lucky that a loud shriek was enough to send the driver away and to bring help.

To revert to my thoughts earlier in this chapter, I have no doubt that the Saudi man's view of women was very much coloured by the image of his mother, his ideal woman. Some of my friends in London, Paris or Madrid have described the way that some rich, as well as not-so-rich young Saudis, attached themselves to young women of a disreputable type – what I might call the low end of the market. I know this was a problem at American Universities. When people spoke to me about this I had fairly simple and direct answer: whenever a young man got involved with a woman for merely physical gratification he would automatically choose one as unlike his mother, his sister, his wife-to-be as possible. We should not forget that the medieval concept of chivalry – the first elevation of the status of women in Europe since the Dark Ages – was a result of the Crusades. In Muslim lands, Christian knights encountered a very different concept of women to the one they had been used to in Western Europe. It is high time that Westerners got rid of the idea of the Harem as a sort of private "maison de plaisir" and recognized it for what it actually was: that part of the house set aside for the untrammelled use of the women and children, where only the husband has the right of entry.

There may have been great changes in Saudi society: I can only speak of what I knew and saw. Even in the late 1970s some Saudi girls who had studied abroad found it difficult to readapt when they returned home. My mother told me there was an above-average suicide rate – something that would not have been revealed to a man. Differences between the educational experience of mother and daughter was part of the problem and another was that there were few posts available in which these young women could make full use of their skills. They could teach, or work with children, or become doctors – an increasingly popular choice with Saudi girls – but a Saudi woman doctor could only work as a gynaecologist or a child specialist. In other countries, nursing is a much-favoured profession for girls, but Saudi fathers disapproved of the idea and would not allow their daughters to train to become nurses.. In the last year for which I obtained – strictly unpublished – figures, the combined Nursing Colleges of Saudi Arabia produced nine female graduates. I will have more to say about this in the chapter on Health.

Women could not work alongside men in Saudi Arabia except – and then only to some extent – on the Radio and on Television: on the English Service of Radio Riyadh we had several excellent Saudi girls working. It must surely have changed by now but in my time businesses could only employ women in their offices if they provided a special entrance, special rooms, separate bathroom facilities and a secure transport arranged with an approved driver. It was hardly worthwhile to provide all this for a handful of women. Surely, however, with the passing of time, Saudi women have been able to replace some of the foreign Arabs who filled most of the clerical posts in the Kingdom.

I wonder whether, today, there are special departments in the Ministries, staffed by women, or even working in the offices of the Girls' Education Department, where, in my time, a beardless youth applying for work there was sent home until he had at least a moustache, making it clear that only men worked there!

CHAPTER 8
Learning and Understanding

Since education was the main reason why I was in Saudi Arabia, this chapter is somewhat more "personal" than the others. I should stress here that I am not going to discuss the vexed question of whether it is wise or unwise to introduce an essentially "western" style of education into a society with very different traditions and values. Rather, I shall write about what I saw and, in the process, recount some of the extraordinary stories of what actually happened, both in school and at the Ministry of Education.

During my long stay in Riyadh, the entire education system was completely changed and reorganized. This was largely due to the efforts of the Deputy Minister of Education, Prince Khaled ibn Fahad ibn Khaled. Prince Khaled was an excellent and efficient man – still young when I first knew him – patient, enormously hard-working yet with time to listen to the problems of the most junior employee: his personal kindness to me was greater than I could ever recount. As the "best" stories come from the earliest days, without further ado, I will start to tell them.

I have already spoken of my Egyptian friends who had come to Riyadh in 1951 to help to set up the new Ministry of Education. It was perhaps a pity they were Egyptian, because they designed a Ministry on an Egyptian model, imposed on the existing Religious foundation. Anybody familiar with Egyptian bureaucracy knows that its main objective is to employ as many people as possible – irrespective of whether they have real jobs to do or not. The Egyptian system reflected earlier traditions, certainly those of the Ottoman Empire and perhaps even those of Byzantium – where the main guideline seems to have been that nobody could be trusted to do anything unless they were checked and double checked, and supervised by other people, who in their turn were subject to scrutiny, and so on *ad infinitum*. This growth found a ready soil in Riyadh.

The original educational "system" had been wholly religious, and this had an important effect upon the early days of "modern" education. As far as I could learn, there had been only two schools in the Kingdom that could have been called "modern": the Mahad Anjal in Riyadh, founded by King Sa'ud for the education of his sons but based on an earlier Royal School where his brothers had been taught; and Al Thaqr School in Jeddah, founded – when Prince – by King Faisal for the education of his sons. In 1964 these two were considered the most "model" schools in the Kingdom.

In 1964 the administration of the educational system was in the hands of two separate bodies: the Ministry of Education, responsible for boys' education, and the Girls' Education Department; reluctantly, the two had agreed to common syllabi and examinations. Later there was to be a Ministry for Higher Education, but in the 1960s all universities and colleges came under the aegis of the Ministry. Inside the Ministry proper there was a Department for Primary Education, one for Intermediate Education and one for Secondary Education. In theory, all children – at least all boys [1] – were supposed to take a six-year Primary Course, moving up year by year according to a system of internal examinations, but ending with a National Primary School Leaving Certificate. In 1964 there were still many remote areas without even a one-teacher village school, but more and more were opened and within a few years the Ministry could boast – with justifiable pride – that every village, however small, had a school. There were also special summer programmes for the educational needs of Bedouin nomads, adults as well as children.

Theoretically the Primary Learning Certificate was necessary for employment in any Ministry or Government Office. In practice, of course, in 1964 and for some years after, this requirement could not be enforced, because many of the older people had had virtually no education at all. Certificates of any sort from a Koranic School carried great weight, but in the old days most of the older men were functionally illiterate. In the Ministry we had some, men who made the tea and carried papers from one room to another, who could not even read the names on the papers they were carrying – so that when they brought a sheaf into my

---

[1] In those days, it was not possible to make female education compulsory; so, although girls' schools were opened, attendance was voluntary. All boys, however, were supposed to attend the Primary School.

office I had to scrabble through the whole lot to find whatever was for me. Naturally their salaries were very low, and there was sometimes resentment against the highly paid foreigners sitting around in their offices. But this resentment tended to be directed against foreign Arabs; it was certainly not directed at me, then the only non-Arab in the Ministry, a creature so strange and exotic that I might just as well have come from outer space and have done with it.

Intermediate Education occupied another three years, and once again the first two years' promotions were based on internal examination, leading to an Intermediate School Leaving Certificate, the possession of which entitled the government employee to gain a higher rank in the Civil Service with a corresponding rise in salary. Since many people had left school and started work with the Primary Certificate, Night Schools were set up, often in the premises of ordinary Intermediate Schools, to enable people to study as External Students and to take the examinations. As I shall explain later, there was considerable pressure on men to gain a higher status. Even in 1964, there were Intermediate Schools in all towns of any size and Intermediate classes added to Primary Schools in some smaller ones.

Those who had passed the Intermediate Certificate were eligible to enter a Secondary School (or, again, a Secondary class added to an Intermediate School). These were only to be found in the main cities, and hence it was quite usual in a Secondary School to find boys who had come from villages or small towns at quite a distance. The Secondary Department catered for the final three years of the twelve-year programme, and the examinations system was the same; but the Final School Leaving Certificate, the Towjahiya, enabled holders to go on to Higher Education in the Kingdom, as a right. A small number, those with the highest marks, were eligible for a coveted scholarship for University Education abroad.

There was one peculiarity about the examinations. They were normally held in June, but it was possible, even at the Final Certificate level, to re-sit subjects failed earlier in September. In the internal stages it was not necessary to pass all subjects. Only passes in Religious Subjects were compulsory – any boy or girl who failed stayed in the same class for another year. If, however, somebody failed English, or some other subject more minor than Religion, he or she was supposed to pass it the following year. Judging by some of the boys I was supposed to be teaching when I first arrived, however, there had been some very liberal marking.

Although the Ministry laid down "rules", Directors of Education implemented its edicts in some two-dozen educational zones; Riyadh and the Eastern Province were two of the biggest. That is why, on that first morning, when Ralph Ellis and I went to the Ministry of Education, we were redirected to the Zone Office. In fact, all members of school staff came under the authority and responsibility of the Zone Office, although the Ministry sometimes intervened. When I was working in the Ministry, a British teacher approached me on several occasions seeking my help to obtain a transfer to another school or another district, or – alternatively – to have such a transfer cancelled. If there seemed to be a valid reason to help I always went to whichever Ministry Authority seemed most appropriate and asked them to intervene with the Zone Office. I think I was successful in every case except one, which was rather interesting, and involved a man who had become a personal friend of mine.

He had been teaching in `Aneiza, in the province of Al-Qassim, north of Riyadh: unlike most people with a degree in Classical Arabic he spoke excellent colloquial Arabic after a year or two in residence. Many Saudis were puzzled by this apparent Saudi with fairish hair and blue eyes, and concluded that he had had a Syrian mother. In his spare time, James Budd sat with the old men of the local families discussing Arabic poetry, history, and the stories of the region and local lore of all sorts. Outside his classes he had little contact with his pupils who would sit, in proper silence, listening to him talking in the evenings to their fathers and uncles. Now `Aneiza had always been a thorn in the Wahabi side – there had been a war to subdue it in the eighteen sixties, a war whose brutality had never been forgotten. But the men of `Aneiza were reputed to be good businessmen, and were also supposed to be less addicted to the gloomier aspects of Wahabism than their neighbours in Bureidah, the most fiercely reactionary religious city. "'Aneiza is the Paris of the Najd!" boys used to tell me, wide-eyed, when I was new; although I think there can have been little similarity between the two cities other than a reputation for a certain *joie de vivre* among their citizens.

For at least a century, students in `Aneiza had been less ready than those elsewhere to attend their local mosque; and in 1969 there was a sort of evangelical mission, led by some zealous Iraqis, which sought to reconvert the city and to discover why mosque attendance was so bad. A report came back: the reason was the presence in `Aneiza, teaching the young, of an Infidel, a Christian, who spoke excellent Arabic, and it was he who was turning the young men against their religion. It was a pretty poor excuse, but it was better than saying that the local boys didn't like the puritan preaching to which they were subjected.

The Ministry acted at once. The teacher must be removed from `Aneiza immediately but, since no complaint had ever been made against him, he should not be dismissed until his contract expired; he should spend his last few months in Riyadh in the Yamama Schools. A deputation came from `Aneiza to ask for his return, supported by a petition signed by his Headmaster, the Zone Director of Education, and by many of the senior men of the city, including some of the religious leaders. The petitioners pointed out that the teacher had spent his time with the old men of the city, learning about poetry and local history and never discussing politics or religion with his students. Sadly the petition was ignored. I did what I could by sounding out various senior officials to see whether we could work something out. One of them investigated and told me: the missionaries had made a report – "and there's nothing we can do," he said, "if an adverse report comes from the Ministry of the Interior or the Religious Authorities it's useless. You can fight it but you won't win."

Below the Directors of Education in the Zone Offices, the Headmasters were very powerful. They made reports on the ability, character and behaviour of all the teachers in their school, which, I imagine, carried a lot of weight. However, I have known instances where a headmaster's well known prejudices were not taken too seriously. "So and so has had a bad report from his headmaster" I was told more than once, "but he doesn't like the English so we'll give the man another chance in a different school." Some of the teachers told me stories that would have made Saudi headmasters a special breed, non-existent anywhere else – like one in Ha'il who forbade an English teacher to use a tape-reorder because he thought that it might be Satanic device. I have to say that the headmasters I worked for in Riyadh would stand comparison with good headmasters anywhere. I remember Dr Hamed Salloum, Head master of the Yamama School, and his deputy, Sheikh Mohammed Abou Saleem, later Headmaster of the Faisal Secondary School. Both had large secondary schools to look after – and that under conditions of some difficulty I shall detail below. Dr Salloum became Director of Education for the Riyadh Zone before I left. Another headmaster was Sheikh Othman Saleh, Headmaster of the Royal School, whose job might have seemed impossible, but who kept his very VIP pupils firmly under control. He enforced discipline rigorously – and absolutely fairly – without respect of person.

I was fortunate to work with Sheikh Jamil Fatani before I left. He was Superintendent of a group of "Independent" schools called "The Riyadh Schools.". These schools were under the aegis of the Ministry of Education but were fee-paying. They were "experimental" and English was to be the chief medium of instruction, except for Arabic and Religion. I left the Ministry proper to become "Advisor" to these schools. Sheikh Jamil – who became a great personal friend – was a brilliant headmaster. Perhaps his greatest achievement was to create an atmosphere like a very good English Independent School. Many English visitors commented on this, and educationalists, especially those visiting our junior and kindergarten schools, described the Riyadh Schools as the one oasis they had found in the Middle East. This was the work of an unusual Arabian headmaster who inspired a real affection among his staff, whom he regarded as partners in a team working for the good of the schools.[2] At that time, the schools in the group were the only ones in Saudi Arabia to teach English from the kindergarten upwards, and to have group teaching, English students grouped by ability, a flourishing music department, both choral and instrumental, a big art and hand crafts department, and a whole range of extra-and leisure–activities ranging from sports of all kinds to learning to type and to repair and service a car. The Riyadh Schools were strongly supported by Prince Khaled, the Deputy Minister, and by Dr Abdul Aziz Quwaiter, a Founder Governor of the Schools who was Rector of Riyadh University before becoming Minister of Education.

Apart from the reports of the Headmasters there was also a corps of Inspectors, so many in fact that they tended to overlap. There used to be a large body of Inspectors in the Ministry who visited the schools and sent in reports on the school and the teachers, one copy going to the Zone Office, one to the Headmaster, and various copies going to the appropriate sections of the Ministry. Then there were the Inspectors who supervised and checked the work of the others, for Primary, Intermediate and Secondary Schools; above them there was another level of Chief

---

[2] When they opened I was sent to London to choose and recruit staff and to buy books and equipment. "What is my budget?" I asked. "How much do you want?" was the reply. "Well," I said, "I don't know, there's so much I could buy. If you gave me a budget I could work within it." "Oh," came the answer, "just order anything you like." There are not many schools where that instruction could be given!

Inspectors. There were Inspectors for all subjects, for buildings, for sports and for administration, whose only function that I could see was to write reports that were then filed by some of the numerous clerks in the Ministry. If there was any real problem, a headmaster would call for a senior inspector to come to his school to see what could be done.

I once had a very good report: it was during my first year and the English Department at the Yamama School was inspected by a very pleasant Syrian gentleman, who asked me if I would take tea with him in the Yamama Hotel. When we were sitting there, drinking tea and eating cream cakes, he confided that he wanted to write his reports – in a special and enormous ledger kept in the school for this purpose – in English instead of Arabic, but was not absolutely sure of his syntax and spelling. Would I therefore go over his reports with him, making any corrections and suggesting any emendations? I was very willing to do so, and as a result I think everybody in the School's English Section got a very fair report, except for myself, for my report would have made Dr Arnold sound like a drop-out from a Teacher's Training College.

It was to the vagaries of the Inspectorate that I owed my one period at the top of my job. When I returned to the Ministry after the 1968 vacation, I learned that I was to be transferred to the External Inspectorate, visiting schools all over the country and reporting on the teachers. As I had written two reports, very critical of the system of inspections prevalent at that time, this presented some problems. Inspectors filled in long forms giving numerical estimates (so many out of ten) on various aspects of a teacher's ability, and – I had been a year at the receiving end – telling me very little about the man. I went straight to Sheikh Ibrahim Al-Hijji, the Director-General and told him that while I was ready to do any work that the Ministry required, in view of my reports on the Inspectorate and the ridiculous forms Inspectors had to fill in, could I be allowed to behave like British HMIs and send their sort of reports? "I don't want you wasting your time going round the schools," he said, "I want you here in the Ministry. You will be attached to my office in the Curriculum and Research Department, and you will come to my office at nine o'clock every morning." So I went upstairs to the Personal Department to tell them to cancel my latest appointment to the External Inspectorate. "That's all very well," said the Head of Personnel, "but I need that in writing." So I went back to the Director General and got the note he wanted. When I took it to Personnel, the Head said, "What is your job title?" and then I had my brainwave. Years before I had much enjoyed Danny Kaye in the film "The Inspector General" and so I said at once "I'm going to be the Inspector General." "There's no such position" was a perfectly true remark, but I countered with, "No, there hasn't been, but there will be and I shall be it." "Then I want that in writing," I was told. I went to see my friends in the Translation Department who wrote out, in faultless Arabic, "Mr David Urch is appointed Inspector General of the English Language for the Kingdom of Saudi Arabia," and I took it away. The Director General was in a meeting and I was told that I couldn't go in, but when a man came along taking tea into the meeting I went in with him, sketched a polite smile to the men sitting round the table, said "I'm sorry Sir" to Sheikh Ibrahim, "it's those people upstairs. Can you sign this chit?" sketched another smile and returned to the Personnel Department.

Three or four weeks later I entered Sheikh Ibrahim's office to find him perusing a newspaper on his desk.

"Good morning, Sir."

"Good morning, Mr David. Who made you Inspector General of the English Language for the Kingdom of Saudi Arabia?"

"Well, you did, Sir."

"Did I?"

"You signed the chit, Sir."

"Did I indeed? Oh, well," he folded the newspaper and put it on one side, "the Official Gazette says that you are the Inspector General so I suppose you are."

And so I was.

***

I have written more about the education of boys than of girls because I knew so much more about the boys. Of course, the religious authorities were opposed to girls' education in schools on the grounds that it was an unwomanly activity, even expressing fears that the whole character of Saudi womanhood would be altered. Under King Faisal, the government's answer was that girls' education would not be compulsory – as boys' education was supposed to be – but "available." In the years after 1964 many more girls' schools were opened and a greater proportion of the educational budget spent on them.

I was myself witness to a curious incident in the early autumn of 1965. At the London interview, I had been assured that there would be plenty of opportunities to give private lessons. I had since learned that officially at least the practice was forbidden – though no one had told me. The only advice I was given was not to give private lessons to boys I was supposed to teach in class. Yet, I soon discovered that, so long as these lessons were kept very "private" and the pupils were confined to relatives and friends of students, then a completely blind eye was turned. But I had also been asked to give lessons to members of the staff at Petromin, and this involved pay sheets and all they entailed. Not wishing to get into trouble, and not knowing that I wasn't supposed to give such lessons, I had submitted an account of my "illegal earnings" for probable income tax. I was forthwith summoned to the office of the then Deputy Minister, Sheikh Abdul Wahab Abdul Wassieh, to explain my peccadillo. While I sat talking to the Legal Adviser I watched a group of a dozen or so elderly men, bearded and austere, their faces scoured by desert winds: they might have accompanied Abraham when he travelled from Ur of the Chaldees. They were very angry and their spokesman kept raising his voice in a loud harangue and interrupting the Deputy Minister every time he tried to speak. I asked the Legal Advisor who these men were and he told me that they were a delegation of religious elders from the fanatically puritan city of Bureidah and had come to protest about the opening of a girls' school in their town. In vain the Deputy Minister tried to repeat what the King had said (they were to see the King later in the day and I wondered whether they listened to him): the school would open for the benefit of families who wanted their daughters to be educated. Those who didn't would not be made to send them. Tea and coffee were served but refused by the whole group – an insult in Arabia – and when they eventually rose to leave and filed past the Deputy Minister, each man in turn ignored the outstretched hand and tucked his own under his cloak, until the last, the leader was reached. With the only truly impolite gesture I ever saw an adult Saudi make, instead of tucking his hands away, he put out his left, or unclean, hand, and thrust it several times, palm forward, into Sheikh Abdul Wahab's face. It was hardly surprising that his Excellency was not in the best of tempers when he had to turn next to an Englishman stupid enough to make public his private lessons: however all that actually happened to me was that I was told not to work for Petromin.

In Bureidah, as everywhere else, Girls' Schools opened, although, at least in Bureidah, and, it was rumoured, in other places, armed police had to be sent in to escort the girls in the first weeks. It was a good move to make a leading opponent of girls' schools Director-General of the Girls'

Education Department: at first the gossip flew around, "Sheikh Nasr will close all the Schools now he's in," but of course he didn't. He was in a position of authority and he could see that there were no dangers in these institutions, while the presence of such a respected figure "in charge" silenced all but the most extreme of opponents. In the end they even opened a Television Station in Bureidah, and many of the more reactionary families simply left the city, to lead purer and less sullied lives elsewhere. Girls' education was never again seriously disputed.

Girls' education, apart from such obviously feminine occupations as Sewing and Domestic Science, ran parallel to the boys'. It was only with some difficulty that this principle was enforced, as to show its independence, the Girls' Education Department wanted to have separate text books and separate examinations. After a great deal of argument it was brought into line. The Inspectorate was another problem until they began to appoint female inspectors, after which men ceased to pollute girls' schools. There were occasional flashes of independence: in the Curriculum department we would periodically get reports from the Girls' Section that they proposed using different passages from some of the set books, to which the only satisfactory answer was that in that case the girls would not be able to answer the examination questions.

In matters of school building and furnishing there was no holding them. When the Boys' Schools – with mixed successes – experimented with prefabricated buildings, the Girls' Department decided to have pre-cast. After the tenders went out there was only one offer, from a company which did not actually want the job, but, just in case, quoted the then astronomical sum of £160.00 per square foot: they won the contract, the money apparently being well spent to be different from the boys.

There was one great weakness of Saudi education, though scarcely the fault of the Government: it was free. It is trite to say that people abuse and don't appreciate what is given to them on a plate; but I remain as certain now as I was all those years ago, that children do not value – and their parents don't value – what is given to them as an automatic right. It was a little different in the private Riyadh Schools, as might be expected, and to be fair, in the "free" schools there were a number of boys – and, I am sure, girls – who worked really hard and very successfully. But for the majority of children – and this possibly increased during the years I was thus involved in Riyadh – going to school was an interruption to their otherwise pleasant lives.

People who have taught in what I must call "poor" countries have told me of the great desire for education and the general enthusiasm for schooling, not least because it can lead to an improvement of life-style and prospects. But in a rich country, such as Saudi Arabia – where it was a function of the State to look after its citizens for the whole of their lives – there is no particular incentive to work. In my early days there was the carrot that especially hard-working students might get a scholarship to go abroad. But as the number and standing of the local universities rose, "foreign" scholarships became increasingly the preserve of those taking post-graduate studies – far too far in the future to mean much to the average school boy or girl. There were always, I found, three problems: to get the boy to school (as girls were always taken that might have been easier), to get him into class once he was in school, and to make him work once he was in class: the last of the three was perhaps the hardest but all were real.

Let me now come down to the basic facts of the Saudi educational system. In theory boys' education, at least at Primary level, was compulsory, and boys' names were entered on a school's roll at the beginning of each academic year and, as in I suppose all other countries, there was quite a lot of competition among parents to try to get their children into schools considered "good" either socially or academically – which wasn't easy, because, as elsewhere, children were normally allocated to the school in the area where they lived. Once the boy was on the school roll he was supposed to attend regularly: if he didn't his name was sent to the Zone Office, from where an Attendance Inspector would be sent to the boy's house to find out what was wrong. This would have been possible when Riyadh (or any other city) was quite small and everybody knew everybody else, but in a city with over a million people, few of whom had an easily identifiable address, it was no easy task. Certainly a lot of absenteeism was truancy: in the Riyadh schools the absentees names were collected from each class and sent to the Secretary, who then spent a pleasant hour or so telephoning parents who had not notified the school of their child's absence. I don't think this happened in State Schools.

In my early days there were a number of simple and basic reasons for truancy, as explained to me by the boys themselves. There might be a particular lesson that they disliked, or a test they didn't want to do, or perhaps a relative had come to Riyadh and they wanted to spend some time with him. But even if everybody had come to school, to get the boys into class was not so easy.

The Staff at Saudi State Schools was divided into Academic and Administrative sections, whose functions not only never overlapped, but sometimes seemed to have no connection with each other. There was a Saudi Labour Law that a certain proportion of employees in any concern must be Saudi nationals; and this caused problems in Saudi Schools before there were enough proper Saudi teachers. In 1964 there were no Saudi teachers in almost all the Intermediate and Secondary Schools, except for those teaching Religion and a majority of the Arabic Language Department. The solution was to employ a lot of "administrators," many of whom had no visible functions other than patrolling the corridors of the school and occasionally forcing reluctant pupils into class. There were also, under "Administration," various Secretaries, the Finance Department, who periodically paid the staff, the Cleaners – a fairly numerous but far from hard-working group – the men who made the tea and those who opened and shut the gates, and stopped the boys leaving early: they also had to stop them from climbing over the walls.

When I arrived, an innocent, from England, I imagined that the biggest secondary school in Riyadh, if not in the Kingdom, would be organized something like an English School – as indeed it was after Dr Salloum had taken over; but I began my Saudi teaching career during an Interregnum, and so such things as class lists were non-existent. I did ask how I was to report absentees when I didn't know who was supposed to be in the class, but got no clear reply. I made my own lists but they were extremely inaccurate. In England I had prided myself that, after teaching a class two or three times, I knew all the boys: in Riyadh I found that after a week I could only recognize a few, and that was probably because they wore thick glasses or squinted, or were especially pock-marked. Most of them were vaguely good looking, with black, flashing eyes, and seemed to have come out of some sort of identikit machine. They all wore identical white robes and white head-dresses which shaded their faces, and they all had names which, if not the same, sounded the same before my ears were attuned to the sound of Arabic, and they refused to sit in the same desk each lesson – in fact it was a major task to make them sit in the same desk though the whole lesson.

I found it very difficult to get any homework. If I had given a piece of homework to Class IIIA, I would ask for it the next time I saw them, to be greeted, as likely as not, by blank incomprehension. As I stumbled through the names on my list, mispronouncing them hopelessly, very few boys seemed ready to answer their names, and the likelihood was that they would have "forgotten my book, sir." When one of the Administrators asked me for some marks I gave him a wild approximation for a series of boys whom he probably had as much difficulty as I in identifying.

The penny finally dropped after several weeks. One boy – I forget in what class – had been particularly bright one morning, and had impressed himself on me more than usual. Later in the morning, when I was teaching a completely different class he turned up, sitting in the front row. I stared at him.

"What are you doing here?" I asked him.

"This is my class, my teacher," he replied, smiling at me cheerfully.

"No it's not. You're in such and such class."

"No, my teacher. This is my class."

"But you were in such and such class this morning." I pulled wildly at my practically useless ledger, covered with question marks and crossings cut. "You got so and so marks on the test."

"Yes, my teacher. You said my test was very good."

"Well then, if you were in that class earlier, how are you in this class now? Have you been transferred?"

"No, my teacher. This is my real class. I came to the other one because I like English so much. And," he added more truthfully, "We had an Arabic test in the first lesson that I didn't want to do, so I came to you instead."

Further questioning, in which several boys joined, made matters clearer to me. There was a definite timetable so that the boys knew what lessons were going on in their classrooms. With some, what I might call "fringe" subjects, especially English, French, history and geography, they would attend if they wanted too, or not if they thought they could get away with it. A boy who hadn't written his history essay simply went to another class. It was obviously easier when new or inexperienced teachers came to the school, and simplicity itself when a foreigner came along, who couldn't even pronounce the names correctly. There were (as I learned later) some boys, theoretically in my class, who had never attended a single lesson, and, in the absence of any school lists, they were completely unknown to me. There were other boys who had come once or twice, decided that they didn't like English, and had not bothered to come again. Sometimes, if I called out a recognizable name of someone who was absent, a refugee from another class would answer his name, and be marked present, although he would smilingly claim to have "forgotten" any work or preparation he was asked for. It was a gloriously surrealist period, but perhaps fortunately, just as I was losing my grip on reality altogether, Dr Salloum established his authority and chaos gradually came to an end.

When I had classes of boys I could actually identify, I learned to get one of the reliable boys to write the names of anybody not present in Arabic for me, and I would send this list to the Administration Office. This sometimes resulted in various boys being yanked out of other rooms and propelled into my class, at intervals during my lesson. Strict attendance was not something to which the boys were accustomed: it took more than a year to get them to school on time – the regular habit being to arrive at school at an hour to have missed unpopular early lessons, and to leave early so as to miss any unpopular later ones. Some form of discipline was gradually introduced – the boys stopped their mass exodus over the walls when the big gates were locked, and school life proceeded on recognizable lines; but there were still an enormous cultural difference which I think I should explain as far as I can.

It was quickly necessary to adjust to a fact I have mentioned – the accepted concept of masters and prefects being in authority, with the rest in a sense bonded together against them, but with both sides playing according to well-established rules of conduct – this was utterly lacking. If a master was not liked in a Saudi school he had a very difficult time indeed: if he was liked, or if he seemed to have the ears of the Powers-That-Be then the boys were all "on his side" and would make shamelessly ingratiating remarks. But in the eyes of the "Powers-That-Be" what made a teacher "good" were the reports they received from the various "spies." I have already written that there were at least three in each class, reporting on the educational, religious and political activities (or lack of them) in every teacher's lessons. Some of the boys, at different times, were identified for me. One – whom in later years I saw from time to time in the most amicable way – reported me to the Ministry of Education for not giving the class enough written homework: as I had been warned about him I was able, when visited by a Ministry Inspector, to whip out my now meaningful mark book and show that I had set enough work, but that this boy had not done it. When I was asked why I hadn't reported him I was able to answer that, as I knew he was a spy, I had left him alone. The matter was dropped.

Palestinian teachers, who were probably the most suspect, had another hazard. There was at least one (about whom I knew), in the Yamama School, and I was told in all other schools as well, who had a regular salary from the Ministry of the Interior in return for political reports on his compatriots. In those early days "The Palestinian Question" was on everybody's lips.

How, then, was one to get the spy-in-the-class to give a good report, especially if you did not know who he was? There were, I learned, certain rules to be observed. To give a "snap test" was absolutely Bad Form. Due warning must be given and no trick questions included. Once, having told a class rather vaguely that they would have a "general grammar test," I sprang it on the boys without adequate warning. Many of them refused to write anything, a few walked out of class – I imagine to complain – and only a small minority attempted to answer some of the questions. After the lesson, two or three of the more responsible boys took me on one side to give me a friendly warning; because, they said, I was generally liked, and had never done such a thing before, this breach of etiquette would be overlooked, but I must promise never to do such an unexpected thing again; and I must also promise to cancel the result of this test as far as marks were concerned. They must not go into my Register. If I would promise this there would be no complaints, or if any had been made they would be explained away as a misunderstanding. I must tell the boys at the next lesson that what they had had was a "run through," give them a couple of days to learn everything up and then I could give the test to a willing and obedient class.

I gave the necessary undertaking and the event passed off. The "test", when it was done, came off quite well, and with no difficulties from anybody. I am sure that had a teacher in an English School knuckled under to what amounted to very odd demands from his pupils, he would have immediately lost any semblance of control over his classes, but in Riyadh it worked in the opposite way. Having demonstrated my willingness to co-operate with them, I found that they were willing to cooperate with me. As long as I was prepared to play the game according to their rather bizarre notions of the rules, they obeyed the referee's whistle without demur.

***

The position of "teacher" used to carry enormous weight, some of which seemed to have been eroded before I left Saudi Arabia, possibly because of the newer and more modern teaching methods; but for those of us who were teaching in the mid sixties, the mystique still existed. I found later that boys I had taught then – when they attained positions in business or government – were always ready to help me, and to accord me a respect to which I had no possible claim other than that I had once been their teacher. There was an old Saudi saying: "If you have taught me only one word, I am in your debt for the rest of my life," and on many occasions I took advantage of this.

I remember one occasion in the mid-seventies when I received a telephone call just as I was leaving home for a dinner party. An English friend, driving somebody else's unlicensed car, had made an illegal "U-turn" and had knocked a Saudi boy off his bicycle: the boy was in hospital, my friend in the Police Station, and could I do something? As the New Zealand couple I was to dine with (as was my errant friend) were not on the telephone I said that I must go to their house; but if after an hour the matter had not been resolved, they were to send me word and I would come.

Sure enough about forty-five minutes later a Police Car arrived at the house where dinner had not yet been served, but several rounds of cocktails had, and I was whisked off to the Police Station. Reeking, I was told afterwards, of Dry Martinis, I marched into the Captain's room to see an old-pupil sitting behind the desk.

"Mr David! My teacher!" he cried. I struck an attitude inspired probably more by the Martinis than anything else. "Ahmed! What is this?" I cried, "My old pupil treating my friend like this?! Where is a private room?" We were at once shown to a private room, a television set was brought in, and tea and coffee were served: I got down to business with my pupil. Could he please release my friend? No, he had to remain in custody until a medical report had been received on the boy, and then a Saudi Guarantor could release him. "I will be his guarantor" I said grandly but the Captain had not so far lost his grip on things to agree to that. No, he said, it must be a Saudi, but he would go himself to the hospital for a preliminary medical report and I could go to the Radio Station (where my friend Peter worked) and get a letter from a Director there. We set off on our respective errands, leaving Peter in a comfortable room watching a film. Luck was with me, because I tracked down the Head of Peter's department, and he went so far as to give me a letter admitting that Peter worked there, but not going so far as to guarantee him in any way. Still the letter was better than nothing, and I went back to the Police Station. Very soon the Captain came back, with a medical report. "It's all right," he said, "the boy has a broken leg but he'll be fine. Now if you've got the Guarantee we can go ahead and release your friend," but his face lengthened as he read the letter. "This isn't a guarantee," he said, "it just confirms that he is under sponsorship of the Ministry of Information." Once more I offered myself, and was rejected. "Well Ahmed," I said, "I insist that you release Peter tonight, so if you must have a Saudi guarantor, you will have to guarantee him yourself, and I will give you my personal guarantee." It is hard to believe but the Captain actually went along with this and the necessary papers were made out – my guarantee being verbal. "Thank you, thank you," we said and as we were going out Peter asked if I had my car with me. I said that I hadn't because I'd been brought in a Police Car, and had then used taxis. "Ask him if I can have my car back," whispered Peter, so I went back to the Captain. "Look," I said, "it's very late, almost midnight. We can't get a taxi now. Can you give me Peter's car keys, please?" He looked aghast. "But the car is evidence," he said, "it has a dent in it, perhaps the boys blood." I summoned up the last remnants of the Martinis of several hours before and faced the Captain dramatically. "Ahmed!" I cried, "I was your teacher and I order you to give me those keys!" The poor man looked quite haggard, "You make it very difficult for me Mr David," he said, pushing the keys to the side of his desk and shutting his eyes, "don't let me see you take them." We said "Good night" again, picked up the keys as quietly as possible and walked out. It goes without saying that in later encounters Ahmed continued to be as friendly and helpful as possible.

***

I began to write earlier about the necessity to appear a "good" teacher in the eyes of the boys. Some people, cynically, said that it was not difficult: if the boys were not asked to do any work they thought that their teacher was "good," but in fact it was not so simple. They were obsessed with getting high marks in tests and in the final examinations, and, when quarterly examinations were introduced – which had a significant effect on the final placing – these too became matters of vital importance. High marks meant scholarships, or at least entry to a foreign university after leaving school; and in the earlier stages it was necessary to do well in the Promotional Exams so as to be put in the "A" stream, where in theory one would have better teaching and a better chance in the final year.

I have already explained that for centuries "education" had been religious and, at least in the Najd, consisted of learning passages of the Holy Koran by rote, without understanding the implications of those passages. As the ability to recite from memory had been the only thing required, the boys needed great mental effort to begin to learn in a different way. For the teachers of some subjects – history and geography for instance – the old method could be used. "Read pages 134-138 in your history book and learn them" was an easy preparation to set, and if the test on the prep consisted of questions on facts taken from those pages, to be answered as far as possible in the words of the book, nothing, except the boys' memories was tested. But it was just not possible to teach English, as a Spoken Foreign Language, in that way, and so the trouble started.

When they boys were reading a prescribed text they wanted an Arabic translation – forbidden by the Ministry of Education but available in local bookshops – plus the exact equivalent of every word new to them in the English version. Character study or analysis of the plot were quite outside the picture, and it was difficult to get them to take the slightest interest. They would answer questions on what A or B did in the book, bur never on why they had done so. Possibly the books themselves were at fault – simplified versions of "safe" nineteenth century books, without sex, religion, or politics, were dull to read: but there was one exception.

During the academic year 1965-66 some bright spark in the Ministry of Education had prescribed a simplified version of Emily Brontë's *Wuthering Heights* to the Literary Section of the final year of the Secondary School. (The second and third years of the Secondary Schools were divided into literary and scientific sections). In England *Wuthering Heights* is not a particularly easy book to teach, full of hate, long-nourished grudges, twisted passions and bitterly divided loyalties. I found it very easy to teach in Riyadh – many of the boys becoming really interested (some referred to it years afterwards in conversation) as I told them stories of Haworth and the people among whom the Brontës had lived, stories gleaned from my step-cousin Winifred Gérin, who, with her husband John Lock, were leading authorities on the Brontë family and whom I had visited in Haworth. I told them of the "spite walls" built to spoil a neighbour's view, of families in the High Street not speaking for generations, of wives abandoned and sons and daughters disinherited, of ragged old men and women who were reputed to have hidden hoards of gold, hidden from their own families, of a twisted society united only in a wall of silence against the outsider; and so we read *Wuthering Heights* and the boys liked it. They discussed it among themselves in class; they understood and even in part approved the behaviour of Heathcliff and Cathy. In every lesson they asked me for more Wuthering Heights instead of such mundane topics as Grammar or Comprehension. It was very instructive to find a work of fiction that really caught their imagination.

I was furious – as were the boys – when we were told, a couple of months before the final examination, that questions would not be set on the book because it was too difficult and most schools hadn't read it. With the unanimous support of the boys, I put in an urgent plea to Dr Salloum for the inclusion of questions on the book, even if they were not compulsory. He must have approached the Ministry officials, because questions on *Wuthering Heights* did appear – although they were so feeble that I suspect that the book must have proved too difficult for the examiners as well.

There was a prescribed book for English grammar – it was quite a good one – with specific sections laid down in the syllabus for study. There were some sections not so prescribed that would have helped the boys to understand the rest better, but it was impossible to get those even looked at. "It's not in the syllabus," they would chorus, and they would not open their books. "Doing" a section meant explaining the grammatical point and giving some examples, which had to be put on the board for the boys to copy. Then came the most important point – the "official" exercises on the section. I always set some of these for homework and they would be done with a greater or lesser degree of competence: then came the crunch. In the next lesson the correct answers were discussed and written up on the board, to be copied and memorized as a "received text." If, a month later, the exact sentences were given in a test many of the boys would score 100%; but if they were changed around so that thought was needed to see how the grammatical point should be adapted, some boys couldn't do it at all. I put this down at the time (and am still of the same opinion) to the stultifying effects, not of the Religious Teaching in itself; but the way in which that Teaching was put across.

Boys certainly had astonishing memories, but it was recollection without understanding. It took a long time to persuade them to stop and think what a question meant before answering it, as a preliminary to being able to cope with questions phrased differently, put back to front, or hidden inside other questions. When, however, I was "advising" the independent and experimental Riyadh Schools, and teaching sample groups of different ages, I still found remarkably good memories but, especially with the seven to nine year olds (and even younger), no inhibitions about thinking for themselves. They were as individualistic as any children of that age in any country, and just as full of "whys." They learned songs and nursery rhymes quite easily, but wanted to know what it was all about. With older boys, particularly those who had not come up through the system, I found attitudes more like those I had encountered in the state schools; but in the Riyadh schools there was the great advantage that all the English sets were according to ability, without concern for what class, or even year, they were in for other subjects. The strain this must have put on whoever had to compile the timetables was not, I regret to say, a matter to which I then gave any thought.

For example, when I arrived at the Yamama School, I found boys in my "top" class who had already taken five years of English. To reach this exalted height, they had taken four internal examinations and the national Intermediate Certificate; but their knowledge of the language was nil, and their only proficiency, if that is the right word, was the ability to write their name in English. These boys were supposed, among other things, to be reading an abridged version of Wilkie Collins's *The Woman in White*. At the final lesson before the examination, I said that I would answer any questions any boy had on any part of the syllabus: one young man, who had passed through the class occasionally during the year, mysteriously and silently, asked me the only question he ever posed, and it was on the book.

"Teacher, what means Woman? What means white?" I heard, years later, that he had described me to someone as "his very good English teacher": perhaps I did teach him these two words. It was in my first year that I realized the farcical nature of these exams. They were to improve enormously, and by the time I left could stand comparison with those in most countries; but for several years I was putting the same sentence in reports: "so long as boys continue to succeed in examinations for other than academic reasons, etc, etc, etc…" for many and various were the ways of getting round the fact that you couldn't answer the questions. I don't suppose the stories that follow will be altogether unfamiliar to those who have taught in numbers of countries, Arab and non-Arab, and the overall attitudes may have completely changed; but what I tell was then a normal facet of Saudi life.

In the Yamama School, we had a very pleasant young Iraqi teacher of English, who was very hard up, with money to send to his family and a student brother to support; by the end of the month he was always on his beam ends. For some reason he was told to set the Internal English Examinations for the Royal School: and the day before the examination two emissaries from the King's youngest brother came to see me. Very politely they explained that that had to find the Iraqi teacher to buy copies of the next day's papers. I told them that I didn't think it would be any good, but I knew the building where my Iraqi colleague lived, and they said they could find him. "But why do you want to buy the papers?" I asked. "I am sure that Prince Homoud could come to some arrangement with Mr Ralph." "Oh no" they said, "His Highness wants to do a very good paper and give Mr Ralph a nice surprise." The Iraqi teacher presumably complied with their request because when he came back after the summer all his financial problems were forgotten. He had got married, took a nice new flat for himself and his wife, furnished it well and bought a Mercedes. I thought the Prince had paid a high price for a whim.

I myself was never asked to set examinations, for my own boys or for anyone else's. This upset me at first and I told some of my Saudi friends, from the families of boys I taught that I was afraid this meant that I was not trusted, or not thought competent by my Headmaster and the Examination Board. A few days later one of them referred to the matter as we sat drinking tea in the evening. "You needn't worry," he told me, "from your point of view it's a compliment, really. You haven't been chosen to set any examinations because it is thought that you would be too strict and would not allow certain people copies of the papers beforehand." I had not at that time adapted myself to local ways.

I did help one boy in a very strange way. One of my more erratic private pupils, one of the Rashid family from Ha'il, came to me and asked me if I could write some model essays to help a Very Important Prince. Thinking little of it, I wrote half a dozen essays on the given topics and forgot all about it in the stress of my own school examinations. One afternoon in the flat – for this was in my first year – Ralph was correcting some papers and gave an exclamation of annoyance. "Look at this damn fool!" he said, "he's got someone else to write his essay and he hasn't even taken the trouble to copy it out in his own handwriting." I looked over his shoulder and recognized the handwriting as my own, and saw the Very Important Prince's name scrawled at the top of the page. One word had been – inaccurately – inserted halfway through. "I wrote that" I told Ralph, "I wrote about six." "I gave them six topics and told them I should set one of them," said Ralph grimly, "and I don't think your essay is worth more than eight out of ten."

Getting work prepared beforehand was a simple way of passing an examination, but there were other ways. Since the purpose of passing the internal examinations was to move into the next year, it was possible to come to some arrangement with headmasters, school secretaries and the administration generally. When the dust had settled in the Yamama School, we had a charming boy in the top class who not only knew no English but appeared to know nothing else either. His father, summoned by Dr Salloum, indignantly detailed the thousands of riyals he had given (and to whom) and described the priceless crate of Scotch that had eased his son's last remove. Did Dr Salloum want more? he asked. Dr Salloum didn't and the boy was removed to another school where he was put in the bottom class of an earlier year: we heard the he remained at the bottom for a while and then sank gracefully into oblivion.

As far as possible, the Internal Examination at the Yamama School was conducted on more or less English lines. We certainly marked rather easy questions generously, but there were still a fair number of failures. I was not altogether surprised when, next term, I found that everybody seemed to have moved up. I thought no more about it, however, until the entire English staff was summoned to the Ministry of Education Examination Department after school. Mystified, we took our old Mark books, as instructed, and turned up – to be harangued by a very stern man who had in front of him piles of last year's Yamama School English Exams, and an enormous sheet of paper covered in columns of figures. It appeared that we were in serious trouble: we were told that the marks – all passes – did not correspond to the marks written on the examination papers. Fortunately one of our members was a very articulate Palestinian, who produced all our mark books and waved them at the stern figure: he showed how we had recorded the marks in our books as they appeared on the examination papers. It was not our responsibility to complete the large sheet of paper containing marks for all the subjects. The stern man was not impressed. The Administrative Staff, he said had filled this in –

we must have given them the wrong marks. Other Arabic speaking English teachers joined in, leaving three Englishmen silent, our heads turning from speaker to speaker like spectators at Wimbledon. We had given in the right marks, they all declared, and there were a number of failures: rather than go to the trouble of having a second examination, the Administration had simply changed the marks – without going to the trouble of covering themselves by changing the marks on the papers! In the end this extraordinary explanation was accepted, and after various cups of tea, we all shook hands and went home.

When the next year's examinations came along, I addressed the whole English language staff, arguing that since the boys were going to be passed anyway, we would do it ourselves. We must explain to the boys that the composition was very important and that they must do it, and must write enough: then, if necessary, we would not take marks off for mistakes but give them marks for what they got right. In addition we would keep back a certain number of marks for "effort" and by these means we should be able to get them all through.

The plan worked better than I had thought possible. While the Mathematics Committee marked every mistake and checked and rechecked every mark and the Arabic Committee argued interminably over grammatical mistakes, the English Committee sailed gaily through piles of papers, bellowing in chorus "Lily of Laguna," "There Was I Waiting At The Church," and other classical gems. We rewarded merit liberally, helped lame dogs over stiles, gave marks for effort whenever possible, and completed our task before most of their others had done their preliminary checking. We had our own reward. Dr Salloum came into the large room where all the various groups were sitting. The English Committee, he said, had already finished, and the results were highly satisfactory. As a result he had asked the Ministry of Education to arrange our immediate release: we could collect our summer salaries and passports and leave immediately on our well-earned vacation. Sensation! All those more serious minded men who had been objecting to learning that "the bulls won't bellow and the cows won't low, the hens won't cackle and the cocks won't crow, the turkeys won't gobble and the ducks won't quack, and I KNOW THEY NEVER WILL UNTIL MY JANE COMES BACK," trumpeted by an irresponsible group of English, Palestinians, Jordanians and Iraqis (our Arab colleagues had picked up all the songs very well), went back to their marking. Perhaps they worked more quickly because of our example.

I am going now to tell two stories about examinations in Riyadh. As it happens I retailed them to a number of people in my later years in Arabia – and they all professed themselves "horrified" by my behaviour. One stout and pompous individual told me that I had prostituted my profession, which was nonsense because a prostitute expects to be paid for his or her services. I know I would have acted differently in England, but at the time in Riyadh what I did seemed right, and I think today that, in the same circumstances, I should again do what I did over forty years ago. To understand the first story, I must explain the Byzantine method by which we avoided errors – and, worse, collusion – when correcting public examinations. All teachers were liable to be involved in this activity, unless specifically released, whether for "good" behaviour (as in the never-to-be-forgotten episode I have just recounted), or for "bad" behaviour (likely to involve a teacher being sent home early due to cancellation of his contract because his work had not passed muster).

A particular Intermediate School in Malaz – off University Street, almost opposite the Canada Dry Soft Drink Factory – was taken over every year. Secondary School teachers from all over the Kingdom were brought to Riyadh to mark the School Leaving Certificate, and we worked in this school. Each "subject", including English, had two or three classrooms allocated to it. Inside our area we were divided into groups of six or seven teachers under a "leader". Each man was given two pens, a blue one and a red one. In one of the rooms was the "top-table" where three or four senior figures sat. (I got there after my third year and after that – when I was in the Ministry itself – I opted out). Each group was told what it had to do – all the extraordinary rules explained – and then waited for the first group of papers.

These arrived in the form of green-covered booklets. The boy's name and examination number had been removed and a new "secret" number had been put on by the Examination Department, who were thus supposed to be the only people who actually knew the ownership of any particular paper. Each group was given a pile of booklets, usually twenty at a time: the members of each group knew how many marks were allotted for each question, and every member was furnished with a paper of model answers in case, I suppose, that he didn't know what the answer to a question should be. The "leader" then appointed one question to each member; if there was a spare man he had the job of adding up the marks, and he should be somebody who could write in Arabic. Everybody then got down to work and started correcting the papers, being careful to show clearly how each mark had been awarded – that having been part of the preliminary instructions. The total number of marks awarded for the paper was forty, and for some arcane reason, we had to mark in half and quarter marks: to pass the boy had to get at least sixteen marks. At this stage the blue pens were used and as each mark was written down it had to have the marker's initials beside it. While the team relaxed the leader checked all the corrections, saw they were properly marked and initialled, and added his own initials in every place – still in blue. If there was nobody totting up the marks, the leader did this himself, and the first mark was written, in Arabic, on the cover. Only very conscientious leaders had the marks written in English and Arabic. These final marks were initialled – in blue – by the leaders and by one other member.

When everything was completed and checked to the leader's satisfaction, he went and found a group doing nothing in particular and gave the pile of corrected booklets to them, finding from somewhere another corrected pile, which he brought back to his team, and now the red pens came into use. Once again each team member was assigned one question, normally the one he had been correcting, and the first group's marking had then to be rechecked. If the original mark was approved all that happened was that a third initial – in red – was added to the two in blue. If, however, the checker did not agree with the original mark then he made a mark (in red) and took the paper to the first marker to query the matter. Should they agree on the change the new mark – in red – was put in the margin. As far as I could see, the old blue mark was cancelled, as it had by then been replaced by a new red one and this new mark was initialled by the checker in red and the original marker and the original leader in blue to show that they agreed. When all the pile of booklets had been checked, the leader went through the whole lot once more, adding his own initial – in red – whenever he saw three initials. Finally he and another member of the group added their red initials to the final mark after having made sure that the addition of the marks was correct.

Every paper now had a minimum of four initials in the forty or fifty places and was extremely difficulty to decipher. Where there had been a dispute it looked like nothing on earth; but it was not yet finished. Each bunch of papers, corrected, checked, rechecked and rechecked again now went to one of the pundits at the Top Table for its final check. As far as it went this was fairly speedy. One used, I think, blue pens and only initialled sub-totals and the final total. When the process was completed the papers went upstairs to mysterious people who entered the marks onto a Final Mark Sheet which we never caught sight of.

All this sounds unnecessarily complicated and time wasting, yet it was typical of the time and of the bureaucratic system that had been introduced to Riyadh – and it didn't work. I believe that the fact that either several people were going to check the work after you or had already checked it before you saw it bred carelessness. When any teacher corrects a test paper, and is responsible for it, he or she will take care and will mark scrupulously. Mistakes may occur but they will not be many. But when one is part of a machine, knowing that at least four other people are going to look at the same beastly question, carelessness doesn't creep in, it's rampant. When I sat among the pundits I sometimes found not only mistakes in addition, or blatant errors in correction, but whole sections of questions over looked. This raises the whole question of responsibility: one could hardly blame Saudi officials in any office referring upwards to some Olympian height. However, what I have just written is not the actual story I want to tell. It is just a preliminary, a setting of the scene because – amazing though it may seem – the correcting process was not yet complete. Beyond even the Olympian heights of the Top Table, unseen by mortal eyes, lurked the Reappraisal Committee.

These Jovian entities were in fact the same people who had previously sat downstairs, busy about corrections. When all the other people were released, a small number (of whom I was one in my first and third years) were requested to stay a few more days. It was pointless to refuse because the penalty for non-cooperation was to have one's passport "mislaid". (In my third year I was in the Zone Office to collect my passport when a Syrian teacher from the Royal School was raising hell because his passport was missing, and was extremely dissatisfied with the bland smiles of the officials who told him to be patient. When he had gone one of them opened a drawer in his desk and pulled out the man's passport. "We've got it here," he told me. "We'll keep him waiting another two weeks. He has been most uncooperative.") The rooms where the Reappraisal Committee sat were very private – only those on the Committee were allowed in through a door that was kept locked against intruders.

Our task was simple. In theory many boys were obvious passes and others were obvious failures: we were supposed to re-examine borderline cases, people within half a mark, or a whole mark of passing. There was never, to my knowledge, any instance of a boy who had scraped through being marked down; but if an extra mark could be found to pass a marginal failure, we were supposed to find it. As every examiner knows, in a subject like English it is usually possible to squeeze out an extra mark for "neatness," or for "effort," or in the composition; and in the first days these were the sort of problems we faced. There were three people to "do" the English papers, and our work was made more interesting by the fact that we now used green pens to scribble our initials all over the already over-decorated papers. In addition we had to sign a form, which – in translation – said roughly the following: "I have seriously and conscientiously re-examined the paper submitted to me and I honestly believe a genuine error was made. In consequence I recommend that the marks be amended as I have indicated, giving a total mark of such and such." We had to sign the paper: the senior member of the English Examination Committee (in my first year AbdulAdthim Sha'aban, the elderly Egyptian who had brought me into the Ministry of Education) initialled all the amendments on the paper in green. He did not initial or sign the form with the solemn declaration.

In my first year I was not only on the Reappraisal Committee but was "asked" to remain behind even later (with my elderly Egyptian) and we sat waiting for something to happen. Suddenly the doors opened and in swept about a dozen important-looking gentlemen, with heavy gold braid on their immaculate cloaks. They were led by a senior Ministry of Education official, the Director-General of Education, whom I had met: he was carrying a single examination booklet, and the whole group made straight for where I was sitting. "Good morning, Mr David," he said in his excellent English, "Perhaps you would be good enough to look over this paper and see what you can do to help this pupil to pass." I opened the booklet and began reading it.

The writing was clear and neat: when one had said that one had said everything. The candidate, who had amassed nine marks, had been given every possible credit. He had written very little, and almost everything he had written was wrong – sometimes he had copied down the question instead of giving an answer; but he had been given full marks for every answer he had attempted, right, or almost invariably wrong. "He does not even deserve nine marks," I said.

The robed gentlemen conferred, while I stared at the markings. Every inaccurate mark had four initials, two blue and two red; but I could recognize none of them. By what arcane group this particular paper had been corrected I didn't know; but it was certainly one far removed from the common herd. The ministry spokesman addressed me again. "Please explain, Mr David." He said, "Why this pupil cannot have more marks."

"Well, sir," I replied, "he hasn't done much of the paper, and nearly everything he has done is wrong; but he has already been given full marks for everything, right or wrong, that he's written. There's no way that I can award him any more marks." There was a pause for more conferring, while I gazed at this ghastly paper and wondered what they would do to me. Then the voice came again.

"You say he has not finished the paper. Why was that do you think?"

"Well, he doesn't know anything," I said rather desperately, "he couldn't write anymore." A silence greeted this unhelpful statement broken by a few subdued mutterings.

"Can you think of another reason?"

The robed figures were in a semi-circle behind my chair. AbdulAdthim Sha'aban was trying to make himself invisible, like shutting a jelly up in a matchbox. I took a deep breath: "Perhaps he didn't have time to finish the questions," I said.

"Exactly!" The tension behind by chair eased, "and what do you think he might have written if he had more time?" This was the crucial question, but at last the penny had dropped and I knew what was expected of me. Unscrewing my fountain pen and drawing the booklet towards me, I looked at the question and began to write. "If he had answered this question," I said," he might have written this answer."

"And what mark would he have been given for that?"

"Half a mark."

So it went on. I wrote answers down on the paper and then corrected them and initialled them in green. When the total reached the magic mark of sixteen most of the figures disappeared. The Director-General thanked me and also departed, leaving the examination people to take over. AbdulAdthim was shaking like a blancmange – he had had to counter initial all the rubbish I had written.

"This is entirely your responsibility Mr Urch," he said, "I have nothing to do with it, lest there should be questions later on. All I have done is to initial that the marks you have written are correct for the question. I have had nothing to do with putting in the answers."

"There's nothing wrong with the answers," I replied, "and nobody could prove that the boy wouldn't have written them if he had more time."

"Do you really believe that he could have done so if he had had more time?" It was a ridiculous question.

"I expect so if he had about a million years of trial and error," I snapped.

At this point I was brought the wretched form beginning "I have seriously and conscientiously re-examined this paper…" which, with a mental *mea culpa* I filled in and signed. "I have nothing to do with that form" shrilled Job's Comforter.

Since this was taking place in the Middle East that was, of course, not the end of the story. The next morning I was visited by three impressively robed men whom I thought had been part of the previous days delegation. The previous day only the Director-General had spoken English: now it seemed that all these three could speak it perfectly well. They produced the wretched booklet again. There had been an error, they explained, implying that it was my fault but that my ignorance would be pardoned. It was a ministry ruling that it was impossible to raise the marks of any paper more than one third, and I had almost doubled them! Would I please immediately re-correct the paper.. "But what is the point?" I asked, "A third of nine is three so he can only have twelve marks: that's no use to him." Nevertheless they insisted, so I sat – still with my green pen because we had gone beyond the rainbow and were now in the realm of pure light – and re-corrected the paper. This, of course was easy: I simply crossed out the marks the boy had been given for incorrect answers and reduced his marks to twelve. I initialled everything again and passed the booklet to my now incoherent Egyptian who silently counter-initialled it. Once more the form "I have seriously and conscientiously re-examined this paper…" was brought to me to be filled in. It had by now no meaning whatsoever and I signed it and sat waiting for the next move. I sat there all day.

The next morning the three gentlemen from the day before were back, with the now all-too-familiar booklet. "To-day," one of them said to me, "you will please re-examine this paper. It now has twelve marks and a third of twelve is four so you can raise it to sixteen." I took the paper in silence, crossed out all the alterations I had made the morning before and restored all the wrong marks. I can't remember what AbdulAdthim did – I think he left the room. In any case there were so many crossings out and initials all over the paper that I doubt whether the most interfering scrutiniser could have made head or tail of it. For the third time I signed a form saying how I had re-examined the paper, making myself out to be the most incompetent marker since examinations were invented.

I wondered then and have wondered since why this charade was necessary. As the careful reader will remember, it was in this same summer that all the failure marks in English at the Yamama School were simply changed on the Final Mark Sheet. Why could something similar not have happened here? Whoever the boy was, he was obviously very important, and all that I could think, then and now, was that those in authority were guarding themselves against any possible enquiry by having the signed papers from an idiotic Englishman which put all the responsibility on him. There was, of course, no enquiry of any sort.

There were other ways of getting people through exams. It must have been at the end of my third year that, during the Examinations, I was paying a flying visit to the Royal School to see that all was well. At the Royal School this was really a formality; but while I was there one of the masters I knew said to me, "Would you like to see Prince Homoud doing his exams? And led me to a small room. Prince Homoud ibn Abdul Aziz was the King's youngest brother, a very charming and polite young man who spoke good English but did not actually attend lessons. In this room I found the Prince with four or five of his friends, "answering" some paper, with a wireless playing Arabic music in the background; the boys were talking in a desultory way. There were, by regulation, two teachers as invigilators but on this occasion there was a third, who was dictating the answers to any of the boys who bothered to listen. I don't know what happened to the others but Prince Homoud got almost 100% in all his papers. On the strength of this he was accepted by the University of Austen in Texas: however, after they discovered that he didn't actually know anything of the subjects in which he had apparently done so well, it was mutually agreed that he (and the vast retinue he had taken with him) should return to Riyadh. I think he was in Texas for six weeks.

***

The second occasion on which I was guilty of deviating from the strictest standards of my profession was the only time I took part in – in fact aided and abetted – organized cheating. Once more, I believe, in the same situation, I should do the same again. One day an old pupil from the Yamama School came to see me (it was the end of my third year): he said that he needed my help, not for himself but for a friend. This man, who was very poor, was working in some Ministry or other, but, because he only had the Primary School Leaving Certificate, his salary was very small. His father was old, his mother ill, and he had two or three sisters and a younger brother to support. It was absolutely essential for him to pass the Intermediate School leaving Certificate, which would lead to an increase of salary. He went to night school and had excellent marks in all subjects except English – here he had a blind spot. For four years he had failed the Certificate Exam because of his weakness in English. If he failed once more he would probably not be allowed to take the exam again. Of course, the man could pay me nothing but still, somehow, I must help him.

Naturally I said that I would do anything I could, but I pointed out that I could not work miracles. If the man had a complete blind spot as far as English was concerned, he was not going to learn everything he needed in less than two weeks – all the time there was before the examination. Abdul Jaleel waved my objections aside: "Come and meet the man," he said.

We went to a small house in a street of poor houses. The Majlis was spotlessly clean but showed obvious signs of poverty. Nevertheless tea, coffee, and a big bowl of fresh fruit were produced and we sat down to discuss the problem. I explained once more that I was ready to do anything in my power, but that I couldn't teach someone English in two weeks, especially somebody with a minus aptitude. Once again Abdul Jaleel waved aside my objections: "he doesn't want lessons," he said," he couldn't understand you anyway. What you have to do is to help him to pass the examination."

The scheme was then explained to me: it was breathtakingly simple. The man was an external student from a night school and would be sitting the examination in the Intermediate School in Wazir Street, beside the Public Library. All the external Students would be taking their exams in the Art School, a large room that held about sixty people; arrangements would be the same as in other years. Abdul Jaleel had already made enquiries and found out that I should be one of the invigilators at that school. All I had to do was to make sure that I was invigilating in the Art School during the English exam, and then I could tell the man the answers to the questions. They both smiled at me: I didn't know what to say.

By the time we had left I had gone so far as to say that I would try and see if it were possible, but I did not feel at all comfortable about doing what was expected of me. Let me be honest and say that it was less a question of ethical considerations than a worry that I should get myself into terrible trouble, in spite of Abdul Jaleel's assurance that nobody would make trouble for me helping a poor man. I was hardly surprised when a few days later I received official notification that I was to attend that particular Intermediate School to act as invigilator. The enquiries had been thorough and the finding correct. I told Abdul Jaleel that I would do my best.

In the school there were a large number of classrooms, about fifteen as I recall, all of which had a group of boys and each of which had two invigilators. On arrival every morning, at some hour like six thirty, one was assigned a room in which one would work for the day, usually for two but occasionally for three exams. It was unusual to be given the same room twice and one never worked with the same colleague – I suppose all this was to prevent collusion. The days went by and I flitted, on the word of command, from one room to another; but I was never in the Art School. The last day of the examinations was the day of the English Exam and on the evening before Abul Jaleel visited me to make sure there would be no backsliding. Again I promised to do my best, but said that there was only a small chance that I would be assigned to the right room. Abdul Jaleel nailed me with his curiously piercing eyes and said "But you have to be there. We are depending on you. I have promised the man's mother and father that you will get him though his English and they are so happy. He knows he has done very well in all the other papers." I went to bed that night troubled, but determined to do everything I could.

The next morning I was at the school before anybody else. As soon as the Supervisor arrived, I said to him "I'm going to be in the Art School today." "No you're not," he said, looking at the list, "You're in room number so and so." "No I'm not," I said, "Please, I want to go to the Art School. I've never been there. Do be kind and change the list." With that I walked out of the room and went to the Art School, where I ensconced myself. Presumably the Supervisor was kind and did change the list because nobody came to turn me out. I counted the desks, saw there was an empty examination booklet on each, with clean blotting paper and ink, and said "Good morning" to an Iranian teacher of something or other whom I had not worked with before. At last the External students filed in, and I saw Abdul Jaleel's friend's face untauten perceptibly when he saw me. He was at the front of the last file but one on the right hand side of the room, so I took up my position on that side and indicated to the Iranian that he should patrol the other. Somebody appeared with the question papers, we distributed them and work commenced.

Most of the candidates seemed able to get down to the papers reasonably well; but some of them had questions about the paper that we were traditionally allowed to answer. My "Private" candidate sat rigid in front of his row and waited to be helped. I leant over his desk, picked up the paper and began to dictate, not word by word but letter by letter, the first words of the answer to the first question.

I had already chosen the questions for him – ones to be answered in the fewest possible words; and one where some mark could be gained with one or two word answers. His writing was neat and he knew the letters more or less. Although I watched "i's" and "e's" getting mixed up, but I thought that this added verisimilitude to an otherwise bald and unconvincing narrative. Unfortunately the man behind him, who was managing a little better but not much (and seemed to be the only other person in difficulties) realised what was going on an began whispering to me to help him. I had therefore to dictate a second – and different set – of answers to get him through, and it was inevitable that I should attract attention. After about half an hour the Iranian teacher came over to see me.

"You're helping the candidates," he said sternly and truthfully.

"I have men here who can't read the questions – I must explain them," I answered, tempering the simplicity of the dove with the cunning of the serpent.

"You're not explaining the question; you're giving them the answers," he accused.

"Shut up and keep to your own side of the room," I said, abandoning finesse.

He went away and I could see him watching me balefully as I spelt out words like AND and THE and calculated how many marks the men would have on their papers. I put in one or two deliberate mistakes and aimed to get them each about two marks above the pass mark. Soon the Iranian was back again.

"If you speak to either of those two men again," he said, pointing to them, "I shall send for the supervisor and report you."

I will not sully these pages by reporting verbatim what I told him to do, and I redoubled my dictating efforts in case I was suddenly expelled from the room.

The next time a man came round bringing a jug of cold water and a communal glass the Iranian spoke to him and the man retired. A few minutes later the Examination Supervisor came in, with the Headmaster of the School and several other men. I suspended my activities and became very busy attending to various other candidates who seemed to be doing quite nicely. After a bit of a talk on the other side of the room the whole lot moved over to me. "Are you helping these men?" one of them asked me in English "Yes," I replied, serpent like again, "they are doing their best but they can't understand the questions unless I explain them. I must give them a chance." They all went and peered at my two hapless candidates and examined their answers (which were of course, different and contained mistakes). Most of the room had by now stopped work to see what was happening. There was a muttered colloquy. And then the booklets were replaced on the desks, the Iranian and I both received pleasant nods and the delegations went out. I hastily resumed my dictation.

The Iranian came over to me for the last time. "I'm going to make an official complaint about you to the Ministry," he said, "don't think you'll get away with this." He then went away and ignored me for the rest of the morning. I gave his departing back the sort of chilling bow I thought a French aristocrat might have given a Revolutionary Judge who had just condemned him to the guillotine.

But it never came to the guillotine. On my return from the summer vacation, I took the trouble to learn the fate of my two candidates: both had passed. Abdul Jaleel told me that his friend's parents were delighted, and that his friend was already getting his higher salary. All that happened to me was that I was promoted to the Inspectorate: the Iranian's contract was cancelled.

***

I remember a very odd incident during my first year at the Yamama School, when, during the final internal examination, we were about to distribute the French papers. The boys were sitting in their desks, with their booklets before them, filling in their names and their examination numbers: there was a long pause, and with my fellow invigilator I kept going to the door to be told "wait." Suddenly, after about twenty minutes, a perfect galaxy of people arrived, among whom were Sheikh Abdul Wahab Abdul Wassieh, the new Deputy Minister of Education, and

Sheikh Abdullah Naim, then Deputy Director of Education and later Mayor of Riyadh, with a number of people carrying piles of papers. Now, we were told, the French papers had arrived and we could distribute them: I hastily shovelled papers onto desks and saw before I had finished hands going up. "Please, my teacher, this is the wrong paper."

I looked at the heading, which seemed to be right – at least the subject, the class and the date were right; but the boys were adamant. I consulted my Arab colleague who went to look for the supervisor. When he came back he looked very solemn, but his eyes were dancing with glee. He addressed a couple of sentences to the boys which in no way satisfied them; and then he whispered to me: "Mr Ramadan," the Egyptian teacher of French, "has sold them copies of the French paper he'd set, and the Ministry got to hear about it. The Deputy Minister had cancelled the paper and has bought a different one. The boys won't be able to answer anything!"

While the boys sat, some looking at the paper, others trying to write a few lines, the authorities interviewed the errant French teacher in the Headmaster's office. I never knew exactly what happened but Mr Ramadan's passport was retained so that he couldn't leave the country, he was transferred to Al-Qassim and fined so much that he had to work for two or three years to pay it. This took time and before it was over the candidates had been released from the classrooms and they all went into the schoolyard to hold a protest meeting. There was a lot of shouting and speechifying – I couldn't understand what was being said, but there were some not very serious threats against the authorities "for making them fail" as they thought. Anyway the dignitaries locked themselves into various lavatories and the Headmaster's Office, and the rest of the teaching staff were told to form a sort of Praetorian Guard and to man the staircase, ready to sacrifice themselves in defence of the authorities. When the time came for the next examination, the candidates came yelling through the doors and up the stairs, but when they reached the serried ranks of teachers (I had prudently placed myself rather far back) they calmed down a little and apart from pushing and jostling – and shouting – dispersed into their rooms and got down to the next examination.

Violence was not a feature in any school I ever saw in Saudi Arabia – as I have already explained, Teachers were really respected. I had an early instance of this when the boys were coming into school to register, the week before lessons were to begin. I had a number of boys in my room, when an argument – I had no idea about what – flared up between a Saudi boy and a Syrian. The Saudi boy picked up a metal chair and raised it over his head to smash it over the other boy's head, upon which the Syrian boy drew a knife. The only thing I could do was to spring between then, arms outstretched, and declaim, in accents Olivier might have envied: "Would you strike your teacher?" I dread to think what would have happened in an inner-city school in England, but in Riyadh it worked: weapons were put down, both boys apologized, and even, under my prompting, shook hands, as they did in all the boy's school story books I had devoured as a child.

I was however told of incidents before my arrival. The winter of 1963-64 had been exceptionally cold in Riyadh, with frozen pipes bursting and two policemen frozen to death on Airport Street. The schools, which had fans for cooling, had no means of heating and had become virtually untenable. In the Yamama School, the boys had thrown desks and chairs over the balconies into the courtyard and made a bonfire of them. Some people told me that they threw on their school books as well – but others said that this was an exaggeration.

More serious was the fate that befell an Egyptian teacher four or five years earlier, when the Yamama School was based at different premises. I don't know what he had done but he must have really displeased the boys – because one day they caught him in the yard after school, locked the gates and then used their cars to run him down and kill him. This was so out of character that I would have disbelieved it, had not so many boys assured me that it was true: that man must seriously have offended public opinion.

In those very early days the purchase of examination papers was a normal way to ensure passing the exam. This practice had largely died out before I left and even in my early days it was the internal exams that were "traded". I doubt whether it ever happened with the Public Examinations (Here, as I have already explained, other methods could be used!) Sometimes it was not so much a question of buying an examination paper as of coming to a financial arrangement with a teacher to ensure that promotion would be gained. This was especially marked in the Royal School, where wealthy pupils seemed to be very willing to subsidize helpful teachers. The whole matter reached such a pitch that in the summer of 1966 Ralph Ellis told all his pupils that, if they wanted promotion, they should pay him a thousand riyals – at that time about eighty pounds sterling – and appointed not only a time but a place, his desk in the master's common-room. There was consternation when a long queue of boys, each clutching a sheaf of bank notes, came up it his desk one morning where Ralph counted the money aloud and then entered the sums in a notebook. Remonstrances from other masters were met with the reply: "You're all doing the same thing in secret. I'm doing it openly." The end result was that he was told that he would be transferred to a school in Jeddah the following year; but as he told me, he had no particular wish to remain in the Kingdom. He said, "It's the Royal School or nothing" and did not return to Saudi Arabia after the vacation.

As I found during a short period when, because of the illness of an English teacher – who returned to England to die – I taught in the Royal School myself, some princes were too important, or imagined themselves too important, to come to school at all. But others, no less important, did come and some of them worked hard. Ralph found one of these persistently stretching his legs out from under the desk and warned him, "I shall kick you every time I see you legs out there. Sit up properly." After several severe raps on the ankle the boy sat up properly and kept his feet under the desk; but a day or two later the Senior Master put up a superb notice in the common Room. It said, in English "Teachers must not kick princes."

Prince Homoud ibn Abdul Aziz, the King's youngest brother, who has already featured in these pages, was one who never came to lessons; but he occasionally came to the class. He always showed the most perfect manners, and would, with great courtesy, beg my pardon and ask permission to speak "to my nephews." Thereupon he would beckon to four or five boys who would go out with him, and that would be the last the school saw of them that day.

It should not be assumed that all princes were idle. Many of them were among the hardest workers in the school, with homework very well done and always handed in on time; almost all of them were notable for their excellent manners.

***

When I look back at the years when I was involved in Education in Riyadh, I can see there was always a struggle between those who favoured modernisation and those who preferred the status quo. I was myself a tiny part of the modernization process and in my earlier years I was strongly in favour of it. Before I left I had become less certain; westernization had become so marked and, in many ways, the quality of life had deteriorated so much, that I felt that I and hundreds of people like me had actually done the Saudi people no favour. One would have expected the opponents of this modernization to have been the elderly, bearded, patriarchal figures like those elders from Bureidah I saw in a meeting in the Deputy Ministers office in 1965 – but in fact I learnt that it was not so. In 1968 there was a deliberate attempt to stop the teaching of English in Saudi Schools, and night after night I went to wait in an anteroom of the meetings of the Higher Education Authority who were deliberating this very point. Night after night I was told that the final vote could go either way, which was interesting because half of the Higher Education Committee was composed of Religious Figures and half of Representatives of Higher Boys' and Girls' Education. Some of the Religious group must have been in favour of English because it was absolutely certain that some of the educationalists were against. I was questioned and cross-questioned by a number of young, western-educated young men, speaking very good English themselves, who seemed, in their own minds, to have weighed the West in the Balance and found it wanting. These young men were polite, if unsmiling, but they made it quite clear that they concluded that an excess of westernization would bring more harm than good. Perhaps they were elitists who thought that such arcane knowledge was not for the mass of the people; but I recorded, before I left Riyadh, a trait I suspect has continued and increased in the years since I left: many of the young men and women who had been educated abroad, particularly in the United States, came home determined to resist the introduction of more western ways into the Kingdom. They displayed a strengthened attachment to Arabic traditions, and a readiness to listen, at least, to the call of what thirty years ago I was calling Islamic Fundamentalism. Friends who had sisters or wives in the Women's College at the University told me that by the late 1970s there was a well-supported movement to strengthen Islamic piety and all those aspects of the traditional Arab woman's life which her western "sisters" were shrilling to change.

The vote in the end went on favour of English, but it was very close. Some of the Religious must have been on the side of English, because our arguments in its favour would not have fooled educated "antis" for a moment. It was agreed that a statement should be inserted in all copies of the English syllabus at all levels to the effect that the sole purpose of teaching English in the Kingdom of Saudi Arabia was to enable the Saudi students to refute the lies of the enemies of Islam in the English language.

After 1968 this was the official reason for learning English: for all I know it still is.

Before I had left there had been a lot of progress in streamlining the bureaucracy, simplifying procedures and producing schools on recognizably western models. Proper control was necessary. One of the most extraordinary sights was in the stores of the Ministry of Education, where there were ranks of dust-covered crates marked "Urgent-Rush", which had sat untouched for years. Well-meaning Saudis, on visits to Europe or the United States, had visited Exhibitions, Schools and Training Colleges, and, fired by what they had seen, had returned and persuaded the Ministry to order materials worth millions of pounds. As soon as "education" became big business, less well-intentioned businessmen flocked to Riyadh, sometimes with and sometimes without success, to sell the latest technological miracle to teaching. Nobody seemed to appreciate that the best aid is useless without teachers able to use it. Before I left the then Minister, Dr Abdul Aziz Quwaiter, was famous for his abhorrence of waste of all kinds, and he had put a stop to this indiscriminate buying – which made him somewhat unpopular (a former Ministry Official, who disliked the Minister, described him to me as the most completely honest man in the Government, and said that because of that it was impossible to work with him). These purchases, or the various "commissions" on the purchases, had provided a useful supplementary income for many officials, which reconciled them to their fairly modest salaries. The Minister, recognising that the aids were useless without teachers able to use them, children accustomed to modern devices, and a stable power supply – not then certain in many places – is supposed to have said in a meeting that until he was sure that every school in the Kingdom had good blackboards, good chalk and teachers who knew how to use them, then, and only then, would he be prepared to talk about other aids. At that time the average Saudi school outside the bigger towns was not ready for the introduction of these innovations. The minister was no educational reactionary. I had talks with him as a Governor of the Riyadh Schools, and from these and from educational reports and articles to which he drew my attention, I soon realized that he was extremely sympathetic to the very latest trends; but that what he considered suitable in a small group of experimental private schools, with well paid specially selected teachers, he was not prepared to introduce into the state system – anyway at that time.

Education in Saudi Arabia changed a lot during my years in Riyadh. Many people regarded education as a means to a higher salary, but, again, many did not need the money. I could see growing in the Kingdom a problem that has bedevilled Absolute Government since the days of the early Roman Emperors, and which must have been exacerbated since: what do you do with an educated and comparatively monied middle class which is without political power? We may learn in the future, but we should not forget that, in Saudi Arabia, some of these "discontents" will be Islamic Fundamentalists.

CHAPTER 9
Enjoying Ill Health

The question of public health and the medical services provided in Riyadh illustrates some of the strengths, weaknesses and – perhaps above all – the peculiarities of the society I found. As with education, the medical service was totally free. Even more remarkably, it was available to anybody, Saudi or non-Saudi, who happened to be in the Kingdom. If, for any reason, the required treatment was not available, the Saudi Government paid for it to be carried out abroad – usually but not exclusively in London, Cairo or Beirut.

The "free" medical treatment, however, was confined to Hospitals. There was no equivalent to a National Health Service that includes ordinary doctors – and so there was a very flourishing Private Sector. In addition, some institutions, such as the Ministry of the Interior/Police, the Ministry of Defence and the National Guard, ran their own Medical Branches, with their own hospitals, for the use of the people who worked for them and their families. In fact, these hospitals would treat anybody in an emergency, or even where no emergency existed. For some reason I cannot remember, my mother once had a tooth most expertly extracted by an Afghan dentist in the Police Hospital; and said he was the best dentist she had ever encountered.

There was no "modern" medicine in Riyadh until the city was opened up in the 1950s. In Jeddah, in Mecca and in Medina, there were Western-trained doctors and one would occasionally be brought to Riyadh to treat a member of the Royal Family or a VIP. Local and primitive methods included searing the flesh with a red hot iron (I myself saw young children terribly marked by this) or – in the case for example of a broken leg – calling in a religious teacher to recite verses form the Holy Koran, and getting him to smear the spittle accumulating in his mouth on the broken limb. The ancient use of spittle, for which we have biblical evidence,[1] certainly survived in Riyadh until after my arrival in 1964, although by then there were many doctors, a quite efficient School Health Service and the Shomaisi, the Central Hospital in Riyadh of the Ministry of Health.

I have said that the Hospitals were free, and this included all drugs dispensed within them. The first and only time that I stayed in the Shomaisi Hospital I had gone in to have a tooth removed – it was trying to grow down rather than up – and some bone had to be removed as well. I was given a very nice room with a private bathroom and stayed four or five days. When I left I asked for my bill, imagining that, as in England, those who were given "private facilities" became private patients. Everybody stared at me; a bill? For what? Of course my room was free! I was there because the Director of the Hospital thought it would be more pleasant for me than being in a ward. They all smiled at my naivety.

There were no private hospitals – at least not in Riyadh – in 1964, but they were coming in the years before I left. The Ministry built more hospitals not only in the smaller towns but even in large villages, and they were not on the old Cottage Hospital model, but fair-sized Medical Centres to serve the surrounding countryside. It is easy, provided you have enough money, to build hospitals, but to run them once built is quite another matter. The great dilemma of the Saudi Ministry of Health was how to attract people to work there. The Saudi medical profession was very small and in those days most of the doctors with Saudi nationality were foreign doctors who had been naturalized. But even then there were some, very good, Saudi-born doctors and dentists who had been trained abroad. I don't think, for example, that I could have found anywhere in London a better dentist than Doctor Ahmed Niazi.

I went to Doctor Ahmed one summer because I knew his brother. He had trained in Germany where he told me it was necessary to get a medical degree before specializing in dentistry. Even in the 1970s, he had a totally automated German Dental Clinic (in fact he had two; but the one "upstairs" was not used because he could find nobody trained to operate it). The third, and only other in the Middle East, was in the Palace Hospital of the Shah of Iran). Dr Ahmed's fees to me were high: what he charged rich patients or members of the Royal Family I did not dare to imagine. If he had a patient he considered "poor" the treatment was free. He would only see two patients in the morning and two in the afternoon,

---

[1] See the Gospel according to St Mark, Chapter 7:33-35.

each visit lasting between ninety minutes and two hours, and during each visit he would only deal with one tooth. It was, he explained, a hobby. "Some people," he said, "collect stamps, some take photographs. I fill teeth. I must do the best work possible, medically and aesthetically." As he wanted to do something to a good number of my teeth, and to adjust the gum-line in some places I went to him every day – except Friday – for almost two weeks. I telephoned to my mother to say I should be a few days late in coming home as I was having my teeth "done". When I reached home she said nothing the first evening but after breakfast the next day said, "You didn't tell me you were having your teeth out and false teeth made." When I told her that I hadn't she could hardly believe that these beautiful, shining and regular teeth were my own, so excellent had been Dr Ahmed's work.

Before I left there were medical faculties at the University of Riyadh and at the King Abdul Aziz University in Jeddah, with a fair number of Saudi students, male and female. As I noted at the time, however, there would still not be enough to staff the ninety-seven hospitals then envisaged by the Ministry of Health; this meant an almost permanent dependence on foreign doctors. In my day most of the foreign doctors – quite a number of whom had trained or had experience in England – were from Egypt or Pakistan, being preferred as coming from Islamic countries. But there is more to running a hospital than hiring doctors; locally, nurses were in even shorter supply than doctors. There may have been some Saudi male nurses, but I never came across any and nursing was not really the sort of profession Saudi men found appealing. There must have been a number of girls who would have liked to train as nurses, but parental opposition drastically limited the numbers. Saudi fathers did not want their daughters to work unveiled in hospitals, and so the Nursing Colleges were virtually empty. There was, or course, no difficulty about finding money to hire nurses from abroad, but a substantial number returned home and spread the word that Saudi Arabia was not the place to work. The difficulties were not in the hospitals themselves, but with the social conditions under which the nurses were expected to live. They were given adequate accommodation, but were expected to keep inside it – being taken to and from the hospital by special bus at the beginning and end of each shift. They were not allowed out except at certain times – maybe once a week – when, in a body, they went shopping. They were not permitted any male visitor on any pretext whatsoever. Sometimes a British nurse might be given permission to visit a British family in the evening, but she must be collected and returned by car, and on each journey the wife had to be in the car. Guards – elderly men so old and respectable that they were considered trustworthy – were the doorkeepers of these semi-imprisoned females, like the fabled eunuchs of the Sultan's palace guarding the womens' quarters, and they kept the nurses in as well as the men out. It was all a very far cry from Monica Dickens *One Pair of Feet*.

As with the doctors, there were many nurses from Egypt and from Pakistan. Many of them, especially the Pakistanis, spoke English, but then the Pakistani nurses didn't speak much Arabic, although, as Muslims, they were at least familiar with the language of the Holy Koran, and the Saudi Government was forced to widen its net looking for girls trained to work in the hospitals. Before I left there were large contingents from South Korea, including, in the Shomaisi Hospital, as I shall relate later, nurses to whose care my mother said she owed her life. While the Korean nurses had a mental outlook that seemed to make them amenable to the discipline and rules imposed by the Saudi authorities, they had one major defect. Only a few spoke English and none spoke Arabic, so that they had to learn two new languages at once. English was widely used in the hospitals. I once had to have a piece of bone taken out from inside my nose to relieve the pressure on the sinus, and the Doctor asked – as it would be under a local anaesthetic – whether I would mind if half a dozen medical students attended to "observe" the operation. I said "No," of course, but was quite surprised when the Doctor, who was a Pakistani, delivered his "lecture" to six Arab students in English. It was a little alarming to hear that, "if I cut too deep here, only the hundredth of a millimetre, I could do great damage," but he didn't, and all went well.

There was a similar problem with hospital administrators. I knew a number of well-trained young Saudi administrators, but they were too few to begin to manage even the hospitals in the Riyadh area. Those I talked to spoke with despair of the conditions in which they had to work, a despair not uncommon in those days with the eager young when they come into contact with Real Life. What those young men had learned about Hospital Administration – mostly in America – did not seem to work in Riyadh, because so many things were totally different. They included the patients, the patients' families, the doctors, the nurses, the engineers, public opinion and the Ministry regulations. Similar difficulties were encountered in other Ministries by young men, who had returned from Europe or America, determined to run their office or department according to the methods they had been taught. They soon sank back into apathy, unable to make headway against the entrenched system.

The answer was to try to set up management contracts with various different nationalities, for the running of specific hospitals or groups of hospitals. This was not easy, as the terms could be onerous. In 1978, for example, the Ministry wanted to make it a condition of each contract that, under penalty clauses, any management company taking over the running of a hospital must guarantee to train enough Saudis to take over the complete management of the hospital within a specified time. Of course, this was something the Ministry of Health itself had been singularly unable to achieve. This nonsense was quashed by the British Advisors to the Ministry, but it showed the thinking that existed in the highest quarters.

In my later years the pride of the Saudi Arabian health system, and also its white elephant, was the much-publicized monstrosity, the King Faisal Specialist Hospital. The original idea was simple, and was largely the brainchild of Dr Kenneth Williams, at the time Senior Medical Officer with Vickers Medical, and a former medical research specialist with the Royal Air Force. Williams had the idea of using some of the Middle Eastern oil money to promote medical research, and also to build a completely modern hospital, utilizing every new technological aid. With a very effective salesman from Vickers, Mr Dermod Knox, after discussions in a number of countries, the idea was "sold" to King Faisal, who gave the land and the money needed initially. John Poulson, the then famous but later notorious architect, drew up the first plan, which was for a simple and probably more efficient hospital than the one that was actually built. The scheme was launched and both Kenneth and Dermod arrived to set up the hospital.

It was not long before the scheme went sour. After the Poulson Scandal broke, other people became involved, and the hospital, like the frog in the fable, grew and grew. No Saudi I spoke to, incidentally, could understand the Poulson affair. Such a fuss made, they said, over such tiny amounts of money there must have been something more behind it. They laughed when I said that the scandal had arisen because in England we like to think that there is no corruption of any sort. There were certain figures who had been near King Faisal, and whom he had trusted, who now seized the opportunity to create, in his name, something not only unique in the world of medicine, but something, bigger, grander and much more expensive than anything else. It also seems to have given a number of people the chance to make money on the side, and on a scale that would have paid all John Poulson's sweeteners for millennia. According to the authorities investigating after King Faisal's death, one of the personages involved was to be asked to account for twenty five million dollars which had somehow got onto his personal account – but he chose to leave the Kingdom without giving an explanation.

It was not only in necessary – and unnecessary – medical equipment the hospital showed itself to be outstandingly lavish. An enormous amount equipment was bought – presumably because of the commission it represented – but was adjudged to be not sufficiently advanced and then set aside never to be used. There were container loads of stores delivered without any inventory being made; a store keeper who arrived three or four years after the goods told me that there were no inventories, no lists, and that much of the stuff had never been uncrated.

The outward appearance of the hospital was incredibly opulent. At enormous expense, a Californian company was flown into in to carve the bookshelves in the library: when an unexpected and unprecedented flood of water ruined part of it, the company was flown back to do it again. Large sums of money were spent – not to the best advantage – to put suites of luxurious chairs in the Reception Hall, to make it look like the lounge of a first-class hotel. Unfortunately, as the various suites did not match they had the appearance of a job lot of furniture (which they probably were) bought cheap (which they certainly were not). A splendid lapis-lazuli portrait of King Faisal by the Pakistani artist Gulgee was commissioned to adorn the Entrance Hall. When it was installed it had diamond eyes but – a sign of the times – they were almost immediately stolen when the hospital was opened, and they were replaced by cut glass.

The patients' rooms were also more like a hotel than a hospital, with special closed circuit television showing a number of daily programmes in addition to the National Programmes. When meals were brought in, the food appeared on elegant china – Rosenthal I was told – and the cutlery was gold-plated. Little of the food so pleasantly presented was bought locally: there was a Management Contract with an American company that flew in food daily from New York. The standard of care of the patients was rather uncertain, and depended on who was working at any one time. The American manager had the power to fire immediately anybody who infringed any one of a host of regulations. These were supposed to conform to Saudi feelings of the decorum proper in social behaviour – but things were taken to excess. It was forbidden for members of the opposite sex to be seen speaking to each other; and six Egyptian nurses, whom I was assured by someone working in the hospital were guilty of nothing more serious than a little flirtatious badinage, were sent back to Egypt with the words "Deported for Moral Offences" written across their passports. One heart specialist was sacked and deported at two hours' notice for having had a woman in his room. Before I left Riyadh, it was the exception, rather than the rule, for a foreigner to complete his contract at the King Faisal Specialist Hospital.

What King Faisal had planned as a boon for the Saudi people – and for others working in the Kingdom – turned out to be nothing of the kind. The Government had to bear the enormously increased costs of the hospital, which was soon charging very high fees to help to cover the running expenses – and this put it beyond the reach of all but a small minority. Of course, if anybody was transferred from a state hospital for the specialized treatment available in the King Faisal, the Ministry of Health would pay; but such was the jealousy felt by the state hospitals towards this riyal-guzzling giant that no hospital wanted to refer patients. The Director of the Shomaisi Hospital used to tell people what medical services he could provide for the city of Riyadh if he had the spending of so much money.

My favourite story about the King Faisal Hospital concerns an occasion not long after its opening. The Shah of Iran was making a State Visit and one morning King Khaled took his guest to show him the most advanced and up-to-date hospital in the world. The Shah was dutifully impressed, and said so; "But where are the sick people?" he asked. Up to that point, nobody, it seems, had realised that, however splendid, the facilities that so impressed visiting dignitaries, had been almost completely unused. A ukase went out: patients were snatched out of other hospitals and brought to the King Faisal, so that it could at least give the impression of a working environment.

Some very good doctors and specialists did go to work in the King Faisal Hospital: not all of them stayed, for it was not a happy place to work. To get into the hospital at all was like visiting a prison and to work there must have been like being an inmate. When one arrived at the gates the guards wanted to know the name of the person to be visited: a list would be consulted and sometimes a telephone call might be put through. Anybody able to penetrate the outer defences was given a Security Pass, which had to be worn at all times. Anybody found wandering through the endless corridors without such evidence of probity could find themselves up against armed American Security Guards, some of whom had the appearance of the extras in a "B" movie exposing police brutality in US prisons.

It is only fair to say that in those early days there were some very sick people who owed their lives to the prompt and skilful treatment received in the hospital. Before I left, however, a number of Saudis complained to me of faulty diagnoses; many, with pull in the right places, were going to the then very modern Ministry of Defence Hospital – which was under British management, and where standards were believed to be higher.

Except for patients in Intensive Care, at the King Faisal Hospital there was always the possibility of being turned out, or transferred to another hospital in the middle of treatment – because a VIP was coming in who needed a whole wing, if not the whole hospital. Late in 1979 the King's elder brother went into hospital and the whole rhythm of the routine was abandoned. Early in 1980 the King himself was rushed in, in a very serious condition, owing to the faulty treatment by his private medical staff. On this occasion the whole hospital was taken over: a number of the King's brothers and senior cabinet ministers simply moved in with their staffs. It was all a very far cry from what King Faisal had envisaged. Nobody, least of all in Riyadh, would have begrudged the King any amount of medical attention; and King Khaled was himself the last man who would have wanted this to be at the expense of anybody else needing treatment; but I was told by somebody who had been sent to examine the Clinic in the Royal Palace, and the Royal Ambulance Plane that the first was filthy and that both were full of time-expired drugs. Perhaps more care should have been given to the King's health from the point of view of preventative medicine.

***

As noted earlier, bodies other than the Ministry of Health ran their own medical Facilities; as a matter of prestige, the Ministry of the Interior, the Ministry of Defence and the National Guard wanted to offer "private" facilities to all men who worked for them and all their families. That this was extended to "friends" was a very Saudi phenomenon. (How else would my mother have gone to the Police Hospital?) In the 1970s there was a move by the then Minister of Health to rationalize the whole thing and cut out unnecessary expenditure by putting all hospitals under the overall control of the Ministry of Health. But Prestige stood in his way –

linked of course to the commissions paid to all members of the various committees involved in the negotiations for the building, equipping and management of these hospitals.

I was told that when the Minister of Health had approached King Faisal, the King agreed that, for example, there was no need to have four nuclear medical centres in the city – as might easily happen unless the Ministry of Health drew up some sort of master plan. The story, which reached me through a Prince who was with Prince Abdullah ibn Abdul Aziz (now the King) at the time went like this. When the then Minister called on the King's brother with a personal letter suggesting that the National Guard should put its medical plans under the Ministry's control, the answer sent back was in these terms: "Tell the donkey who is bringing this reply back to you that the National Guard Hospitals will not be under anybody's control;" after which, as was natural, there was no holding back the Ministry of Defence, although it was eventually agreed that the Ministry of Health would approve offers from international bidders. In fact the Ministry was given no freedom at all in this regard. It was widely believed and reported in Riyadh that, when bids for a hospital were being discussed at a Cabinet Meeting and one bid was on the point of approval, the Minister of Health was suddenly presented with another and very much more expensive bid from the German company, Philip Holzmann. He was told to approve that bid within two weeks. At subsequent Cabinet meetings the Minister was said to have protested that there was nothing in the offer to justify the increased price, and the company were not specialists in hospital building. After a few weeks, however, a paper was slammed down in front of him and he was ordered to sign it at once – thereby approving the Philip Holzmann offer, not only for the Military Hospital in Riyadh, but also for five other hospitals as well.

The cost of some of these hospitals was staggering. I knew something of the private hospital sector because I knew people who were involved, or were planning to become involved in it. I was told – and noted down – that at 1979-1980 prices it was possible to build and equip completely a hospital of European Standard in Saudi Arabia for a cost of half a million Saudi Riyals per bed – exclusive of land and housing for Doctors, Nurses and Ancillary workers. It should therefore have been possible to build a 500-bed hospital for two hundred and fifty million riyals. Given the land and staff housing, plus some fancy additions – and commissions which would undoubtedly be paid – it would probably be reasonable to revise the price upwards to five hundred million riyals. Yet when – by what chance I cannot now recall – I had sight of Philip Holzmann's bid for the housing (only) at the new Hofuf General Hospital, the price, including a twenty-five million riyal "contingency fund" was over seven hundred million riyals – a sum for which any company working under normal Western conditions could have built the housing and the hospital and equipped the hospital completely.

But even these sums are petty when compared to the costs of the National Guard Hospital. One of the National Guard Officials told me the total overall cost was four and a half million per bed; and commissions had to be paid to some very high personages indeed, both in Saudi Arabia and in Belgium. I could not then and obviously cannot now confirm the figures but it is certainly true that the Belgian Consortium, after taking its down payment, immediately went bankrupt and the rescue operations became a very involved affair, not really solved by the time I left. The chief result of this was that a lot of officials had a lot more money than they had had before and some very rich men because even richer. Incidentally there would – in time – have been an improvement in the medical care of quite a lot of people, but I don't think that I am being unduly cynical in saying that this was incidental. I shall be returning to the question of this payment of commissions in a later chapter.

***

In Riyadh and other cities with sizable populations there were large numbers of private "clinics" which in England would be called surgeries. At least nominally, the Ministry of Health was in control, and it did regulate fees: but in my day there were unscrupulous doctors who got round this by charging the fee for the "consultation" – which might be no more than the question, "What's the matter with you?" – and a second fee for doing something: a harmless injection was a favourite ploy. From time to time, the Ministry would introduce new regulations, which might for example make it illegal for a doctor working in a Government Hospital to run a private clinic on the side – because the excessively long hours he would be working might affect his efficiency; but usually such regulations fell into abeyance. The doctors' surgeries always seemed full, in spite of the obvious attractions of the completely free Outpatients' Department at the local hospital: in Riyadh, at the Shomaisi Hospital, the numbers attending the very large outpatients' department literally ran into the thousands every day.

I have never seen it stated – and may seem rather critical – but it is my opinion that a lot of Arabs are hypochondriacs. I can understand completely why so many Saudi women go "to the doctor": it is a legitimate outing and they can sit in the waiting room for ages talking and gossiping with their friends. I was told, and I have no reason to disbelieve it, that some women went to the doctor every day.

What makes me stigmatize a whole race with the term "hypochondriac" was the regularity with which my friends and colleagues sought medical advice. After I had been a few weeks at the Yamama School, I was mildly rebuked for missing one day. The fact was that I had been in bed with a sharp bout of influenza. On the following day, still feeling very much under the weather, I struggled back to school, not wanting to miss the classes I had to teach that day. I had to see the Headmaster who asked why I had not been at School the day before. When I explained that I was ill in bed at home with a fever, I was told that that was wrong. I could not be ill in bed without a doctor's certificate; and to get such a certificate I had to come to the school to collect a letter from the Headmaster – which I must take to the doctors in the Zone Office, who would then issue me with the certificate. It was in vain that I pointed out that if I had been well enough to do that, I should have been well enough to come into school and take my classes. My arguments were dismissed as irrelevant. The Ministry had laid down certain regulations and, willy-nilly, I must obey them. Some years later there was an English teacher who was really ill but who had not followed the regulations; and he was to be fined for was called in officialese, "lack of cooperation," until I managed to get a doctor's letter authenticated by the Zone Office. I was able to save his salary but not his reputation.

But what took me a long time to come to terms with was the way some of my Arab colleagues at the Yamama School would come in looking reasonably well; but, after sitting chatting for a while they would say something like, "I had a bad night," or "I've got a sore throat," or "I'm not feeling very well – so I'll get a letter from the Headmaster and go to the doctor's." Sometimes they would come back from the doctor and would sit talking to their friends and drinking tea before departing on sick leave, which would last for two or three days. Having been brought up in the tougher tradition that if you could keep on your feet you could go into class, this attitude was incomprehensible to me; but perhaps it is now found nearer home than Saudi Arabia.

This preoccupation with health perhaps explains why private doctors' surgeries were so full. I could not then and do not now believe that all the people who thronged them were actually ill: I have already surmised that many of the women patients went to the waiting rooms for social rather than medical reasons. We have heard stories of doctors' waiting rooms in England unnecessarily crowded; but in England these are National Health Service patients, and their visit is free. In Riyadh each visit was costing at least several pounds, and there would inevitably be prescriptions for medicines (did the doctors and the pharmacists have some private arrangement?) These surgeries were very informal by western standards, and no idea of confidentiality ever seemed to occur to anybody. I have sat talking to doctors while patients came and went: the average consultation might be three or four minutes, while the money piled up – rather like a City of London wine bar at lunchtime. I have seen a workman whose fractured arm had been set for about sixty-five pounds – a considerable sum thirty-five years ago – refused permission to leave until one of his workmates had gone off to find the money and brought it back to ransom him.

But these strictures should not detract from the fact that, during my years in the Kingdom, the Ministry of Health did an excellent job in creating what was then becoming an efficient service under very difficult circumstances. By the time I left Riyadh I felt that anybody who lived in a major town could get very good medical treatment. There was talk, at the beginning of the nineteen eighties, of imitating Australia by providing a Flying Doctor service. I don't know what happened but it would have been a great benefit in the country districts, for although most people were within reach of a well-built and lavishly equipped hospital or clinic, it had not been possible to find good staff to live and work in the backwoods. It was a Muslim who pointed out to me a fact, so obvious in itself that I had never noticed it, that Islam does not provide the same sort of missionaries as Christianity does. There are, of course, plenty of missionaries in the purely religious sense; but Islam has no equivalent to the teaching or medical missions so long a feature of Christianity. I think now as I thought then that Christian non-proselytising orders could have come and set up medical centres in "unsocial" places; but the Saudi Arabian authorities, heavily influenced by the Religious Leaders, would never have stood for such a thing.

Before I left, the Ministry of Health was working well – and successfully – in the area of "Rural Health" and sending teams out all round the Kingdom to undertake health surveys. A friend of mine who worked at the Shomaisi hospital spent several weeks in the North as a member of a mobile X-ray team, visiting the remotest villages to administer compulsory Tuberculosis checks. The Ministry of Education Health Department also did much good work in their efforts to screen all school children for dental and optical problems. Eyes were a major problem in Saudi Arabia, especially in the country areas, and in some villages they found a very high incidence of trachoma. The Ministry had the records by the early nineteen eighties, but that didn't mean that the work of cure and prevention was far advanced: too often urgent programmes were stultified by the sheer bureaucratic process. In the meantime the situation could deteriorate: a condition ignored will get worse – but not so badly or as quickly as one wrongly treated. For example, in a village hardly fifty miles from Riyadh, a team of medical students from Riyadh University not only discovered that, to a greater or lesser degree, 90 per cent of the children were suffering from trachoma, but also that the only treatment given by a semi-trained Nursing Aide (who could only read Arabic) was a cream marked – in English and in red – "DANGER. NOT TO BE USED NEAR THE EYES."

I cannot complete this chapter without describing an occasion when, quite fortuitously, I played a small part in medical developments in Riyadh. In an earlier chapter I wrote about a time when I was ill with food poisoning for a long while – but did not then give any medical details. Because I was taken ill at the beginning of the holidays and could not see the Ministry of Education doctors, I went instead to a British doctor with Airwork, a company working at the Airport with Saudi Air Force planes, who told me that there was a new French miracle drug. The dosage depended on body weight, so I was duly weighed and told that I must take forty tablets, four a day for ten days. In fact, as I discovered later, he had got the decimal point in the wrong place and had prescribed ten times the proper dose. I sent my houseman to the chemists with the prescription, but when he came back he had only tablets for three days as the chemist had refused to give him more.

Having been brought up with the idea that you did whatever the doctor told you, I duly took the tablets for three days and, although I was feeling very bad by the end of the third day, I sent my houseman back to the chemist – where, again, he was given a three days' supply. On the fourth and fifth day I felt really ill, with a sort of paralysis coming over me. I couldn't eat any solid food, and just sipped liquids through a straw:

the tablets had to be put on the back of my hand from which I could take the tablet into my mouth as I could not use my hands at all. On the sixth day an Anglo-Dutch couple[2] came to see me and said they would take my mother straight to the doctor. He didn't come to see her but sent a nurse to say, "Tell David to stop taking the tablets." I stopped, and after a few days began to feel better. After two or three weeks I felt able to visit a local private hospital where I knew the Syrian Director. I told him what had been wrong with me and what medicine had been prescribed. "Quite right," he said, "I should have prescribed it myself." When I told him I had been told to take it for ten days, he said "Nonsense. No doctor would tell you that. You can't take it for more than one day." When I produced the prescription and handed it to him silently he looked at it and said, "Good God! Well, if you'd have taken all those you'd be dead. In fact you would probably have died before you finished the course!" Shortly afterwards, I was shown the English version of a notice from the Ministry of Health to all doctors in Riyadh, in fact possibly throughout the Kingdom. It was to this effect: "In Saudi Arabia there are a wide number of drugs available from different countries, and there may be some which are unfamiliar to you. Great care should be taken if you are prescribing a drug which is new to you, as there has recently been a near-fatal accident in the over-prescribing of an unfamiliar drug." I felt at the time and still feel that I must have been the "near fatal accident" which didn't happen, and I hope – as a result of the Ministry's notice – nothing like that happened to anybody else. I may say that the British doctor who had made the mistake never came near me to ask how I was, and, in any social gathering, kept well out of the way of my mother and myself.

There is no doubt in my mind that the Saudi authorities were sincere in their attempts to improve the health of the people, and I am equally sure that they were generally successful. The extravagances I have mentioned were good subjects for local gossip, but, because the authorities had huge sums of money at their disposal, they did not in any way hamper the progress the Ministry of Health was making. The Ministry deserves great credit for its work in those years when I was in Riyadh – and I am sure this has continued ever since.

---

[2] They were the Boswinkels, who might have been described as being "prominent socially" in Riyadh. Adele Boswinkel, who was a great friend of my mother, was the sister of George Blake, the Russian Agent. This became public knowledge when he was spectacularly "sprung" from prison by the Soviets: the British Embassy in Jeddah were thrown into panic.

I cannot end this chapter without telling the story of how the South Korean nurses saved my mother's life – or so she believed. She was taken ill one morning and I took her straight to the Shomaisi Hospital where an English doctor diagnosed a heart attack. He said, however, that she would be happier at home, and so she should go home – but if there was any reoccurrence of the trouble I was to bring her back to the hospital immediately. Sure enough, two or three days later, she had another attack in the evening. Jordanian neighbours procured me an ambulance and, on arrival at the hospital, Mother was rushed into intensive care.

Normal visiting is not considered appropriate in Intensive Care but the doctors and nurses gave me a white coat and a clipboard and, so disguised, I spent most of each day beside Mother's bed. But one morning I was barred: the Director of Intensive Care, who had been away, returned, and said I could not see my mother. She sent a message out to me by one of the nurses: if I couldn't get permission to visit her she would discharge herself and go to die at home. I saw Dr Saddiqui, the Edinburgh trained Head of Cardiology to ask his help, but he could do nothing as he and the Intensive Care Director were of equal rank. "You must go to the Director of the Hospital," he said, "he can arrange it for you." So I went off to wait until the Hospital Head was giving public audience. When he arrived I explained the situation and asked him to overrule the Intensive Care Director. He thought for a moment.

"No," he said, "I don't think that is a good idea. If your mother was in the VIP wing you could live there with her and your servants could bring in the food your mother would like."

I pointed out the obvious snag, "but my mother is not a VIP."

He looked at me slightly coldly. "In my hospital," he said, "I decide who is a VIP and who is not." He spoke rapidly into the telephone to two or three people. "Well," he said, putting down the telephone, "I have arranged a room in the VIP wing for your mother. Do you know it? On the top floor turn right when you come out of the lift."

"Thank you very much!" I said, "and when do you think they will move her?"

"If you go up there when you leave here" he said, "you might meet her on the way."

I tried to articulate my thanks and to say how grateful my mother would be, but he held up his hand. "You are not like a Westerner," he said, "You care for your mother like an Arab. You're doing your best for her and so we must do our best to help you."

I did not actually live in the VIP suite. My mother insisted that I should go home on alternate nights, but Abdou and his wife brought in our meals. Mother was nearly three weeks there; having had a third, mild, heart attack in Intensive Care, she had a fourth – also mild – on the VIP wing, but she made an amazing recovery. She herself put this down to the care she received from the South Korean nurses. They were, she said, the most efficient nurses she had ever come across and by far the kindest and most caring.

She was, of course, in bed when she got home, and remained there for months. We had an Egyptian doctor who came twice a day, between seven and eight in the morning and about seven o'clock at night, and took her blood pressure and prescribed medicines – from a stock of over twenty – which I should give her during the next twelve hours. Every four hours (except at two o'clock in the morning if she were asleep) I took her temperature, and, in one of those large Office Diaries with a page for each day, I entered all those medical facts.

Life became, in a way, increasingly bleak, and Mother did seem to be "sinking": I was told that she was in a gradual decline, and would pass away very quietly, "anytime, but no longer than eighteen months from the first attack." Then, one day, Mansour Shalhoub came to see me. "The top heart specialist in the world," he said, "dealing with older people is being flown in from the Heart Centre in Houston, to see six elderly princes and princesses. Would you like him to see your mother?"

"I'd love it." I replied, "But I can't afford top specialist in the world flown in from Houston."

"Oh, you wouldn't have to pay anything," he declared, "the princes and princesses aren't paying. It's the Cabinet Office which is paying. If you agree I'll speak to the prince" (that would have been Prince Ahmed ibn AbdulAziz) "and he'll have your mother's name put on the list."

When the World's Top Expert came he was a most charming young man. He talked to mother for over an hour and examined the medical records I had kept. He cut out most of the drugs completely and advised her on her diet; "Eat and drink what you enjoy. At your age you will benefit most from what you want to eat. If someone tells you something will be good for you, and you don't like it, it wont be." This advice seems to be so sensible that I stick to it myself religiously. He also said that he would notify the hospital and the airline that she would be fit to travel after a month, and he gave me a prescription for tablets to be taken, one per day, for thirty days. "Can I get more after thirty days if we need more?" I asked. "No," he said, "You may not take these tablets for more than thirty days."

The next morning I took the prescription to my local pharmacy, where it was taken away into some back room. After a short time the pharmacist returned, and said he couldn't dispense this drug. I should have to go to another pharmacy – which he named – at the bottom of Airport Street. I duly drove down there and, once again, the prescription was taken into a back room. This time, however, the man came back and asked me to call for the tablets the next day after six o'clock.

"But you're closed at six o'clock," I said.

"Yes," he replied, "please come after we are closed."

I couldn't understand this but did as he had asked. When I arrived at six o'clock the next evening I vaguely noticed a Police Car parked close by but thought nothing of it. I knocked at the door, which opened and I went into a darkened shop. On the counter was a large ledger which, after I had been given a small bottle containing thirty purple tablets, I was asked to sign. Then, again in a sort of hushed silence, I was ushered out of the shop. As I drove up Airport Street I became aware that the police car was following me: in fact it followed me until I stopped outside my own front gate, after which it just drove away. What were those purple tablets, that I had to collect when the pharmacy was closed, and which necessitated a police escort?

Whatever they were, they worked. After a week my mother said: "I've been living in a fog. Now my mind is clearing," and she was her acutely intelligent self before she had finished the course. As for living only eighteen months, she actually managed eighteen years. But she never forgot the kindness and the excellent nursing she had received when she needed it, from those South Korean nurses in the Shomaisi Hospital in Riyadh.

CHAPTER 10
Safely Through This Foreign Land

The subject of security is so wide that I have decided to divide it into two parts – unlike Caesar, who divided Gaul into three – and so in this chapter I shall think about my personal position and that of people both in Riyadh and elsewhere in Saudi Arabia. I go on to discuss how the situation deteriorated in the course of my stay and how, in my last years, I came to the sad conclusion that the total security of earlier times had been undermined, largely due to the prevalence of dishonesty. I should stress that, even then, conditions were much better than those in, say, London or New York.

I put deteriorating standards of those later days squarely down to the influx of "foreigners" – not so much to the fact that they had "corrupted" the Saudis, as that much petty crime was committed by those same incomers. I do not say that no Saudi ever committed a crime, but by 1980 it was certainly difficult to convey to newcomers that, in 1964, it was not just common honesty that prevailed, but rather an honesty of the most scrupulous and highest order. It had been a boast in the Kingdom that if anybody put a bag of gold down in the street and forgot it, he could come back a day, a week, a month or even a year later, and the gold would still be where it had been left, - unless it had been moved to the side of the street to stop it blocking the way. That might not have been the experience fifteen years later; but I would like to give a few examples of the sort of standards and behaviour that were the norm in my early days in Riyadh, examples of things that happened to me personally. The first is from the summer of 1965, when I had been at work all day correcting examination papers in the school in University Street described in an earlier chapter. I was going to dinner with an English friend, Brian Walters, who lived near the Shomaisi Hospital. That day the teachers had all been paid – in cash of course – and with my salary in my briefcase I hailed a taxi and was driven to Brian's house. I had, as I have said, been working hard and I was tired. I put the briefcase behind me on the rear window - and forgot it. We were drinking coffee after dinner when the front doorbell rang, and shortly afterwards Brian's houseman appeared. There was, he said, a taxi driver at the door: he had found a briefcase with a lot of money and some papers in English. He had had only one foreign passenger whom he had brought here, and it must be his briefcase. The driver wanted to know whether the man was still here or where he could be found. There was some three thousand riyals in the case: six months salary to most of the Saudis employed in government ministries, while the standard fare for a private taxi was two riyals for any journey within the city limits, irrespective of length. Such a sum meant a lot to me, but I had still forgotten it – but, although the driver finally accepted a very small "reward", he brushed aside my thanks saying that it was only his duty to look for me and return my property. I spoke about this to several Saudis who also could not see why I was making such a to-do about what was, to them, a perfectly natural occurrence. That was nothing, they said; Sheikh Mohammed Al-Rajhi, Sheikh Saleh's brother, had put a brown paper parcel, containing several hundred thousand riyals, on the roof of a taxi, while he looked for change to pay the driver. He also forgot it, and only realized, a little later, that it was missing. His distressed report to the Police Station coincided with that of an equally distressed taxi-driver, who had brought in this large sum of money left behind by an unknown passenger. I told everybody that I doubted very much if a London taxi-driver, finding a lot of cash and some papers in Arabic, would be ready to spend his time driving round looking for the owner – in fact if he handed it in to a Lost and Found office the owner could consider himself fortunate.

Two or three years later, I was down town with my mother in the Kuwaiti Suq. This was a covered market on the southern side of Bat'ha whose name derived from the fact that, at one time, the goods sold there had come from Kuwait. My mother had been asked to furnish and equip two large "boarding houses," intended for British workers with the Airport and the Air Force who were out on "Bachelor Status." We were looking for towels: we wanted a lot and so I had several thousand riyals in my pocket, and had already made a few small purchases at other stalls. Having reached the stall we were looking for, we asked the stallholder to see his towels and soon there were twenty or thirty different ones displayed in a great heap. My mother chose three or four and asked for a large number of each. The stallholder dug around in boxes and produced what we wanted. I dug around in my pocket and found it empty.

I knew perfectly well that I had had the money because I had bought things at other stalls, and all I could think was that I had somehow left the wad of banknotes at the last one: I knew I must go back for it. Trying not to alarm my mother, I said something like, "I must go back to the last stall, I must have left my money there," and turned to the stallholder who was putting the towels into parcels the market porters could manage: "Please wait a minute," I said. He had either understood my looks or the English word "money" because he said, "If you want your money it's here. You put it down when you came in," and, hauling away the pile of towels, he scrabbled underneath and produced my money. He told me I had had the notes in my hand and had put them down on the side of his stall before asking to see the towels. Once again when I told my Saudi friends about the incident they could see nothing in it that was not perfectly normal; but I still cannot help reflecting that not every (every? any?) stallholder in an English market would have been so scrupulous if a foreigner "forgot" over a thousand pounds in cash - for I had had absolutely no idea of what I had done with the money until the man told me and showed me where I had put it.

Perhaps a third personal example is enough. I had gone to the Riyadh Supermarket – the first supermarket in the city – at the bottom end of Airport Street. I don't know why I was in a taxi because in my mind's eye on my return I can see my shocking pink Cadillac outside the house. Anyway I was in a taxi, which had been loaded by boys from the supermarket. A visitor had just arrived at the gate and, what with paying the taxi-driver and greeting the visitor, I took no notice of the houseboys as they carried the numerous parcels of food into the house. The visitor stayed only long enough for a cup of coffee; and I went into the kitchen to see that everything had been put away properly. Opening the door of the freezer I found almost nothing there. I called the cook.

"Where's all the frozen food." I asked him.

"What frozen food?" he said

"There was a whole carton of frozen food." I began to enumerate: "meat, fish, sausages, peas, beans, strawberries and some other things."

"There was no frozen food," he said decidedly. "You bought a lot of tins, tea, coffee, sugar, butter, biscuits and some jars of pickles. No frozen food."

A minute later I was in my car on the way back to the supermarket, where I told my story. The manager remembered most of my purchases and summoned the boys who carried the goods out to the taxi: they were sure I had not left a carton behind.

I was very vexed by this loss but it was not a very serious one; so I repeated my order and duplicates of the missing items were duly bought to the cash desk. There, however, there was an argument. The owner-manager refused absolutely to let me pay for the goods. I didn't have them when I reached home, he said, and so they must have been left outside the Supermarket by the carelessness, if not by the actual dishonesty of his employees. (There was no suggestion that, after buying the goods I was then responsible for them and should have kept an eye on them myself). It was, he insisted, the duty of the supermarket to make good my loss. The degree of trust that this showed was something that has not existed in the West for a long time.

The story, of course, did not end there – this was in the Middle East. I had hardly got home and seen the second lot of frozen items safely in the freezer before the first lot turned up. My taxi-driver had taken a fare to the Airport, and when he had unloaded the luggage he had found a carton of food. Remembering where he had taken an earlier fare from the supermarket, he automatically came round to my house, full of apologies for not having checked all the cartons had been taken out when my houseboys were taking the food into the house. Once again, here was an example of a man going out of his way to perform an act of honesty – the sort of behaviour we had grown to expect in those simple days.

For my own sake I should add that I went back to the supermarket the next morning to tell them what had happened. The manager was relieved to find that his staff were blameless, and therefore accepted payment for the second lot of goods.

In case it seems odd that I should walk about with several hundred pounds in cash stuffed carelessly into a pocket or clutched absent-mindedly in my hand, I should like stress that this underlines my main point. My rather careless attitude was the result of living in a society such as used to exist in Riyadh, where I felt so totally "safe" that the idea of anything unpleasant happening didn't enter my thoughts. I knew, subconsciously - for one just didn't "think" about such things – that if I dropped a wad of notes in the road somebody would pick it up and run after me to give it back. I suppose that this atmosphere of total honesty did make me careless. I was reminded of this sometime in the late 1970s, when a complete stranger came up to me in Heathrow Airport to tell me that I had a lot of money sticking out of my breast pocket, warning that I was likely to be robbed in London if people saw me with so much cash. The reason was that, in the Middle East but especially in Saudi Arabia, we lived in a cash society: cheques were never used for ordinary purchases, and, although credit cards were coming in, and would, I am sure, have been accepted in the Intercontinental Hotel, no ordinary Saudi shop would have recognized their validity. We lived, as I said, in a cash society and we paid cash for what we bought.[1]

I used to read accounts in the English newspapers of people convicted of shoplifting while they had a lot of money on their persons; quite often they were from the Middle East. They were not only used to carrying a lot of money on them, but, alarmed perhaps by the stories of lawless London, were afraid to leave their money in their hotel. This does not mean that I am condoning shoplifting in any sense; call it whatever you like it is stealing. There used, however, to be a convention that when one had made a number of purchases in a shop, one received a small gift from the shopkeeper. In the larger supermarkets this was not the practice – at least with Western customers; but both there and in smaller food shops one saw parents helping their children to sweets or small ice-cream cones in full view of the manager and the staff, and I have myself, on a hot day, drunk a can of chilled lemonade or cola handed to me by one of the assistants as a "perk" for buying from that shop. I remember when my mother had bought a lot of soft-furnishings from a shop in Wazir street for a small compound she was equipping for a British company, the Syrian manager not only presented her with two large and beautiful arm-chairs, but asked me whether he might give her a personal present, and, when I said "of course", took both of us to a nearby jewellers where my mother chose a particularly attractive – and expensive – gold bracelet.

There was however, even remembering the custom of getting a "reward" for shopping, no excuse whatever for shoplifting. The number of offenders from Saudi Arabia used to be very few indeed and, on the

---

[1] My mother did not shop a lot but she was what might be called an "impulse" buyer. In other words, if she saw something she liked she would buy it. When she lived in Riyadh this meant that she always carried a good sum of money "in-case." When she visited England she no longer, of course, had the monthly accounts to which she had been accustomed – accounts which were sent to her bank who paid them for her: this meant that in London she always had a lot of cash. I remember her horrifying some of the family by saying airily at a family party "I don't feel comfortable unless I have at least a thousand pounds in my purse."

rare occasions when a Saudi National was caught, critical reports in the English newspapers were nothing compared to the apocalyptic denunciations appearing in the Saudi press. I was assured that one Saudi, in a reasonably responsible government post, who had been convicted, with his wife, of shoplifting in a London store, was stripped of his post on his return to the Kingdom, banned from any future government employment and his passport, together with that of his wife, was confiscated - so that they could never again travel abroad, and while in another country, bring such disgrace upon their own.

So far I have been describing the almost idyllic situation in which those of us lucky enough to be in Riyadh in those early days lived. Things had changed – very much for the worse – before I left; but, as I explained at the beginning of this chapter, I put the deterioration down to the "foreigners" who had flooded into the Kingdom. There were break-ins, burglaries and lots of thefts from cars. Before I left there had been no reports of muggings or robberies involving any personal violence, although there were rumours of pickpockets.

The thefts from cars were not just from those parked in lonely or isolated places. On Sitteen Street, close to my house in Malaz, where one could drive around for ages waiting for a car to move away and leave a parking space, cars were robbed regularly. A friend who lost his brief-case containing money, papers and passport, was assured at the local police station – where he encountered several others who had lost items from their cars on the same street and in the same morning - that the thieves could probably find some way of returning the papers and the passport, because all they wanted was the money.

Small items were regularly taken from cars at night – hubcaps, the caps of petrol fillers, windscreen wipers – those were the sort of things that vanished. Sometimes windows were forced open and car radios or cassette players removed – plus anything of interest in the glove compartment. I lost a number of cassettes that way myself. In a time of petrol shortage (yes, improbable though it sounds, owing to some mishandling of supplies, on more than one occasion we did have a petrol-shortage in Riyadh) petrol might have been siphoned out of a car at night. All this, however, was as nothing compared to the story told to me by the resident of a fashionable flat on Campden Hill, whose neighbour had her Jaguar steadily vandalized, night after night, until there was little but a shell left – even the wheels had gone.

Such thefts were not necessarily at night. One evening in '77 my driver had come to collect me from an office down town, and brought his wife, who was sitting in the back of the car with their baby. It was about half past nine, and in those days all the shops were open, lights were blazing and the pavements thronged with people. While my driver came upstairs to tell me the car was there, his wife saw a hand come through the window and open the glove compartment. The girl naturally screamed and the hand vanished at once; but when we came down a few minutes later we found a sandal left in the gutter between the car and the kerb. Presumably there was a sneak-thief with one foot bare roaming Riyadh that evening.

There must have been thefts from cars in the "good old days" but they were very rare and caused quite a sensation. When an American friend, Bill Royer (then the United States Information Service man in Riyadh, and later a hostage in the American Embassy in Teheran) visited Dara'iyah he had had a number of items taken from his car, parked beside the ruins, including, as I remember, the light meter from his camera. He reported the theft to the local authorities, and saw an elderly man who was the local governor. After one or two people had tried to make out that Bill must have been mistaken, it became quite plain that everybody had a very good idea of who the culprit was. It was suggested that Bill should leave the matter in the governor's hands and that his belongings would be returned to him, while the boy who had taken them would be suitably punished: so he did, and they were, and so, presumably was the boy. We decided that it was probably a case of kleptomania, because Bill felt sure that his had not been the first complaint, and that the village regarded the whole episode as a disgrace and something to be kept quiet.

I don't know how the boy was punished. A lot has been said and written about the barbarity of the amputation of a thieving hand. It was a punishment occasionally inflicted, but it was not as simple or inevitable as it has been made to seem. Certainly, in the old days, in the absence of a confession, the proof of theft required the testimony of at least four "reliable" witnesses. On conviction, for a first offence, the thief was fined, and had to make restitution: after a second conviction the punishment was the same, with a short term of imprisonment added. Only such a thief so persistent as to be convicted a third time had his hand amputated.[2] Incidentally the theft of food by a man who was

---

[2] I once encountered a taxi-driver – with an automatic car – who had both hands missing. I didn't like to ask him whether he had been convicted of theft four times!

himself really hungry or had a really hungry family was not considered as theft.

In the old days I never heard of a burglary but in 1977 I heard of two within ten days. In the first a British couple, whom I knew well, went to their local supermarket after their evening meal and were away about three quarters of an hour. They may not have locked up properly because they had been so long in Riyadh that they were accustomed to leaving everything open. When they returned home the house seemed to be in order, but one or two items in the bedroom were out of place; and investigation showed that the wife's jewellery – including some recently inherited from her mother – had disappeared. The thieves seemed to have known exactly where the jewellery was, which suggested that somebody had made a careful investigation.

A few days later I was starting to tell this shocking story to my old friend Sheikh Mohammed Al-Khamis when he stopped me saying that it was nothing compared to what had happened to him in his house two nights before. He and his wife and their baby slept in a room upstairs, and the next room, into which there was a communicating door, was his dressing room. Both rooms had doors opening onto the landing; and in the dressing room there was a freestanding safe containing a lot of cash and his wife's not inconsiderable collection of jewels. On the previous morning he had woken up at the usual time and gone downstairs – the servants were already in the kitchen. On entering the sitting room he found the safe, open and empty, in the middle of the room. The thieves had entered the house, gone upstairs, carried the safe – which was very heavy – downstairs and had opened it quietly at their leisure. Suspicion – perhaps naturally – fell on Mohammed's new Egyptian servants, (whom I admit I had not liked) but nothing could be proved. In fact, the police were sure that the servants had had nothing to do with the theft itself, but suspected that they had somehow been involved in giving the necessary information to the real thieves. Suspicion often fell on the servants whenever there was a theft, and I suppose this was inevitable because there were two kinds of servants. There was the sort who worked for one master for years and became almost part of the family; but there was another sort who moved from household to household, never staying anywhere for more than a few months, perhaps only a few weeks. Most, even of the best sort, were not above taking advantage of the odd "perk." I was told by the manager of the Riyadh Supermarket, in the days when it was the only one in the City and nearly all the foreigners shopped there, that there was a small discount for ready cash, which was given to housemen who had come in to do the shopping, or just to push the trolley round. Only Abdou, my incomparable Yemeni, refused his percentage commission - instead beating down the price and passing the benefit to me.

Organised gangs had certainly arrived in Riyadh before I left, but I am positive that Saudis themselves were not involved. I think there was so much money about (even if the amounts were exaggerated in the stories that circulated) that it served as a magnet to petty, and to not so petty criminals. They must have thought that the openness with which money was treated in Riyadh made it a paradise for the thief. The way money was carried about must have been unlike the practice anywhere else. I myself saw a man cash in a large cheque in the Arab Bank: when the cash came – which I guessed to be something more than a hundred thousand pounds sterling – and was placed in great piles on the bank counter, the man began by trying to stuff it into a big plastic bag. Eventually the bag broke and the money fell to the ground. Nothing daunted, he looked around for a suitable receptacle and found a large metal waste paper bin: this he casually emptied onto the floor, pushed his money into the bin and walked out of the bank with it. Another time, when I was in the same bank, waiting for something or other as the bank was officially closed, there was an altercation at a side door, and an elderly Bedouin pushed in, followed by a younger man who looked like his son. Both were wearing very expensive cloaks and the younger carried a sack, which he heaved onto the counter.

"What's this?" asked a clerk.

"Put it on my account," said the old man, turning to go, followed by his silent son.

The clerk began to expostulate, asking him to wait while the money was counted, to sign for it, to receive a receipt, but the old man wasn't interested.

"I told you to put it on my account," he said, and walked out. The clerk opened the sack: "There's millions in here!" he said.

The most extraordinary sight was in the Malaz Branch of the National Commercial Bank, and I didn't see it myself. A very reliable Saudi friend, however, was in the bank cashing a cheque when two very poor men came into the bank. They were wearing dirty, torn robes, and one was barefoot: they looked like beggars, completely out of place in a bank. One pushed to the counter and asked if they had the money for the cheque he had brought in the day before: my friend was rather puzzled, and the clerk asked the beggar man to wait a moment and disappeared. After a minute or two, two men appeared carrying piles and piles of cash. It mounted up on the counter and fell over. One of the "beggars" went to a nearby shop and came back with a number of empty cartons into which - uncounted - the money was stuffed. More and more money appeared, more and more cartons were brought in and filled. When the floor of the small branch bank was so crowded as to impede the movement of other customers, the "beggars" began to carry the cartons out to a small open truck, which, in turn, began to be filled. When the money was finally paid out, the cartons were piled up in the back of the lorry, with money spilling onto the floor: my friend said that there must have been millions of pounds sterling, but everybody felt completely safe. In 1980 I wrote, "Securicor vans have not yet been seen on the streets and I hope they never will be."

But, as I said, there were gangs; one was based at the Airport and its operation was explained to me by the Airport Police. The Police had built up a pattern from the accounts of victims. Almost invariably, a man, reasonably prosperous-looking, arrived alone in a taxi - which implied that likely targets were spotted by watchers outside. The man was usually in a hurry and concerned only with getting on his flight, and while checking in would put his briefcase on the ground. There was always a press of people around, with a bit of pushing, but the same people seemed to be there all the time. After a minute of so when the checking in formalities were completed, the briefcase would be missing. The Police were convinced that the actual thief merely passed the case to someone else, who sent it down a chain of people and away. The Police were about to mount a vast plain-clothes operation to monitor the check-in points and either catch the thieves or frighten them away.

***

Of course, this story raises the question of the role and position of the all-powerful police. I was often asked how I could live – and enjoy living – in a police state. I always answered that the words "Police State" were emotive, and suggested a place very different from the reality of Riyadh. Of course I was living in a country where the Police were extremely powerful and very thorough, where Police Spies and informers were everywhere, and where the Police had the power to imprison or to deport without a trial. But, as I said repeatedly when challenged, as far as I could see the Police exercised their powers with tact and discretion. They were kind and helpful to anybody who was trying, more or less, to keep on the right side of the law, and they did their best to act as Protectors of the Peace. I was all for them and see that I wrote in 1980, "I don't want the Police in Riyadh one iota less powerful or numerous that they are." I must write now that all my encounters with them have been entirely to their credit. A couple of examples will show what I mean.

There was an English friend of mine who lived across the road from my house in Malaz; and when he left another English friend took over the lease. He was going back to England for the university vacation, and so arranged for a houseboy to move in and act as caretaker while he was away. I knew this boy quite well because he came from the same town in Yemen as my houseboys, and had often visited them. I never knew the full story, but there was an "entry" of some kind and various articles, including a stereo–player, were stolen. The boy reported this to the Police and, in the absence of any other evidence, they arrested him for inviting "undesirables" into the house - as they were probably the ones who had stolen the goods.

I knew the boy to be rather stupid but honest, and his friends, led by my own houseboys, asked me to do something to help him, or he would be left in custody at the Police Station until the end of the Vacation. Not even knowing any of the officers, I went to the local Police Station and asked to see the Commandant. He received me courteously and asked my business. I explained that I was a friend and neighbour of the absent tenant of the house which had been "burgled" and that I knew quite a lot about the boy who had been arrested. I said that I was sure that he was innocent and asked whether he could be released - if I guaranteed to keep him until my friend returned, when he could then decide what he wanted to do.

The Police Captain thought for a moment and then sent for the boy: what followed was pure Terence Rattigan. The Captain accused the boy of theft, of complicity, of betraying his trust: the boy, frightened but firm, stood up straight and denied everything. After about two minutes hectoring the Captain stopped, smiled, and said to me (in English), "I agree with you. I think the boy is innocent." He told the boy that he would be freed immediately, but that he must keep in touch with me as I would be responsible for him. "Do I sign a guarantee?" I asked. "No," said the Captain, "You can't, you're not a Saudi. You just sign a letter that if the owner of the missing property wants to bring an action against the boy, you will produce him here in my office." There was no more formality: I scribbled a few lines, which were approved, signed them, and we walked out of the Station with no further ado.

My second story concerns a car accident. I was driving to the Riyadh Schools one morning and was in the front of a line of cars waiting at a red light. When the lights changed I was very quick off the mark and almost collided with a Mercedes trying to shoot the red light against it. We both swerved at right angles, the Mercedes driver shooting down the road I had been aiming for, while I hit the near fore wing of a car just moving off in the other direction.

The driver of the car I had hit was a Pakistani who worked for the British Aircraft Corporation, and he wasn't very happy. I apologized and told him that, although I myself couldn't have helped the accident, he was absolutely blameless and I accepted 100% liability. He asked for this in writing, which I gave him, and in the ensuing pandemonium – for any sort of accident attracts even more people in Riyadh then in London – he disclaimed any interest in knowing anything about my Insurance Company and I found myself agreeing to go with him to the Traffic Police. Various masters from the School arrived, alerted (and alarmed) by boys who had seen that I was involved in some sort of an accident, and had spread such a garbled story that my colleagues seemed surprised that I was not stretched out on the ground expiring in my own gore. I told them that I would have to go to the Traffic Police and would not be at school until the matter was settled. "Two days I expect," said the Senior Master, judiciously, and off we went in our respective cars to the Police Station.

A very civil senior officer met us and told us, immediately, that we had done wrong. The cars should not have been moved, because the Police needed to examine them *in situ* to help determine the degree of responsibility of each driver. He read my written acceptance of total responsibility: "Never write anything like this" he said, tapping it with his forefinger. "Never admit responsibility. It is the work of the Police to decide that."

"But in this case," I protested, "there can't be any dispute. The driver who caused the accident escaped - but this man" (I pointed to the other driver) "was completely innocent. I hit his car, and his car had every right to be in that place."

The officer smiled at me, kindly but a shade pityingly. "Leave it to the Police," he said, "we will look after you better than you can look after yourself." If he had known enough English to say, "You don't know enough to come in out of the rain," he probably would have said it.

In the case of a motor accident, the Saudi regulations were that three estimates must be submitted from approved garages. The police would choose the cheapest, the expense being borne by one or both of the parties according to their degree of culpability decided by the investigating officer. After leaving the Traffic Police I contacted my Insurance Company who said that they would make all the arrangements and have three estimates ready for me by the following morning – the cars having been left at the Police Station. During the afternoon the other driver telephoned my house – I had been mad enough to give him my number. He insisted that I should meet him at the house of a senior Saudi military officer, who worked with BAC as a fixer of problems. When I arrived I found him with two other Saudi officers, both very drunk, and the Pakistani. I soon realised that they were trying to pressurise me into agreeing to a rather expensive out-of-court settlement. I accepted a few drinks, to keep everything friendly; but I absolutely declined to do anything except through the Insurance Company. When the officers discovered that I was not refusing to pay, as they had been led to believe, and that I had said I would pay whatever the Saudi Police decided, they lost interest and relapsed into a sort of coma. My opinion of the crash "victim" sank towards absolute zero.

The next morning we all met at the Traffic Police Station. The Insurance Agent handed me three estimates from approved garages, all for a few hundred riyals. The other car-owner produced an estimate from a notoriously expensive garage and said he had already ordered them to collect the car from the Police and to do the work. He himself was not insured and I must pay: the amount was several thousand riyals. My Insurance Agent refused to pay any other sum greater than the smallest of the three estimates: the Police Captain considered the position.

Finally he spoke: "According to regulations I authorize this garage to do the work," he said, picking up the cheapest of the three estimates. "If the owner wants a different garage to do the work, then he is entitled to that, but he must pay any difference in price."

The other man produced my wretched admission of responsibility. "I have this," he said, "Is an Englishman's word worth nothing?"

The Police Captain motioned to him, "Give me that," he said, and the "letter" was handed to him. He read it again and then tore it up. "Now it's gone," he said, "It should never have been written in the first place."

The man, not unnaturally, burst into a storm of English, Urdu and Arabic, denouncing this high-handed proceeding, suggesting collusion between myself and the police, and declaiming against the well-known perfidy of Albion. I was rather distressed: "I'll have to pay him," I said.

The Police Captain ignored me; but dropped the affable air he had worn hitherto throughout both our meetings. "Be quiet!" he said to the voluble one, who did as he was told.

"Now listen," the Captain said; and he turned to me. "This man has tried to cheat you. He was involved in an accident a few weeks ago – I had a man check our records and the car last night. This man was awarded damages and received cash from the other driver, but the repairs have not been carried out. The damage you did as you described the accident, and from the marks on your car - which are slight - make it plain where you hit him, and the damage you did was confined to one headlamp and the wing. He is trying to make you pay for your accident, the previous one, and various bumps and scrapes the car has had at different times." His face broke into a smile, as he added, "I told you we would look after you better than you could look after yourself." After a short silence he added, "However, since you did sign the paper and since you have more money than he has, I suggest, but I do not order, that you pay him one hundred riyals out of your own pocket, over the amount your insurance will pay." This I of course agreed to at once, the cash (including what I would get back from the Insurance) was handed over, and the man was made to sign a letter disclaiming any further charge against me. After much shaking of hands and mutual exchange of courtesies, I left the Traffic Police, with the matter satisfactorily settled, and my admiration for the Police set to "very fair."

Curiously enough I met that Police Captain again nearly two years later. I had stopped at the traffic lights at the bottom of Sitteen Street, ready to turn right into University Street, and beside me was a juggernaut van towing an enormous trailer. As the lights went green the lorry driver cut across me and, although the van missed my car the trailer hit me and carried me onto the pavement. The driver continued down University Street, pursued by a crowd of Saudi drivers, all blaring their horns. I inspected the damage to my car, which was minimal, really only affecting the front near wing, and then proceeded down the road to where a crowd of cars and police surrounded the Juggernaut. My car was inspected, some rough and ready work eased the wing away from the tyre, and I was given permission to take my car to the Traffic Police, where I saw my old friend, the Captain.

The next morning I went to the station and the captain called me into a side room. "Look," he said, "the lorry-driver is 100% liable, but he is a poor man, who drives for a Kuwaiti Company. He will be delayed over this business, and would probably lose his job even it there were no fines and damages to pay. Are you prepared to withdraw your claim against him so that we can let him go?" Of course I said that I would – I certainly didn't want to help any man to lose his job, so we returned to the Main Office where the man was sent for. When he arrived the Captain made a short speech explaining the Englishman's extreme kindness and generosity and telling the man he could go straight out to his van and could drive it away. The man fell upon me and made such remarks to Heaven about me that I am sure the Recording Angel took it with a pinch of salt.

When he had gone the captain smiled at me. "As you know," he said, "we always try to look after people in a fair way."

Even if things do not go right at the Police Station, Justice will not only be done but be seen to be done – as revealed in a story told to me by Sheikh Mohammed Al-Khamis in the late 1970s. One morning one of the Yemenis failed to turn up to work in the Al-Khamis office, and on enquiring it turned out that he was in prison at a Police Station after an accident. Mohammed went straight off to see what could be done, and learned an astonishing fact: when driving his car, the man had been hit by a large and powerful car driven by a very high-ranking Saudi General. The General had first taken the Yemeni to the Hospital to see that he was all right and then had gone with him to the Police Station to report the accident - where he assumed full responsibility and promised compensation. After that, presumably because of his high rank, he had been allowed to go home; but the young officer on duty, possibly feeling that somebody should be in the cells, shut the innocent Yemeni up for the night. Sheikh Mohammed could not believe the evidence of his ears and insisted on seeing the Commandant of the Station. This officer said that it was a most unfortunate error, but that nothing could be done until the officer who had committed "the prisoner" agreed to his release. After a further display of incredulity Sheikh Mohammed went off to the Head of the Traffic Police and demanded instant action to release his employee. Once again, he came up against "regulations," which were, apparently, as had been stated: even the Head of the Traffic Police could not sign a release. After saying that he didn't know how such a regulation could ever have been made, Mohammed went away again, by now having spent most of the morning on the affair. Finally he managed to find the Deputy Minister of the Interior. When informed of the facts, Dr Awaji made a number of telephone calls, and asked Sheikh Mohammed to meet him at the Police Station at sunset, when the whole matter would be settled, personally by himself.

At sunset all the *Dramatis Personae* gathered: the Deputy Minister, Sheikh Mohammed, the Head of Police, the Captain of the Station, the Officer on duty the night before, the General who had caused the accident and of course, the prisoner. The Deputy Minister addressed them at some length on the miscarriage of justice and also said that, although up to a point the General had acted correctly, he should have made sure that the Yemeni was all right and should not have left him at the Police Station. He therefore proposed that the General should pay adequate compensation for the car, plus something over for the trouble and discomfort that had been caused to its driver. He should also spend the same period in a cell as the victim, a suggestion to which the General agreed, although without any marked enthusiasm. The senior Officers were told that they should have sought such higher authority as was necessary to get an innocent man released without delay; but the real punishment was reserved of the young man who had shut up an innocent man rather than risk offending a powerful one. The man was not demoted, but reduced with immediate effect to the most junior officer of his rank in the Kingdom, thus losing all his seniority. He was also to be transferred as soon as possible to one of the Border Posts, which were considered "hardship postings." Islamic Justice is no respecter of persons.

In the early 1970s, I heard another and somewhat similar story from friends working at the Airport. One of the King's brothers arrived on a scheduled flight and when he came through the Terminal, a Customs Official saw that he was carrying in his hand a publication that was on the banned list. Respectfully, he drew the Prince's attention to the fact that this item could not be taken into the Kingdom. A row, in every sense a Royal Row, ensued. The Prince insisted on his right to bring in anything he liked, while the Customs Official stuck to his guns and refused to allow the publication through. In the end, in a towering rage, the Prince took the man's name and said he was going straight to the King to complain: the man should be dismissed and disgraced. Everybody waited to see what would happen, and sure enough, in about an hour, there was a call from the Palace: the King wanted to speak personally to the Head of the Airport.

King Faisal said that he had heard that a junior Customs Official – he had the name – had prevented a brother of the King from bringing a certain publication into the Kingdom because it was on the banned list. Was this so? The Airport Director replied that, yes, the officer had done just that, acting according to what he thought were the regulations. Exactly, the King said, and the Officer concerned would receive a Letter of Thanks from the Palace, and was to be promoted immediately, not one but two ranks, for "exemplary service." A notice would be sent to all personnel at the Airport stating what had happened and reminding them that nobody, however important or powerful, was outside the laws of Islam or the Kingdom. Everyone should know they had the personal support of the King at all times when doing their duty - irrespective of who might oppose them. This was a very different picture to the stories in the Western Press about royal princes who could do anything they liked.

***

Riyadh was comparatively small when I was first there, and the Police were very much in evidence; this was especially noticeable at night when they seemed to be on every corner. When you drove though the streets after dark, a whistle would be blown at every intersection; and if you were walking, armed figures would loom up out of the darkness and demand to see your papers. But these police, visible and uniformed (and often armed) were only the tip of the iceberg. The plain-clothes police and informers were legion, and there was no means of knowing whether any – or indeed all – of one's friends were informers. I suppose I must have lived a pretty law-abiding life in Riyadh because I always felt that the Police were on my side and were there to protect me.

When I moved into a mud house in the Old Town in November 1965, I was, apparently, not only the first European to live in that particular area but also the first non-Saudi. Various Saudi friends helped me to move in and I had a Sudanese cook who came daily – except for Friday – and "did" for me. I lived alone for a good time and revelled in the size of the house and the peacefulness at night, the only "sounds" were when I would sit on the roof in the dark, with subdued lighting in the pillared courtyard, and the strains of Mozart, Beethoven, Wagner or Monteverdi rising to engulf me. After I had been there about six weeks, some friends said casually one evening, "Oh, by the way, if you want to have whisky or anything in your house you can now, because the watch on you has been withdrawn." I didn't know what they were talking about and asked them to explain, so they told me: when I moved into the Old Town, the authorities had been anxious about my behaviour and feared I might prove a disturbing influence in such a quiet and orthodox neighbourhood. They had therefore ordered a twenty-four hour watch on the house, with everything and everybody going in or coming out being noted. There had been no signs of drink, or drinking, no parties, no problems with neighbours, no behaviour they would consider anti-social; and so I was not considered "an undesirable." I swore that they must have made a mistake, because I had never seen a sign of a policeman anywhere near the house. My naivety was a source of general amusement; of course, everyone said, I hadn't seen anybody! What would have been the point of a watch if I had known about it? There must have been many times when I had seen men, alone or in pairs, especially at night, sitting in cars within sight of the front door: old men sitting idly doing nothing in particular for hours: boys playing football up and down the street. All those I was told, had been keeping an eye on me all the time. There are three points of interest in this story; two struck me immediately, but the third only a long time afterwards. The first was the enormous ramifications of a police system that could call on everybody from old men to boys as plainclothesmen – except that it was far more than that. It revealed one of the great strengths of the Saudi state: these people were not "police" at all. If necessary the Police could call on the whole population to assist them when the matter could be expressed simply as Saudis versus the Others. I am sure that all my neighbours constituted themselves into a kind of special Constabulary for the occasion, even though we were then, and remained, on amicable terms, minding our own business and keeping a proper distance. The second point was that once I had been, as it were "accepted," I became far less of a foreigner than before, although I did not in fact alter my way of life and suddenly indulge in a series of drunken orgies.

The third point, the one that didn't occur to me for a long time, was that my friends must have known about the twenty-four hour surveillance all the time – yet they never gave me the slightest inkling of what was happening. They told me when the "danger" was over and were, I am sure, genuinely glad that I had passed the test. But their loyalty to me as a friend came after their loyalty to society as Saudis, and I am convinced that, if I had failed the test, our friendship would have been forgotten as soon as possible.

***

I believe that the authorities in the Ministry of the Interior used to have detailed files on every foreigner – especially foreign Arabs - in the Kingdom.[3] When there were so many thousands of foreigners it must have been almost impossible; but as companies had to put their foreign workers into compounds - or into blocks of flats, which were like a compound - they were at least isolated from the Saudi community. When there were only a few of us we could be watched more easily.

Foreign Arabs were always more strictly monitored than Europeans and Americans, because with the latter there was a language barrier between most of them and all but the most educated Saudis. The worst they could do was to provide an example of a different lifestyle that might lead to an alteration (which meant a deterioration) in the standards of young people. Where there was no language barrier, there was a real danger that religious or political propaganda hostile to the establishment might be circulated. Hence, travellers with publications in English were normally waved through (including my Bible and Prayer Book!) unless these publications could be considered even mildly pornographic – such as a magazine with a somewhat scantily clothed girl on the cover. Travellers with publications in Arabic were much more carefully scrutinized. This seemed to be especially true of religious works: a Jordanian friend told me that his copy of the Holy Koran had been confiscated to make sure that it was an authentic copy as it had not been printed in Saudi Arabia.

Some idea of how thorough the Saudi Police can be is shown by the story of a Palestinian who had a Canadian wife. I knew him quite well

---

[3] A friend in the Ministry of Education once came to me: "I've been in the Ministry of the Interior, looking at the Secret file of somebody, and, quite by chance, I came upon your secret file!" "What did it say?" I asked anxiously. "It says that you don't drink or smoke, you don't run after boys or girls, you don't talk religion or politics, you work hard and always did your best for your pupils." "Who wrote that?" I said. "I can't imagine," he said candidly, "but it must have been a good friend of yours. Anyway, that *is* your "official" character and nobody now can go against it!"

and I shall call him buy his first name, Khamis. This in itself shows something of the complexity of Arabic nomenclature, as many names may be "given" or "family" – and Khamis also means "five" and "Thursday." This man and his wife came to Riyadh in 1970, and were soon well known to the authorities because of the unstable personality of the wife. The husband, a Financial Consultant, got on with his job of representing various North American Finance offices, worked hard and was liked by all with whom he came into contact; but his wife could not cope with the changed living conditions and began to act very erratically. She would walk around the streets with her baby, asking complete strangers to help her, as her husband (who was in his office not half a mile away) had gone to Jeddah, and she had no money, and must contact the Embassy. Discussions about the poor woman took place between British Embassy officials – who looked after Canadian interests – and people from the office of the Governor of Riyadh, but nothing had been decided when, one day Khamis returned at lunchtime to the block of flats where they lived to find the whole place seething with Police and all the male occupants of the flats being questioned. He was stopped as he entered and, when he gave his name, an officer told him that his wife was in a state of collapse after having been attacked by a group of men who had tried to rape her. He was naturally distressed, but also doubtful whether such an attack had actually taken place, remembering his wife's problems and her peculiar imagination. Sure enough, when talking to him – with a policeman unobtrusively in the background - she changed her story from "attempted rape" through a number of gradations, until it appeared that she had gone out shopping and that when she had been crossing the road four men had looked at her. They had not, it seemed, spoken to her, gone anywhere near her, or even looked at her in an unpleasant or suggestive way, but they had looked at her, and that had started the whole thing.

Khamis apologized to the Police, who withdrew. He then went round to each flat in the block and apologized for the unpleasantness caused and then decided to spend the rest of the day at home with his wife. Quite late in the evening he answered the doorbell to find a plain-clothes officer. The man apologised for the lateness of the hour, but asked Khamis, as a matter of urgency, to come to the Ministry of the Interior to discuss the day's events with a Saudi General in charge of aspects of security.

They went to an office behind the Ministry of the Interior where an elderly Saudi in plain clothes awaited them. It was really important, he said, to discuss the problem of Khamis's wife, who was now causing too many scandals. Khamis began a long-winded explanation to try to minimize what his wife had said or done, but the General waved him to silence. "Don't tell me these stories, Mr. Khamis," he said, "we know exactly what has been happening. We know everything." He paused. "As an example," he went on, "we'll leave your wife and talk about yourself."

He opened a large file, which was conveniently beside him, and began to detail Khamis's career. It was not just a recital of his life and activities in Riyadh, but went back many years to when he had been a student in Cairo. It listed his addresses, his friends, and the clubs he belonged to, his academic achievements: the most trivial details were faithfully recorded and Khamis told me, were absolutely accurate. The saga moved to Germany, where he had gone for further studies and training in financial affairs. Again there was the same remorseless attention to detail – his landlords, his girl friends, his lack of political involvement, the cafes where he ate regularly, his favourite foods were all listed – nothing was omitted and nothing was incorrect. The General moved on to Canada, where now the file included not only everything concerning Khamis himself but, when he became engaged, also embraced his wife's family: her father, a prominent academic, her own sociological work, and after their marriage, their friends and his work in Canada – everything was listed. Finally the tale moved to Saudi Arabia where every fact, especially every indiscretion, had been noted and registered; and not only the details of Khamis and his wife, but also details of relations who happened to be working in the Kingdom.

At last the General shut the file "Tell me one thing Mr. Khamis," he said "you have two cousins with exactly the same name, one in Jeddah and one in Damman. I always forget which of them is a non-smoker. Which is it?" Khamis told him.

"Now Mr. Khamis," the old man leant forward, "You see, we do know what we are talking about, so now let's get down and talk about what should be done about your wife."

The most interesting part of the story to me is not that the Saudis had the mass of information – surprising enough in itself – but rather the extent of international cooperation Khamis's file revealed. Clearly, Egyptian, German and Canadian information about a Palestinian had been made readily available to the Saudis. The whole thing may have been financed with Saudi money but, as it involved a Palestinian, other Gulf States may have contributed - because of a general fear and the belief that all Palestinians should be kept under observation. In Khamis's case it had been going on for a good many years, and if a westernized financier, completely law-abiding and totally apolitical, was subjected to such scrutiny, what about the politically active?

On the subject of where most of this information came from, I have an idea that amounts to certainty – it all came, originally, from other Palestinians. Just as in the Yamama School one of the Palestinian masters had a supplementary salary from the Ministry of the Interior to report on the activities of his colleagues, so that pattern must have been repeated with endless variations wherever two or three Palestinians gathered together.[4]

***

Most of the time I lived in Riyadh the Traffic Police were the most obvious branch – there were a lot of them and, on the whole, they did a good job under extremely trying condition. In 1964 we were told there were some ten thousand vehicles in the city; and that comprised private cars, taxis, trucks, vans and lorries. Fifteen years later – if one went by registration numbers on the cars - well over a hundred thousand new vehicles were coming onto the streets of Riyadh every year. To use a commonplace phrase, traffic became "nose to tail", whereas in my early days cars passed only occasionally as one walked. People familiar with the traffic in Teheran or Tokyo used to tell me that it was worse there; and I myself have vivid memories of Beirut before the troubles, and of down town Karachi at rush hour, which were terrible. In Riyadh the situation was aggravated by the amount of road-works that were carried out non-stop. New roads were laid, only to be dug up again immediately, and the very busy streets in the town centre were permanent worksites. Water pipes were laid underground, as were drains, electricity cables and telephones. As in most countries, there was no co-operation between the different authorities, and the same stretch of road might be dug up four

---

[4] A point has struck me forcibly during recent years, especially since the Palestinians were divided into Fatah (the West Bank) and Hamas (Gaza). We often have been told that an Israeli helicopter–gun ship has fired a rocket at a car travelling from A to B and that a senior Palestinian official (almost always Hamas) and his aides have been killed. I have never seen any sort of query in any branch of the media as to how the Israelis were able to identify the exact time, route, and the actual car they targeted. It could only have come from Palestinian sources actuated, I am sure, not by any backing for Israel, but by a greater hatred for a rival Palestinian group.

times in six months. It was sometimes tempting to think that the roads were dug up so that the contractors could see how the pipes and cables were getting on. One friend, a very senior government official - I think he may already have been a Deputy Minister - told me he had been shopping and had left his car in a street off Wazir Street. He was away about forty-five minutes, and when he came back a deep trench had been dug across the road in front of his car. As there was another car parked immediately behind his he couldn't move it, so he went to find somebody to whom he could complain. This took some time and the outcome was not very satisfactory, and when he returned the car behind had vanished, but another trench had been dug across the road behind his car. He had to leave it there two or three days until the trenches were filled in.

Police cars also used to patrol the streets at night, but the foot patrols, ubiquitous in my first days in Malaz, seemed to have almost died out after a few years. Quite early in my time there the Police came to my house one morning and spoke to my servants.

"Why does the Englishman have his gate open at night?" they asked.

"His dog likes to be able to go in an out at night," was the answer.

"Other people," said the Police, "keep their dogs inside or outside at night. Tell him he must not leave his gate open. We cannot stop anybody we see going in if the gate is open, even if we think it is someone who shouldn't be there. For his own security he must shut his gate: then we can protect him."

***

No mention of the Saudi Police would be complete without a mention of what happens to people who are caught breaking the law and then punished. As far as British Nationals are concerned, the offences are almost always connected with alcohol, either drinking or manufacturing. There are clear distinctions in Islamic Law between committing a sin, helping someone else to commit one – which is worse – and profiting by exploiting another's weakness, which is worse again. It is recognized – there is much common sense in Islamic law – that human nature being what it is, some men will drink alcohol if given the chance. That is really something between themselves and God. But the man who produces the drink and sells it to the weaker brethren is the one who must bear the heavier punishment.

When I used to get my English newspapers in Saudi Arabia, any adverse criticism of the Kingdom had been cut out by the censors (which was partly why our papers were always a day late). From what I was told, however, it seemed that British readers were given a very unfair picture of Saudi Arabia. In London we expect foreign visitors to obey British laws, so it seems only right that visitors in Saudi Arabia should obey Saudi laws – or, if they deliberately break them, be prepared to suffer the consequences. There is also the point that, in most cases, Britons imprisoned for alcohol related offences have not just been caught drinking – rather they have been producing and selling alcohol, sometimes for several years. It can be a lucrative business, capable of making not just thousands, but tens of thousands of pounds. Many of those caught made no complaint; but the Saudi authorities had reason to be angry at what seemed to be a well organized and orchestrated chorus of protest against the application of the laws of Saudi Arabia to British workers – a protest that condemned punishment by "lashes" as barbaric. In fact the Saudi application of the lash was not especially violent – it was a humiliation rather than a physical punishment. Certainly any reader old enough to remember a prefect's beating at school, or the application of his Scottish tause, would have thought nothing of it.[5]

Although "against" drinking, the authorities were apt to turn a blind eye to the habits of Europeans and Americans, and indeed others. Back in 1966-67 there was, and had been for some time, a government employee cooperative where groceries and household items could be brought at very reasonable prices. One such store was in the basement of the Ministry of Agriculture and, I think, was open most afternoons. I never went there myself, but for some months, I had a German friend and his American wife, the Guerins, staying with me and he was, by the standards of the time, very well paid. There was then a limit on salaries of 3000 riyals a month, except by the special order of a minister, who could authorize a salary of up it 4500 riyals – above 4500 it needed the signature of the King. Jean Guerin had 4500 riyals a month, and this entitled him to a special privilege. Beneath the Ministry of Agriculture, through the cooperative store, there was an inner room, to which only those on a salary of 4500 or more were admitted. Until or unless the guards knew the

---

[5] I was asked, about 1980-81, by Sheikh Abdullah Blehed, then the Deputy Governor of Riyadh, to write a rebuttal of the stories appearing in the British Press, and gave the facts as I have put them here. I don't know whether the rebuttal was ever sent. It seemed to make no impression in England if it was.

individual, a copy of the contract stating the salary was needed to gain admission to the Holy of Holies. Inside there were all the forbidden goodies – crates of whisky and crates of gin, English beer as well as German beer, and hams, packets of bacon, joints of pork and frozen pork chops: we bought so much that I had to buy my first deep freeze to hold all the stuff.

When houses where alcohol was manufactured were about to be raided, the Police usually managed to "tip off" the tenant. There was an Englishman with whom I used to play bridge, and he had a still going day and night in his flat. He was "shopped" by some other Briton who had been caught with a quantity of drink on him – and being drunk in charge of a car was as serious in Riyadh as in London. Word was passed to the still owner by some means that his flat would be raided, but, unfortunately, he refused to heed the warning - because he had a number of well-placed friends and his wife gave lessons to some princesses. He was sure that nobody would ever touch him.

When he was in prison I happened to be talking to one of the Police Officers who had carried out the raid "we had given him three days," he told me, "three days to get rid of the evidence. We thought we were going to go to the flat, look round, and make a report that the accuser was mistaken, and that there were no signs that alcohol was being made. Nobody could have been more surprised than we were to walk in and find the still bubbling away."

This particular Englishman stuck to his opinion that by producing alcohol he was performing a public service. The expression of this opinion in court brought him an extra year "for arrogance." (The proper way to behave in such circumstances was to plead guilty and to apologize for offending against the laws of the Kingdom). He actually served a little over eighteen months in the main prison in Malaz. I don't think conditions were ideal, but as the prisoners were organized in "messes" and he had a very good Pakistani cook in his mess; he said that the food was much better in prison than he got at home. Boredom and lack of exercise were probably the worst evils.

When I left Riyadh an old friend – who produced the best "Siddiqi" in Riyadh and from whom I must have brought an incalculable amount over the years - was serving a three-year sentence in a new prison. His view was that he had known the risks and had enjoyed a long run for his money. He seemed to have been caught almost by chance: the police were actually investigating a Saudi neighbour for possession of alcohol, when somebody apparently said "It probably came from this Englishman's house," and they entered without the preliminary warning, to find, as usual, the still in production and a large quantity of liquor stored ready for sale. Desmond's report on the conditions of his gaol was rather favourable. He said that he had a decent bed and the bathrooms and lavatories were clean; he had plenty of books and a friend sent him in *The Times* each day with the Crossword untouched. His wife was allowed to visit and talk to him when she wanted, not only at the official times when there tended to be a swarm of people. If you had to be in prison, he said, it could be a lot worse. (Another friend who had been in prison in Kuwait on an alcohol charge told of terrible conditions and beatings: the Saudis were much more civilized).

In spite of the laws, telescopes, as I have already said, were regularly turned to blind eyes. From the beginning there had been an arrangement whereby the American Corps of Engineers were given the right to bring in materials – some of which were doubtless military items not to be seen by unauthorized eyes – without going through the Saudi customs. I don't know whether everybody working for the Corps was entitled to a ration, but certainly the senior staff had a monthly allowance of alcohol – and quite a generous one. One English couple were moving and I was helping them, and just when we felt like dropping, in marched an American couple. The husband was a Senior Corps officer, but the couple hardly drank at all and took their ration for the benefit of their friends. On this occasion, they brought a complete supper, with a four-pound ham as the centre-piece and, as a house warming present, a bottle of Scotch, a bottle of Gin, a bottle of Brandy, a bottle of Vodka and two bottles of wine, all of which they shrugged off with: "It's from our ration – we rather you had it."

BAC actually promised its senior staff that there would always be drink available; indeed its willingness to pay over the odds to keep that promise did more than anything else to drive up the price beyond the reach of ordinary mortals. The Company was given tacit permissions to run "clubs" and to serve drinks there – the "Sultana" for the supposed officer ranks, and the "Turki" for the others. For some reason, the British Embassy took exception to these clubs and the British Military Mission - attached to the National Guard – was told not to go to them. I had just been invited to join as an "Outside Member," but an officer from the Mission was quite definite: "You're a sort of permanent inhabitant,

David," he said, "and I think you had better not go to it." As I respected Major Harms's opinion, I never attended either club.

There were numerous "bars" which lasted for a longer or shorter time. There was one run by BAC personnel, which I went to occasionally – often to meet Saudi Police at the entrance. They told me that I could only go in if I wore European clothes, as otherwise the BAC people might be in trouble for selling alcohol to an Arab.

I cannot resist telling one story involving me directly. In the mid seventies - long before he went to prison – I received an urgent telephone call from Desmond; could I go round to his house at once. It must have been about half past midnight, because I had been on the evening shift at the Radio Station until twelve. At that time Desmond lived in the street behind mine in Malaz. Although it was little more than a hundred yards I was sufficiently tired to get into my car and drive there. Even though it was so late there were a number of people about, and several cars. I parked outside Demond's house and went inside.

Desmond explained that he had to move because his landlord had become alarmed at the thought of a house he owned being a centre for illicit distilling; somebody had blown a whistle. The still was dismantled and packed, and gallons of perfectly good drink had been flushed down the lavatory; but Desmond had a crate of Scotch ("I got it very reasonably from a taxi driver") that he could not bear to destroy. "Whenever I leave," he said, "I shall be stopped and searched. I can't conceal the Scotch. So I want you to take it and kept it for me until it is safe for me to have it. And you can keep two bottles for yourself." I agreed and we settled down to wait for the activity outside to die down. Meanwhile, on the principle of Pooh Bear giving a pot of honey to Eeyore, we thought we should make sure the whisky was good and actually drank a good deal of a bottle before Desmond's houseboy came in to say that everyone had gone away. He was told to put the crate into the boot of my car and I gave him the keys. In those days, the boot of a Cadillac could not be opened from within the car, and it had a different lock to all the others.

When the houseboy returned my keys and said the whisky was in the boot I rose to leave. It must have been at least half past one, and I went out into darkness and silence; but as soon as I had switched on my lights other sets, three or four, came on and my car was bathed in lights. I slammed my foot down and shot down the road and round the bend at the end. I didn't, of course go home, but quickly got up onto the main road to the Eastern Province, with Police cars thundering after me. This was in the days of my shocking pink Cadillac Eldorado, which was supposed to do 120 mph, but the Prince who had had it before me – on loan from his elderly cousin the Princess Sara bint Abdullah (who had certainly herself never been in it) - had had an engineer tinker with the engine, so that it was actually quite a bit faster. At that time there was no Police Car in Riyadh that could live with me if I let the car out: so I did.

After several minutes, I slowed down, and stopped. The Police were no longer chasing me, and I could see no sign of anybody or anything, so I turned the car and drove back towards the city, hoping that the Police were now looking for somebody else somewhere else. But, alas for my hopes, two or three miles outside the city limits I came upon a Police barrier across the road and people with lights signalling me to stop there. I can't imagine what possessed me, but I didn't want to be caught with the whisky in my boot: the main road was not built up but was level with the desert, and so as I came up to the barrier I suddenly swung right, onto the sand, drove round the barrier back onto the road and behind it and streaked for home.

The distance was too short for me to have anything but a very brief advantage. I reached home, rushed into the house to tell the houseboys something of what had happened. My mother, perhaps fortunately, was in England, and my incomparable houseboy, Abdou, was on holiday in the Yemen, but a friend of his had come to help Mohammed, my second boy, to look after me. Having told them I was on the run from the Police, I took the key of the car boot off the key-ring and put it in a jar of, as far as I can remember, Extra Strong Mints. I had hardly done this before there was a prolonged ring on the front gate bell. "I'll go," I said.

Outside the gate were a lot of Policemen and, I think, three cars. They had, of course, all known exactly where I lived. The young officer who seemed to be in charge was perfectly civil.

"Would you give me the keys to your car?" he asked.

"Of course," I said, and handed him the ring. A policeman made various attempts, unsuccessfully, to open the boot.

"The key's not here," he said.

"Is the key to the boot not on the ring?" the young officer asked.

"No," I said, "it isn't."

"But you opened the boot earlier tonight," he said.

"No, I didn't." I replied, truthfully. "I haven't opened the boot tonight."

"No, he didn't," said one of the policemen: "it was somebody else who opened it."

We seemed to be at an impasse, and I could not think what was going to happen next, when another police car drew up and a very big fat sergeant got out.

"Aysh h'aardha, aysh h'aardha, aysh h'aardha?" he said, which might be translated "Wotsallthis, wotsallthis, wotsallthis?"

Several people explained, and he grabbed me by the arm and walked me down the road. "Now," he said, "Between ourselves and no witnesses, you've got drink in the boot haven't you?"

"Between ourselves and no witnesses," I said, "Yes I have."

"But you haven't got any guns." He said

"Guns!" I exclaimed, "No, of course not!"

"We're supposed to be checking up on guns," he said. "Now go into the house and bring out the key." So I went into the house, retrieved the key from among the mints, went outside and handed the key to the fat sergeant, who opened the boot. There were a number of cries and fingers pointed at the whisky. "No guns there" he said and slammed the boot shut.

There followed a fairly mild altercation, after which all the policemen got back in their cars. "What happens now? I said.

"Nothing" said the Sergeant, handing me back all the car keys. "Nothing'll happen."

I said goodnight to him and went indoors, to where the houseboys were naturally worried. "Well, that's over," I told them, putting the boot key back on the ring. "While I have a shower, bring the whisky in and put it on the chest in my bedroom. I think we need a drink."

Emerging from my shower I retrieved a bottle from my bedroom and met the houseboys in the dining room. I had just poured out three (very) generous whiskies and we were raising our glasses when there came another long ring of the bell at the gate. I put down my glass. "Get rid of these," I said, as, again, I went to open the gate.

There was another policeman and a plainclothes officer, who spoke excellent English standing outside. "I believe you have had a little difficulty tonight," he said, "Would you mind opening the boot of your car?"

I opened it and, of course, there was nothing to see. "You have taken the crate indoors," he said. "I should like to see it, please. I have no order to do, although I can get one, but it would be easier…"

"Of course," I said, "please come in and I will show you."

We went into the house where the boys had made themselves invisible in their own quarters and made our way to my bedroom, where I showed the policeman the crate sitting on a chest in the window. The officer took out, and replaced three or four bottles. "This is all good stuff," he said, "We have to look out for home-made alcohol. Some of it is very bad, in fact some is actually dangerous to drink."

He wrote busily in a notebook for a minute or two. "I suppose he said, "You can't tell me where you got this whisky?"

"I know it sounds like a story," I replied, "but I am looking after it for a friend." (A fact I am sure he already knew!)

"He said he got it from a taxi driver."

"You don't know where the taxi driver got it?"

"No, I don't?" I said, "I expect he got it from that Swedish company beside the Police Station."

"That's quite likely," he said, and then I saw him staring across the room behind us. "Do you always drink out of three glasses at once?" he asked.

I turned round and there, on my bedside table, were three large glasses of whisky. "No." I said, "But tonight has been very traumatic. I need some comfort and once I have got into bed I don't want to have to get out again to pour myself another drink."

He wrote all that down: "Well, that's all," he said, and turned to go. I went with them outside the gate where we all shook hands. "Please," I said, "what will happen to me?"

"To you?" he said, "Nothing at all. Good night."

I returned in and I hope shared the glasses of whisky with the houseboys. I have wondered since if someone at Police Headquarters, an old pupil, say, hearing what was going on gave an order that I was not to be unduly troubled.

But, remember, I was in those lands from which the Arabian Nights took their name. Scheherazade never ended a story at night; the ending had to come later. About two weeks after my exciting night I was coming out of the Passport Office with my visa-decorated passport when there was a screech of brakes and a police car came to a halt. Out of the front window leaned the big fat sergeant. "Hello!" he called, "Are you going on holiday?"

"Yes," I called back, "the day after tomorrow."

"Where are you going?" he asked.

"Egypt," I replied.

"Have a good time," he shouted as the police car moved away. Can the reader wonder that I have very friendly memories of the Saudi Police?

Of course the Police couldn't please all of the people all of the time. I went to the Airport once with a member of a highly respectable and respected family, to see one of his younger brothers off to America where he was studying. On arrival, he put the car in the middle of a line of parked cars where there happened to be a space. Up came a policeman who banged lightly on the roof of the car, and said, "You can't park here."

"Of course I can," said the Sheikh, "all these other cars are here."

"No, you can't" said the Policeman, "Please move your car."

The Sheikh expostulated: if there was a row of parked cars, his car wasn't doing any harm. Yes it was answered the Policeman, because all the cars were in the wrong place and if he had seen them parking he would have stopped them.

The Sheikh then said that he only wanted a few minutes to say goodbye to his brother who was leaving for months, if not years. As the policeman went on refusing, I drifted away to avoid any imbroglio and to make my own farewells to the brother. In the end the Sheikh had to move the car and joined us barely in time to say a hasty fraternal good-bye as his brother went though passport control. In a sulphurous silence we went back to the car. "What this town needs," said the Sheikh as we started off with tremendous jerk "is a hydrogen bomb on it with" he added changing gears noisily, "all the people inside it."

I have written particularly about the police in instances in which I was directly involved or had at least some direct knowledge. When I think of the way Middle Eastern security forces have been portrayed over many years, I am sure that my view is not the normal one. But then, as I must stress to the reader, I am not just telling stories from hearsay but giving true accounts of what actually happened. It is no wonder that my sense of security and protection was so solid during those happy years in Riyadh.

CHAPTER 11
Soldiers Of The King

This chapter, dealing with Saudi Arabia's national security, is shorter than the previous one – perhaps something that needs explanation. Of course, I realise that the security of a nation is more important than that of any individual, but this book is about how Riyadh affected me and, on a day-to-day basis, my own sense of safety mattered more to me than any ideas I may have had about the security of the government. But the two things are not so easily separated; I understand now that – at least to some extent – I could feel safe because Saudi Arabia itself was safe.

When I lived there, Saudi Arabia was defended by soldiers, sailors and airmen – all under the control of the Ministry of Defence. A large American military mission advised and assisted in the training of the soldiers, while the British had a major role with the Air Force. The Navy was small but, in the early 1980s, a huge contract – to include training – was signed with the French. It was typical of the Saudi authorities not to put all their eggs in one basket, but to involve different countries – all of whom were allies – in various defence projects.

But, as I made clear in earlier pages, set against the regular Army was the National Guard, and I use the words "set against" quite deliberately. When I was first in Riyadh we used to call the National Guard, "The White Army". It was a force of Bedouin, advised by a small British Military Mission, and it was generally believed that it would rally to the King and the Al-Sa'ud family in the event of internal conflict. Indeed, I was assured that it had been specifically created to provide a balance to the Regular Army and that, during the crisis of 1963 – when there had been talk of forcing King Saud to leave the country before he bankrupted it – the National Guard had actually been ordered to surround the Nassariyah Palace Complex to protect the King against an anticipated move by the Regular Army.

It would, however, be an oversimplification to describe the Army and the National Guard merely as counterweights to each other, or even to follow the old rule of thumb that the Army came from the towns and the National Guard from the Tribes – although most of the Guardsmen actually were Tribesmen. Rivalry between the services and between regiments is common to all significant military establishments; in Saudi Arabia, this rivalry took the form of a competition to acquire the most advanced and sophisticated "hardware". There were, however, a number of tasks specifically reserved for the Guards. For instance they were responsible for security in most government offices; their presence was especially visible at the Radio and Television stations, where security was extremely tight.

On the other hand, the Coastguards and the Frontier Control came under the aegis of the Ministry of the Interior, as did the Security Forces at the Ports and the Airports. There were also various different branches of the Police, and – because they were all armed and wore special uniforms – laymen found it difficult to distinguish them from the military proper. It was actually quite hard to work out who was what.

Threats to National Security come from two directions: they can come from the Outside (and the next chapter will discuss Saudi Arabia's relations with neighbouring powers) or they can come from the Inside. A quarter of a century ago, I thought the danger from Inside was much the more serious – as, indeed, I still do.

In the early chapters of this book, I explained that the Kingdom of Saudi Arabia was in itself an artificial conglomeration of different states (why does the name Yugoslavia spring to mind?) consisting of: the central province, the Najd, a very conservative and ultra-puritan religious area, now the dominant partner as it were, but previously perhaps the least important area in the Arabian Peninsula; the western province, Hejaz, more liberal and cosmopolitan, but for centuries the most important because it contained the Holy Cities of Mecca and Medina; the southern province, Asir, with closer ties with Yemen than with Riyadh; and the Eastern Province, Al-Hasa, with a long history of trading by sea, and which now contained the oil wealth of the Kingdom. Al-Hasa was also the home of the Shi'ite minority, who, in my early years, had been very definitely second-class citizens and were only cultivated after the massacres accompanying the Mecca incident. The "official" state of Saudi Arabia had been formally established only in 1932. Of course, to say that a state is "artificial" is not the same as saying that it is unnatural or necessarily doomed to failure. To a greater or lesser extent, all states are "artificial", in the sense that a good deal of "art" – even "artfulness" – has been applied to bring previously distinct and antagonistic elements together. After all, even England was once a Heptarchy.

But did Saudi Arabia face an external threat? While I knew that envious eyes were turned on the Saudi oil fields, especially by Iraq and Iran, I also knew that there was no actual danger. Was not the Company that controlled Saudi oil called Aramco? And did that not stand for the Arabian American Company? And was it even possible to imagine that the American government would do nothing if those oil fields were attacked? There seemed to be no possibility of such an attack. But when my thoughts turned to trouble inside the Kingdom, things seemed much more worrying. In the 1980s, I really believed that there was a serious possibility of insurrection.

The main danger then seemed to come from the Shi'ites – who could look to Iran for material and moral support. Perhaps I exaggerated this danger and underestimated the other. This came from the extreme religious zealots – and there had been plenty of those around ever since the eighteenth century. They objected to ever-greater adoption of western values – although they should not have been too concerned with commercialism, because Arabs have always been shrewd businessmen. But changes were being made to what might be called the "traditional" way of life. These included changes to the role of women and – doubtless to the puzzlement of Western enthusiasts for "women's rights" – women themselves emerged as some of the strongest opponents of change.[1] Anyway the possibility of "trouble" existed, and in those days, it seemed that, in the event of conflict between "traditionalists" and "reformers," the National Guard would be on the side of the traditionalists and the Army on the side of the reformers.

Foreign Arabs used to speak rather slightingly of the expensively armed Saudi forces; but except for the Egyptian army, which performed well against the Israelis in 1973, regular Arab armies have never covered themselves in glory – however effective some of the irregulars may have been. In the late 1970s, when there was an Arab Peacekeeping Force in Lebanon, the Saudi military detachment won golden opinions from the civilian population – not, however, for its warlike qualities, but for its

---

[1] It was while I was writing these pages that I heard the – to me – amazing news that a woman had attained ministerial rank in Saudi Arabia. She may be concerned with "women's affairs" but the appointment seems revolutionary.

politeness and courtesy. I am now going by what I was told by Lebanese friends during my visits to their country; but of all the Forces soldiers, the Saudis were favourites, followed by the Yemenis and the Sudanese. The Syrians were generally disliked, even by the various groups with whom, from time to time, they seemed to be allied. At this time, my mother and I took a number of holidays in the Lebanon and there were military checkpoints all over the place – sometimes only a hundred yards apart. At some there was what might well be described as mild harassment, but, if we were stopped by Saudis, they smiled, examined our papers and waved us on with a quiet "God be with you!"

In the years before I left, I had no doubt that there were some foreign governments who did their best to foment trouble in Saudi Arabia – in those days Colonel Qaddafi of Libya had replaced General Nasser of Egypt as leading trouble maker. There is certainly no doubt that weapons were smuggled into Saudi Arabia, although exactly to whom was never entirely clear. But weapons were smuggled and the authorities were seriously concerned. On the night of my adventure, described in the previous chapter, the police were looking for guns. Smuggling was easy over the land frontier; after all, Bedouin tribes must be allowed to travel at will regardless of frontiers drawn on maps. Smuggling was relatively easy when it was just a matter of crates of whisky, but more sophisticated methods were needed when it came to modern weapons. The simplest thing to do was to send them in by sea, labelled as something innocuous, in a container filled with – mostly – genuinely innocuous items. At that time so many containers were piling up in Saudi ports that it was impossible to search each one thoroughly. [2] In 1979, however, the Port Authority issued an order to the effect that, after a given date in 1980, containers of the normal pattern would no longer be acceptable; shippers would have to obtain new containers of an approved design that allowed all four sides to be opened for easy inspection.[3] I remarked to a Saudi

---

[2] As I write this I hear that the number of containers coming into Britain means that they cannot be properly searched for illegal drugs – and, of course, illegal immigrants sometimes come in like this too.

[3] There were simpler ways of smuggling: I was at a Royal Wedding in one of the Nassariyah palaces when I saw a new Ford sports car parked outside. Ford cars were then banned because of some Ford plant in Israel. I pointed it out and was told that it belonged to some young prince I didn't know. He was produced and I asked him how he had got the car into the country. "I drove it in from Kuwait" he said. "But you can't bring a Ford in." I said to him. "Oh, on the form I said it was a Mercedes," he

businessman that the order had probably been designed to enable some people to make a "good thing" out of the sale of the new containers. While he did not completely exclude this possibility, he insisted that the real reason was that masses of weapons (guns and ammunition) were being brought in to the Kingdom under false manifests. Sometimes it appeared these were consigned to highly respectable – and innocent – companies: the materials just went "missing" before they were actually delivered.

Apparently a cache of weapons had been discovered only as a result of a random search; even with the new design it would not be possible to search all the containers. British Intelligence had been called in to help the Saudis to establish the origins of the weapons and the routes by which they entered the Kingdom – and no doubt similar requests were made to the intelligence services of other friendly states. I am sure that a lot of weapons were detected – but equally certain that a greater number were not.

All this was happening before the Mecca crisis of 1979, and obviously a proportion of the arms were intended for that incident. But they continued afterwards and I was sure that many were destined for the Shi'ites of the Eastern Province. There resentment about the 1979 massacres was very strong, and many – dare I say most? – families had a blood feud against the "Authorities." And there was another disturbing factor, which I might describe as "boredom." Many people had a lot more money than they or their forebears had had. True, they could afford to buy all sorts of luxury goods but, apart from that, they had virtually nothing to do. They had no political or cultural outlets and who can be surprised if some were tempted into subversive activities? We all know who it is that finds work for idle hands.

Of course in "The Old Days" there had been "nothing to do" either and in an earlier chapter I described the regular evenings spent in the Shalhoub Majlis. It was not "exciting", but it was traditional, and interesting – at least to the people involved – and I don't think that in those early days any of us wanted anything different. I learned that while the men were in the Majlis, the women were in their quarters, alternately boasting and complaining about their men folk, their children and their servants. It was not until western ideas and – even more – a lot of money came in that a general spirit of dissatisfaction began to appear.

---

explained, "I was sure that the man on duty wouldn't be able to read FORD in English, and he couldn't."

I am sure that most of the Saudi population, like majorities everywhere, wanted to live comfortably and quietly keeping their heads down and quite ready to obey whatever government was in power. Indeed, for most Saudis, loyalty to the Royal Family sprang more from the fact that they were the government than from any great devotion to the Al-Sa'ud family as such. This attitude changed when one mixed with higher social and educational circles; indeed, the higher the circle, the greater the level of dissatisfaction. Large numbers of young men – and women – who had been educated abroad did not want to see things they had encountered in other countries introduced to Saudi Arabia – and they did not like what they found at home either. They did not want changes in the household, but they also disliked the hidebound activities of the "official" life. I have already described the frustration many felt when they went to work in one or other of the Ministries. They had intended to make real improvements but now found themselves baulked at every turn.[4]

All governments fear the consequences of unemployment, not least because civil disturbance is more likely to occur in places where a lot of men have no work and hence have unlimited time on their hands. Trouble is less likely in places where most people are in gainful employment, and men know that they can provide for their families. I am sure that this is the reason why government offices in some countries, including Saudi Arabia, are over-laden with superfluous clerks who, being in receipt of a regular income, are not likely to make trouble.

At this point I digress slightly to discuss the jobs Saudis were prepared to do and those they regarded as demeaning and unacceptable. Any branch of the Police or Armed Forces was considered good, all the more so perhaps because automatic entry was not assured. I have already mentioned the officers' plot in which my alcoholic neighbour was, perhaps unwittingly, involved and the defection of Saudi airman at the time of the Yemeni Civil War. No government wants to arm or train young men who might turn against it. When I was first in Riyadh, both the Police and the National Guard seemed to be in a mess – this, the reader will remember, was at the end of the King Sa'ud's reign – with ill-fitting uniforms and unsuitable boots. When I asked, back in 1964, why they looked so awful, I was told that their pay was always in arrears and

---

[4] It was a rule (sometimes circumvented) that Saudis who had been educated abroad at Government expense should work for the same number of years in a Government Office.

they had to pawn or sell their boots and uniforms to get money. I can't vouch for the truth of this story but I heard it from a number of people – and it is hardly something anybody would want to make up. Later, realizing the necessity of a contented and efficient defence force, the authorities raised both standards and pay.

Although service in the armed forces was perhaps more prestigious, employment in a Ministry or Government Department was quite acceptable. People in such posts were generally "loyal" subjects and unlikely to make trouble. The fact that they were not doing anything really vital mattered less than their loyalty to the government. Of course, it was perfectly respectable for a man to drive a car, because driving a camel had been a traditional activity of the Arab male for millennia. It was not unknown for grossly under worked clerks in the ministries to slip away for an hour or two to double as taxi-drivers. There was certainly a large number of taxis, all, I believe, driven by Saudis. In my day, there were two sorts of taxi. The first was the "private" taxi, which one flagged down and which drove one anywhere within the city boundaries for the sum of two riyals. For destinations outside the city, the fare was a matter for negotiation, to be completed before the journey began – but I never knew a Saudi driver dispute an agreed fare.[5]

"Business" was also a perfectly acceptable occupation, because buying and selling seemed to be a part of Arab life. Being in business, however, meant working for oneself or a member of one's family. To be really "respectable", however, it was necessary to work for one of the very big Saudi or foreign companies – employing hundreds, if not thousands of people – but only if this involved a post in the administration. Any kind of manual work – unless for oneself – was to be avoided at all costs. Avoidance of manual labour extended to farm work, unless one was working on one's own, or a family farm. I imagine that an exception would be made for work on the experimental farms in Al-Kharj, because they were owned by the Ministry of Agriculture and hence all posts there came into the category of "Government work."

---

[5] I once took a taxi in Cairo for a journey, the cost of which I had been told in advance. The driver – whose brother was with him in the front of the cab said, "Pay me what you will" when I asked him how much he wanted. When we had completed the journey I thanked the driver and gave him the money. He and his brother immediately started shouting and appealed to passers-by for help against this cheating Englishman. Luckily by then my command of Arabic was enough for me to hold my own, and eventually to win over to my side the growing crowd and the Police who turned up.

As well as driving taxis, working class Saudis – perhaps a somewhat inaccurate description – might take jobs as "drivers" to the Ministries, Government offices, Saudi families or Saudi and foreign companies. By any standards, many Saudis were excellent drivers, but some were not, although – even in my day – the Police were becoming stricter over licenses. In 1980 a thump announced that something had run into the back of my car and, on investigation, this proved to be a Post Office van. We suffered only a cracked rear light but the Suzuki van was severely buckled. The driver, who seemed dazed, said that he hadn't been able to stop because he couldn't remember where the brake was. It appeared that his knowledge of driving had been almost nil before he had been sent out in the van that morning to deliver some parcels.

Although I may seem to be wandering from the question of security, it is important to stress that popular attitudes have a strong bearing on National Security. Because I think it may interest my readers, I will mention two occupations, both of which would put a man Beyond the Pale. One, for no good reason I ever discovered, was that of a butcher. All Saudi men were prepared to kill and dress an animal for a family dinner, but the killing and preparing of animals to be cut up and sold in the market was something that made a man almost "untouchable." I was told that the children of a butcher could only marry into the family of another butcher – they really were a caste apart. One saw many of these men in the meat market, but if one went to a Supermarket with a fresh-meat counter, the men who served would not be Saudis.

Another "impossible" job was that of barber. Here, I believe, there was a feeling that it was unmanly to be a barber. The very numerous barbers' shops, to which Saudis flocked as much as other Arabs, were staffed by men from almost every other Arab country – where there was no such feeling. I was told that "Hairdressing" was taught in the Vocational Schools; but I could never get any figures for the number of students, although I am sure nobody went on to practice the skill they had acquired. I was told a story – for which I cannot vouch – of a man in Ta'if who had married the daughter of an important local man. He wanted a divorce but could not make any progress because his powerful father-in-law opposed it. However, one Friday before Prayers, this man set himself up outside the main mosque with a chair, hot water, razors, soap and towels and began to shave the worshippers before they entered the sacred building. When the father-in-law came along he was horrified: "What are you doing?" he hissed. "This is my new trade," said his son-in-law. After

Prayers he was summoned to the in-law's house where a divorce settlement was speedily arranged. Nobody could permit his daughter to be married to a barber!

I mentioned above the Vocational Schools, which were based on the excellent idea that young men should be taught a useful – and necessary – trade. When I lived in Riyadh I questioned whether these institutions did much good – because very few of their graduates had any intention of practising the trade they had been taught. In my first office at the Ministry of Education there was a very well dressed youngish man who made the tea. He told me he had been trained in the Riyadh Vocational School – I forget for what – but never had any intention of practising the trade, which, in any case, his father would have forbidden. He had two or three large American cars and said he enjoyed the work – which meant that he could meet his friends every day, and didn't have very much work to do. I knew another man who had been trained as a plumber in the vocational school, but he too never had any intention of practising his trade. The idea of being a sort of superior bathroom cleaner – virtually the same as a lavatory attendant – was quite beyond a joke. This man was offered a well-paid job by Aramco as a Maintenance Plumbing Engineer for their villas, but turned it down without hesitation in favour of a more lowly-paid job making tea in the Ministry. The uninitiated might wonder why these men bothered to learn a trade they had no intention of following: yet things become more understandable when it is realised that students in Vocational Schools received an allowance. In Qassim, where there was a Vocational Training Course, I saw an abstract of a report that revealed that almost none of the students had gone on to practice the trade for which they had been trained: nearly all had saved their allowances and either bought a taxi or stock for a shop.

When I made the original notes on which this book is based, the future of Saudi Arabia seemed more uncertain than has actually proved to be the case. I think it is worth pointing out that the country, only thirty-two years old when I first entered it, is now seventy-seven years old. What was still in the process of "settling down," is now firmly settled, and the Saudi Royal Government's policy of making life as comfortable as possible for its citizens has been remarkably successful.

Of course people complain, usually about things that affect them personally. In a country like Britain people have the – theoretical – possibility of removing an unpopular government at a General Election; voters seem to vote against a government rather than for an opposition.

While this was not possible in Saudi Arabia, at least disgruntled citizens had an opportunity unavailable almost everywhere else. They could go straight to the Mayor, the Governor, a Minister or even to the King himself — with the certainty of being heard and in the knowledge that, if their case was just, they would receive justice.

There used to be stories — in the foreign media — about dissatisfaction in Saudi Arabia, stories from foreign visitors who had talked to "Saudis." At the time I discounted these stories because they seemed to come from "untypical" Saudis. Of course, there were some who frequented the houses of foreign Arabs, Europeans and Americans — possibly for the ease with which alcohol could be obtained — but these were not your average Saudi. I read in my notes that, while I could not claim to be omniscient, in the 1980s I thought that I knew more about the "ordinary" Saudi than any other Westerner. I used, sometimes, to invite a Saudi friend — even a Saudi friend and his wife! — to a party. He would always ask whether any other Saudi would be present, and if so, who would it be? This "typical" Saudi did not want to be seen frequenting a European house (and possibly drinking alcohol) by any other Saudi, except — possibly — a very close friend.[6]

I am sure that, by now, the chances of a military coup are minimal.. There was certainly a possibility of a coup in the 1960s when Nasser was peddling his ideas of Arab Socialism. Nasser wanted to make the Arabs once more one of the most important political groups in the world — but I don't think a coup on these lines would have succeeded. A violent Islamic Fundamentalist rising was far more likely; as Al-Akhwan showed, there have always been a lot of people of that ilk in the Kingdom — and their most potent fulminations were always against those Muslims who did not live up to the Fundamentalists' very high standards. When I was in Riyadh it seemed likely that the Shi'ites of the Eastern Province would be ready to join any religiously–inspired uprising. But they have now been quiet for a good many years and I am inclined think that this possibility has vanished.

---

[6] I had an odd experience in 1979. I drove one evening to the house of a middle-aged Saudi friend and we were joined by some western businessmen. Our host had produced a generous amount of whisky when suddenly an elderly cousin was announced. He joined the party, greeted the guests, and accepted not one, but five or six glasses of scotch. Soon the cousins began laughing: although they lived within a few miles of each other, and had been friendly all their lives, neither had known that the other drank alcohol. Such is the degree of secrecy many "ordinary" Saudis preserve about their lives.

There must be a lot of people in Saudi Arabia who – secretly perhaps, or in small groups – admire Osama bin Laden. Perhaps they are even proud he is a Saudi and a son of the man who built the Mecca – Ta'if road and embellished and restored the Grand Mosque in Mecca. I believe that the more extreme of these people do want a religious change that would also involve some political change; but they are up against a difficulty. I am sure that the great majority of Saudis have become so accustomed to a comfortable and "westernized" life that they would be loath to return to the primitive simplicity of half a century ago. Furthermore, those who seek reform must be divided; should they concentrate their anger against the army of foreign workers who weaken the Islamic character of the country, or against the Royal government that admits those workers?

It is a fact that for very many years, ever since "real" money came into the Kingdom, more and more non-Saudis have had to be recruited to perform the necessary jobs Saudis won't do. I have already mentioned the non-Saudi barbers but, because of the numbers involved, other categories have been even more significant. There are thousands and thousands of labourers who work on the huge number of major construction works. There is no question that – even if kept segregated in camps or compounds – the presence of a large number of people of other races does change overall attitudes and patterns of behaviour. In England we have only to look at the changes brought about by the reluctance of British men, in the years after the war, to do the more menial jobs on the railways and on the buses. Many of those jobs were given to immigrants from the West Indies, particularly from Jamaica, and so began a profound change in British society. The situation was different in Saudi Arabia, where foreigners were forbidden to own property, but the outlook and attitude of the people had changed before I left, and must have changed even more now.

During the early 1980s, there was much talk of a crisis and people spoke, if not openly, at least privately, of the possibility of a coup. Criticism focussed on the behaviour of some of the more extravagant princes and princesses,[7] with stories of vast properties bought abroad and

---

[7] The mother of one of my pupils wanted to get home for King Faisal's funeral (she was in America). As there were no immediate flights she chartered a Boeing from Air France and flew back to Riyadh, buying the plane on arrival. She then had the interior redecorated to include a bedroom and a marble bathroom with solid gold taps. In the most exclusive apartment building in Paris she had two complete floors, the whole being furnished (at what expense?) with the best antiques her interior designer could find.

collections of diamonds locked up in Swiss Banks. Even at the time I did not see anything sinister in this: it applied only to a limited number of the Royal Family and the super-rich. In any case, opportunities for investment in the Kingdom were still limited and, if the purchase of foreign properties had been banned, the result could only have been to push the already exorbitant cost of land and buildings even higher. In short, it could be argued that investment abroad was almost a patriotic duty. I knew some members of the Royal Family who, as well as investing abroad, poured money into as many local developments as the market would stand. I think that there was a sense of unease, if not actual nervousness, in high places; but I also noted that with the majority leading quiet, God fearing lives (which, unpublicised, ignite no headlines) the chances of the regime surviving were much better than some people supposed, and, I am thankful to say, I have been proved right.

There were, I think, always some senior members of the Armed Forces who looked enviously at the political power exercised by the military in other Arab States. I have already referred to the officers' plot in the 1960s and to the behaviour of some members of the Air Force at the time of the Yemeni troubles. But such men were a minority and the senior officers were always strong supporters of the regime. As it happened, I knew many more Police Officers than Military men but none of those I knew – ordinary middle-class men with young families – were interested in what might be called "politics."

I must tell of one odd incident in 1978. One day, a Jordanian friend came to my house accompanied by a fairly senior Saudi Air Force officer, who made a remark that was either extremely unguarded or – perhaps – deliberately provocative. This officer admired my very handsome dog (Chico was a cross Virginian Sheepdog – like a Collie/Alsatian) and asked if I had brought him from England? I explained that Chico had been born in Riyadh, one of a litter of nine, but that all the other eight had gone to Europe or America. "Ah," said the officer, addressing the dog, "so you're the unlucky one, boy. You've had to stay behind here." As

---

When she took her three sons to see it they said it was too old fashioned, so she told her designer to get rid of the antiques and do up the whole place in a modern style. She also had an apartment – I am sure a very luxurious one – in Geneva, and at each city she kept a fleet of three Mercedes, a 600, a 450 and a 300. When I was told this I asked my pupil why she needed so many cars, and why have duplicates in Paris and Geneva? The answer was that she didn't know what car she wanted to ride in on any one day; and it was too long to drive to Paris from Geneva. Now that she had on her own Boeing she could fly more quickly.

some reply seemed to be expected, either from myself or from the dog, I answered for both of us and remarked on the advantages of living in Riyadh, with security and stability and with many old friends. The subject was changed smoothly, but I wondered at the time and have wondered since, whether the remark was some sort of test: was I a foreigner to whom a certain amount of steam could safely be let off, or, more sinisterly, was it a test remark to see whether I was one of those foreigners who were critical of the regime? I never saw the officer again and never asked my Jordanian friend anything about him or about our meeting. I suppose that when I lived in Riyadh I adopted the local – and prudent – policy of not concerning myself with, or even referring to matters "political."

I think today as I thought all those years ago, that the Saudi regime is secure, and that there is no realistic danger to Saudi National Security.

CHAPTER 12
A Band of Brothers?

All those years ago, when I was making the notes for this chapter, I wrote that readers would probably find some of my views rather cynical. Of course, the political situation has changed enormously in the past quarter of a century, and in any case, what I wrote then – which is in fact what I am writing now – was my own interpretation of what I saw and heard; this was sometimes rather different from the "official" line given in newspapers or on the radio or television programmes. In those days, there was constant reference to "The Arab Nation," "The Arab People," and "Arab Brotherhood" – phrases heard less frequently today. I always remember a letter from Viscount De L'Isle that I had received on my first arrival in Riyadh. De L'Isle argued that hatred of Israel was the only thing that kept the Arabs together; while like many families, the Arabs tended to unite against outsiders, the normal state of relations in the "Arab Brotherhood" resembled those of the Nickleby or Chuzzlelewit families at their worst. I noted then that what was to follow was (and is) based on what "ordinary" Saudis told me over many years of continued conversations – and what they said was often the almost exact opposite of the "official" line.

In the first chapter, I made the important point that, throughout my sojourn in Saudi Arabia, the people of the Najd really did think that, by the grace of God, they were superior to others, especially to other Arab Muslims. Non-Muslims were so far beyond the Pale that they didn't enter into consideration – they were doomed to the Fire anyway. I was conscious of a sense of "apartness," or "election" – if I may use a word with a religious association – that still pervaded much Saudi feeling. Even those who travelled abroad fairly frequently and led quite cosmopolitan lives tended to travel much as rich Englishmen travelled in the nineteenth century. Their attitude to the inhabitants of poorer, non-oil producing countries was probably not so different to the way the "Milord" regarded those Kipling called "The lesser Breeds without the law". In both cases, those at the receiving end must have found the experience profoundly irritating.

When talking to me, many Arabs from other countries used to complain about Saudi "arrogance," and I suppose there was arrogance, if only unconsciously, because they did feel themselves set "apart" by the purity of their religion and by their great wealth (that really is having your cake and eating it!). Yet they did not claim to be better than others in a personal sense; their superiority came from the fact that they were Saudis – especially if they came from the Najd – not because they were Mohammed X or Ahmed Y or Abdullah Z. They were nationalists, and, I'm afraid, racialists par excellence.

I must say a word here about "Racialism" in Saudi Arabia. I suspect it probably had much to do with the fact that slavery had been normal until not long before my arrival, and many middle-aged men had been slaves when young. Most of the slaves had been brought from Africa by Arab slave-dealers and it was indicative of the prevailing attitude that the word "African" was used in a casual and disparaging way – with no attempt to differentiate between different black races. Some remarks I have heard could easily have come from a group of slave owners in the American Deep South. For instance, when asking questions round a class, I would come to a dark-skinned boy; "Don't ask him sir," would come a chorus, "he's black. He won't know." All I could do was to say "Don't talk such nonsense," and immediately ask the question of a pale-skinned boy whom I was sure would not be able to answer; and, when he failed, get the answer from the dark boy. Apart from thanking him for his answer it would have been counter-productive to make any more of the incident. As the years went on and the memory of slavery receded, I think attitudes towards "blacks" eased somewhat – but students and even Police Officers and Government Officials have told me they were ashamed of their colour. They really believed they would have done better and gained quicker promotion if their skins had been paler. I should add, however, that there were some very senior dark-skinned officials in the ministries.

I was told a story on this theme, concerning an incident at which, obviously, I was not present. A former senior official of the Ministry of Education was involved: he was dark-skinned but not black, and he was a particularly kind and civilized man. It seemed that he had had to review the promotions of various officials and among these were a several religious figures who drew substantial salaries for occasional attendance at meetings of the Higher Education Committee. One of these gentlemen had applied for promotion to a very senior grade indeed and, since there was no possible justification, his request had been turned down. He stormed into the office of the dark-skinned Director, ignoring the meeting that was taking place and the large number of people present – one reason why the story raced around the Ministry so quickly. He then slammed the letter rejecting his request down on the table and said that he was not going to have a "black" stop his promotion. He was Sheikh So-and-so from such-and-such a family, and if a letter confirming his promotion was not written immediately, while he waited, he would go to the King and the "black" would be out of a job.

Rather regrettably, he got his letter and his promotion. This little story is not very edifying, but what struck me were the reactions of the people who retold the tale. The general opinion was that the King would have sent the petitioner off with a flea in his ear; but, in the late sixties, the inferior status of the "blacks" was so ingrained that the senior official buckled under the pressure. Actually, it was the way the story was told that was rather shocking – if one allowed oneself to be shocked by behaviour patterns in a different culture – because there were hints that most of those present, who liked and respected the Director, still felt more sympathy for the outrageous demand of a religious bully, greedy for a material advancement he did not deserve, than for an administrator trying to preserve a balance of fairness and justice. It was not so much what the tellers actually said, but the tone of their voices and the half admiring laugh as they described the old Sheikh's hectoring voice and domineering manner.

This racialist view must have coloured Saudi dealings with countries such as Sudan and Somalia, both in those days poor and in receipt of Saudi aid. There were quite a lot of Sudanese who had been employed as upper servants in the palaces, and the image still clung, although many had now been seconded to Ministries and there were quite a lot of – efficient – Sudanese teachers. Friends assured me that the Sudanese authorities – though urgently in need of aid – disliked the role of supplicant for Saudi bounty and preferred to find other sources of assistance if possible. They explained that, despite the Islamic prohibition on the charging of interest, the various "charges" imposed by Saudi Arabia made its money more expensive than most, while its "conditions" were exceptionally onerous. For a long time, Somalia barely figured at all: it was black, African and linked to Russia. As soon as the President abrogated the treaty with Russia, Somalia became politically "interesting" and it received some

Saudi aid. Many Somalis (like their predecessors, the Eritrean refugees) came to work in the Kingdom, but usually as domestic servants or in other humble occupations. Yet since the Somalis are not really Arabs, they hardly belong to this chapter at all. They are included only by virtue of the fact that Somalia then belonged to the Arab League.

In much the same way, the North African States of Tunisia, Algeria and Morocco were, as it were, "Arab" by courtesy. Their people spoke Arabic, but in such a different dialect that many Saudis claimed not to understand a word they said; in an earlier chapter I recounted a language problem I had in Morocco. Apart from some Saudis going there on holiday – Prince, now King Abdullah, used to go to Morocco as a favourite holiday destination – there was little contact with "Barbary". There was some affinity with Morocco as it was a Kingdom, and the Tunisian government was sufficiently right wing and pro-Western to permit good relations with Saudi Arabia. The position on Algeria was more equivocal: its government was left wing and seemed to subscribe to socialist views totally rejected by the Kingdom, but – since Algeria did not meddle in affairs that affected Saudi Arabia – the official line coming through the press was one of guarded semi-approval. As far as the man-in-the-street was concerned, these countries were so far away that they were rarely so much as given a thought.

When, however, I turn to Libya we come to a horse of a very different colour. In those days, Colonel Qaddafi was officially regarded as a dangerous lunatic, yet it cannot be denied that he appealed to some people, particularly those who wanted to grumble about the government. The fact that Qaddafi had come to power by overthrowing a monarchy hardly commended him to the Saudi authorities – even if they had not given King Idris their whole-hearted support. This benevolent Senussi ruler came from Cyrenaica, or Eastern Libya, and had been imposed on the country by the victorious allies when it became independent after the end of the Second World War. Britain and the United States had preferred Idris to the Princes of Tripolitania, or Western Libya, who were the choice of the majority of the people. This family had been living in Saudi Arabia and had Saudi citizenship – one of them actually became the Saudi Ambassador in Paris. Hence it is possible that Qaddafi's initial revolution, although deplorable per se, was not entirely unwelcome.

However, in his early days, Colonel Qaddafi's championship of every conceivable Arab cause, his defiance of America and "The West," his insistence that all visitors' passports should be in Arabic as well as any other language, all struck a chord to which Arab hearts responded. Whatever their private feelings, the Saudi authorities joined in the general adulation of Qaddafi, seconding his calls for more unity against Israel, and for the oil-rich states to help their poorer Muslim neighbours. They echoed him until it became obvious that Qaddafi was not entirely unselfish, and that he aspired to the mantle of General Nasser. He tried to use his oil money to form indissoluble alliances with Egypt, Sudan, Tunisia and Syria, but all failed. Worse still, from the perspective of orthodox Muslims, Qaddafi's flirtation with atheistic Soviet Russia destroyed his credibility as a religious leader. His gross interference in the internal affairs of various west African countries was of no real interest – except, perhaps, to businessmen like Sheikh Jamil Khojeer, who had a cosy arrangement with the President of Gambia – because they were a long way away. However, late in 1980, Qaddafi stepped up his attacks on the Saudi monarchy to the point of suggesting that it was allowing American aeroplanes to pollute the holy cities of Mecca and Medina by flying over them and spying on them. This was too much; an official protest had to be made and diplomatic ties were severed.

However even at this stage, I could not detect any sign that ordinary people shared the indignation felt in official circles. Qaddafi was regarded as an *enfant terrible*, who might say and do frightful things, but still things with a germ of truth in them. His pronouncements might be greeted with some disapproval, but this would be accompanied by a reminiscent chuckle – suggesting that Qaddafi scarcely shocked the Arab people, however much he alarmed the Arab Leaders. His action in ordering the murder of his enemies living in other countries was certainly considered "A Bad Thing," especially if it involved women and children; but the Arab mind does not look on a personal vendetta, a blood feud, in the way it is seen in Western Europe.[1]

I happened to know two people who had known Qaddafi. One was a British Army Officer who had trained him on an English course; the other

---

[1] A Jordanian friend, whose father was the Police Chief in Amman, told me the following story. Amman came into being after Transjordan was formed in 1919 and many Circassians, including his grandfather, came south to settle there. It was pretty lawless: people looked after their own, and one night out in their orchard, his grandfather shot and killed a man who was trying to steal fruit. More than fifty years later my friend's cousin, an American graduate home on leave, was drinking in a bar in Amman when a man came in and shot him. The killer was the grandson of the man shot so many years before. The family offered "blood money" but said that they were quite ready to continue the feud, and the other family could now try and kill one of them.

was a young Saudi who had been for a time a fellow student in Italy: both gave identical opinions. They said that Qaddafi was intelligent and that his pleasant manners made him quite well liked. He was religious, sometimes to quite a fanatical degree, and he could be intractably stubborn. Once an idea was fixed in his head no reasoning could alter it. At the same time his mind was illogical, and he seemed capable of holding two contradictory opinions at the same time. As the two people's opinions were so very similar I think they must be regarded as accurate.

But whatever the Saudi authorities thought about Libya and its seemingly eccentric leader, ordinary Saudis were generally indifferent. They were interested, and probably secretly supportive, of some of Qaddafi's more outrageous attacks on Israel and "the West," but of the Libyan people they hardly thought at all. Saudis who had met them at conferences tended to dismiss them with few words, not seeming to consider them important. Libya, again, was a long way away and posed no threat to Saudi Arabia, which had more oil and more money than Libya. It is when we come "nearer home" that interest quickened. Egypt, the Yemen, the Gulf States, Iraq, Syria, Lebanon and Jordan and, above all, the Palestinians, were people who were known. Men of these nationalities, often with their families, came to work in Saudi Arabia, and Saudis travelled to see these countries, to do business or go on holiday. They were "real" people and hence interesting, and the man-in-the-street had definite opinions about them. These opinions, not overtly political in the narrow sense, were perhaps more interesting than the official line – not least because, since they were not political, they changed less than the view of the government.

I have already argued that hatred of Israel was the one thing that bound the Arab States together. When I lived in Riyadh I was sure that the successive efforts to achieve the much-talked-of "lasting peace in the Middle East" had failed because most of those involved knew perfectly well that it would be nothing of the sort. Few actually wanted war, but the uneasy state of neither war nor peace suited a good many. There were too many interests tied up in the maintenance of a state of acute tension to allow "peace" to come without a struggle.

As Egypt is next door to Libya, I will start a survey of Saudi nearer neighbours there. In one sense Nasser was right; Egypt is a natural leader of the Arab world – although not strictly an Arab country – because of its population and because of it geographical position, forming a bridgehead between Asia and Africa and being quite close to Europe, both in terms of location and tradition. Arabic is of course the native language of Egypt and, in the past, its inhabitants achieved a higher general standard of education than most other Arab states. Egyptians, too, were not afraid of work, and anyone who questions this should go and watch the peasant farmers at work in the Nile Delta.

The relationship between the Saudis and Egypt can best be described in the hackneyed phrase of "love-hate." Since the days when an Egyptian army – in which, Saudi historians like to point out, there were actually no Egyptian soldiers – crossed the desert and destroyed the first Saudi state, relations between the two countries have always been ambivalent. In the first chapter, I described the sort of things that were bound to cause deep resentment and antagonism; yet at other times the connections were quite close. When King Abdul Aziz (or possibly, his advisors, because by 1950 the King was an old man) decided to "modernize" his administration, he turned to Egypt for expert advisers. At the time when education in Saudi Arabia was largely confined to religious subjects, most Saudis who left to study abroad went to Egypt. Many married Egyptian girls and brought them back to Saudi Arabia. By the time I arrived in Riyadh however, the relationship had soured once more. When there had still been a King of Egypt, there had been a certain affinity between feudal Riyadh and Cairo, which, if not feudal, was at least not a centre of republicanism. Nor had there been any of the tension of the kind that complicated relations with Iraq and Jordan, whose Kings were the sons of that Sherif of Mecca who T.E. Lawrence had supported and whom King AbdulAziz had driven into exile. However when King Farouk was overthrown and a Republic proclaimed, relations became strained: Neguib – bad enough – had been succeeded by Nasser, who was far worse. Saudi fears that their world was crumbling had been exacerbated when the United Arab Republic was set up, incongruously composed of Egypt, Syria and – before the revolution – the Kingdom or Imamate of Yemen, a state so reactionary that it made Riyadh seem Avant Garde. At first, the UAR did look quite a serious threat to the Saudi regime, but it did not last long, soon falling apart from the sheer incompatibility of its components.

During the Civil War in the Yemen, the Egyptians did their best – unsuccessfully, even with Russian support – to foist a left wing republic on the country, while the Saudis, equally unsuccessfully, attempted to keep what I must call a corrupt and enervating regime in power. At that time, the rivalry between Egypt and Saudi Arabia seemed very one-sided in that

Saudi Arabia was still virtually unknown.[2] Even though oil-revenues were increasing, it did not have much influence and such importance as it possessed was due to the fact that Mecca and Medina, the twin shrines of the Muslim World, were situated within its borders. Only gradually, under the leadership of King Faisal, did the country begin to achieve anything like the enormous international eminence it has enjoyed in recent years. Thus, when Nasser was at the height of his power, the Saudi authorities made no effective reply to the scurrilous attacks, broadcast nightly by Egyptian Radio, on the characters and morals of the Saudi Royal Family. These attacks, delivered between the songs of the aging Diva, Omm Chelthoum, were listened to by hundreds of thousands of Saudis.

At this time there were many Egyptians working in Saudi Arabia. Many, if not most, claimed to be members of the Muslim Brotherhood, a strict religious group outlawed in Egypt, where they opposed Nasser's Arab Socialism – as later they were to oppose Hafez Assad of Syria. I was never sure how many of the Egyptian workers were actually members of the Muslim Brotherhood. Some spent their summers in Saudi Arabia, or travelling circumspectly, but not going "home" for fear of reprisals – these I felt probably were members. But I had my doubts about those who returned to their homes and the bosom of their families in Egypt every summer. The point was that if someone could claim to have been persecuted for "religious orthodoxy", they had a better chance of obtaining a more or less permanent and comparatively well-paid job in Saudi Arabia.

There were times when feeling ran high. In 1966 I planned to travel to Cairo in one of the holidays, but Saudi friends warned me that the authorities intended to cancel the contract of any foreigner who had an Egyptian visa in his passport. I don't know whether this was true, but I did learn that the contracts of two teachers who had gone to Cairo had not been renewed. But even if Saudis did not travel to Cairo, the average Saudi rather admired Nasser for asserting some of the old glory of the Arab Empire – and for defying the West.

After Nasser's death, relations took a turn for the better. Once more, Saudis took their holidays in Egypt in droves and, in the other direction, came droves of Egyptians – teachers, doctors, engineers, clerks, even domestic servants and farm labourers. Friendship was in the air, but in

---

[2] Readers may remember my mother's difficulty in early 1965 when the head of International Cables at the Main Post Office in Worthing had never heard of Riyadh and, for some time, refused to believe in its existence.

many cases "in the air" was exactly where it stayed. I knew a lot of Egyptians and, of course, hundreds of Saudis. I liked most people of both nationalities very much, but to listen to Egyptians talking about Saudis and Saudis talking about Egyptians was to hear about people quite unlike the ones I knew. According to the Egyptians, the Saudis who took their holidays in Egypt were purse-proud, arrogant, hypocritical, uncultured, uncivilized and immoral – a picture of the Saudis not unlike the one presented in some sections of the British press. This unflattering picture might have been true of a small minority, but it is always the untypical minority that makes the headlines. I knew some middle class families who spent a couple of months each year in Cairo and Alexandria and was certain they never behaved badly. On the other hand, according to Saudis who had suffered at the hands of extortionate landlords, the Egyptians were rapacious, greedy, untrustworthy, untruthful, arrogant – and servile – and immoral. On the surface – which I learned not to trust in the Middle East – it was hardly the basis for a happy association.

Politically, all seemed to be going reasonably well in my later years. Egyptians working in Riyadh used to complain that they were treated like second-class people because they were from Egypt, but this was not true: they were treated like other non-Saudi Arabs. The man-in-the-street, whom I cite so often, tended to speak badly (from hearsay) of the Egyptians in general, but to except any individual Egyptians he happened to know. When Sadat went to Jerusalem, most people in Riyadh greeted the news with indifference or acquiescence. Only when it became clear from the line put out by the Ministry of Information that the visit was "a Bad Thing" did it become fashionable to decry it. Luckily the visit was in November, so that everybody could declare virtuously that they would never again visit Egypt – at a time when they had no intention of going there anyway. By the following summer, when I was tactless enough to ask some of them why they were going back to Cairo, they just shrugged their shoulders, murmuring that, with all the family and dependents, Europe was too expensive and, after all, it was easier for the women in an Arabic speaking country. I don't believe that verbal condemnation ever led to fewer Saudis going to Cairo – or to less money being spent there.

In the early 1980s, there were regular reports that all flights to Egypt were to be cancelled, that the contracts of all Egyptians working in Saudi Arabia were to be terminated, and other similar harassment – but it always came to nothing. There was a face-saving formula – which was also more or less true – that the "quarrel" was with the government of Anwar Sadat, and not with the Egyptian people, and that therefore no move should be made which might hurt them. Many of those employing them in Riyadh also declared that if their Egyptian members of staff were repatriated, the Ministries would grind to a halt and the schools would close; but some of the same people told me that the atmosphere had become less friendly and thought the Saudis were becoming increasingly xenophobic. Certainly most Saudis spoke harshly of Anwar Sadat; but his frequent broadcasts and statements were aimed at an Egyptian rather than a foreign audience, and he was not trying to please public opinion in Saudi Arabia or elsewhere. Sadat also used to say and do what he thought, and did not change his coat with every suspicion of a change in the weather. All this rather set him apart as a ruler in an area once part of the appropriately named Byzantine Empire.

***

When I left Riyadh, Yemen was still divided between a moderately pro-Western North and a hard-line Soviet South. The Yemen used to be the richest and most prosperous part of Arabia – its Roman name was Arabia Felix – and its wealth came from the spices that passed through the eponymous port of Mocha. If there was any one trait that proved that the Yemenis were pure Arabs, it was surely their inability to agree among themselves – but they were always very open and forthright about their disagreements. The Civil War of the sixties, when Nasser supported the Republicans and the Saudis the Royalists, was not just a struggle on political lines; it was also a continuation of a long-drawn-out fight, which had been going on for centuries, between the tribes of the Northern mountains – generally more conservative and allied with the tribes of the southern province of Saudi Arabia – and those of the central plains and the coastlands, who were more outward looking. North Yemen, in particular, was backward and desperately poor. The South, however, should have been much better placed; it included the fabulous valley of the Hadrhamaut (which had been vaguely "controlled" by the British) and, in Aden, it possessed a port and oil-refinery, which, under any normal government, should have provided the basis for a reasonable national economy; under the Soviet-controlled rulers, however, it was anything but. Since the latter's independence, relations between Saudi Arabia and South Yemen had varied between bad and very bad, and, for much of the time an unreported sort of border war continued in one form or another. The ill feeling was aggravated by the Saudi practice of giving shelter to all refugees, including former tribal leaders, who were awarded pensions, apparently given on the understanding that the former leaders would organize harassment operations against the South Yemen government. There was a time during the late seventies when tensions eased a little: by a judicious use of money the Saudi authorities tempted some members of the South Yemen government away from their Soviet masters. Embassies were reopened, direct air services were resumed, and all looked set for reconciliation and some sort of merger between North and South Yemen – all under the benevolent auspices of Saudi Arabia. Unfortunately the Russians moved quickly and decisively, as they were to do in Afghanistan. The South Yemen president was murdered in a coup and more obedient vassals were installed. All prospects of a merger ended abruptly when the President of North Yemen was killed in his office by a bomb carried by a Peace Envoy from the South. Riyadh gossip maintained that the Envoy had not known what was in the package the Soviet agents had given him to take to Sana'a, and as he had been himself blown to pieces, he couldn't be questioned.

Saudis considered the Hadrahmis to be the "wide boys" of the business-world. Certainly many of the leading businessmen and bankers – all with Saudi nationality – were of Hadrahmi origin. They were thought hard working and were generally quite popular – but there were not many of them. Later refugees received sympathy because they were fleeing from an atheistic tyranny. Feelings about the "Yemenis", by which Saudis meant people from North Yemen, were more equivocal.

In the first place there were an awful lot of them and they could come and go in Saudi Arabia without needing a Saudi sponsor. Thousands went backwards and forwards though the mountains without troubling the frontier posts at all, so that it was impossible to tell at any one time how many Yemenis were in Saudi Arabia. The often-quoted figure of one million was probably about right, and these numbers had a profound effect both on the Kingdom and on the economy of their own country. Originally, they went into Saudi Arabia to take labouring jobs, working on roads or on building sites, or to become servants, especially with those families who could not afford the more expensive Sudanese. Thus, they were looked down upon because they were prepared take jobs Saudis felt "beneath them", but local traders also became increasingly irritated when they found their market taken by harder working Yemenis who cut prices. There were all sorts of regulations, designed to compel Yemenis to trade only through Saudi "owners" – but even so many Yemenis amassed considerable fortunes even by Riyadh standards. Before I left, even those who worked as "labourers" (and it was difficult to find a plumber or an electrician who was not a Yemeni) were making a great deal of money and they did not endear themselves to the Saudis – or others – by their exorbitant charges. There was an electrician who, every year at the beginning of summer, would come and spend the best part of a day checking and preparing the air-conditioners. He always charged a sum (in sterling value) of fifteen pounds, but suddenly in 1977, he put his charge up to a hundred and fifty pounds. One Saudi friend told me that on the same day he had called three men to his flat: one had to make an adjustment to an air-conditioner; one had to change a washer on a tap; and one had to change the lock on the front door. Each one had charged him seventy five pounds for coming to the flat in the first place, plus exorbitant charges for the "parts" they had to go and buy. The effects of this "wealth" when sent back to the Yemen were rocketing land and house prices in a country where many people were very poor; there was actually a consumer boom in items like television sets and refrigerators (all imported) when many people had hardly enough to eat. So many men had gone to Saudi Arabia to work that not enough remained to till the land – hence not enough food was produced and so prices rose and food had to be imported.

When men wished to return to the Yemen, especially if they were of military age, they might be refused permission to leave – although so long as they could cross the mountain passes at will such a ban was virtually meaningless. On the other hand if a man did not want to go that way it could prove difficult and expensive to travel legally. In 1979 Abdou, who had looked after us for many years, took his wife and son back to Ibb in the Yemen for a holiday: since his wife was in "a delicate condition" he decided that it would be unsuitable for her to travel over rough roads and tracks. In any case, they had their return air-tickets and, at great cost, he had obtained official exit visas. On arrival at the airport, however, he found that he had to distribute as much again to the airline officials and the airport guards before he was allowed to board the plane.

It would not be true to say that Saudis despised Yemenis; rather they despised the manual work Yemenis were prepared to do, work which the Saudis would not do themselves. They were, however, ready to admit that Yemenis were "real" Arabs who spoke the nearest to classical Arabic and had played an important part in the History of "the Arab Nation." On the debit side – at least from the perspective of strict Najdis – was the fact that the Yemenis were regrettably liberal-minded Muslims and were split into many sects. They had maintained a large Jewish community until the state of Israel had been founded, whereupon the Imam had ordered the Jews either to leave for their new homeland or to convert to Islam.

Yemenis, who are also sometimes looked down on by expatriates – of the sort I must designate as ignorant – are among the most fiercely independent of the Arabs you are ever likely to meet. In part, this explains why the Civil War lasted so long; to demonstrate their independence, some tribes took money from both sides, and fought for both at different times. Unlike many Arabs, a Yemeni does not automatically side with the stronger party – indeed, he is more likely to help the weaker. At the height of the Civil War, when the Saudis were making their maximum, and nearly successful, effort to crush the Republicans, a senior Saudi general visited John Habib, the American liaison officer with the Ministry of Defence. When the Yemeni houseboy came in to bring coffee, the General asked him where he came from, and, hearing that he was from Yemen, asked if he was a Monarchist. It was definitely a question that expected the answer "Yes," but it didn't get it. The boy looked the General up and down and said: "No, I'm a Republican. Do you want anything else?" and left the room. The General turned to his host: "By God," he said, "The Yemenis are a fine people. That boy knows that I could have him arrested just like that" – he snapped his fingers – "but he doesn't care. That's why the Yemenis will never be beaten."

The Yemenis tended in their turn to look down on the Saudis as "uncivilized", which is unkind, but perhaps understandable if the architectural splendours of Sana'a are compared with the crudity of Wahabi Riyadh. Visually, Riyadh was austere in the extreme; and with the exception of fine carpets, there was little of beauty in the traditional house – although I would make an exception for the chaste simplicity of the wooden bowls in which food was served. They pleased me very much, although sadly they were already being superseded by plastic when I arrived in the city. It is very bad form, and vulgar, to criticise hospitality honestly given, and I must ask the reader's forgiveness if I now describe two Ramadan breakfasts to which I was invited on successive days. This meal, after a day of fasting, is something of a special celebration, and I give this description as an illustration of what were two different cultures.

On the first day I was invited to the house of a fairly well to do middle-class Saudi, not a man whom I knew well, but who worked in the

Ministry of Education. The meal was served in an inner hall, totally bare except for a green Wilton carpet that almost filled the room. The meal was served on a sort of thick brown paper placed in the middle of the hall, and a mass of food, evidence of the host's hospitality, was spread on the paper. The various china, plastic and enamel dishes were so close together that they overlapped and couldn't be put down properly. There were fifteen or twenty of us and we ate ourselves to a standstill, yet there still seemed enough food left to feed an army. I particularly remember one large – and very expensive – fish remaining untouched. I feel ashamed for criticising this meal, but it throws into greater prominence the breakfast I attended the following evening.

This time my host was a Yemeni, who had a small shop in the market, with a tiny two-roomed mud house in a little street behind it. The main room was about fifteen feet long and seven wide: it was covered in oriental carpets and had patterned velvet cushions around the walls on which were hung a number of framed photographs of mountain scenery in the Yemen. Instead of using fingers there were spoons, knives and forks in every place – not only for myself, a courtesy to which I was accustomed – and a white cotton or linen cloth was spread. When the food came it came by degrees: first a cup of coffee with dates, the traditional beginning to a Ramadan breakfast. A dish of soup followed, with a number of plates of various savoury pastries – my favourite part of the meal – and a meat and macaroni dish, served separately, preceded the creams and fruits that ended the meal. In short, it was a civilized, even elegant meal. In fact I was so struck with the cups used for coffee before the meal, and with others from which we drank tea afterwards, that I found out privately from a fellow guest where our host had bought them. The following day I went out to buy myself a dozen of each.

One final example of why I still think of the Yemenis as "civilized" concerns the incomparable Abdou, who has figured before in these pages. I was in the market with my mother looking for a new carpet for my majlis. Both my mother and I prided ourselves on being able to "dress" a room to advantage; and, after looking through twenty or thirty carpets, chose one I still remember as being especially beautiful. I asked Abdou what he thought and he said "It's a fine carpet but you can't put it in the Majlis. The blue of the curtains will kill it. It would look nice in the dining room though." Needless to say, when we got the carpet home, he was perfectly right. In the Majlis, with its blue curtains and midnight blue ceiling, the carpet looked to be nothing at all, but once in the dining room it drew admiration from every guest.

To sum up, I think now as I thought before, that while relations between the Saudis and the Yemenis cannot be easy when one is so rich and the other so poor, that does not alter the fact that these relations were, and I believe still are, generally good. Basically, the two people understand each other and have common interests; and there was a sufficient degree of interdependence, because – for different reasons – neither could do without the other.

***

When we turn to the countries of the Gulf – which I was brought up to call "The Persian Gulf" but learned to call "The Arabian Gulf" after 1964 – the situation is again different. Kuwait, Bahrain, Qatar, the United Arab Emirates (that amalgamation of six formerly feuding British-protected Trucial States) and Oman all have a good deal of money; indeed Kuwait was the first state to reach a per capita income which made all its citizen's rich. There is, therefore, no way in which any one of them can be financially dependent on Saudi Arabia, but they can never forget their great neighbour, like Big Brother looking over their shoulder. It must be difficult for those who just look at the map or read about the notorious high spending in the area to realize just how few people actually live there, and how empty these lands are outside the "capital city." The people do resent what they regard as Saudi interference. In the late sixties, when Bulgaria was a hard-line Communist country, I met a rather maudlin Kuwaiti businessman in the All-Night Bar of the Balkan Hotel (where the good communists sold only champagne, Scotch whisky and English gin), and he accused me of siding with the Saudis against him: "You're bullies," he kept saying, buying another round of gin each time, "you're all bullies. Saudi Arabia wants to bully us because it is so much bigger. We don't like you!" I don't say that all the inhabitants of the Gulf felt the same, but those countries where alcohol was on sale – especially Bahrain – disliked the continued stream of advice and admonition coming from Riyadh. Perhaps they had some reason to resent this "abuse", especially since the first thing rich Saudis usually did on arriving in their hotel rooms was to telephone Room Service and order drink by the bottle. There were, however, and I am sure still are, two facts to remember about these Gulf States; there are many Wahabis among them – particularly in Qatar – and there are also a lot of Shi'ites. Many Iranians went to work on the southern side of the Gulf after the oil-money began flowing, joining the families of Persian origin who had lived there – in some cases for centuries. In fact, Iran used to claim Bahrain; in 1968 I had to get a special new passport for a visit to Iran, as the Iranian embassy in Jeddah would not put a visa in my old one which showed evidence that I had visited Bahrain. King Faisal later negotiated with the Shah and Bahrain's "territorial integrity" was confirmed; but after the Islamic Revolution and the overthrow of the Shah the question was again raised. Now, the "interference" took the form of a call to all Bahraini citizens of Shi'ite origin to rise against their Sunni rulers and to institute the Rule of the Saints.

There was also, in my early years, trouble over the oasis of Buraimi, especially when it seemed possible that oil would be found in the region. Various people told me about Buraimi but none of the explanations struck me as convincing or coherent. I was told that it was "Saudi" because, in the third quarter of the nineteenth century, a governor had been sent from Riyadh – although nobody was sure whether he had really governed. The odd thing about this story was that this was supposed to have happened at time when Riyadh was in a state of conflict between King Abdul Aziz's uncles; it seemed unlikely that anyone would have had the leisure to think of extending Riyadh's influence to such a distant place. By 1964, although Riyadh meddled partly for the sake of meddling, the real dispute was between Sheikh Shakhbut of Abu Dhabi – whose son, Sheikh Zeid, was then Governor of Buraimi – and Sheikh Taimur of Muscat, the ruler of Oman. It will be appreciated that both these states were "protected" by Britain, which brought Britain into a verbal dispute with Saudi Arabia. Diplomatic relations were broken off, but as I recorded earlier, Britain's support for the Yemeni monarchists in the Civil War restored relations, although British troops were helping to guard Buraimi.

The situation was made more complicated in Oman because Sheikh Taimur was fighting a prolonged war with the Imam of Oman, a cleric of the type of the Norman Bishop Odo. However the British helped the Sheikh to pacify the area, and then arranged for his removal in favour of the Sandhurst-trained Sheikh Qaboos. At the same time they arranged for the retirement of Sheikh Shakhbut. The arrival of two reasonable, pragmatic and competent rulers meant that there was no more fuss. Abu Dhabi asserted its permanent right to Buraimi by the simple expedient of building a multi-lane motorway between the capital and Al-Ain, the main town of the Buraimi oasis, and then putting up a Hilton Hotel there.

Saudis in general – as opposed to those in the Government – don't talk much about their neighbours in the Gulf. They think of them rather as younger brothers, and so perhaps the charge of "bullying" is reasonable, because what is permissible in an elder brother is impermissible in somebody from outside. The smaller states are jealous of their independence, and some Saudis were liable to resent independence in both young people and in young states. Many more resented what they saw as the enormous wealth of the Gulf States, not appreciating that they had few people to spend it on and did not have to sustain anything like the same defence expenditure as Saudi Arabia. "Why can't we have free water, electricity, and telephones?" They would say with some envy.

Before I left Riyadh the problem of the Shi'ites was a major concern that brought the Saudi and Gulf Governments together. The Iran-Iraq war made matters especially difficult, as Riyadh was forced to side with a left wing, Russian-allied (but Sunni) power against the dangers of destabilization posed by Iran: they were, all of them, nervous about the effects over zealous support for the Iraqi cause might have on their Shi'ite subjects.

***

During my stay in the Middle East, Syria and Iraq were at daggers drawn, so it may seem incongruous to consider them together. However they were similar in at least one respect: their "popularity" – or its opposite – with the Saudi authorities fluctuated wildly and on no particular principle. I explained in an earlier chapter how the Syrian teachers in the Yamama School (and in others) were all withdrawn in one day – and without prior warning – on "political" grounds. The presence or otherwise of Syrians in the Ministries and schools ebbed and flowed. There were, on the other hand, many Syrians who lived permanently in the Kingdom, refugees from the revolutions that were a regular feature of Syrian life until the strongman, Hafez Assad, took over. Each change of government brought a number of senior military or government officials to take refuge in Saudi Arabia, a country which, as likely as not, they had been reviling only weeks earlier.

To a lesser degree, the same was true of Iraq. There had been revolutions, but not with the regularity of the Syrians, and the flow of refugees was therefore smaller. There were Iraqi monarchists in Saudi Arabia, most of whom had been granted Saudi nationality, and Iraqis were regularly seconded to work in the schools or the ministries; but, as with the Syrians, their employment was liable to sudden termination on political grounds too arcane for the ordinary mortal to follow. Even those in the Ministry of Education, who were considered comparatively secure, every summer awaited with nervousness the publication of the "Haraka", or Movements list, detailing not only the people transferred from one school or one office to another, but also those whose contracts would not be renewed. Every year there were rumours that one or more nationalities were to be expelled; and sometimes the rumours were true. I never tried to understand the intricacies of Arab politics.

Saudi public opinion — by which I mean what people actually said to one another rather than what the papers claimed they said — was very different in relation to Syria and Iraq. It goes without saying that Saudis were very critical of both, but the reasons were not the same; Iraqis were seen as a "hard" people, and in some respects their oil-wealth put them on a par with Saudi Arabia. Even ordinary Saudis feared Iraq's expansionist aims, and until her military incompetence was shown up in the Iraq-Iran War, they had been afraid of her military power. It was not so much that the Saudis wanted to dominate the Gulf, but — particularly on the southern side — they wanted no rival protector of the smaller states. The reaction to the Iraq-Iran war was interesting: ordinary people did not share the government's (tentative) support of Sunni Iraq, but preferred Iran, declaring that Saddam Hussein was a madman: few, if any, regarded it as a struggle between an Arab and a non-Arab power.

The war itself did not surprise me, and perhaps I may be allowed to introduce a personal note. In the summer of 1957, I was working at a language school, where cadets from the Royal Iraqi Navy were taking an English course before going to the Royal School of Navigation at Southampton. The Headmaster's wife was removing all the money to set up her own school in Bournemouth and there was no money for anything (except to pay a good chef). The Headmaster, sensibly, had a nervous breakdown and I found myself as Acting-Headmaster with no domestic staff — who liked to be paid — except one young Italian man who had lost his work-permit. I explained to the students, only about half of whom were from Iraq, that they must make their own beds, clean their dormitories and do other tasks in rotation. The three (rather important) Iranians at the school objected – one insisting on calling his Ambassador – and when I demanded that they should do their share the eldest boy said, "Why should we do this work? You have Iraqis here. Iraqis are servants. Let them clean the classrooms." The next day I assembled all the students in the Hall after prayers, sent for a broom, and began myself to sweep the floor. Before I had completed one length the eldest Iranian came forward to take the broom from my hand. There could, he said, be no disgrace in doing the work if his teacher could do it, but the mutual scorn and loathing felt between the Iraqis and the Iranians persisted, and I have not forgotten it.

The Saudi opinion of Syrians was rather curious. Lord Curzon classified them as outstandingly sharp businessmen and this was the most marked traits of the Syrians I met in Riyadh. They wanted to become involved in every business deal they heard about. If I mentioned to a Syrian friend that I knew somebody wanting a villa, he would tell me that he knew exactly the right one and make an appointment to show it the next day. He then apparently would spend the rest of the day going round looking for a suitable villa and arranging his commission with the owner.

The local slang word for a thief is (because of a rhyming association) rather unfairly applied to the inhabitants of Damascus, who are considered the sharpest and keenest businessmen of all. There is certainly one thing to say in favour of their business methods: they succeeded because they worked hard. If you asked a Syrian about anything, from a villa to a car to a second-hand wireless, he would start to look immediately. I have known them to pick up a telephone to start enquiries almost before I had finished speaking. They never minded how long they worked, and were willing to live in very uncomfortable conditions for years, with or without their families, in order to to make and save the money they eventually hoped to spend in ostentatious luxury and entertaining.

Generally, Saudis did not like their Syrian brethren, but I must make one important proviso. In nearly every case – as with other nationalities – they would except an individual or individuals they knew personally. These were "very good men," even if the nation as a whole was condemned.

***

As I noted long ago, it was difficult for anyone who knew and loved the Lebanon before the Civil War to talk or write about it later. It was the favourite summer resort of thousands of Saudis who used to go up into the mountains; Aley was their centre, as Bhamdoun, further up the Damascus road, was the centre for Kuwaitis. It should not be supposed that all the Saudis went to the Lebanon just for the cabarets and the nightclubs – although there were many who did. I knew strictly teetotal Saudis who used to go to the Lebanon every year for the mountain air and good weather, but who would have died rather than set foot in a nightclub. Together with other oil-rich inhabitants of the Gulf, Saudi visitors contributed quite a lot to the Lebanese economy.

When I was first in Riyadh there were not many Lebanese there except for a few businessmen. There had been a special regulation promulgated, I think by Royal Decree, before 1964 – later abrogated but I don't know when – that had exempted Lebanese from the normal requirement to have a Saudi sponsor. Some of those who took advantage of the decree were able to amass great fortunes. Most of the Lebanese I knew were at least trilingual, with fluent Arabic, English and French, and many seemed to have enough Italian and German for day to day needs. Their language skills made them well placed to become company secretaries, office managers and or private and confidential secretaries to Saudi businessmen and princes. Another advantage was that the Lebanese – who are not really Arabs at all – were the most Europeanized of all the Arabic speaking peoples and most at home when dealing with Western businessmen. Of course, the advantage worked both ways and, as I have just noted, many Lebanese made large fortunes: like the Syrians they were prepared to work hard under difficult conditions for a long time in order to render their later years comfortable.

During the Civil War in Lebanon, the Saudi government followed the very sensible policy of trying to defuse the situation and thus restore some sort of normality. This task was made especially difficult because people seemed to change sides with amazing rapidity. On the one hand were the Muslims, who were fighting for their rights and to free themselves from a political settlement, dating from the French mandate, that favoured the Christians; the Christians were now in a minority. On the other hand these same Christians were murdering the Saudis' Islamic brethren. But – and as so often in the Middle East I loved so much – there was a "but": the Islamic brethren were left-wing, and were supported by Communists and by the Saudis then *bete-noir*, Colonel Qaddafi of Libya. The Christians, on the contrary, were right wing and had the tacit support of Saudi Arabia's allies. Throughout the Lebanese troubles the Palestinians – about whom more later – were a major problem. The Muslim left wing alliance was basically pro-Palestinian and the Christian right wing basically anti-Palestinian: this caused heart searching in Riyadh.

Ordinary Saudis, unless they were in business, thought of the Lebanon in terms of a holiday destination and having to spend a lot of money – for the Lebanese are mercenary as well as shrewd businessmen.[3] Most Saudis naturally theoretically preferred their co-religionists, but actually trusted the Christians more. After the Civil War and the subsequent troubles that made life in Lebanon so difficult, more and more Lebanese made their way to Riyadh and to other Saudi Arabian cities. The influx of so many Lebanese might have caused resentment, particularly as – with little justification – many of the refugees behaved as though they were slumming it and yearned loudly and publicly for the superior attractions of the country they had themselves destroyed. As I noted at the time – without denying the evil done by the Palestinians and the Syrians – it was the Lebanese themselves who had wrecked their own country.

There is an old story; but some readers will not have heard it and so I think I can repeat it here. A snake and a scorpion were on the bank of the Dog River, north of Beirut, and both wanted to go across. The snake could swim but the scorpion, of course, could not, and so the scorpion asked his old enemy, the snake to carry him across on his back.

"But I don't trust you," said the snake, "You might sting me and kill me."

"If I did that," said the scorpion, "I should drown, so, of course you can trust me."

The snake agreed and the scorpion climbed on its back, and the snake began swimming across the river. A little more than halfway across the scorpion could no longer resist temptation and stung the snake in the back of its head.

"Why did you do that?" cried the dying snake, "You have killed us both!"

"Because I'm Lebanese," said the scorpion, and they both sank beneath the waves.

---

[3] I once asked a Beirut Muslim businessman what would happen if the Israelis attacked and occupied Lebanon. "Let then come," he said, "They've got a lot of money and we're better businessmen. We'll have it off them!"

***

Of all the neighbouring Arabs it was with the Jordanians (the Real Jordanians as they hastened to explain) that the Saudis felt most in common. This was not surprising since, like many of the Saudis, the "East Bank Jordanians" – as they used to be called – were of Bedouin origin, with many tribes living in both countries and crossing the border at will. Nevertheless the Hashemite Kingdom of Jordan always followed its own programmes and in no sense "followed" Saudi Arabia. In the early seventies, for example, King Hussein was far more forthright over the Palestinians than the Saudis dared to be, and in 1980 Jordan's pro-Iraqi stand went far beyond the cautious and somewhat reluctant support given by her neighbours. However in general the countries agreed and the fact that both were monarchies was a further tie. Individual Saudis usually spoke of the Jordanians with approval and liked King Hussein, not least because he was thought to possess "Baraka." This is not an easy concept to define: it is more than just "Good Luck," but the word "blessedness" has the wrong connotation for a western Christian. Perhaps it would be best to say that it means that God is keeping a benevolent eye on the person concerned, and keeping him out of trouble. Otherwise (as with King Hassan of Morocco) there seemed to be no way to explain the survival of a king known to be surrounded by enemies who were plotting his death.

***

I have deliberately left the Palestinians to the last of the Saudi "neighbours". In my time, the Palestinians had no homeland of their own and occupied many sprawling refugee camps. In their way, they were the most important – and importunate – of all the Arabs. The Arab-Israeli struggle is not really a part of this book, but I cannot ignore it. Then, as I suspect now, it dominated life in the Middle East. That is not to say that people talked much about it: they didn't, but it was always there, looming over their shoulders. I don't suppose the villagers who live on the slopes of Mount Etna or Mount Vesuvius talk much about the volcanoes, but they are always behind them.

When I read over the notes I made twenty-five years ago I am surprised at my own vehemence, but as I re-read them I am still find my old views convincing. I wrote then that the so-called "Palestinian Problem" was artificial and was maintained for political reasons. There had never been a country called "Palestine," as, since the collapse of the Ottoman Empire in 1918, the area had been under a British Mandate. Most of the population were Muslim, with a fair number of Palestinian Christians, and a substantial Jewish Minority. Jews from the ghettos and camps of Europe flooded into Palestine as soon as the war was over and began driving "Arab" Palestinians off their lands even before the United Nations accepted the Zionist established state of Israel, with quite unsustainable frontiers. During the next years, the Arabs tried to drive the Jews into the sea, but failed spectacularly and ended by losing those regions of Palestine that had been allocated to them. I felt then (and have not changed my view) that it was a disgrace to the "Arab Nation" that so many Palestinians lived in refugee camps. With so much money available from oil there was no reason to keep them in squalid camps – except perhaps that the sight of Palestinians living without running water made good propaganda at the UN and might stir the consciences of Western countries. It seemed therefore that there could only be a political explanation for the otherwise inexplicable cruelty of keeping so many people in abject and terrible conditions.

There were atrocities committed by Jews against Palestinian Arabs, and nobody in his right mind could deny that – although in the last days of the Mandate the British were pilloried for their "cruelty" to the Jews when they tried to keep out illegal immigrants, who were committing these atrocities. It is also perfectly true that once the state of Israel was a reality many more Arabs fled for fear of further atrocities. What most readers probably don't know, however, is that the first camps for Palestinian refugees were set up outside Beirut in 1917, and therefore had nothing to do with the Israelis. These refugees, whose families were still living there half-a-century later, were the victims of their fellow Arabs. In reality, as a race, Palestinians were hated and feared by other Arabs; this is a strange fact, yet I think many Palestinians would acknowledge that it is true. I couldn't, and can't explain the reason for this. Most of the many Palestinians I knew over the years were pleasant people – although with big chips on their shoulders. The Arab world seemed to regard them rather like Europeans long regarded the Jews. With the Palestinians, as with the Jews, the words "hated" and "feared" seem the most accurate. Indeed the similarity extends further; it does not surprise me that, like the Jews in the days of the Mandate, the Palestinians turned to terrorism. One evening a group of Yeminis told me that the solution to the Problem would be to send all the Palestinians back to Palestine and let them settle matters with the Israelis, "because, Israelis or Palestinians, they are all one people so that they can fight it out among themselves." Perhaps the Yeminis were right. Maybe if that had been done in 1949 it could have worked: sixty years on, however, it couldn't.

During the British mandate the Palestinians had the advantage of a very good education system, and so a lot of those I knew in Riyadh worked as secretaries and managers. Compared to the Lebanese they usually lacked French but that was all. The Palestinians retained their identity in a remarkable way, rather like the Jews of the Diaspora, and even those born "in exile" – and whose passport might identify them as Jordanian, Syrian, or Lebanese – would always say, "I'm Palestinian," if asked. Of course, like other people, most Palestinians wanted to keep their heads down and live quiet lives, bringing up their families safely and minding their own business. But the business was no longer their own: it had been taken over and become a part of a political scenario. Back in 1980 I noted that the whole scene had got totally out of hand.

When I was first in Riyadh in 1964, there was a good deal of sympathy for the refugees and a genuine desire to help them. The very word "Israel" was forbidden, and Western Atlases that showed it either had the page torn out by the censors or the offending word had been blacked out with special ink. On maps printed for Arab consumption the former mandated territory was firmly labelled "Palestine," and sometimes illustrated by the Palestinian flag.[4]

I think that public opinion in Saudi Arabia changed after the Palestinians were driven to terrorism. Even then I don't think there was any underlying change, it was more that people felt more free to express their true feelings – at least in Riyadh. I was told that in some of the Gulf States, where there were as many or more Palestinians than locals, the fear was greater and it provoked reticence, except behind closed doors. I never met a Saudi who, when pressed, would deny that he disliked the Palestinians. And the Palestinians were aware of this, which only fed their despair. The situation has eased now that fledgling Palestinian states are emerging. I am talking of the time a quarter of a century ago; in those days Palestinians often told me they were better treated by the Israelis than by

---

[4] Those who blame Israel for non-adherence to United Nations Resolution 242 should remember that the Arab states themselves refused to accept the United Nations Resolution which established Israel in the first place.

other Arabs. Since such a statement seems so extraordinary and unlikely, I must give some examples. I couldn't recount all the stories I was told or this chapter would never end: so I will only look at the way the Palestinians were actually treated – as opposed to the way the propagandists said they were – in various countries.

In Egypt, for example, even under Nasser, they were never given much freedom; and it must have been from the Egyptian Secret Service that the Saudi General, described in an earlier chapter, obtained all his information about the student life of my Palestinian friend Khamis. The Palestinians were spied on, confined, and made uncomfortable, and they knew what the Egyptians thought of them. In Jordan they attempted to usurp the government. The population on the West Bank, as it was called, was greater than that of the East Bank (which had been the old Kingdom of Transjordan – the "Trans" having been dropped) – and Palestinians were prominent in government. Unfortunately, egged on by extremists, they began to hijack planes to the Jordanian desert, to draw attention to the plight of the refugees, and in general to act as bullyboys, as they did in Lebanon. King Hussein acted decisively, and what followed was a sort of Civil War, the Palestinians against the East Bank, and the latter won. Many refugees remained in camps, which had been the *casus belli* in the first place. But a lot more fled to Israel where they felt they would be safer; curiously this interesting fact has received very little publicity.

Syria always pursued a devious policy toward the Palestinians – holding them up with one hand and smacking them down with the other. In Syria, Palestinians were never allowed the same sort of freedom they enjoyed in Jordan and Lebanon. Thus, visitors to Damascus were spared having to make enforced charitable contributions to the Palestinian cause; there was nothing like the gun-toting collectors who demanded donations on the streets of Beirut or in the lobby of the Philadelphia Hotel in Amman.[5] During the Civil War in Lebanon, Syria sided first with the Right wing Christian Militias – until they had smashed Palestinian resistance in the centre of the country – and then changed sides, stepping in to protect the rest. Having given sufficient evidence of their

---

[5] Once, in Karachi, my hotel room was entered by three or four young men brandishing rifles and asking for money for the Bihar Liberation Army. I gave them enough to make them go away but asked them not to go to my Mother's room, as it would be improper for them to enter the room of an elderly lady. They were at least well behaved terrorists, and did not bother her.

ruthlessness, the Syrians became the effective controllers of the P.L.O, so much so that, at the Amman Conference of 1980. the P.L.O was forced to agree that Syrian troops would surround their camps in Lebanon. Such behaviour went by almost unremarked – except by the Palestinians themselves, many of whom I talked to.

In Lebanon, where some had been since 1917, the Palestinians ran a state-within-a-state. Inside the camps the Lebanese writ did not run. The Lebanese people, both Muslim and Christian, wanted to curb the powers of the Palestinians, but it was left to the Christian Militias to take active steps. In the early stages of this "war" the Lebanese army and air force made all-out attacks against the camps – and I never knew what pressures were brought upon the Lebanese authorities to stop this – but it led to more widespread sectarian clashes afterwards. Yasser Arafat bestrode the stage and was acknowledged by the United Nations as the Palestinian Leader; but all the Palestinians I knew in Riyadh laughed bitterly at what they called this "posturing."

There were events that could, I feel, only happen in the Middle East. In the Riyadh Schools we had two teachers of English from Lebanon: one was a real Lebanese and the other was a Palestinian, from a refugee camp outside Beirut. They were both good teachers – I wouldn't have recruited them otherwise – but for their sins they shared a flat, and however calm things may have been at the beginning of the year, relations deteriorated as the tensions mounted inside Lebanon. They actually came to blows in sight of the pupils when the fighting began. There were several Palestinian teachers in the Riyadh School, and it was easy to see where their sympathies were; but there were also a number of Egyptian teachers, who made little secret of their support for the Lebanese. By a sad chance both the English teachers were personally affected by the war. The Palestinian's family was in one of the camps that was strafed and bombarded – very accurately we were told – and for many days he had no idea whether they were dead or alive. One could hardly blame him from resenting his Lebanese colleague's triumphant reading aloud from the accounts of the success of the bombing. On the other hand the Lebanese had just received news that his parents' farm – which was the patrimony of himself and his brothers – had been completely destroyed by Israeli bombing. It interested me very much that in no way did he blame the Israelis. His parents had been turned out by Palestinian guerrillas – who, he said, took whatever they wanted in Southern Lebanon – and the farmhouse became the local Palestinian headquarters. Therefore he thought that the Israelis had a perfect right to bomb it. Both men spent a lot of time talking to me and complaining bitterly of their lot – the Lebanese because his country was not truly independent with all the Palestinians in it; and the Palestinian because he and his family felt helpless, with every hand against them and nowhere to turn to.

Of course in the days before the acts of terrorism became frequent there was more open sympathy. Ritual noises of support for "our Palestinian brethren" were made and collections for Palestinian charities were frequent. A certain amount of arm-twisting went on to get teachers and Ministry officials to donate to the Palestinian cause from their salaries; the British, perhaps naturally, objected, but nothing like so loudly as the Saudis. In most shops there were green collection boxes standing on the counters, mute reminders that there were refugees in need. Only very occasionally did I see anyone put in a coin.

Periodically there was a more official collection for the Palestinians. Various members of the Royal Family made large donations, which were duly reported in the newspapers to encourage other people to give. I asked one collector who came round the school how I could be sure that the money would actually go to the people in the camps. He told me, virtuously, that I could specify what the money should be used for, and I think I wrote "children;" but I had no real confidence that any of the money collected in Saudi Arabia would ever reach the refugees. I met one Saudi prince who, before the Civil War in Beirut, wanted to reserve a table at the "Fontana" the best of the Lebanese nightclubs.[6] He was told he could only have a table at the back – because all the tables around the stage were permanently reserved for leading Palestinians. When the head of the prince's office pointed out to the managers that the Saudi royalty were not paupers and would doubtless spend very generously he was told, "Yes, His Highness would spend a lot of money for one or two evenings; but the Palestinians are here every night, week after week, month after month, and they have unlimited money to spend, always." That particular prince, I was told, advised his relations that their charitable contributions did more to support Lebanese bars and nightclubs than to alleviate the lot of refugees.

From the beginning of my time in the Yamama School, many Palestinian teachers went back to "Occupied Palestine" every summer, and returned laden with goods made in Israel, which they swore were

---

[6] I have myself, in my salad days, had a "hostess" dancing on my table in the "Fontana."

much cheaper than anything they could buy in Riyadh. None of them pretended that their families were anything but contented under Israeli rule – but all asked me to keep this secret and not to tell anybody what they had said. They were quite ready to join in the regular denunciation of the Israelis, and some of them told me that in theory they would prefer to live under an Arab government – "but the Israelis are so much more efficient." They all admitted that it was the money that had brought them to Riyadh, and that they were not happy there.

In 1967, a Palestinian teacher in the Royal School asked me to have some German documents translated for him. He had heard that he was eligible to apply for a scholarship to do research for a doctorate, and these were the forms he had to fill in. I had them translated and found to my surprise that this was one of a series of scholarships for Arabs – particularly Palestinians – paid for by Jewish groups. I took him into a deserted classroom and imparted what I was sure he would find shattering information out of the corner of my mouth. He posed as a very militant Palestinian and so I fully expected him to reject the scholarship along with Satan and all his works. To my surprise he knew all about it: "They give lots of scholarships for us," he said. "I don't mind who pays for me." Not long afterwards the 1967 War broke out; and there was a lot of anti-British (and American) feeling for a short time, owing to propaganda lies that the British – among other things – had sent planes to help the Israelis. The marking of examinations was about to start and the Palestinian was walking about calling on all Arab teachers to boycott the British and to refuse to correct papers with them. Luckily he was smaller than I, so I got him into a corner and told him that I still had copies of the correspondence about his scholarship, and that if he didn't shut up about the British, I would show the papers to all his Arab friends to prove that he was taking money from the Israelis. I was amazed when he actually began to shake. He begged me not to tell anyone, and he certainly never said another work – in public – against Britain.

There was a Palestinian secretary I knew, who worked for one of the lawyers in Riyadh. If not fanatical he was at least a strong proponent of the rights of his people, and occasionally took it upon himself to lecture me on the lack of interest and concern shown by the Western countries – particularly Britain and France – for the plight of the refugees. He would brush aside as irrelevant my protests that the Arab countries should look after their own, and that they shared as least as much of the blame. I met him and sat talking to him for a long time after the Syrians had withheld reinforcements while the Christian militias pounded the fortress-camps near Beirut into submission. He was resigned but despairing: "Now we know that we have no friends among the Arabs," he said "The only thing to do is to come to terms with the Israelis."

I was sure that, if left alone, the average Palestinian would have done precisely that, but with the professional troublemakers (in those days Libya, Syria and Iraq played the part that Syria and Iran play in 2009) egged on by the then Soviet Russia, constantly intimidating and stirring up the young men, there was little chance of a compromise. I remember my friend, Olof, from the Swedish Embassy, bringing to my house two broadcasters from the Swedish Radio and Television, a husband-and-wife team who produced foreign affairs programmes and who were on a Middle-Eastern fact-finding tour. They had visited Jordan in the aftermath of King Hussein's campaign against the Palestinian guerrillas; and they had also visited Israel where they had met many Palestinians who had fled from, or been driven out of Jordan. The impression they had received was that the new refugees had been very pleasantly surprised at the conditions. The Palestinians seemed to think they would be better treated in Israel than they had been in Jordan, and many had decided to change their stance.

One of the most extreme Palestinians I knew in Riyadh was an Art master who had his origins in the Gaza Strip, and who was definitely pro-Israel. He told me that he attended summer camps run to bring together young Jews, Christians and Muslims, and he had extremely liberal views on religion. Until "restrained" he would have numbers like "Put your hand in the Hand of the Man from Galilee" playing on the stereo through his art classes. He said that all his family agreed that it would better for the Palestinians to work with rather than against the Israelis, thereby taking advantage of the improved social and economic conditions that would ensue. Naturally, in the climate of Riyadh, he had to be extremely careful to whom he propounded his opinions; but he told me – although I never met them – that he had several friends in Riyadh who thought the same way.

Far more forthcoming, however, was a young Palestinian Games Master who had been trying for two or three years to get one of the Arab organisations to give him a scholarship to take up a training course in America. He was eligible and successful completion would open up a whole world of new job possibilities. One day, he showed me a letter he had just received: as he had been born in "Occupied Palestine" – and his family still lived there – his uncle had taken up his case with the Israeli authorities. With very little delay they had agreed to give him a scholarship – a scholarship more generous than the ones he had been asking for in vain – and he was to take it up at the start of the next academic year. "When I've finished the course," he told me "I may work in America or I may work at home, but this it the last time I shall work in an Arab country. I'm tired of being a second-class citizen."

***

I have dwelt at some length with the Palestinians, and their "relations" with Saudi Arabia, not just because their problem was the central one in my years in Riyadh, but also because nothing seems to have changed. Events that have unfolded while I have been writing this book have only emphasised the depressing fact that the situation is very much the same.

The point I want to stress – and which I think is important – is that the "Palestinian Problem" is largely an artificial one, created decades ago and kept alive by interests that are both many and diverse. I have no authority for saying what I do other than my own gut instinct, which was and is based on personal impressions gained by living among the people and talking to them – often when nobody else was present.

The Palestinians were feared by other Arabs because they were intelligent, hard-working, and traditionally well-educated. After the establishment of the state of Israel the "plight" of the Palestinians – the pitiful refugees living in camps – was a stick with which to beat the Israelis. This is an important reason why Arab oil-money – even in my time – from such a pro-Palestine country as Libya, was never used to provide a homeland for these unfortunate people. Of course, there was the question of where such a homeland should be sited; – no Arab country was willing to take in people who might flex their muscles and take over. But, as with so many struggles (I think of the sectarian problems in Northern Ireland) it is a question of Power. Where there is confrontation the top dogs will have power, and, dare I say it, money: a peaceful settlement is in the interests of the vast majority of the people, but it is not in the interests of those calling the shots. I have cited conversations with Palestinian friends over thirty years ago; but I believe that the feelings they confided to me in private – but were not able to make public – must be felt now today by an awful lot of ordinary people.

Like my friends, their real sentiments are probably the opposite of the views they have to subscribe to in public.

CHAPTER 13
Tales and Adventures

This is not going to be a proper chapter like the twelve that have gone before. Those all dealt with a particular aspect of life in Riyadh as I knew it. As I look back over the years, however, there are numbers of incidents that I can remember with amazing vividness, but that don't fit in with any of the chapters. I have decided, therefore, to add a few stories and incidents – partly because I think that readers will enjoy then, but, let me admit, even more because I want to write about them!

I have told earlier how the Shalhoub boys insisted that I should wear Arab dress when presented to their Grandfather, Sheikh Mohammed Shalhoub Al-Kebir. It was so comfortable that I took to wearing it regularly and, after I suppose another year, hardly ever put on European clothes. One thing I liked particularly was that I felt I was blending into the background; and, although most people probably knew who I was, I felt myself more and more accepted as "one of them." I soon began to wear it when I travelled, first to other Arab countries, and, very soon, everywhere. In the Arab world it may have helped and, even outside, in all those years I can only remember three occasions when being dressed like an Arab was a disadvantage; and here they are.

I was on holiday in Pakistan staying in Peshawar and had been invited to dinner at the Peshawar Club by a fairly senior local banker. Now this Club had been the Military Club in the days of the Raj, and my eldest cousin, Niall Annett had been a member in the 1930s. There were, I discovered, no English members at the time of my visit, but I was banned from entrance because I was in "native dress." Apart from ceremonial occasions, when the local Prince and his entourage, in full Court Dress, might attend, only those dressed as an "English Gentleman" were admitted – a decent jacket, collar and tie being the minimum. It struck me that it was a remarkable instance of the influence of the British, that such a regulation should still be in force, more than a quarter of a century after Independence.

The second time I found my dress a handicap was in New York. I had booked (and confirmed the booking) a decent room in the Waldorf – Astoria Hotel, and duly arrived there on a flight from Paris. My arrival at the hotel seemed to disconcert them, and I was asked to wait a moment. In a short time a very apologetic young man came to me and explained that there had been a most unfortunate case of double-booking; but they had secured for me an excellent suite across the road at the Lexington Hotel, where they would take my luggage. The trouble, I learned later, was that there were a series of secret meetings between the Palestinians and the Israelis taking place in the Waldorf-Astoria, and security had been thrown at the appearance of an Englishman dressed like an Arab. I might be a spy, I might even be a terrorist, or I might just be barmy, or any combination of these: in any case I would be better off in a different hotel – and so to the Lexington I went.

I remember two things about the Lexington: on the first evening I was quite late, the restaurant was on strike and so I looked at the magnificent Room Service Catalogue with two or three pages of delicious sandwiches. I rang Room Service and ordered gin and tonic, coffee and two sandwiches. Unfortunately the ones I wanted were "finished," and in fact they only had two sandwiches left (neither of which I would have chosen). After a short time there was a knock at the door and a voice called out "Room Service" so I opened the door. A coloured waiter looked at me disapprovingly.

"You shouldn't open your door like that," he said, "It could be anybody."

"But you said Room Service," I expostulated, "and I was expecting you."

"Anybody can say Room Service," he said, "You're in New York now. Keep the door on a chain until you can see who it is."

The very pleasant memory I have of the Lexington was that in the Restaurant on my last evening, Yma Sumac, the Peruvian singer with an astonishing range, gave a recital. I hoped my bouquet of flowers was the biggest she received.

The third occasion when my clothes betrayed me was very small beer indeed, but I tell it. For reasons I could not have explained at the time, I went to Harrods to have my hair cut and a very courteous barber asked me where I was from? When I said "Riyadh" he asked if I would be in London for long, and I said I was going home in a few days. When he had trimmed my hair he walked with me to the cash desk and said to the girl there "the Gentleman will pay ten pounds." The gentleman duly paid ten pounds and gave the obliging barber two pounds as a tip. On my way out I saw, by the door, the Pricelist: the charge for a haircut or trim was £2.95. I wondered then – and I still wonder – how often foreigners are ripped off in London, especially if they are believed to have plenty of money. It is not a pleasant consideration.

***

Many of my old memories have to do with travelling either to or from Riyadh. The process of actually getting away was quite a problem. I have already told how Ministry employees had to give a substantial financial guarantee before they could leave on either of the holidays. But there was another difficulty: contrary to instructions from the British Embassy, we all had to surrender our Passports. In every ministry there was one official who looked after them, procured exit and return visas and issued the orders for air-tickets at the end of each annual contract. In the Ministry of Education, the young man in charge of Passports was Abdullah, the same Abdullah who, in an earlier chapter, refused to issue me with air-tickets because I was "too late." The trouble with Abdullah was that he took so long to get the visas that people frequently missed their flights. One time, it must have been in 1968, I decided to go away on holiday rather late and wondered how I could get Abdullah to produce visas. A Saudi friend in the Ministry advised me what to do, and so, when I went to Abdullah with my request and my permission to leave; I also carried, well wrapped up, a bottle of Scotch, which he inspected without comment. I hoped that he would produce my visas in two or three days instead of the usual week or ten days or more. To my surprise Abdullah turned up at my home that evening, to bring me the passport and to thank me for the Scotch. One or two unnecessarily strait-laced English friends maintained that I was wrong to "bribe" the man, as it only encouraged him; but I disagreed. I think that a bribe is payment to do something which the recipient ought not to do: I see nothing wrong in giving a "douceur" to encourage the recipient to do his job well, after all, if we are expected to tip a waiter or waitress for good service – what is to stop us giving the tip before the meal, to ensure good attention? Of course, in later years, when the numbers of people in Riyadh increased enormously, the Passport Office was submerged in a flood of passports, and getting a seat on a plane was difficult: companies used to book several seats on every flight so that their employees could fly more or less when they wanted to. After I left the Ministry proper and was in charge of my own passport, the situation – although much worse in general – was a lot better for me. I only had to take my passport to the Passport Office to see Abdul Rahman, my old pupil, who was now the Deputy Director, and, while we chatted and drank tea and coffee, some minion had the necessary visas put in my passport. Then I would go off to the Airport to see another old pupil, Dakheel, Head of Security at the Airport, to ask for a seat (or two if my mother was with me) on that evening's flight. After a talk, and more tea and coffee, some minor official would bring me back my passport, tickets and boarding passes!

Unfortunately this engendered a spurious sense of superiority which let me down badly once in London. I decided that I would return to Riyadh by that evening's flight, and went along to the Saudi Arabian Airlines office in Regent Street, where a rather supercilious young woman informed me that all seats were booked on all flights for ten days. "Well," I said, "I have a First-Class ticket but I don't mind travelling economy if necessary." "Economy seats," she said rather smugly I thought, "are fully booked for two weeks." I asked to be put on the waiting list and was told that all the waiting lists were full as well.

Now I knew that the Saudi Embassy always had a few seats reserved for them which they released half-an-hour before the flight if they weren't needed, so I decided to try my luck. I had a friend at the Embassy but knew he had just gone to New York, although I can't remember why. I took a taxi to Belgravia, where I entered the Embassy and asked for Abdul Raheem. An obliging young Saudi told me that he was away, and so I did the most theatrical gesture, flinging up my hands and clasping my brow. "Oh God!" I cried, "I'm in such a difficulty! Abdul Raheem would have helped me!" The young Saudi looked doubtful, "Well," he said, "if there is anything we could do…" I could tell by his expression that he thought I had probably lost more money than I could pay at a casino the night before, or something like that, and had come to borrow money from Abdul Raheem: that was an eventuality that sometimes happened to young Saudis in London. When I explained my predicament his face cleared and he smiled: "Of course I can get you a seat!" he said, "If you can give me your ticket and your passport." He went away for about five minutes and came back with my documents. "All's well," he said, "You have a seat on tonight's flight. You can go back to the Airlines office."

I thanked him very sincerely, went outside and took another taxi back to Regent Street. By chance I found myself with the same girl who had refused me a seat a little bit earlier.

"I believe you have a seat for me tonight now," I said. She looked at me with distaste. "Yes," she said "we have had orders from the Embassy to give you a seat. Somebody with a confirmed and reconfirmed seat will be turned off the flight."

Of course I knew that this wasn't actually true because I had been given one of the Embassy's reserved seats, but I just said – somewhat mendaciously – "Well, it's very important that I get back to Riyadh tonight," and we parted in an atmosphere of armed neutrality.

**

One of the most trying journeys I ever had was my journey home in 1967. The War had, as mentioned in the last chapter, caused a certain amount of anti-British feeling; and I had booked from Riyadh to Beirut, and thence possibly by British Airways, or possibly Middle East airlines, to London. Job's Comforters – of whom there were many – warned me of likely unpleasantness at Beirut Airport, but I went ahead. The journey was complicated by the fact that somebody – I think it must have been the Shalhoubs – had given my mother a rather large and very beautiful kitten. I think the breed was called the Turkish Cat. Mother's cat was called Sophie and she was white with black paws, black markings on the face and a black tail. Mother left the cat behind with me, with instructions to bring Sophie with me when I came home on leave. The idea was that Mother would make Quarantine Arrangements, although, as I was rather vague about the exact date of travel, she didn't do so.

The situation was made more difficult by the fact that Sophie grew up and, forty-eight hours before our departure, gave birth to three kittens. These forty-eight hours were very uncomfortable, because she had the kittens in my bed – which meant I had to sleep on the floor while during the day she took them into the kitchen behind the oven – which meant that nothing could be cooked all day. There was also the problem – how was I going to transport a cat and three kittens on the plane? As usual, when faced with a problem, I went to the Shalhoubs.[1] They had a

---

[1] One year, just before she was going to fly home, we discovered that my mother's Inoculation Certificate was out-of-date. We went to our doctor but he said that, although he could give mother the inoculation, he could not issue the certificate, as that

solution at once – a large birdcage. "Put towels in the bottom," they said, "and you have the bowls for milk or water." It seemed a possible idea so I took the cage home. I can't remember the time of my plane in the morning but it was fairly early, and I told my houseboys to call me in good time.

I woke in the morning to find them both sitting looking at me. I looked at my watch, and found out that it was almost time I should be leaving for the Airport. "Why didn't you call me?" I cried. "You looked so tired," was the answer, "we didn't like to disturb you." I leapt up, washed perfunctorily and (I hope) cleaned my teeth – there was no time for shaving. I sorted out what I wanted to take, told one houseboy to pack my case and sent the other for a taxi. I myself had the task of putting Sophie and her kittens into the birdcage. It was not easy: I put in one kitten and while I was picking up he second Sophie took out the first. When I put in the second and went to retrieve the first she took the second out. Eventually I got one of the houseboys to hold Sophie while I put all three kittens into the cage. Then she joined them quite happily and we put milk in one bowl and water in the other. Too hot and bothered to be hungry, I climbed into the taxi and departed for the Airport.

When I reached the Airport it was completely deserted. There was literally, nobody at all about, not even a guard. I explored all over the place and finally – I can't imagine how – ended up in the Control Tower. "What's happened to the plane for Beirut?" I asked. "Oh," came the reply, "you are the passenger, are you? I'm afraid the plane was coming up from Jeddah and the pilot said that as there was only one passenger to collect, it wasn't worth landing so he's flying over." I asked what I was supposed to do, and "could I see the manager?"

The Manager, who turned out to be American was still in his bedroom at the Sahari Palace Hotel, beside the Airport, and, when I spoke to him, said he would be right over. It took him about half an hour so I imagined he had some breakfast; but when he came he was profuse with apologies: it was all most unfortunate, but it would be better if I went home and flew another day. I said that this was impossible because I had closed my house for the summer and my servants were on holiday. He must reroute me. More apologies followed: there was nobody in the Airport capable of

---

had to come from the Hospital. Knowing that the Shalhoubs had clout at the Hospital, I went to them for help. They pooh-poohed the idea of any inoculation, and produced a bunch of certificates, all signed and stamped. "Just write in your mother's name and the date," they said. I may add that, once back in England, mother did have the inoculation.

making out a new ticket correctly. I would have to go to Dharhan and get it done there. He would write, "Involuntarily re-routed" on my ticket and sign it. I could take the next plane down to Dharhan. When would that be? I asked. The Manager didn't know but when I pointed to a plane just landing he said that it must be the one. Formalities were hurried through: they included weighing the birdcage and contents, because, apparently, they had to travel as "excess baggage." We boarded the plane and arrived in Dharhan.

Here the second part of my adventure began. The Manager, whom I asked to see at once, was very helpful but very cautious. There was a plane that afternoon going to Beirut, but he was unwilling to let me go there to change planes, with, possibly, a long wait: "There is so much bad feeling at the moment," he said, "that you might not be safe." He consulted some timetables. "Your best plan," he declared, "would be to take the afternoon flight to Bahrain. You can stop overnight at the Airline's expense and take a British flight tomorrow morning to Beirut and London. You needn't get off the plane in Beirut." I had a good lunch, procured food for Sophie, who attracted an enormous amount of attention and revelled in it, and waited in transit for the Bahrain flight. This was the only time in my life that I flew in a Dakota, the flying workhorse.

In those days there was only one "western" style hotel in Bahrain, the Bluebird, which was owned by the British Overseas Aircraft Corporation. It had an alcohol license but was only supposed to serve alcohol to Western travellers. Actually, as Saudi friends told me, they sold it to Arabs too, but charged them two or three times the proper prices. I took a room, chargeable to the Saudi Airlines, and explained I was carrying a very valuable Turkish cat, who might harm her kittens if upset. Nobody, chambermaid or other, must go into my room for any reason. I could turn down my own bed. Once in the room, I let Sophie out: she explored thoroughly and decided that the bed, under the top sheet, would be the best place for the kittens, and transferred them there. I foresaw another night on the floor.

Dinner that night was not a gourmet's paradise but it was perfectly satisfactorily, and it was a treat to drink wine with it. The night was not too uncomfortable and in the morning, after breakfast, as there was some time before the London flight, I hired a taxi with an English speaking driver from the Hotel and asked him to drive round the island for an hour – and very interesting I found it. Back in the hotel I put Sophie and the kittens into the cage and saw the awful mess they had made in the bed. The only thing was that nobody could go into the room until I had left the hotel, and so I arrived safely at the Airport. There was a slight hitch as BOAC did not carry animals in the passenger section; but as I refused to fly at all unless the cats were actually with me, and as there were very few passengers, I was told that I could have them with me if I sat right at the back of the plane. Of course I agreed and the only result was that most of the other passengers also moved to the back to admire my feline friends. I did have one fright: we were, I suppose, waiting for clearance before take-off when a uniformed man came aboard and spoke to the Air-hostesses. An announcement was made for "Mr David Urch" and with horror I recognized the uniform as that of a commissionaire from the Bluebird Hotel, and felt sure that they were going to ask me to pay for new bed sheet – but I need not have worried. The man came up to me with a smile: "You left this on your bedside table," he said. It was my rosary!

These were the days when passengers normally debarked at each airport where the plane stopped and so, in spite of warnings, I got off at Beirut. There was no unpleasantness: one young man in Lebanese Airways uniform gave me some money and asked me to go into the Duty Free Shop and buy some particular perfume for his girl-friend, which I did. Nothing else happened.

Things did not go so smoothly at London. The Cabin Crew explained to me that, as I had not arranged for the cats to be quarantined I was, technically, smuggling them into the country. I said that I hadn't known what flight I would be using, they were my mother's cats, and she ought to have arranged quarantine. Well, I was told, I would have to wait on the plane until the Police arrived: they would "escort" me to the Quarantine Kennels. Sure enough, some fifteen minutes after arrival, a large jovial young policeman arrived and joked – somewhat unnecessarily – about putting me under arrest. Then he explained that the Quarantine Kennels were the far side of the Airport: I could go there by taxi and he would "escort" the taxi: he was fascinated by Sophie. At the kennels there was a good deal of paperwork and I think I had to pay for two or three weeks in advance (for four cats!) and said my mother would send a cheque for the rest. Then I wanted to get back to the Airport proper so that I could catch a train to Victoria. Could the kennels telephone for a taxi? No, their telephone was out of order. Could the Policeman send a taxi for me when he went back? No, he was going to stay with Sophie for a while.

What was I to do? Well, I was told, if I went across the field next to the kennels and then the next field beyond that, I would come to a road where there was a bus stop where the Green Line buses for Victoria stopped.

It was fortunate that in 1967 I was still wearing European dress outside Saudi Arabia, or I dread to think what would have happened. There had been quite a lot of rain because both fields were extremely muddy. There must have been stiles, because I have no recollection of fighting my way through hedges, and when I reached the road, where there was a proper bus stop, both I and the two cases I was carrying were very muddy. I had to wait barely ten minutes before a Green Line bus arrived on its way to Victoria. When I reached my destination I decided to take a coach down to Worthing, because the Victoria Bus Station was much closer than the Railway Station, and, once in Worthing, my mother's sea-front flat was within easy walking distance of the Bus Station.

I had not been home for many minutes before my mother asked me how, on a flight from the Arabian Desert to Heathrow, I had managed to get my shoes caked in mud, and why I was splashed with mud up to my knees.

***

Thinking about Sophie and the kittens being weighed as "excess baggage" reminds me of an incident in Karachi Airport, when my mother and I were trying to get back to Riyadh. It was 1979 and we had decided to go "abroad" from Riyadh to do our Christmas Shopping. We had decided on Hong Kong, because my young cousin Claire (who was my mother's god-daughter) and her husband Guy Howells were stationed out there. Guy was in the Navy and, unfortunately, before we could go to Hong Kong, he was posted back to Portsmouth, and Mother didn't want to go to Hong Kong if Guy and Claire were not there; and so we looked for somewhere else to go. Before Christmas the flights were getting booked up, but there were seats available to Karachi, and as I liked Pakistan, we decided to go there.

We had a very pleasant stay (during which came the incident I have already cited of members of the Bihar Liberation Army extracting Danegeld from the guests) and we bought and bought. One problem was that, having bought some object and taken it back to the hotel to decide who to give it to, we would decide to keep it – and then had to go out again and buy something else. When the time came to go back to Riyadh we had amassed a formidable lot. We had bought rugs, and tables and chests and carved boxes and bowls both wooden and copper and lamps and other copper items and quite a lot of books. We had to leave the hotel at some ridiculous hour like seven o'clock in the morning, and when the hotel porters had assembled all our goods in the foyer, everyone agreed that we needed two taxis to take our entire luggage and leave enough room for ourselves. The taxis – from the hotel of course – duly delivered us to the Airport and the drivers carried in all our belongings, which made quite a long queue behind us, and I proceeded to check in.

Now on a previous visit to Pakistan, my good friend, Sheikh Jamil Fatani, Superintendent of the Riyadh Schools, had asked me to visit his cousin who was the Saudi Arabian Consul-General in Karachi and to bring back certain family items. On arrival in Karachi I had telephoned the Consul-General at his home and had then gone there to see him. He had received me very kindly, and asked about my return flight to Riyadh. I would not, he said, want to carry a lot of things round Pakistan with me, so he would meet me on the day of my return at the Airport and give me the things then. He met me as arranged and gave me various parcels, telling the check-in clerk that I was not to be charged any "excess baggage", "and," he said when we had turned away, "any time you are in Karachi and you have been shopping, just tell me and I'll see that you aren't charged excess baggage for anything." It was with this in mind that I approached the check-in counter. I presented our passports and tickets.

"Are all those your luggage?" asked the clerk, pointing to the long line of packages.

"Yes, they are," I replied, "but I don't pay excess baggage on Saudi Airlines."

"Everybody pays excess baggage," he said firmly.

"Most people do," I agreed, "but I don't. If you don't believe me, then telephone the Consul-General."

"The Consulate doesn't open until nine o'clock."

"Then telephone him at home."

"I don't know the number."

"Oh but I do," I said placing a paper with the Consul's home telephone number on it in front of the clerk. "Call him and say that David Urch and his mother are in the Airport and need his help. Or I can speak to him."

The clerk looked at me with dislike. "Oh very well," he said as he stamped out passports and tore the relevant pages out of the tickets.

"I'll need two porters," I said, "to carry my luggage onto the plane."

A pleased look came over his face. "There aren't any," he said, "It's too early. You'll have to manage by yourself."

"Well dear," my mother said, "I'll go ahead and see about our seats. You'll have to ask other passengers to carry our luggage on," and she disappeared.

And, dear Readers, that is exactly what I did. I can't think now how I had the face to do it, nor why so many of the other passengers were so long-suffering. It took eight or nine of them to get it all on board – in the end I don't believe I carried a thing myself. We flew back to Riyadh via Dubai and at Riyadh, of course, there were no problems. I had telexed Dakheel, the Head of Security, from the Karachi Hotel, and he was there to meet us and to take over. Porters were summoned, all our worldly goods assembled and waved through customs. I can't remember exactly how but Dakheel had everything put into some vehicle which followed us home – my own car having been brought to the airport.

I suppose that the moral of this story is that if you have enough cheek and self-confidence you can get away with almost anything.

***

I must tell one more story of a travel experience, a return from London to Riyadh that must have taken more than two weeks. It was really all the fault of the Saudi Authorities who – it must have been in 1978 – decided that foreign employees, that is all non-Saudis, could not have Dependents with them. I'm not sure if exceptions could have been made for a man to have his wife and children with him – and certainly strings would have been pulled; but there was no question of somebody like my mother having a visa or a free flight. I only discovered this in London when I went to get her visa and both our tickets, so I bought a ticket for my mother when I collected my own. I booked our flight first to Madrid, were we had good friends and the Ritz was my mother's favourite hotel anywhere; and then we would fly to Paris. The brother of a friend of mine was the Saudi Ambassador to France and I was sure he would arrange a visa for my Mother; and then we would fly to Beirut and Riyadh. It all looked straightforward, as indeed it would have been if everything had gone to plan; but we know what happens to the best laid plans of mice and men.

The first hitch was in Paris, where the Ambassador was away in Saudi Arabia. However we spent three or four days, sightseeing and eating some rather good food. I felt sure that I could arrange something once we were in Beirut. We were booked on a Middle East Airlines plane leaving at a reasonable time in the morning and, suspecting nothing, we duly turned up at the Airport – it must have been in good time – only to learn that MEA was on strike and no planes would be flying for some days. Nor would any other planes be flying to Beirut that day as the entire Airport staff was also on strike; but it would probably be open the next day.

There was a desk where passengers could take their problems and by good chance there was then on duty a Frenchwoman who was very kind, efficient, and who spoke much better English than I did French. I asked whether we could get nearer to Beirut, say to Athens or Nicosia? But it seemed that all flights to those destinations were already overbooked by people who had known about the problems before we had. What about Istanbul? Yes, she checked, there was a flight with seats that afternoon but we would miss the Beirut flight even if it flew without MEA – and we might be left two or three days in Istanbul. Well I asked, having an inspiration, was there a flight to Damascus? If we could get to Damascus we could take a taxi to Beirut. She checked and spoke rapidly on the telephone, and then turned to us, smiling: there was a Syrian Airlines Boeing 747 going to Damascus that afternoon with a number of seats free and she had reserved two for us. With very sincere thanks we left her and went to the Syrian Airlines desk. Here our names were entered on the manifest, and, although they wouldn't take our luggage they did give us our Boarding Passes, and told us to come back at two o'clock. There was nothing to do but to have the best luncheon we could find in the Airport. I can't remember anything about it, because my memories are all about what happened at two o'clock.

We returned to the Syrian Airlines desk, calm and looking forward to getting somewhere within reach of Beirut, to be met by a bombshell. The Syrian official was most apologetic, but we would not be able to fly that day. Instead of the Boeing 747 Jumbo jet, the Airline had sent a Caravelle which had only 140 something seats: therefore – he showed us the manifest, with a line drawn across it – only those at the head of the list could fly, and our names were well below the line. I thought quickly and spoke: I don't know if what I said was actually good law, but it made sense and at least sounded legal, not only to me but to the Syrian official. We had been booked on that flight, I said, and had been given Boarding Passes: we were therefore the responsibility of the Airline; and if they couldn't fly us out that afternoon, we must be accommodated, at the Airlines expense, at a first-class hotel, until they were able to take us to Damascus. There was a hasty conference behind the desk and then, rather grudgingly we were told that we could take the flight after all. I suppose two people who had been above the line but who didn't have boarding passes were put off the list.

The flight was, as it happened rather delayed, but we got away mid-afternoon. We reached Damascus soon after sunset, and I bought – rather expensive – transit visas and set about finding a taxi to take us to Beirut. There were a number of drivers ready to make the journey, and, having negotiated and agreed a price, I settled for a very comfortable and warm Mercedes: our luggage was put into the back, and we began our journey. It was not long: I don't think we drove for more than twenty minutes and were on the outskirts of Damascus, when the car stopped the driver got out, asked us to wait a moment, then disappeared. We waited nearly a quarter of an hour before he returned with another driver and a different car, a Mercedes, but a much older model. (And one that was much colder than the one I had chosen.) They explained that the newer car was only used around Damascus, and never taken into Lebanon; but the other car would take us there safely. As they transferred our luggage from one car-boot to the other, there didn't seem much we could do so we smiled and said goodbye to our first driver and at least we set off again in a pleasant atmosphere.

After we had negotiated the frontier we came soon to the mountain range which runs north and south inside Lebanon. The road goes up steeply and there is a high pass on the Beirut and Damascus road, which can be blocked by snow. There were a lot of cars stopped at the bottom of the last stretch: the driver got out to see what was happening; and when he came back he said that the was snow and ice, and the going was "hazardous." I pointed to a few lights of cars which were coming towards us: it must have been possible to drive up. "I'm willing to try," the driver said, "it's up to you." I asked Mother, what she thought, "Oh for goodness sake, let's try," she said, "the sooner we get to the hotel the better." So we pulled out of the line of cars and started off up the hill: I noticed that as we went past several cars also pulled out and followed us.

Up near the top of the pass the driver had to go very carefully but it really hadn't been dangerous, and the other side of the pass, going down towards Beirut, was a lot easier. As we approached the Lebanese capital dawn broke and everything became clear as we entered the southern suburbs, where there had been a lot of fighting. At first glance the streets looked intact, but as we came close it was evident that the buildings were just shells, windowless and doorless, although evidently there were people living there. There was less damage near the city centre, but there was some everywhere. It was a relief to find ourselves at our favourite Cadmus Hotel, which was more or less undamaged.

I hadn't been long in my room when my mother called me on the telephone, and asked me to come to her room, which was on the floor above. When I got there she pointed to the wall above the bed and the ceiling which were both riddled by bullet holes. I was horrified and told her that I would get her room changed but she said it was a room she liked and it wasn't likely to happen again. "Anyway," she said, "they have to fire from down below: I wouldn't get hit, and the worst thing that could happen would be a shower of plaster." They don't make people like my mother's generation now.

A visit to the Saudi Embassy was not successful. There was a very civil Civil Servant who told me that there was no possibility of them issuing a Visa for my mother. What I must do was to go back to Riyadh myself and get someone to sponsor her privately: then they would give her a visa immediately. This made good sense so I went straight to the airport to book a flight. Alas! It was in the Christmas period and all the flights were fully booked. I explained the situation and as usual – outside London – the Saudi Airlines staff were very helpful. They promised to call me at the Hotel if they had any cancellation and as so I went back to the hotel.

It must have been two days later, just as we were finishing lunch, when a waiter hurried up to the table. There was, he said, a telephone call from the Airport. They had had a cancellation on the afternoon flight to Jeddah. If I wanted it I must go at once. Asking him to get me a taxi, I went to my room, grabbed my passport, air ticket and more money and rushed off: I didn't need any luggage as I was going home. At the Airport thy were expecting me and I was soon on board the aircraft: there was another – unexpected – delay but, being on the plane I didn't trouble myself, and waited patiently until we took off and flew into Jeddah, where I immediately made enquiries about flights to Riyadh. There were two that evening, but both were overfull. There were, however, seats available on the first plane out in the morning leaving at about dawn, so I booked myself on that and went to change my money into Saudi Riyals.

Here came the next hitch in my adventure. For some arcane reason which nobody explained to me, Lebanese Lira had become unacceptable in Saudi Arabia. None of the money-changers still operating would even look at them, and with apprehension I approached the restaurant. I had not quite finished my lunch in Beirut, and I was in for a long night. Could I get anything to eat and drink? The restaurant management were polite, but firm: if I had only Lebanese Lira they could not serve me. Luckily I then had a brainwave: Could I have a glass of water?" Of course I could (I rather think that it was the law that any place serving food or drink had to provide free water to anybody who asked for it) and I knew that for some reason or other I had in my pocket a tube of orange-flavoured vitamin C tablets, which dissolved in water. So I duly dissolved a tablet in a glass of water and had a refreshing drink. During the night I repeated this action twice more.

In the early morning I flew to Riyadh and took a taxi home – I knew there was Saudi money in the house. While I showered, shaved and changed, Abdou prepared a very substantial breakfast; and after I had satisfied the Inner Man, I set out to get a visa for my mother. I did not go straight to the Shalhoubs because they would have had to go to a Prince or Princess, and it could have taken more time. I decided to go to the Ministry of Education and, on arrival, discovered that Prince Khaled, now the Deputy Minister was in the Ministry, and would hold "public audience" at half past eleven; and I waited in his anteroom with about a dozen other people until the double doors opened and we filed in. The Prince was standing, and shaking hands with each person. When he saw me he said, "Hello David, what are you doing here? How's your mother?" "It's my mother I've come about Khaled," I said "She's stuck in Beirut." He motioned me to sit beside him, which actually was a considerable privilege, while the other men sat on chairs round the walls of the room. Prince Khaled consulted a list which must have put the names of the men in the order they had arrived, and he asked them one by one to come up to his desk. It did not take very long to deal with their problems, and when the last had departed he turned to me, "Now," he said, "what is this about your mother being stuck in Beirut." I explained the situation and he wasted no time. "She can't come in as your dependent," he said, "so she must come in on a private visa as a visitor to my wife and myself."

"What about me?" I asked. "I have to go back to Beirut and bring her back."

"You can go on a special mission for the Ministry," he said, "I am Deputy Minister and can authorize it." Well, I knew he could: had not Sheikh Ibrahim Al-Hijji, when only Acting Deputy Minster, sent my mother and I on a special mission to London?

We chattered about this and that for about half an hour while the secretary prepared and registered the necessary letters. Then, with many very sincere thanks, I went to the Passport Office to get my visas and then to the Airline Office to buy my ticket to Beirut and back. Once more I hit a snag. All seats on all flights were booked until after Christmas, and, most of all Dakheel was away. I had to depend on myself and the men in the Airport Office. To them I disclosed that fact (as I do now to my readers) that December 22nd was my mother's birthday, and I had to get to Beirut on that day. It was then December 19th, and, as I think with most Arabs, and certainly with all Saudis, the fact that a mother was involved made the matter urgent. All the men in the Airline Office promised to do anything they could to get me to Beirut on time. I said that if I couldn't get a flight to Beirut I would fly to Damascus, and take a taxi: if I couldn't get to Damascus I would fly to Amman and take a taxi from there. There was no available seat on that day, or on December 20th or on December 21st. On the 22nd, before I could call the Airlines, they called me. "We've got a cancellation on the morning flight to Cairo," a man said "would that be any good to you?" "I'll take it" I cried. Cairo was not Beirut – it was not even in the right continent – but it was nearer and anyway, I felt that I was doing something, I had to pay a little more for my ticket "Riyadh – Cairo – Beirut" but I was ready to pay anything.

Naturally, because this was the Middle East, there was another problem in Cairo. For a reason nobody could or wanted to explain to me, Egypt Air were not flying to Beirut, and the Middle East Airline planes were all absolutely fully booked. It looked as if, with no luggage and only the clothes I was wearing, I might be stuck in Cairo. Suddenly, however, as I wandered, perplexed, round the Airport, I saw a face I recognized – it was a man who had for years been the KLM Man in Riyadh. I rushed up to him, "Khaled," I cried, "thank goodness you're here. I need your help!" Then I told him my position, how it was my mother's birthday (Khaled knew her quite well) and how I must get to Beirut. "I'll see what

I can do," he said. "You'd better wait in the bar," which seemed a sensible place to stay. I suppose it was about half an hour before he came back. "All right," he said, "I've fixed it. There are two MEA planes going to Beirut, one this afternoon and the other early evening: you'll be on the second. It will get you to Beirut before seven o'clock." I began to pour out my most grateful thanks, but he cut me short. "You must stay in here," he said, "and people from MEA will come here for you. Don't go outside the Bar." It was just as well that the bar sold tea and coffee and snacks as well as alcohol or I might have been barely able to make the flight.

Sometime around four o'clock a young woman in MEA uniform came into the Bar, and looked around her. She came over to me and asked, "Mr David Urch?" I admitted the soft impeachment, and she asked for my passport and air ticket. With these she disappeared for a while, but returned quite quickly, gave me back my papers and a boarding pass. "Shall I go to the Transit Lounge now?" I asked. No, she was emphatic; I must not go to the Transit Lounge or the Boarding Gates: I must stay where I was and somebody would come to take me to the plane. So I thanked her and tried to wait patiently.

It was some time later that I heard the MEA flight to Beirut called; but nobody came for me. The call was repeated several times and then came the last call. Still nobody appeared and I now rather admire my self control in just sitting there. About ten minutes later a young man wearing a MEA uniform appeared: he came straight up to me. "I've come to take you to the plane", he said, "You have no luggage?" I said that I hadn't and he took me outside onto the tarmac where a car was waiting. We got in and he drove me over to where the plane was, apparently, waiting for me. Certainly the gangway was taken away as soon as I had boarded the plane. All the seats were taken but there were little fold back seats for the cabin crew and on one of these I was settled and strapped in. Obviously rules had been bent to get me to Beirut on time.

The flight was uneventful and I was able to be the first off the plane when we landed – probably the Cabin Crew were glad to see the last of me – and hurried through passport control. As I had no luggage I went straight to the taxi rank and took a cab to the Cadmus Hotel. I expected some sort of a hero's welcome, with smiles and congratulations and a general atmosphere of euphoria: I didn't get it.

"You're very late," said the clerk in the Reception Desk reproachfully. "You're mother is already changing for dinner and she has ordered the meal."

I fled up to my room to collect the birthday present I had prepared, went to my mother's room, kissed her, wished her many happy returns and gave her the present – which pleased her very much.

"But you must be quick and get ready for dinner," she said, "I'll be ready in a few minutes."

"But I telexed you about the difficulty in getting a flight," I said, "how could you know I would come?"

She looked at me in mild surprise. "It's my birthday," she said, "I knew you'd get here somehow or other."

***

We spent Christmas in Beirut and on Christmas day went to Mass at the Shrine of Our Lady of Lebanon. Then we collected my mother's visa and took a flight to Riyadh. I learned that on each of the four evenings when I was away the Manager of the Cadmus Hotel had sent a waiter to escort my mother to a cinema of her choice, where he bought her ticket and one for himself, not, of course, beside her, which would have been very improper, but in the seat immediately behind her, where a good servant should sit, in case she wanted anything. The cost of these nightly excursions did not appear on my bill.

I remember another story about Cairo Airport, which happened on my first visit to Egypt. The financial regulations were very strict and no Egyptian currency was allowed outside Egypt, and on entry one had to detail all the "foreign" currency one was taking in, down to the denominations of the notes and coins. I had bought, for about a third of the official rate, quite a lot of Egyptian pounds from Sheikh Saleh Al-Rajhi's stall in the main square, which I stuffed inside my socks – and damnably uncomfortable it was – and did not include on my financial declaration. On arrival I had ostentatiously changed some dollars or sterling, I can't remember which, in the Bureau de Change in the Airport, and once more during my stay I changed some money "officially," but most of the time I spent – rather lavishly – the money I had brought from Sheikh Saleh. This, however, did not quite suffice, but I had acquired a guide from Shepherd's Hotel, who took me round the sights of Cairo (for a fee) and had also introduced me to certain shops in the Souq where rather good examples of tourist goods were available (and where, obviously, he got a commission on what I bought). But he also intimated that, if I wanted to change any dollars or any pounds sterling he could take me to a shop where I could get a much better rate of exchange then the official one; and, twice, I availed myself of this service. When I came to leave – I was flying to Beirut to meet my mother but why we were not together in Egypt I can't remember – I went to the Airport and found myself faced with another financial declaration. I changed back the few Egyptian pounds I had into Sterling; and then filled in the Declaration. It seemed better to be honest, so I listed in detail exactly what foreign currency I had on me; and then found I was to give in the Exchange Slips from the Bureau de Change: I only had the two "official" slips, because in the shop where I had changed money illegally there had been no paperwork. Anyway I had my luggage rather cursorily checked and handed in my papers, and proceeded to the Transit Lounge. I had been there about fifteen minutes when a voice – in flawless English – came over the tannoy. "Will Mr David Urch, passenger on Flight such-and-such to Beirut, please return to the Customs Hall." I returned and found the vast hall empty, except for one official standing beside a pile of my luggage. In some trepidation I approached. "What is the matter?" I asked.

He explained that the two official exchange slips were not enough to cover the amount of money I had – from my declarations – spent. I was in a dilemma, because I could not explain about my illegal transactions in the Souq, and thereby get other people into trouble, and so I stood in silence. The official went on: "You were staying at Shepherd's Hotel," he said – how did he know? The Secret Police? "And it is quite expensive. Perhaps when you were leaving this morning you needed more money," and as I remained in silence, "that is possible isn't it?" I broke my silence – "it is possible," I said. "I think that is what happened," he went on, "and in the hurry about leaving you forgot to pick up the exchange slip. Now, the next time you visit Cairo, as I hope you will, just put down, on your declaration when you leave, just these exchanges you can prove," he smiled kindly. "We're not going to search you." Of course he had known all along what had happened, and I have very pleasant memories of that benign Egyptian Customs Official.

The thing I remember most about the Shepherd's Hotel was the amount of baksheesh I had to distribute. There were very few tourists in Cairo then, and the Hotel Staff all wanted tipping, although the amounts involved were always very small. I made a note at the time of the "worst" occasion, when I arrived back at the Hotel in a taxi with a very small parcel – I think it was two or three English paperbacks – and a smiling man in Hotel Uniform came across the pavement to open the taxi door and help me out: a second man in the same uniform came and took my parcel from me – in fact he carried it for me to the lift. When I was inside the Hotel a pageboy ran to the Reception to collect my key, which he also carried to the lift, while a second pageboy had run to the lift, to summon it and have the door open so that I should not be inconvenienced by having to wait a few seconds. There was, of course, a boy operating the lift and when I reached my floor there were two more pageboys. Once of them took my key and ran ahead to open my door, the other took my parcel and walked, correctly behind me to my room. So, to get from the taxi to my room with a small parcel, I had to "tip" seven people. That morning was rather exceptional.

***

I have several times in these pages mentioned Abdou, my Major-Domo, cook, driver, organizer, and his wife Kheriya, who, between them, ran the house and managed everything for my mother and myself. We built up a very unusual relationship, as I learned one day when I had to see one of the Sudairi princes, who was a junior minister – although I can't remember what I had to see him about. I knew him because I had taught his son in the Riyadh Schools, (he was the boy whose Aunty had a suede-covered Rolls-Royce) and I knew that his wife was American. When we had finished whatever the business was, the Prince said to me: "Did your houseman, Abdou, tell you that I had sent for him?" Surprised I said that I hadn't known. "Well, I did," the Prince went on. "I told him that as he and his wife knew all about running an English house I would like them to come and work for me and my wife. I said I would pay him double what you did. And do you know what he said?" I shook my head. "He said "Mr David doesn't pay me: he gives me what I need. He paid for my marriage: he gave me a car afterwards. We are a family. His job is to go and work to make the money we need. Our job, my wife's and my own, is to run the house and look after him and his mother." Now that," the Prince went on "is how it used to be in the old days. It's getting rarer and rarer, and I have never known it with a foreigner."

I had, of course, had other servants before Abdou came to take over everything. The most memorable of these was a Sudanese chef, Saleh, who worked for me for a few months when I was in the first big mud house in the Old Town. I had to get rid of him – with great reluctance – because he was nearly bankrupting me. I call him a chef rather than a cook because that is what he was: he had been the second chef in the Belgian Embassy (and Belgians know what good food is) and I believe that they had got rid of him on account of some misunderstandings over financial and other matters. He had a friend, Ahmed, also a Sudanese who was an Embassy-trained houseman. Saleh would not work anywhere unless Ahmed was with him – Ahmed could lay a table properly and could wait at it, so Saleh knew that his food was properly presented. He always cooked three courses at lunchtime and four courses in the evening, each course with all the side dishes, sauces and dressings needed, but naturally, if there was a luncheon party, then there were four courses then: he never repeated a dish unless he was asked to, and every dish was a masterpiece. It is hardly surprising that people often dropped in to see us a little before a meal was to be served.

It was one day after a dinner party. I was going to be alone, as my mother was going to some American Women's Lunch. After breakfast I said to Saleh, before I went to work, "Look, I'm going to be alone at lunchtime. After that dinner last night I don't want a big meal. Just give me cold meat and salad." When I returned home at about half past one the house was full of the most delicious cooking smells. I crossed the courtyard, went through a sort of tunnel into the second courtyard where the kitchens were, and found the oven going full blast, with four saucepans bubbling away and every other sign of the usual elaborate preparation for a meal. "What is all this Saleh?" I exclaimed, "I told you to give me cold meat and salad for lunch!" He stared at me, and then, with his left arm, swept the four saucepans off the stove and onto the floor: then he stormed out of the house. There was a silence. "Please bring me bread and cheese and fruit, Ahmed," I said, "and a cup of coffee. And then clean up this mess." I wondered what was going to happen that evening. In fact at six o'clock Saleh and Ahmed returned and Saleh apologized for his behaviour. "But I am an artist," he said, "and you cannot ask me to produce cold meat and salad."

Three or four weeks later we had a luncheon party and my mother and I were going to be alone that night. My mother said that she really didn't feel like another meal in the evening, so I went to Saleh and said, "Now, don't get angry! You have just given us a wonderful meal. My mother and I really don't want another big meal tonight. You've spoken about a very special lobster omelette. Could you make us that tonight, and something delicious as a sweet?" He smiled and said, "Very well, I won't get angry. Yes I can make you that omelette and I'll think up a special sweet dish to follow it."

At about half past six I was for some reason going into the Yamama Hotel – then the main Hotel in Riyadh. I heard my name called and, turning, saw in the left hand corner of the foyer, Olof, the Swedish Middle East Trade Commissioner, who was standing up and waving to me. I went across to him. "I'm so glad to see you David," he said, "I'm taking these gentlemen" – he indicated five dark suited men – "round the Middle East. They are Swedish businessmen. I've told them all about your house and the way you and your mother live. Can I bring them to dinner tonight?"

"Of course you can, Olof," I replied, "my mother will be delighted. Shall we say seven thirty?"

I hurried home, told my mother the somewhat alarming news, and went into the Kitchen to see Saleh. "There's a crisis," I said. "You know Mr Olof from the Swedish Embassy?" he nodded, "Well, he's got five businessmen with him and he wants to bring them to dinner tonight. Can you manage something?"

He thought for a moment and then said, "Yes, I will give you a good dinner; but it will take some time and you must not hurry over any of the courses. I'll go now and get the things I shall need."

At half past seven the six visitors duly arrived and came into the Majlis for drinks, which Ahmed served. Soon afterwards he came and announced that Dinner was served and we went into the Dining Room with its beautifully laid table for eight. I remember the first course, it was a salmon soufflé, and after eating it everyone agreed that it was the best soufflé they had ever eaten. I can't remember the next four courses, but each one was delicious, had every possible side dish to go with it, and followed on perfectly from the previous dish. The sixth course consisted of three different savouries, and the last was three different sweets. As we were drinking Saleh's excellent coffee Olof spoke. "What did I tell you?" he said, "David and Mrs Urch were alone this evening. Six uninvited guests turn up and look at the dinner they are given! There isn't a private house anywhere in the Middle East with food as good as this one!" After they had left with many thanks for what one guest called "a gastronomic experience" my mother and I looked at one another in silence and cast our eyes up to Heaven.

But, of course (we were in the Middle East) that is not the end of the story. Four or five weeks after that rather memorable night, Olof called again, probably at a mealtime. The King and Queen of Sweden, he said, were going to Jeddah on that day, and on the next were coming to Riyadh for a State Dinner with the King. Could he bring them, and the Swedish Ambassador and his wife, to luncheon first? We professed ourselves very honoured, and I went to tell Saleh. He was genuinely pleased, and surpassed himself on the next day. It is the only time in my life that I have entertained European Royalty in my own house!

***

One of the great advantages of living in Riyadh in those early days was the number of interesting people whom one met. There were so many that if I could remember all of them and wrote about them this book would become impossibly long. There are two, however, whose stories were so surreal, as they told them to me, that I think I should share them with my readers. But before I start on them I must mention an elderly Saudi whom I had met, and whose "business" had been described to me by friends. For a reason I could not understand even at that time, he called at my house in the Old Town to say good-bye because he was going abroad. When he had left my mother said "What a nice old man! Who is he and what does he do?" When I told her that, as far as I had been informed, he was the last slave-dealer to the Royal Family, and he was still – illegally – procuring slaves for some of the Princes and Princesses, she changed her opinion of him.

The first of the larger-than-life figures I am going to write about was Jean Guerin, who has appeared briefly on earlier pages. His tale is so extraordinary that I have to give it as he gave it to me. I liked him very much, but I remember my mother saying once, "I can never decide, Jean, whether you are bad or just mad." Anyway, this is his story. He was born in Alsace, the second of three brothers, and his mother was from the de la Rochefoucauld family. When the Germans occupied France in 1940 they gave the people of Alsace the opportunity to take German Nationality. Jean's mother and father, and his elder brother remained French but he and his younger brother became Germans. The Alsatian-Germans received special treatment – although liable for military service they were allowed to complete their studies, including any university studies. Jean was able to complete an engineering degree and, incidentally, to marry a niece of the Cardinal Archbishop of Paris.

When he was called-up he was immediately put on "special duties." The war was moving towards its inevitable end, and it appeared that the German High Command had a particular problem, which I am sure has not appeared in any regular History of the Second World War. There was, in France, fighting with the Germans, a Polish Brigade, which consisted of fanatical Catholics who were prepared to fight for the Germans against Atheistic Communists. As they could obviously not be stationed on the Eastern Front, where almost every Pole would have been against them, they had been sent to the West, and there were still over two hundred of them surrounded, with some thousands of Germans, in the region of Grenoble. Now the German soldiers could, in time, surrender and become prisoners-of-war; but what would happen to the Poles if they surrendered? The German High Command took soundings through their embassy in Stockholm: the Russians said they should be shot as traitors, while the French and the Americans said they must just take their chance whatever happened to them. Only the English were prepared to be helpful, and said that, if the Germans could get the Poles into British hands, they would be taken to England, enrolled as part of the Free Polish Army stationed in England, and could therefore return eventually to a liberated Poland as acceptable patriots.

The question, of course, was how? With the help of the Vatican, it was proposed to get these Polish men to Rome, where Cardinal Salmino would issue them with Vatican City passports. With these they could travel openly to Ostia where they could be embarked on an English boat waiting for them. Jean, who of course spoke perfect French, was set to get information about codewords and petrol coupons. Attacks were made (this doesn't make pleasant reading) on American soldiers who were killed for their uniforms – the excuse being that they hadn't been ready to help these Poles – and it was not long before all the Poles were fitted out in American Uniforms. At that time all armies had a somewhat miscellaneous collection of lorries and trucks, and so it was not difficult to assemble a convoy to take the Poles south to Rome. Jean, through the French Underground, had obtained enough petrol coupons to get the convoy to its destination, and the military codewords for that week and, if necessary, the next. Under cover of a particularly hard German offensive, the trucks slipped out of Grenoble and went South, English speaking drivers having been found for each truck. The operation was successful, Rome was reached, the Vatican City passports were issued, and the Polish contingent made their way safely to an English ship, and thence to England. Jean managed to return to Grenoble and was there captured and became a P.O.W. But before that he had been awarded the last Gold Cross of the War: there were a lot of Iron Crosses given, but very few Gold ones.

Jean was sent to a Prisoner of War camp in Texas which he didn't enjoy. He heard that his wife's uncle had used his considerable influence and had had his niece's marriage annulled by the Vatican: Jean had also been condemned to death, in absentia, for "collaboration," and could never return to French territory. After a number of months Jean escaped – it was not difficult, he said, because the guards were very lax, and he had just enough money to buy a one-way ticket to New Orleans on a Greyhound bus. At the first stop everybody got out to the Refreshment Room; but, as he had no money, Jean sat still. One of the other passengers spoke to him. "Not hungry?" he said?

"No," replied Jean.

"No money?"

"No."

"Escaped prisoner from back there?" with a backward jerk of his head.

"Yes," said Jean, because it seemed useless to lie.

The man didn't say anything but slipped Jean a dollar bill, but he must have spoken to other people because at each stop a different passenger passed him money, and when New Orleans was reached he was directed to the Docks and advised to find a boat going to South America. He found one going to Venezuela and was able to work his passage. . He told me that he remained several years in Venezuela, and was doing very well when, in one of the many revolutions, he was involved on the wrong side and had to escape for his life on a boat he fortunately owned. He sailed North and it was, I think, as he sailed into the harbour at Havana that he saw a tall girl walking on the Promenade and made up his mind at once – "That's the girl I'm going to marry!" She was Frances Merrick, a descendent of Joshua Coffin Chase, and her money was controlled by the Chase Manhattan Bank in Jacksonville. She was a Secretary at the American Embassy and was engaged to marry a most suitable young Ivy-league fellow diplomat, but, as soon as she met Jean, she discarded her betrothed and married Jean. They stayed more than a year in the West

Indies, spending some time in Haiti, from where they had disturbing stories of Voodoo.

However Jean wanted to do some "proper" work and he heard of an opportunity which exactly suited him. It was on Bathurst Island, North of Canada, and concerned the construction of an Early Warning System for the American Military. There was however, a major snag: there was no chance of the American Military employing a German engineer, who was condemned to death in France and was an escaped prisoner of war from America. The only thing, Jean told Frances, was to go to Rome and see Cardinal Salmino and ask for his help – in return for those Catholic Polish boys he had saved: to Rome, therefore they went.

Cardinal Salmino received them but would not give them Vatican Passports. He pointed out that these Passports were "given" to people and were not documents many people had from birth. In such a sensitive area as Military Security, anybody claiming to be a citizen of the Vatican would be carefully investigated. They should, he said, go to the Captain-General of the Jesuits, to whom he would give them an introduction. This, in Latin or Italian, said simply, "This man has done well and deserves your help," and so they presented themselves to the House of Christ, the Jesuit headquarters in Rome. The Captain-General listened to their story and said that he could help, but that he would have to make some enquiries first. They were to come back in three or four weeks – I forget which.

When they returned, the Captain-General was very business like. From his appearance and colouring Jean could be a Scandinavian, and so he should become a Norwegian. There was on Bathurst Island nobody who spoke or understood Norwegian and steps could be taken to ensure that none were appointed. All that remained was for Jean to choose his new name – he should keep the same initials. As Grieg was the only Norwegian name he could think of beginning with G he became Jan Grieg. He would, he was told, be issued with a Passport, a Birth Certificate, Educational Certificates and Diplomas and Suitable References. It would perhaps be as well also to have a Marriage Certificate, as there would be no connection with the West Indies in his CV. Jean was pleased, but a little doubtful.

"With all these papers he good enough?" he asked, "The Americans may examine them carefully."

The Captain-General looked disapproving. "The Jesuit Order," he said rather coldly, "does not deal in forged documents. All the papers you receive will be originals and they will be genuine. We have our sources."

He went on to tell them that on their journey to Bathurst Island – he had no fears that Jean might not get the job, perhaps he knew that it would be arranged – they would have to make a number of stops. At each stop, a Jesuit priest would meet them and keep them away from any chance encounter with a Norwegian speaker. Jean, of course, got the post and the journey was made without a hitch. It was, as he and Frances told me, an uncanny example of the power of the Catholic Church in general and the Jesuit Order in particular. The work on Bathurst Island proceeded successfully and they were there I think about two years. When Jean's contract was over there was no difficulty in applying for another post and he chose one in New Zealand, to work on the extension of Wellington Harbour, but, of course, they were still Mr and Mrs Grieg. Their son, Edward was born there and when I knew him was in possession of no less than four "legal" passports, which his parents maintained for him in case he ever needed to become another person. He had dual nationality as Edward Guerin, and had by virtue of his parents, German and American passports, but when he was born he had been in New Zealand, of apparently Norwegian parents, and so he also had (valid) New Zealand and Norwegian passports as Edward Grieg.

The Guerins did not enjoy New Zealand: I shall probably annoy any potential New Zealand reader by saying that Frances described the country to me as "lower middle class," but I am quite sure it is very different now. I am writing of the 1950s and the great feature of New Zealand life then was the stranglehold which the Unions had over everything. One thing they noticed particularly was the obsessive pride everybody else took in the appearance of their garden and their road – a fact that the Guerins ignored: their garden was literally, a blot on the landscape; and as they ignored any request to beautify their plot, the neighbours, in desperation, "did" their garden for them, so as not to let the neighbourhood down. Frances told me that it was quite normal for her and Jean to sit in deck chairs sipping gin and tonics while their neighbours mowed and weeded and pruned all around them.

I wrote, a few lines back, that the Unions completely controlled New Zealand at that time, and that was why the Guerins left. One day, when Jean was in his office by the harbour, horses were being unloaded from a ship. The method used was to put each horse in a sling, upon which a crane would lift the horse up and over and deposit it gently on the ground. Suddenly, while a horse was suspended in mid-air, the whistles or sirens blew signifying that it was the lunch break, when all work must stop. The crane operator shut off his crane, leaving the horse hanging in the air. Jean rushed out of his office and told the crane-operator that he must bring the horse down. "I can't" the man said, "The Union says we must stop whatever we are doing the moment the whistles go." "Then," said Jean, "I'll do it: I can operate a crane." "If you touch that lever," the man told him in all seriousness, "you'll have the whole of New Zealand out on a General Strike. You aren't allowed to touch that crane." Jean went back to his office and wrote a letter of resignation, explaining exactly why he refused to work there any longer. The Guerins returned to Germany and resumed their proper name. Jean worked some years in Germany: I can't remember the name of the company but it was based at Bochum and he told me one interesting anecdote about his years there. There was a very big contract from the American Military, ostensibly for vast underground vehicle parks, but actually a line of defence against a potential Soviet attack. There were some dozen or so German Companies invited to tender for the contract, but one – again I do not remember the name if I ever knew it – was much bigger and more powerful than the others. This company invited representatives of all the others to a meeting and explained that they were going to win the contract, and that they proposed to sub-contract parts of the work to each of the other companies. Most of the smaller companies were pleased to go along with this arrangement but Jean, as he told me, representing his company, said that they proposed to put in a bid for the whole contract, knowing that on their own, they could submit a lower offer.

Time went by and the tender was carefully prepared. The offers had to be handed in to the American Military Headquarters in Frankfurt by noon on a particular day. Early the day before, Jean left Bochum with a copy of the tender, and went in the opposite direction to Frankfurt. He spent twenty-four hours travelling in an enormous semi-circle, ending up on the far side of Frankfurt from Bochum and, sometime after eleven o'clock in the morning, made his way to the American Headquarters and submitted his company's tender. Meanwhile two other engineers, with copies of the tender, left the Company Offices early in the morning, one going by car and one by train. Unfortunately there was some hitch on the railways, and no trains were able to leave Bochum in any direction, until after twelve o'clock. The man going by car fared no better; Army manoeuvres, with tanks and army trucks all over the place, made it impossible for any cars to get from Bochum onto the autobahn, and this caused such a traffic jam that cars could not get out at all until, again after twelve o'clock, the situation eased and traffic again began to flow normally.

The Americans, of course, had no part in this at all, and, incidentally, awarded the contract to Jean's Company. The interesting part of this story, as Jean told it to me, was that the very big company, which was apparently able to disrupt the train services and to organize military operations, was jointly owned by the German Chancellor and the Cardinal Archbishop of Cologne.

Jean's arrival in Saudi Arabia was not effected under the most favourable circumstances. He was recruited by a Palestinian-owned company that had secured a major contract to build roads in Saudi Arabia. Jean was to become the Manager of the whole project in the Kingdom. He settled Frances and Edward in an apartment in Beirut, and came to the country to begin the work, with what he said was an adequate workforce. Unfortunately the Palestinian owners had a very different idea. Having obtained a considerable down payment from the Saudi authorities they disappeared with most of it, and left Jean and his workforce in an extremely difficult situation. Jean managed to get the workers repatriated, but, as the Local Manager and the only person of substance available, he himself was detained, indefinitely, while proceedings were taken against the company he had involuntarily to represent. He was in no respect ill-treated, and was in fact living in the Yamama Hotel when I met him; and because he was such an interesting person we became great friends. Eventually, I suggested that he should bring his family to Riyadh, and they could come and live in my large mud house, to which my mother was shortly due. Frances and Edward did come, and for quite a time we shared the house, until Jean's situation was resolved and he was given a well-paid post in the Ministry of Agriculture, mention of which I have made, for it was Jean's salary which entitled him to buy the forbidden dainties in the secret room in the basement of the Ministry. Another "dainty" he managed to procure for us at Christmas was a *bourriche* of oysters – twelve dozen – which meant that we not only had oysters *au natural*, but oyster chowder, and on Christmas evening, a large turkey stuffed with oysters by Saleh. It was a memorable feast.

After a time in the Ministry, the Guerins moved to a villa in Riyadh but made plans for the future. It was all very mysterious and seemed to encompass taking over the administration of, as I remember, Thailand. The money was coming from the German Trade Unions and there seemed to be the possibility of a great deal of money to be made. It all seemed to depend upon very delicate timing, and was, I was sure then, probably something of a confidence trick – although the benefits to the local people would be considerable. Jean had sketched in for me a position in the Ministry of Education, where I would be in charge of all the teaching of English in the country; but, he told me, I should not resign from my post in Riyadh until I got a definite assurance from him that all was well. I didn't, as the plan fell through. I think there must have been something illegal about it because not long afterwards I had a man from Interpol asking me if I knew where Jean was. I told him that I didn't, although I guessed it would be somewhere in South America; but I also told him that Jean was a friend whose address I would not have given him even if I had known it.. He did not seem to be upset in any way by this and we parted civilly. I never heard of Jean Guerin again.

***

Another character whom I met, very briefly at this time, was a remarkable Swiss figure, Hans Griesharber, whom I first saw in the Sahari Palace Hotel near the Airport. For some reason I can't now remember, I was at the desk making some enquiry or other when this elderly figure came in, marched up to the desk, and said, in rather heavily accented English, "I wish for a room. I am the Peruvian Consul in Zurich."

The Sahari Palace was sorry but there were no rooms free: a clerk knew that the Yamama Hotel was also full, and so he recommended the Semiramis. Now that hotel had been alright for Ralph Ellis and for me on our arrival, but it would hardly do for a Swiss diplomat! I said nothing at the time but went straight home and told Jean Guerin about this unusual visitor. Jean knew (how? I never really knew) how to get a room at the Sahari Palace which would be "free" in every sense, and, having visited the Sahari Palace to arrange the room we then drove to the Semiramis.

There we found the gentleman wearing lederhosen and a sort of Tyrolean hat with a William Tell feather in it. We introduced ourselves and said that we had been able to arrange a room for him at the Sahari Palace, as I had heard him being refused one earlier. He thanked us and Jean intimated, very discreetly, that he would not be expected to pay for the room. At the time it seemed rather odd that Griesharber took the whole affair so matter of factly. It was, after all, rather unusual in a foreign city to be approached by two complete strangers and offered better – and free – accommodation; but by no word or even look did the Swiss gentleman show the slightest surprise. He behaved as if our encounter was perfectly normal. We drove him to the Sahari Palace and left him there, having invited him to luncheon on the next day.

"I'm sure I've seen that man before," Jean said on the way home. "When he comes tomorrow let me have half-an-hour alone with him. I want to talk to him on my own."

The next day Jean duly took him aside in the Majlis and they only emerged when luncheon was announced. They were both smiling: "Ah," said Herr Griesharber "we are among friends – we can speak freely!" It appeared, during luncheon, that Jean had met the Consul during the war, when he was in the German Army. In a somewhat equivocal way, Jean had helped a number of Jewish families to escape from Occupied France by arranging for them to buy passports of different nations from the Peruvian Consul in Zurich. I am sure that Herr Griesharber made them pay very highly for this accommodation; and I expect that Jean himself got some commission on the sale, although he never gave me the slightest hint of that. It seemed that our guest's main occupation was moving gold from one country to another – and especially to India. He was, also, the President of a major Swiss Re-Assurance Society, which covered Insurance Contracts all over the world. He had bought the Peruvian Consulate in Zurich in 1939, so that he could travel with a diplomatic passport. In fact he had two – one Swiss and one Peruvian. "Rightly or wrongly" he chuckled, "my Minister thinks that I am an honest man, and so I can do as I like."

He told us that his greatest achievement during the war when, in Switzerland, he had a railway wagon full of gold. "I sold it to the British for cash," he said, "and then I sold it to the Germans, and they paid too, and I kept the gold for myself and didn't give it to either of them!" Had he been in a Television Serial there would have been a race between British and German hitmen to eliminate him.

Hans Griesharber's great passion was travel – he had been round the world more than two dozen times. He had visited nearly every country in the world and now he had been to Saudi Arabia there only remained Tibet. He had just received permission from Peking to visit Lhasa, and he explained that he had been doing business in China for decades, from long before the Revolution. "The men in charge of the money in China," he said, "are still the same. Some of the men I used to know have died but it is now their sons who have taken their place."

Before he went to China and Tibet he had another journey planned. His wife had accompanied him until her death and now his daughter was to be his companion. They were to sail around West Africa to the Cameroons, go up the river – by canoe – to Lake Chad, and then fly home before setting off together to the Far East. They never made it. Flying home from Chad in a French airliner the plane crashed in the desert and everybody was killed. I heard about the crash but had no idea that the Griesharbers were on it, until I received a black edged notification of the death from the Zurich office.

In one way I missed out over his death. He had assured us – and he was the sort of man who did know things – that there would be a war in the summer and things might get very unpleasant, especially for Americans and the British, who would be accused of helping Israel (this, of course, turned out to be perfectly true). My mother would have gone back to England before the great heat, and the Guerins had German passports and would be alright, but he was worried about me. "You should have a second nationality," he said, "in case of an emergency. You will find one very useful, and, in any case, to have an extra passport is always a good thing. What country would you like?" I thought for a minute and the said "I would like a Nicaraguan passport." He looked at me quite shocked. "Nicaraguan!" He exclaimed, "I wanted to give you a proper passport in return for your kindness to me. Why have you chosen Nicaragua?"

I said that it was a pretty name and he actually snorted. "Through diplomatic channels," he said, "I could arrange a genuine passport for you for a great number of countries. However, if you want a Nicaraguan passport I can of course get you one." Unfortunately because of that air crash, I never attained even temporary Nicaraguan citizenship.

***

I have mentioned Radio Riyadh, or at least its English Service, on a number of occasions, and for many years it played a large part in my life. When the Saudi authorities decided that, with more and more English speakers in Riyadh, there should be an English language service on the Radio so that people would not have to listen to the BBC World Service and also would hear the official Saudi version of the News, they brought out an advisor from the BBC Arabic Service in London to help set it up. By this time the British Council was firmly established in Riyadh and they asked the local head, Bill Charlton, to bring all the British teachers under his auspices to a voice-trial to pick the best person to be the first British Announcer. Bill asked me to go along as well and at about half past six one evening we all met at the Radio station. We were asked who wanted to go first, and as nobody seemed anxious I offered to set the ball rolling because I was taking my mother to a cocktail party and wanted to get away in good time.

I was handed a copy of the *Daily Telegraph* and told to choose two items and to read them into a microphone. The first was some moderately interesting political story but the second was a marvellous piece to read. There may be some readers who remember a cat food called "Arthur," which featured a white cat called Arthur on each tin. It appeared that Arthur was owned by two men who had quarrelled – presumably over money – and one of them had taken Arthur to the Soviet Embassy and had asked that the cat be given political asylum. This was a splendid piece to read and gave ample opportunity to the reader to inflect his voice. Having read my two pieces I took my leave.

It seemed that after I had left the BBC man had himself chosen two passages – much duller ones I was told – and everybody had to read the same ones. Perhaps it was not altogether surprising that, some two weeks later, I received a letter saying that I had been selected to be the first announcer on the new programme.

Working on the Radio was quite an experience. While we were allowed to express ourselves as we wanted when we introduced a programme this only meant a very few words. Most of the programmes were from the BBC in the early days, but we were soon encouraged to write and produce our own, as more and more people were recruited to work in the English programme. Programmes had to be submitted to the censors for approval and then recorded – people were not normally allowed to speak "live" on the radio. When, after five or six weeks, we began a news bulletin, it consisted mainly of Reuters news flashes, with some additions of a local character. The Reuters items had to go to the censors, and sometimes words or phrases were crossed out – any mention of "Israel" was always censored. On one occasion I had to read an item in which the word "not" had been inserted, to give the exactly opposite meant to the real one.

What had been approved was supposed to be read exactly as written. I remember once there was an item about some meeting attended by a number of members of the Royal Family. Their titles and names were supposed to be mentioned in turn and in full: His Royal Highness Prince A, His Royal Highness Prince B, His Royal Highness Prince C and so on. To save time in quite a long bulletin, the newsreader David Sidell, a good friend of mine, said "Their Royal Highnesses Princes A, B, C, D..." and so on. Before his stint was over senior officials from the Radio and I think – but I may have been exaggerating – one or two guardsmen arrived. David was removed from the studio and threatened with the direst penalties. He was suspended and it was only after we had all pulled whatever strings we could and he had written a letter expressing his deepest apologies that he was allowed back on the air having been given a Final Warning.

One thing had been a puzzle from the beginning: all the Arabic language broadcasts started with the words "Bis M'Allah Al-Rahman Al Raheem," – "In the Name of God, the merciful, the compassionate." There was a suggestion that it should be said in Arabic at the beginning of each day's broadcast, but that did not find favour; nor did the idea of saying it in English: it didn't sound right and many people were worried at the idea of "infidels" saying it, who might not really mean what they were saying. Then an acceptable solution was found. The broadcast should begin and end with a reading from the Holy Koran. I was at once told that I must record the whole of this sacred work in the approved English Translation: I already a two-volume copy – it was given free to any English speaker who applied to the Imam's Office, and I had gone there within a few weeks of my arrival. It was an excellent translation, as the Palestinian translator had evidently studied the language of the Authorized Version of the Bible.[2]

It took quite a number of afternoons in the Radio Station to record the whole of the Holy Koran in suitable length segments. I think it was because of the language of translation that it felt very like reading in church. I suppose I used to think about different priests while I was reading, because my mother claimed to be able to recognize some of them. "You were being Father so-and-so today," she would say, "last week you were being Father such-and-such. I was told that tapes were sent to many of the Gulf States so that they could preface each English

---

[2] I think that the King James' Bible is the most beautifully written work in the English language.

broadcast with a reading. I confess to liking the idea that English speaking people were in this way being introduced to the Islamic Scriptures. After a good number of years the Authorities decided that they would like a new recording, with three readers. I was again asked to organize this and so again divided the book into suitable passages in groups of fourteen, so that each "voice" gave the readings for a week. Apart from myself, one of the readers was that Desmond Smith who has featured in earlier pages as the maker of the best home-distilled alcohol in Riyadh.

Over many years I wrote, edited, produced and presented a large number of programmes, usually about three a week. Many of those were musical, and for a long while I had a weekly "abridged" opera night in which I narrated the story of the opera and played all the main arias and choruses, the operator introducing pre-recorded applause in all the right places. I also copied the BBC and introduced "Book at Bedtime." For a while I had to choose short stories or serialize books, in fifteen minute segments. The difficulty of editing such works was that they must not contain any references to anything religious (a character could not even "turn right past the church") or political. Any romantic interest had to be played down, and there must be no reference to alcohol – if people were having a drink I had to make it clear that they were having coffee, or a cup of tea. I found detective stories the easier to edit, because there was nothing against a good juicy murder. But I sometimes found it easier to write the whole story myself.

Of course before any programme was recorded it had to go before the censorship section – whom I never met – although I suspect that they were much more concerned with the Arabic language broadcasts. But if I had proposed a programme that would be a serial then all the episodes had to be submitted at the same time. I think that I never had a series, or even a single script rejected. I had also sometimes to edit the scripts of other contributors. I remember one man in particular, a very pleasant and intelligent man who wrote a number of interesting programmes. What I remember about him in particular is that his English was, grammatically, very uncertain. He had, however, been awarded an MA in English from Dayton University, Ohio. I then understood why many Saudis preferred to go to American Universities rather than British or European ones, where they would be expected to compete on equal terms with native students. It appeared that in America all sorts of allowances were made for Foreign Students, who were not expected to reach the standard of their American fellow-students.[3]

As everything had to be scripted I feel it to be an honour that I was – the only non-Saudi so distinguished – allowed to give an unscripted sports programme on Saturday evening. Sometimes people said they could not receive the BBC World Service and they missed the Football Results. Later I expanded this into a general survey of the sports' news of the week. When the Olympic Games came on I used to give three programmes a day, updating the results and the medals tables. I have already mentioned the 1972 Munich Olympics when the Israeli team were kidnapped and – mostly – murdered, and I had to be allowed to use the word "Israeli."

I have a very vivid recollection of one News Broadcast (we had copied the then BBC times and had our main news at nine o'clock in the evening) when the Americans had landed on the Moon. It was when they were due to return but there was a doubt as to whether or not they could blast off the Moon's surface. The first item of news from Reuters was a well-written and informative explanation of the difficulties and dangers: then, about five to nine, I was handed a news flash giving the news that the astronauts were safely off. I decided to ignore this, and at nine o'clock read the original first item, and began to read the second. Then I stopped, said: "Excuse me," and rustled a paper by the microphone, and then said in an excited voice, "I've just been handed a newsflash from Reuters and its good news!" And then I read the flash and made some appropriate comment. Then I said: "I must now return and reread the item I interrupted." In this way I thought my listeners got the most interest and satisfaction out of that news item.

***

In earlier pages I have animadverted on the subject of "commissions," paid not only to agents who had done some work but also to others who because of their rank or position felt entitled to receive – as if by some

---

[3] There was a department in the Ministry of Education which looked into the Educational Qualifications of anybody coming to work in Saudi Arabia. I was there shown a large book which was turned to the USA. There was on one page a column of Universities as good as European ones, and a whole page of others which were not so good but which were "recognized." There followed a number of pages of so-called Universities and colleges whose degrees were not recognized in Saudi Arabia.

sort of Divine Right – some remuneration in the awarding of a particular contract. I was myself involved – although, I must say, merely as an "observer" – in one such negotiation. I think it is a story worth telling, and, from an English point of view, it is actually quite important. There was a rather surprising move about 1980 to introduce Public Buses into Riyadh, and thereafter into other parts of the Kingdom. There was a lot of talk about this; and, naturally, a good deal of opposition. The buses were single-deckers, divided into a slightly larger front portion for men, and a slightly smaller one at the back, for women; this was perfectly reasonable because many more men would be likely to travel. Payment, when the buses did arrive, was made in the front part, and a man bought tickets for the women of his family who were in the rear part of the bus. I don't know whether any women, even escorted thereto by a male, would have gone alone onto a bus. What happened if a group of women, three or four, were so bold – fortified by numbers – to travel without a male escort, I just don't know. I imagine they travelled free because there used to be no means for them to pay. I wonder how many rich young ladies who, under normal circumstances, would have died rather than travel on a Public Bus, borrowed old clothes from their maids and, as if for a dare, enjoyed such an adventurous escapade.

One day, when every one knew about the forthcoming introduction of these buses, I received two young visitors. One was one of my best pupils, a boy whose father had been a religious refugee from Egypt, and was now perhaps the leading Islamic Theologian in Saudi Arabia. He seemed to me to be scholarly, pious, humane and broad-minded, and I liked both his sons very much. The elder brought with him another undergraduate at Riyadh University who was a particular friend, because they wanted my help. The friend's father was the man who had to decide on the award of the contract for the buses: this initial contract was worth millions and would grow enormously over succeeding years.

This man had studied all the offers carefully and of all the tenders he preferred that of British Leyland, for he had to choose the most suitable and was in no sense constrained as to the cost. There was, however, a snag: if he were to accept the Leyland offer he wanted a small percentage for himself – I think it was two and a half per cent. This sum, he said, could be added on to the existing offer, it need not come from British Leyland's profits. The boys did not know how to get in touch with British Leyland: it seemed that other contenders for the contract had already made suitable arrangements through their agents. But the British

Leyland Saudi agent had made no approach and the man was reluctant to approach the agent directly and tell him blatantly to add the two-and-a half per cent. Could I help? Could I tell then who to go to? The only thing I could suggest was to contact the Commercial Attaché at the British Embassy, because in those days the Embassies were preparing to move from Jeddah to Riyadh, and many had some offices in Riyadh already. In the case of the British, it was that of the Commercial Department. I knew the Commercial Attaché quite well, and a very nice and helpful man he was. I went to see him to explain, rather wondering whether he would hold up his hands in assumed horror and say that no British Company could behave like that, but he took it all as a fact of life and asked me to bring the boys to see him, which I did the next day. The son explained that his father didn't want anything in writing: a private intimation would be enough, because the British could be trusted. The Commercial Attaché said he would contact London at once. The contract was to be awarded in about ten days and the representatives from British Leyland would be in Riyadh a few days before that.

We possessed our souls in patience, or tried to: almost every day the boys came to see me to ask for news, and every day I visited or telephoned the Attaché. All he could tell me was that British Leyland now understood the position and would come to a decision when they were on the ground: and so they came. Neither I, nor the boys met them – we did not think that would be appropriate, because we were not really involved in any way. But the Attaché saw the BL representatives, and, he told me, spelt out the situation to them in no uncertain terms. They maintained that their agent was sure that they were going to win the contract, and so there was no need to become involved in any action which might be questioned later. This the boy passed on to his father.

After the British Leyland people arrived they were not very cooperative. The day before the decision was to be made public, the man concerned said that all he needed was for them to make a "courtesy call" on him, and to shake hands: no word need be said about the contract – he would trust them. This was communicated to the head of the Leyland group who replied that his Agent had now "guaranteed" their success, and there was no need to involve this Saudi official. That night, after talking to the boys, I told the Attaché that even at this eleventh hour it was not too late. The contract would be awarded at eleven o'clock the next morning: if early in the morning, the Leyland people made a "courtesy call", their agreement would be understood and they would win the contract. If they did not it would be awarded to another, more compliant company. The Leyland people dismissed this as "quite unnecessary" – they already had the contract

The contract was awarded, at eleven o'clock to a German company (was it Mannesmann?) and I was telephoned with the news a few minutes later. Ten minutes after that I was in the Commercial Attaché's office to tell him the news. He was not pleased. He told me that he had given London a full and frank report, pointing out that he was the man on the spot whose job was to help British businesses. He had told these people exactly what to do and they had completely ignored his advice. I was told later that the loss of this contract signalled the end of the line for British Leyland Buses, which, made it significant in the British economic history of the time.

Of course, we were, after all, in the Middle East, and all sorts of unworthy thoughts came into my mind. Why had the Leyland Agent persisted in giving his clients quite the wrong advice? More than anybody, such an agent would know whose bread to butter. Could it be that he had been bribed by other companies' agents to give his clients the wrong advice? Perhaps by that means he had made more money than he would have received had Leyland won the contract! Believe me, nothing was impossible in Riyadh at that time!

***

Thinking about the British Embassy in the early days of my Riyadh residence I am reminded of a certain British Consul (who shall remain nameless) who had what I might tactfully refer to as a drink problem. I only met him on one occasion, in the Sahari Palace Hotel. My mother's passport expired while she was in Riyadh and it had been necessary to apply to the Embassy in Jeddah for a new one. We were told that the Consul would be coming up to Riyadh and would bring the new passport with him; he would see us both at a stated time in the Hotel.

People had warned me of the Consul's little weakness, and had told me he always travelled with a fair amount of luggage, a good deal of which consisted of bottles of gin. "He never gets through an interview without going away for a drink," they said, " he will say that he had left a paper he needs in his room and will have to go and get it." This seemed to me at the time to be something of an exaggeration – surely, after all, the "interview" couldn't take more than half-an-hour at the most. In the event we met the Consul at the appointed time and he received us very courteously, offered us coffee, and for a time we exchanged small talk and he asked me sensible questions about my work and about Saudi education in general: but as soon as we got down to the matter in hand, my mother's passport, he found that he had left a paper in his bedroom and must go to get it. My mother and I exchanged glances and found it difficult to find topics of conversation as we sat and waited a good ten minutes for the Consul's return. When he did come back he seemed exactly the same – nobody would have thought that he had had a drink and there was certainly no smell of drink on his breath. The business of giving my mother her passport, which involved her signing two or three papers, should only have taken a few minutes; but somehow the time seemed to drag on and everything was done very slowly – so slowly in fact that the Consul had to return to his bedroom again to look for something or other. Again he was away for a good ten minutes and on his return seemed to be a trifle distraught. However my mother had then a valid British passport, which had been the point of the exercise: the "interview" had taken an hour.

A friend told me that on the evening after our interview the Consul had returned to the hotel from some party or other and had fallen over and passed out in the foyer. This story did not surprise me.

Far more serious – although I think it is a better story – was what happened in Jeddah around the time when we were pulling out of Aden. The Consul had a completely "blank" weekend, during which period of insensibility he lost the Consulate keys. When access was regained it was found that more than a hundred British passports were missing, together with the official stamps and seals. I was told, but have now forgotten, how much people in Aden would pay for a British passport. The question had to be faced by the Embassy, as the numbers of missing passports were known. Should they be circulated worldwide and be declared illegal? In one sense that ought to be done, but explanations would have to be made and there would be a resulting scandal; and so in the end, it was decided to let a hundred and something Hadrhamis have valid British passports, and not to report to the world the Consul's lapse. As far as I knew he wasn't even disciplined.

A last Ambassadorial incident was a favourite story of my mother's who told it many times especially in England. The British Ambassador had come up to Riyadh for some reason or other and was staying with Brigadier Adrian Donaldson, head of the British Military Mission to the

National Guard. Adrian's wife, Edith, a great friend of ours and a general favourite, was famous for speaking her mind forcibly and bluntly. My mother and I were among half a dozen people invited to drinks and to see the Ambassador. It was a pleasant party and after about half-an-hour Edith's voice echoed loudly through the room. "Oi, David, get off your arse! Can't you see his Excellency's glass is empty?" She was, as I have just said, famous for her "plain" speaking.

One final memory: my mother and I were in the Shalhoub house and Mansour's mother said to my mother: "When David is in Riyadh he is David Shalhoub. When my sons are in London, you are their mother." I hope I am not making an unjustifiable claim when I say that I understood Saudi people better, and was closer to them, than any other Englishman. That is my excuse for my presumption in writing this book.